The Law and Economics of Class Actions in Europe

NEW HORIZONS IN LAW AND ECONOMICS

Series editors: Gerrit De Geest, *Washington University in St. Louis, USA*; Roger Van den Bergh, *Erasmus University Rotterdam, The Netherlands*; and Thomas S. Ulen, *University of Illinois at Urbana-Champaign, USA.*

The application of economic ideas and theories to the law and the explanation of markets and public economics from a legal point of view is recognized as one of the most exciting developments in both economics and the law. This important series is designed to make a significant contribution to the development of law and economics.

The main emphasis is on the development and application of new ideas. The series provides a forum for original research in areas such as criminal law, civil law, labour law, corporate law, family law, regulation and privatization, tax, risk and insurance and competition law. International in its approach, it includes some of the best theoretical and empirical work from both well-established researchers and the new generation of scholars.

Titles in the series include:

From Economic to Legal Competition
New Perspectives on Law and Institutions in Europe
Edited by Alain Marciano and Jean-Michel Josselin

New Perspectives on Economic Crime
Edited by Hans Sjögren and Göran Skogh

Law, Economics and Cyberspace
The Effects of Cyberspace on the Economic Analysis of Law
Niva Elkin-Koren and Eli M. Salzberger

Games and Public Administration
The Law and Economics of Regulation and Licensing
Georg von Wangenheim

Law and the State
A Political Economy Approach
Edited by Alain Marciano and Jean-Michel Josselin

Democracy, Freedom and Coercion
A Law and Economics Approach
Edited by Alain Marciano and Jean-Michel Josselin

The Economics of Courts and Litigation
Francisco Cabrillo and Sean Fitzpatrick

Transport, Welfare and Externalities
Replacing the Polluter Pays Principle with the Cheapest Cost Avoider Principle
Dieter Schmidtchen, Christian Koboldt, Jenny Helstroffer, Birgit Will, Georg Haas and Stefan Witte

New Trends in Financing Civil Litigation in Europe
A Legal, Empirical, and Economic Analysis
Mark Tuil and Louis Visscher

Comparative Contract Law and Economics
Mitja Kovač

The Law and Economics of Class Actions in Europe
Lessons from America
Edited by Jürgen G. Backhaus, Alberto Cassone and Giovanni B. Ramello

The Law and Economics of Class Actions in Europe

Lessons from America

Edited by

Jürgen G. Backhaus

Krupp Chair in Public Finance and Fiscal Sociology, Erfurt University, Germany

Alberto Cassone

Università del Piemonte Orientale, Italy

Giovanni B. Ramello

Università del Piemonte Orientale and International Programme IEL – Institutions, Economics and Law, Italy

NEW HORIZONS IN LAW AND ECONOMICS

Edward Elgar

Cheltenham, UK • Northampton, MA, USA

Published by
Edward Elgar Publishing Limited
The Lypiatts
15 Lansdown Road
Cheltenham
Glos GL50 2JA
UK

Edward Elgar Publishing, Inc.
William Pratt House
9 Dewey Court
Northampton
Massachusetts 01060
USA

A catalogue record for this book is available from the British Library

Library of Congress Control Number: 2011932878

MIX
Paper from responsible sources
FSC® C018575

ISBN 978 1 84720 803 3

Typeset by Columns Design XML Ltd, Reading
Printed and bound by MPG Books Group, UK

Contents

Contributors

Jürgen G. Backhaus holds the Krupp Chair in Public Finance and Fiscal Sociology at Erfurt University, a post he has held since November 2000. Between 1986 and 2000, he held the chair in Public Economics at Maastricht University. In September 2004 he was awarded an honorary doctorate by the University of Thessaly (Greece). He has published 68 books and monographs, more than 200 articles in refereed journals and book chapters, some 30 scholarly notes and more than 60 reviews. His research interests span economics, but also neighboring disciplines such as law, fiscal sociology, and environmental sciences. In 1994 he founded (with Frank H. Stephen) the *European Journal of Law and Economics*, of which he is the managing editor.

Having edited the *Elgar Companion to Law and Economics* (1999, 2005), he has published – together with Richard E. Wagner of George Mason University – another reference work, *The Handbook of Public Finance* (2004).

Judge **Guido Calabresi** was appointed United States Circuit Judge in July 1994, and entered into duty on 16 September 1994. Prior to his appointment, he was Dean and Sterling Professor at the Yale School where he began teaching in 1959. He continues to serve as a member of that Faculty as Sterling Professor Emeritus and Professorial Lecturer.

Judge Calabresi received his B.S. degree, *summa cum laude*, from Yale College in 1953, a B.A. degree with First Class Honors from Magdalen College, Oxford University, in 1955, an LL.B. degree, *magna cum laude*, in 1958 from Yale Law School, and an M.A. in Politics, Philosophy and Economics from Oxford University in 1959. A Rhodes Scholar and member of Phi Beta Kappa and Order of the Coif, Judge Calabresi served as the Note Editor of the *Yale Law Journal*, 1957 to 1958, while graduating first in his law school class.

Following graduation, Judge Calabresi clerked for Justice Hugo Black of the United States Supreme Court. He has been awarded some 40 honorary degrees from universities in the United States and abroad, and is the author of four books and over a hundred articles on law and related subjects.

Judge Calabresi is a member of the Connecticut Bar.

Alberto Cassone is Full Professor of Economic Policy at the Università del Piemonte Orientale, a post he has held since 1991. He is currently the Head of the Department of Public Policy and Public Choice – POLIS, Italy. He was previously a professor at the University of Torino and Messina.

He served as Pro Rettore of the Università del Piemonte Orientale (1998–2004), and as Dean of the Faculty of Political Sciences (1992–2002).

Besides economic policy, he taught applied economics, economic dynamics, public economics, environmental economics and institutional economics. He was a Visiting Professor at the University of Pennsylvania, USA, University College of Buckingham, U.K., Université de Reims, France, Université de Rennes 1, France. He is a member of several academic societies and a referee for several economic journals and reviews.

His main research interests are about microeconomic policy analysis, public choice, law and economics and the economics of higher education.

He has published many articles in journals such as *Review of Law & Economics*, *Public Choice*, *International Review of Law and Economics*, *European Journal of Law and Economics*, *Journal of Institutional and Theoretical Economics*, *Journal of International Economic Law*, *Public Finance/Finances Publiques*.

Dr **Marta Silvia Cenini** is a Tenured Researcher of Civil Law at the Faculty of Law in Milan. She graduated with first class honors cum laude at the Faculty of Law in Milan under the guidance of Professor Pietro Trimarchi and completed a Ph.D. program at the University of Turin. She was visiting scholar at the University of Minnesota, where she carried out research in Comparative Law and Economics with Professor Francesco Parisi. She is author of numerous publications in major law journals, and recently she has been exploring the relationships between Law & Economics and the Humanities.

In September of the same year, she sat the open competition to attend a Ph.D. program in civil law at the Faculty of Law in Turin and she obtained a Ph.D. on 14 April 2008. The thesis she presented on that occasion has been recently published by Giuffrè Editore.

In April 2006 she won the open competition for Researcher at the University of Milan and she was given tenure, and since then she has been working as tenured researcher. She has had several articles published both in Italian and in English, often co-authored with Francesco Parisi.

Bruno Deffains is Professor in Law and Economics at the University Paris 2 Panthéon Assas and European Business School at Wiesbaden, Professor in Economics at the University Paris Ouest and Associate Professor at Sciences-Po.

From 2002 to 2006, Professor Deffains was Vice-President (Scientific Council) of Nancy University. From 2004 to 2008, he was Director of a CNRS research unit, BETA-REGLES (Bureau d'Economie Théorique et Appliquée) at Nancy University, and from 1998 to 2002, Director of the Doctoral School of the Faculty of Law, Economics and Business.

Professor Deffains gained his Ph.D. degree in the area of applied microeconomics in 1991, more precisely the topic was the 'economics of producers' liability'. He has strong research achievements in several of the topics relating to the fields of law and economics, industrial organization and public economics. During the last 15 years, he has conducted and published research related to the economics of law and regulation. Moreover, as a member of the Steering Committee of the European Association of Law and Economics and as a member of the Board of the French Association of Applied Microeconomics, he has promoted the development of an economic evaluation of legal systems. As a researches supervisor, Professor Deffains has developed a program to analyze the economic impacts of legal rules, particularly in the fields of civil liability, litigation and judicial procedures, corporate law, labor law and, more recently, public law.

Francesco Denozza is a Professor of Commercial Law at the University of Milan (Faculty of Law), a post he has held since 1986, and is also a member of the Milan Bar Association.

Graduating from the University of Milan in 1968, he became researcher at the Juristisches Seminar of the Tuebingen University from 1971 to 1972 and Visiting Scholar at the University of California at Berkeley (1996).

Denozza was Professor of Industrial Law at the University of Ferrara and at the University of Modena and later Professor of Commercial Law at the University of Brescia. From 1990 to 1992 he was Director of Institute of Commercial Law (University of Milan) and from May 2001 to November 2002 Director of the Milan University School of Specialization for the Legal Profession.

He is co-editor of the legal review *Giurisprudenza Commerciale*. His publications include the following books: *Responsabilità dei soci e rischio d'impresa nelle società personali*, Milano (1973), *Contratto e impresa nell'assicurazione a premio*, Milano (1978), *Licenze di brevetto e circolazione delle tecniche*, Milano (1979), *La disciplina delle intese nei gruppi*, Milano (1984), *Antitrust – Leggi antimonopolistiche e tutela dei consumatori nella CEE e negli USA*, Bologna (1988), *Norme efficienti. L'analisi economica delle regole giuridiche*, Milano (2002), *Appunti di diritto commerciale*, VI Ed (2006) (co-author).

Nuno Garoupa is Professor of Law and the H. Ross and Helen Workman Research Scholar at the University of Illinois College of Law. He received his Ph.D. in Economics from the University of York (UK) and also holds an LLM from the University of London. He has a long-established research interest in the economics of law and legal institutions. The results of this research have been published in the *Journal of Legal Studies*; *Journal of Law and Economics*; *Journal of Law, Economics and Organization*; *American Law and Economics Review; Journal of Empirical Legal Studies; Oxford Journal of Legal Studies; American Journal of Comparative Law; Journal of Comparative Law; Journal of Law and Society; International Journal of Law, Policy and Family; Berkeley Journal of International Law; Columbia Journal of Transnational Law; European Business Organization Law Review; Maastricht Journal of European and Comparative Law* among other journals. Nuno has served as Vice-President of the European Association of Law and Economics (2004 to 2007), Member of the Board of the International Society for New Institutional Economics (2006 to 2009), and co-editor of the *Review of Law and Economics* (2004 to 2010). He currently serves as a Member of the Board of the Latin America and Caribbean Law and Economics Association.

Antonio Gidi is an Associate Professor at the University of Houston Law Center, where he teaches Civil Procedure, Class Actions, and Comparative Law. After graduating from the University of Bahia, Brazil, Gidi obtained his masters and doctoral degrees from PUC University in São Paulo, Brazil. After that, he obtained his SJD degree from the University of Pennsylvania in the United States.

Gidi served for several years as the Associate Reporter and Secretary to the ALI/UNIDROIT project on Principles of Transnational Civil Procedure, a project geared to producing uniform procedural rules for international litigation and arbitration. He also served as a co-reporter in a project sponsored by the Ibero-American Institute of Civil Procedure to create a Model Class Action Code for Latin America. Gidi also helped draft comprehensive class action legislation for the Mexican Senate and the Brazilian Ministry of Justice.

Gidi has written several articles and books in Portuguese, Spanish, English, and other languages. Most recently, Gidi published the Civil Procedure chapters of *Schlesinger's Comparative Law*, 2009.

Fernando Gomez is Professor of Law and Economics at Universitat Pompeu Fabra, Barcelona, Spain, having previously taught at Universidad Complutense, in Madrid, and regularly at several European and US institutions. His main research interests lie in the economic effects of legal rules and institutions in the fields of Torts, Contracts, and Law Enforcement. Among his recent publications are, 'Realistic Standards. Optimal Negligence with Limited Liability', 37 *Journal of Legal Studies* (2008), and

'Cashing by the Hour: Why Large Law Firms Prefer Hourly Fees over Contingency Fees', 24 *Journal of Law, Economics and Organization* (2008).

Mariana França Gouveia is a Professor at Lisbon University (Law School), a post she has held since 2003. She has a graduate degree in Law from the Law School of the Lisbon University (1997) and a Ph.D. in Civil Procedural Law awarded by the Law School of the Lisbon New University (2003). She teaches Civil Procedure and ADR and is also a consultant at the Lawyers Firm 'Soares Machado & Associados' in Lisbon. She has published work on Portuguese Civil Procedure and ADR methods. Her most important publications are: *A Causa de Pedir na Acção Declarativa*, 2004; *Regime Processual Experimental Anotado*, 2006; *Meios de resolução alternativa de litígios. Negociação, Mediação e Julgados de Paz*, in Livro comemorativo dos 10 anos da Faculdade de Direito da Universidade Nova de Lisboa – Volume II, Coimbra, Almedina, 2008, pp. 728–58.

Sophie Harnay is Assistant Professor at the University of Paris Ouest Nanterre La Défense and researcher at EconomiX-CNRS. She received her Ph.D. in economics from the University of Paris I Panthéon-Sorbonne in 1999. She has published several articles in the field of law and economics. Her main fields of interest include the economic analysis of the judicial system and judiciaries, with a special emphasis on judicial decision-making. Her current work focuses on the history of the economic analysis of law and the market for lawyers in the European Union.

Samuel Issacharoff is the Reiss Professor of Constitutional Law at New York University School of Law. Prior to joining the NYU faculty in 2005, he held chaired appointments at the University of Texas School of Law and Columbia Law School. Professor Issacharoff is a graduate of Yale Law School and worked as a practicing attorney before entering the academy in 1989. He works across a number of fields dealing with procedural questions in law, and also with constitutional law, particularly as concerns elections and the political process. Professor Issacharoff served as the chief reporter for the American Law Institute's recently published Principles of the Law of Aggregate Litigation. He continues to appear in courts, primarily for appellate arguments. He is also a Fellow of the American Academy of Arts and Sciences.

Eric Langlais is Professor in Law of Economics at EconomiX, Centre National de Recherche Scientifique and Paris Ouest University-Nanterre, a post he has held since 2008. From 2008 to 2010 he was Visiting Professor at Institut National de la Recherche Agronomique (Laboratoire d'Economie Forestière, Nancy).

His research interests are in the areas of law and economics, economics of risk and uncertainty, public economics and economics of environment. He is Co-editor of the *Journal of Advanced Research in Law and Economics* and he has published many articles in academic journals including *Economics Letters, International Review of Law and Economics, Journal of Public Economic Theory, Public Choice, Theory and Decision.*

Jörg Luther has studied law at the University of Göttingen (Dr. juris) and Milan (dottore di ricerca) and worked as 'Professore Associato' at the Law Faculty of Pisa University. He is Full Professor of Institutions of Public Law at the Faculty of Political Sciences of the University of Eastern Piedmont, member of the Department of Public Policies and Public Choice (POLIS), the Italian Association of Constitutionalists, Societas Juris Publici Europeae and of the Guarantee commission of the Region of Piedmont. His research on class action is based on studies regarding access to constitutional justice, public comparative law and fundamental rights issues. For recent works see *A World of Second Chambers*, Milano 2006; *Europa constituenda*, Milano 2007; *Modelli giuridici europei nella Cina contemporanea*, Napoli 2009 (co-editor G. Ajani).

Alain Marciano is Professor of Economics at the University of Montpellier 1. He is the author and editor of books in economics and philosophy (and the co-editor of the *Elgar Companion to Economics and Philosophy*) as well as on the economic analysis of law. He has recently published a *Reader in Law and Economics*. He has also published many articles in journals such as the *Economic Journal*, the *Journal for Economic Behaviour and Organisation, Public Choice, Constitutional Political Economy*, the *European Journal of Law and Economics* or the *International Review of Law and Economics, History of Political Economy*, the *European Journal of the History of Economic Thought* or the *Journal for the History of Economic Thought*. His research interests include law and economics and more specifically the history of law and economics, which is the topic of the book he is currently working on.

Geoffrey P. Miller is an author or editor of ten books and more than 200 articles in the fields of financial institutions, contract law, corporate and securities law, constitutional law, civil procedure, legal history, jurisprudence, and ancient law. Miller received his B.A. *magna cum laude* from Princeton in 1973 and his J.D. from Columbia in 1978. After clerkships with federal judges, including Byron R. White of the U.S. Supreme Court, he worked as an attorney adviser at the Office of Legal Counsel of the U.S. Department of Justice and as an associate at a Washington, D.C., law firm. He joined the faculty of the University of Chicago Law School in 1983 and

NYU School of Law in 1995. Miller has been a visiting professor or visiting scholar at Columbia University, Harvard University, University of Minnesota, University of Basel, University of Genoa, University of Turin, University of St. Gallen, University of Frankfurt, University of Sydney, University of Auckland and the Bank of Japan. Miller is a founder of the Society for Empirical Legal Studies, a scholarly organization devoted to promoting statistical and other empirical techniques in the study of legal institutions. He is founder and director of NYU School of Law's Center for Financial Institutions, co-convener of the Global Economic Policy Forum, a member of the board of directors and audit committee of State Farm Bank, and a Fellow in the American Academy of Arts and Sciences.

Francesco Parisi is the Oppenheimer Wolff and Donnelly Professor of Law at the University of Minnesota, Law School and a Professor of Economics at the University of Bologna, Department of Economics. From 2002 to 2006 he held a Chair in Private Law at the University of Milan (Statale), where he was appointed *Professore Ordinario per Chiara Fama*. From 1993 to 2006 he taught at George Mason University where he served as Professor of Law and Director of the Law and Economics Program and as an Associate Director of the J.M. Buchanan Center for Political Economy. Professor Parisi received his D.Jur. degree from the University of Rome 'La Sapienza', an LLM and a J.S.D. and an M.A. degree in Economics from the University of California at Berkeley and a Ph.D. in Economics from George Mason University. He is the author of ten books and approximately two-hundred papers in the field of law and economics. Professor Parisi is currently serving as Editor-in-Chief of the *Review of Law and Economics* and served as Editor of the *Supreme Court Economic Review* from 2002 to 2008. He is a member of the board of editors of the *International Review of Law and Economics*, the *Journal of Public Choice,* the *American Journal of Comparative Law*, and he serves on the Board of Advisors of the *Social Sciences Research Network.*

Giovanni B. Ramello is Professor of Industrial Economics at the Università del Piemonte Orientale and associate fellow of the International Centre for Economic Research (ICER) at Villa Gualino, Torino. He is currently chairing the International Programme IEL – Institutions, Economics and Law – run by a pool of well-known US and European universities and located at Collegio Carlo Alberto. Professor Ramello has been research fellow at the Fondazione Giovanni Agnelli, Torino, and visiting scholar and visiting professor at the Banff Centre for the Arts (Alberta, Canada), UC Berkeley, University of Venice, Polytechnic and University of Turin. He has served as an advisor for many governmental and international institutions including the European Commission and the Italian Presidency of Ministries Council, and as an expert for a number of antitrust cases. His research interests mainly concern industrial economics and law and economics, with a special focus on competition policy and law and economics. On these topics he has published a number of papers in national and international journals and books. Professor Ramello was Vice-President and then President elected of the *Society for Economic Research on Copyright Issues* (2006 to 2010); he is now a Member of the board of the Italian Society for Law and Economics (SIDE) and co-editor of *the European Journal of Comparative Economics*. He is a member of the board of editors of the *Journal of Industrial and Business Economics* and of the *Review of Economic Research on Copyright Issues*.

Lorenzo Sacconi, laureate cum laude in Philosophy of Economics at the University of Pisa, is Full Professor of Economics and Unicredit Chair in Economic Ethics and Corporate Social Responsibility at the Department of Economics of the University of Trento, where he leads the LaSER – Laboratory of research in Social responsibility, Ethics and Rationality. He is also member of the teaching boards of the Ph.D. program in Law and Economics, run jointly by the Universities of Siena and Trento, and the Economics and Management Ph.D. program at the University of Trento.

At the end of 2004 he was appointed as the scientific director of EconomEtica, an interuniversity centre of research, gathering over 25 Italian Universities and located at the University of Milano Bicocca.

He is also a member of the International Society of New Institutional Economics (ISNIE). In the past he served as chair of the Italian business ethics network, Italian chapter of the EBEN (European business ethics Network). His research subjects are the foundations of game theory, ethics and economics, new institutional economics, theory of the firm and incomplete contracts, corporate governance and corporate social responsibility. His publications include books entitled *The Social Contract of the Firm: Economics, Ethics and Organisation* (2000), *Social Capital, Corporate Social Responsibility, Economic Behaviour and Performance* (edited jointly with Giacomo Degli Antoni, 2011) and *Corporate Social Responsibility and Corporate Governance: The Contribution of Economic Theory and Related Disciplines* (edited jointly with Margaret Blair, Edward Freeman, Alessandro Vercelli, 2010).

María Isabel Saez is Associate Professor in the Department of Commercial Law at the University Autónoma de Madrid, Spain. She has researched in several German universities with the support of an Alexander von Humboldt fellowship – and she teaches courses in corporate law and law and economics in various Spanish and South American institutions. Her fields of interest are corporate governance, take-overs and corporate law. Some of her later research is available at the ssrn website.

Frederic M. Scherer is Aetna Professor Emeritus at the John F. Kennedy School of Government, Harvard University. He has also taught at Princeton University, the University of Michigan, Northwestern University, Swarthmore College, Haverford College, the Central European University, and the University of Bayreuth. From 1974 to 1976, he was chief economist at the Federal Trade Commission. His undergraduate degree was awarded by the University of Michigan; he received his MBA and Ph.D. from Harvard University. His research specialties are industrial economics and the economics of technological change, leading inter alia to books on *Industrial Market Structure and Economic Performance* (third edition with David Ross, 1990); *The Economics of Multi-Plant Operation: An International Comparisons Study* (with three co-authors, 1975); *International High-Technology Competition* (1992); *Competition Policies for an Integrated World Economy*; *Mergers, Sell-offs, and Economic Efficiency* (with David J. Ravenscraft, 1987); *Innovation and Growth: Schumpeterian Perspectives*; *The Weapons Acquisition Process* (two volumes, one with M. J. Peck); *Industry Structure, Strategy, and Public Policy*; *New Perspectives on Economic Growth and Technological Innovation*, and most recently, *Quarter Notes and Bank Notes: The Economics of Music Composition in the 18th and 19th Centuries* (2004). His personal web page is found at the Kennedy School of Government faculty profiles site.

Luca Toffoletti is Senior Lecturer of Commercial Law at the University of Milan (Faculty of Law), a post he has held from May 2000; Lecturer in Competition Law and Economics at the University of Castellanza (Faculty of Law) from 2001; and member of the Milan Bar Association from 1995.

He received his Law degree, *cum laude*, from the University of Milan in 1991; during the 1993 to 1994 academic year he was Visiting Scholar at Yale Law School and he obtained his Ph.D. in Commercial Law from Bocconi University in 1999.

He was Adjunct Professor in Commercial and Company Law (1999 to 2000), at the Faculty of Economics, then of Industrial Law (2000 to 2002) and Economic Analysis of Law (2003) at the Faculty of Law of Castellanza University.

His research interests include antitrust and competition, dispute resolution and arbitration industrial and intellectual property and he is author of several publications in the field of antitrust law.

Thomas S. Ulen is Swanlund Professor of Law at the University of Illinois at Urbana-Champaign and Director of the Illinois Program in Law and

Economics. He received his bachelor's degree from Dartmouth College in 1968 then studied PPE (philosophy, politics, and economics) at St. Catherine's College, Oxford from 1970 to 1972. He successfully gained a Ph.D. in Economics at Stanford University, in 1979. He became affiliated with the Institute of Government and Public Affairs in 1987 and officially joined the Faculty of the College of Law in 1989. He was a Visiting Professor at Fudan University in Shanghai in Spring, 1989, and has also taught at the Katholieke Universiteit in Leuven, Belgium, the University of Ljubljana, Slovenia, the University of Bielefeld, Germany, the University of Hamburg, the Universidad Torcuato Di Tella, and the University of Ghent. He was one of the founders of the American Law and Economics Association, in 1991.

During the 2000 to 2001 academic year he served as Chair of the UIUC Chancellor Search Committee and co-chair of the Dean Search Committee at the law school in 2008 to 2009. In March, 2003, he was appointed a Swanlund Chair, one of the highest endowed titles on the Urbana-Champaign campus.

His scholarly interests have been in the economic analysis of legal rules and institutions. He has published three books on law and economics and over 80 articles, essays, and book reviews. His textbook with Robert D. Cooter, *Law and Economics*, is now in its fourth edition and has been translated into Chinese, Japanese, Italian, Spanish, French, and Russian.

Mikko Välimäki is a research fellow at University of Eastern Piedmont, Italy and an Adjunct Professor at Helsinki University of Technology, Finland. He teaches technology and intellectual property law and is the author of four books on intellectual property. Mikko Välimäki holds an LLM from the University of Helsinki (1999) and a Ph.D. from Helsinki University of Technology (2005).

PART 1

Class action litigation: the origins and its main features

1. The law and economics of class action litigation: setting the research agenda

Jürgen G. Backhaus, Alberto Cassone and Giovanni B. Ramello[1]

1. MAKING SENSE OF AGGREGATE LITIGATION

In 1961 an influential contribution by Guido Calabresi, 'Some Thoughts on Risk Distribution and the Law of Tort', challenged the then-prevailing assumption that spreading losses was more efficient than concentrating them just because 'the real burden of a loss is smaller the more people share it' (p. 517).

Just a few years later another seminal work, *The Logic of Collective Action* by Mancur Olson (1965), provided evidence that the uncoordinated action of individuals can sometime be less efficient than coordinated action. Olson's contribution then became a prominent explanation of the formation of groups and, as a by-product, of the emergence of specific institutions whose purpose it is to make that coordination possible.

The two researches were not related; yet, it is here argued, they provided two pillars for explaining the emergence of aggregate litigation and class

1 The research contained in this volume has been favoured by the brainstorming occurred at the conference 'Introducing Class Action in Europe: A Comparative Law and Economics' held in Alessandria in January 2007, organized by two of us with the help of two other colleagues. The insights provided by this venue has proven to be crucial for gathering the list of book contributors and identifying the topics herewith discussed. We are also grateful to the sponsors of the previous event including the Regione Piemonte, the City and the Province Councils of Alessandria, the MIUR. We are finally greatly indebted to the many colleagues that provided comments and suggestions and to the International Center for Economic Research (ICER), Torino that supplied a very stimulating environment for finalizing the manuscript. The usual disclaimer applies.

action in the legal procedure, and the reason why they can be a powerful device for promoting social welfare when other institutional arrangements seem to be ineffective.

Actually, in a number of cases, torts systematically spread losses over a number of individuals, and in several circumstances individual action through the court system seems to be ill-equipped for tackling them. This has become one of the main reasons for amending regulation, precisely intended as an alternative (substitute or complement) to legal action working on behalf of a multitude of interested parties (Glaeser and Shleifer, 2003).

In selected circumstances, the court system can to some extent be leveraged in order to bring legal actions in collective name and in coordinated fashion, as with criminal lawsuits involving a number of victims or litigations fostered by a public company, which involve, although indirectly, all the investors. However, this is limited to particular situations and does not offer a general solution.

On the whole, in a number of cases where there are large numbers of individuals characterized by a common interest and none of the previous instruments is able to work, a substantial failure seems indeed to emerge. Such situations involve the spread of losses and the lack of individual rights enforcement – in other words, fragmented and meritorious claims will neither be litigated because of the imperfection of the legal systems, nor tackled by the regulatory systems. Moreover, social welfare will also be affected as the provision of deterrence will be sub-optimal and the systematic under-protection of victims will necessarily influence firms' choices and performance (Chiou, Lee & Lee, 2010; Porrini & Ramello, 2011).

In all such situations, the question naturally arises whether a solution exists that can ameliorate those shortcomings by permitting some coordinated action in the judiciary. The problem is not a trivial one as one of the reasons for the failure of the judiciary is precisely the structurally high cost of coordination.

Class action is an affordable, though controversial, solution as it provides a powerful means for gathering dispersed interests and channelling them into a type of action in which the different parties concur to promote individual and social interest (Hensler et al., 2000). It can restore the full working of tort law by promoting (private) compensation of defrauded victims and thereby encouraging minimization of the social cost of accidents (Porrini and Ramello, 2005).

This opportunity, coupled with a situation of systematic under-protection of victims, has led to pressures for the introduction of class action into several legal systems. A number of countries have already introduced it with varying success; others are currently experimenting with class action-like devices, although lacking some of the constituent features of the original procedure; still others are considering its introduction. While there is no lack of critical voices, especially from the side of the would-be defendants (Hensler et al., 2000), the systematic under-protection of victims is urging national lawmakers to find an adequate answer to the incompleteness of liability systems, whether this be class action or something different. This is for instance one current focus of the European Commission, which recently launched a public consultation about the issue of collective redress.[2]

One stream of the debate revolves around the technical possibility of transplant, as class action is a legal device developed within the US common law system and this of course makes enactment of the US model elsewhere far from trivial. The answer to the question is provided by comparative law scholars, who have already shown how many changes in legal systems can in fact be primarily explained by legal transplants and how this process of cross-fertilization is vital to legal development (Mattei, 1994; Ewald, 1995).

The other stream, leaving ideologies aside, focuses on whether class action is the best device for achieving the expected results and what the proper design should be to make the system work (Dam, 1975).

The aim of this book is to provide firm ground for discussing the introduction of class action in jurisdictions different from the USA and other common law countries, using the benchmark of the recent and ongoing European experience. This aim has been pursued by gathering a panel of distinguished legal scholars and economists, all of them sharing a specific interest in the law and economics approach. Although the overall attitude coming out of the volume is in favour of class action as an instrument for enhancing justice and social welfare, the extensive and yet critical discussion provided in the following pages offers food for thought for readers to make up their mind on whether class action can be an adequate solution for meritorious but non-litigated claims.

2. CLASS ACTION: SKETCHES OF RESEARCH

The chapters of this book are intended to provide a broad perspective on class action, starting from its origins and most extensive application, that is to say chiefly the US case, and then disentangling its constituent features, its role and its effects on the larger society. They then move on to address

---

[2] 'Towards a Coherent European Approach to Collective Redress', SEC(2011)173 Final, February 4, 2011.

current developments, looking at class action-like devices introduced or soon to be introduced in other legal systems. Overall the volume summarizes what could be called the law and economics of class action.

We start from the historical backdrop of the US experience sketched out by Guido Calabresi, which reminds us once more of the role of class action in avoiding loss spreading and thereby links the current discussion to his seminal 1961 article. This contribution provides a good window through which the reality of class action today can be observed and the main concerns about its costs and benefits can be raised.

Frederic Scherer provides the perspective of an economist who works on matters of public interest and who has participated as an expert witness in several class action lawsuits, especially in the antitrust domain. Professor Scherer develops the two goals that this litigation procedure is supposed to promote, and which underlie the analytical framework within which law and economics scholars work: to do justice on the one hand and to deter wrongdoing on the other hand.

Samuel Issacharoff and Geoffrey Miller begin to set forth what then becomes the leitmotif of the subsequent discussion, by making explicit some of the doubts surrounding the introduction of aggregate litigation mechanisms into continental European legal systems. Their conclusions call for further research on the topic, such as is in fact provided by the authors that follow in the book: the main resistance to collectivist measures of adjudication is somehow linked to 'a deep-seated belief in the importance of rationalist expertise in top-down administrative decisionmaking'. Many continental legal cultures are in fact experiencing an impulsive reaction when it comes to entrusting to private actors the collective responsibility that they have traditionally reserved for the state. Subsequent chapters are therefore devoted to critically show how and when the spontaneous order provided by class action can, in a given setting, be the better way to solve the problem and promote efficiency when the state is unable to do it.

Juergen Backhaus tries first to shortly introduce the significance of class action litigation with respect to the twofold issues of market failure and forensic dynamics. These are somewhat diverging issues that should be jointly addressed if the goal of efficiency is to be pursued while avoiding the emergence of symmetric market failures.

Thomas Ulen extends the discussion by giving the reader a comprehensive law and economics framework designed to summarize the theory and practice of class action litigation in the USA. He sketches out at a general level the economics of this idiosyncratic device of American legal procedure in order to allow assessment of its efficiency, which is the focus of law and economics analysis.

The second part of the volume is intended to provide further insights into the law and economics of class action litigation. Alberto Cassone and Giovanni Ramello's contribution attempts to carefully disentangle the economic rationale of class action by considering the procedural mechanism as a technology, though of a 'legal' sort. This stylized description permits to highlight its productive features with regard to attorneys', victims', and society's interests. From a production perspective – and in accordance with a large body of mainstream economic literature – class action can thus be understood as legal machinery designed to efficiently address judicial market failure and promote social welfare.

One of the main features of this idiosyncratic new market is that it makes it possible to shift risk among parties, which according to Juergen Backhaus' chapter is indeed one of the main contributions of class action. This result can be achieved by changing the financial arrangements governing the lawyer-plaintiff relationship from fee-for-service to contingent fee arrangements, even though, of course, cases exist in which class action itself can fail.

Francesco Parisi and Marta Cenini examine the effect of alternative procedural regimes on the effectiveness of punitive damages and class actions. On the one hand, their findings can help explain the slow motion that characterizes the introduction of class actions in Europe, on the other hand they strongly suggest using class actions and punitive damages in order to create optimal deterrence.

Bruno Deffains and Eric Langlais take an information theory approach to the study of a setting in which market failure characterizes the production of evidence, testimony and expertise. When victims are injured by the same offender, a system relying upon individual action makes the first mover benefit subsequent plaintiffs, while class action is a way to internalize the informational externality, yielding some welfare improvement.

Lorenzo Sacconi, however, reminds us that all that glitters isn't gold, as contingent-fee remuneration schemes have their own shortcomings. His argument relies upon principal–agent modelling and his results underline that everything depends on whether the conduct that complies with fiduciary obligations is supported at the equilibrium. When this is not the case, according to Sacconi, lawyers may fail to maximize their clients' interests.

A similar alert comes from the chapter by Alain Marciano and Sophie Harnay that discusses the possibility of using class action as a rent-seeking technology in the judicial system when rent-seeking technologies in the political market are not available or inefficient.

The third part of the book provides a specific spotlight on the European case. The chapter by Francesco Denozza and Luca Toffoletti introduces the part more focused on legal issues and precisely on legal transplant. Their chapter, in particular, deals with the new opportunity afforded European countries by the Green Paper of the European Commission, on *Damages Actions for Breach of the EC Antitrust Rules*. This is an opportunity to enhance the role of private enforcement as a complement to the publicly enforced competition policy.

In a similar vein, though in a different domain, Fernando Gomez and Maria Isabel Saez analyze the role of private enforcement via shareholders' class action vis-à-vis public enforcement in corporate governance, and particularly in the field of passivity rules. They conclude that in that field the solution is doomed to fail as an effective deterrent because of idiosyncratic elements that characterize the continental European legal systems.

Joerg Luther further extends the comparative perspective by addressing constitutional law and its enforcement. After offering a broad and multifaceted survey of the European legal tradition and the early experiments in collective action, the focus then zooms in on the impact of class action on constitutional justice, especially in the Italian case. This necessarily involves a comparative perspective, since Italy recently introduced a watered-down version of class action-like procedure, which is in fact a de-powered version of the American legal institute.

A similar analysis is contained in Mikko Valimaki's study of the Finnish case. His conclusion for this case supports the argument that introducing amended class action-like devices without the proper foundations can lead to a new kind of failure, namely a law-making failure. This occurs not just for lack of understanding, but as well because the legislative process is easily captured by specific stakeholders in the public choice sense. In this respect, the law and economics approach can provide an *ex-ante* remedy to legislative capture.

A difference from American-style class action similarly characterizes the collective redress institute recently introduced in Portugal, as presented by Mariana França Gouveia and Nuno Garoupa. Once more, their analysis supports the conclusion that if on the one hand the differences are justified on grounds of legal system specificities and legislators' desire to move away from the US model, on the other hand a regularity emerges, and that is the failure or ineffectiveness of the class action device.

However, criticism can be sterile if it is not followed by some normative suggestion. That is why the book concludes with a practical proposal by Antonio Gidi, who provides a model of class action code for civil law countries. While this is of course a personal proposal by a scholar who is well acquainted with both common law and civil law systems, it is thought-provoking. Policy-oriented reflection should focus on properly specified drafting of class action procedures, in order to overcome the systematic under-protection of victims that still exists in Europe. That, in essence, is the ultimate aim of this book.

REFERENCES

Calabresi, G. (1961), 'Some Thoughts on Risk Distribution and the Law of Tort', *Yale Law Journal*, **70**, 499–551.

Chiou, W.J.P., A.C. Lee and C.F. Lee (2010), 'Stock Return, Risk, and Legal Environment around the World', *International Review of Law and Economics*, **19**(1), 95–105.

Dam, K.W. (1975), 'Class Actions: Efficiency, Compensation, and Conflict of Interest', *Journal of Legal Studies*, **4**, 47–73.

Ewald, W. (1995), 'The Logic of Legal Transplant', *American Journal of Comparative Law*, **43**(4), 489–510.

Glaeser E.L. and A. Shleifer (2003), 'The Rise of Regulatory State', *Journal of Economic Literature*, **41**, 401–425.

Hensler, D.R., B. Dombey-Moore, E. Giddens, J. Gross, E. Moller and M. Pace (eds, 2000), *Class Action Dilemmas. Pursuing Public Goals for Private Gain*, Santa Monica, CA and Arlington, VA: Rand Publishing.

Mattei, U. (1994), 'Efficiency in Legal Transplants: An Essay in Comparative Law and Economics', *International Review of Law and Economics*, **14**, 3–19.

Olson, Mancur (1971) [1965]. *The Logic of Collective Action: Public Goods and the Theory of Groups* (revised edition), Cambridge, MA: Harvard University Press.

Porrini, D. and G.B. Ramello (2005), 'Class Action for Financial Losses: Deterrence Effects from Ex Post Regulation', Working paper, Università del Piemonte Orientale, Alessandria.

Porrini, D. and G.B. Ramello (2011), 'Class Action and Financial Markets: Insights from Law and Economics', *Journal of Financial Economic Policy*, 3, 140–160.

2. Class actions in the U.S. experience: the legal perspective

Hon. Guido Calabresi

A couple of days ago, literally as I was about to leave for this conference, I received two cheques in the mail, one for sixty dollars and ninety-eight cents and the other for six dollars and twelve cents. They were my shares of a class action suit brought against my insurance agent. This was originally a local agent who had bought insurance for me on most all I have – from my house to my car to everything else. The insurance agent many years earlier had been bought by a national company. I hardly knew any of this, but someone had brought a class action suit against the national company, claiming, apparently correctly, that these agents (who are supposed to be *my* agents) instead of presenting me with the various available insurances at the lowest prices were simply signing up me – and people all over the United States – with those who gave the agents the greatest profit margins. The suit successfully led the national company to settle very quickly.

I was a bit aware of the existence of this suit; I sort of knew of it, but barely. Until the suit, I had not known of these practices of the agent. And, to this day, I have no idea what proportion sixty dollars and ninety-eight cents, for one thing, and six dollars and twelve cents, for another, were of the extra charges that I had paid because of the wrongdoing on the part of the agent. I had no concept of that at all. I also have no idea what the representatives of the class or the lawyers received. I do have – because I just did some research on it – figures on percentages of what lawyers get in class action suits, and I'll tell you about those later, or in the question-and-answer period. On the other hand, when the matter was brought to my attention, with the right to opt out, I didn't think for one moment of opting out and bringing my own suit, for the same reasons that I previously had no knowledge or interest in the wrong that had been done me. It was too small for me to think in any way of bringing an individual suit, so of course I didn't opt out. I waited and finally received a total of sixty-seven dollars and ten cents with which I could, probably, buy myself a good bottle of wine, or something of that sort, a better bottle of wine than I would have bought otherwise.

The interesting thing is that even before the class action suit settled, when I was scarcely aware that there was a class action suit, the practices of the agent changed dramatically. For the first time in years they called me and said, 'We would like to go over all of your insurances'. When they had said that generally in the past, it had been to charge me more, but this time they said it was 'because we think we can get you the same coverage far more cheaply'. I went, and they did. And they've been extraordinarily nice ever since. So something happened, and I think it was because of the class action suit.

All of this highlights some of the issues concerning American law and class actions. There is a difference in class actions between the purpose of deterrence – through a social accounting function that forces individuals to be aware in their decision-making of the costs they cause – and the compensation function of redressing the losses of those who have borne them. So who gets the amount recovered in the class action may be highly important if we are concerned with compensation and with redress. But it may not be very important if we are concerned with social cost accounting for deterrence.

There is, of course, a question of the adequacy of knowledge of the class. I knew virtually nothing of what was going on in this case and of the quality of the representation. In fact, I still don't know who my representatives were and, frankly, wasn't interested in spending my time or money to find out. There is a question of the capacity and knowledge to opt out, how important that right really is, and in what kind of case. And there is a question that I understand is very much alive in Europe. That is, the difference between a lawyer-driven, representative type of class action where someone assembles the group of people who otherwise would not have done anything, and the aggregation type of class action where there already are many torts suits being brought and they are simply put together into an aggregated suit, combining suits that would have been there anyway but may be brought a lot more cheaply by aggregation.

Not at issue in my sixty-dollar cheque were other key American issues that are not yet alive in Europe but, I think, will be. In the United States, an essential feature of class actions is the extent to which these are local-state class actions versus nationwide class actions in federal court. I am not sure how much these are issues in Europe today. Yet at some point a key question will be whether class actions, if they are allowed, are to be brought in Italy, Germany, France, Luxembourg, or what have you, with the class being able to choose where it brings the suit and what law is most favourable, or to what extent, instead, they must be brought under some universal

European law, perhaps in European courts. In the United States that is a major issue today between state and national federal class actions.[1]

Today, I hope, not too boringly, to describe the history and current status of class action rules in the United States since that is the topic that was assigned to me. And then I will turn for a few minutes to something that interests me rather more, which is a comparison between class actions and another form of extra-compensatory damages – punitive damages – as means of doing the same thing. Interestingly, neither punitive damages of this sort, nor class actions generally, have traditionally existed in civil law systems. They both – and at least one particular form of punitive damages – can be made to vindicate, from an economic view, the kind of social cost accounting goals that I earlier mentioned class actions can accomplish. Since I have written about punitive damages of that sort, both in an article and more authoritatively in an opinion, I will speak a bit about that.

1. HISTORICAL BACKDROP

What is the history of major developments in class action law in the United States? First it goes back a very long way. Class actions seem to have been permitted at common law, but they were, in any event, codified in 1849 with the Field codes of New York and California.[2] So, with the Field codes, two major states allowed class actions, albeit in the most simplistic of ways: where there is a common interest in law or fact, a class action may be brought.[3] Very simple, no details, not much used. The first key moment in class action history came in 1938 when class actions became part of the Federal Rules of Civil Procedure. These Rules completely revised civil

---

[1] *See, e.g.*, *Schwarm* v. *Craighead*, 233 F.R.D. 665, 658–660 (E.D. Cal. 2006) (noting the federal court's discretion to decline to exercise supplemental jurisdiction over a claim that raises a novel or complex issue of state law but finding, in the instant case, that 'comity counseled in favor of the [federal] Court retaining supplemental jurisdiction') (internal quotation marks omitted); *see generally* Issacharoff (2006); Issacharoff and Sharkey (2006, pp. 1415–1419) (exploring the potential for the Class Action Fairness Act to make federal courts the 'centralized forum for all national market class actions, … provid[ing] an impetus for the development of a coordinated body of substantive law to address the particular concerns of these cases').

[2] *See* Subrin (1988) (explicating the history of the Field Code).

[3] The New York Field Code of 1848, for example, as amended in 1849, provided: 'When the question is one of a common or general interest of many persons, or when the parties are very numerous and it may be impracticable to bring them all before the court, one or more may sue or defend for the benefit of the whole.' Conte and Newberg (2002, pp. 399–400).

procedure in the United States and created a whole new system which, because of the influence of the people who wrote the Federal Rules of Civil Procedure, came to be adopted as the rules of procedure of many, many states.[4] The father of that was Charles E. Clark, my predecessor, as professor, as dean at Yale, and then as a judge on the United States Court of Appeals for the Second Circuit. The Federal Rules of Civil Procedure, adopted in 1938, included Rule 23, which specified that class actions could be brought. This rule was generally adopted by the many states that enacted the Federal Rules of Civil Procedure. But it did not follow that the states gave the same meaning to that rule as the federal government did. And this was very important in the history of class actions in the United States, as each state – while they adopted the same generalised statute – was then free to interpret it in its own way.

The federal rule came to bear its full meaning only forty years ago in 1966, and it did so in the context of civil rights. 1966 was the great moment of the civil rights movement, and the movement was faced by a powerfully important question: how does one avoid having to bring multiple suits for integration, suits for redress against discrimination, especially in the South? The answer was found in class actions; and the need for this answer became the locomotive force for giving new meaning to the class action.[5] The changes that were made to Rule 23 in 1966 were not enacted in order to further the suits that make class actions so important today.[6] And that's an interesting and important historical fact.

Under the revised Rule 23, there was a functional test for when multiple possible actions could be certified as a class – there had to be: a) numerosity (that is, enough people that the class action was worthwhile); b) common questions of law and fact; c) representatives who had an interest or claims

---

[4] *See* Subrin (1989) (providing an historical examination of the development of the Rules on the fiftieth anniversary of the development of the FRCP).

[5] As Professor John P. Frank, a member of the 1966 Advisory Committee on Civil Rules that proposed amending Rule 23 to its current form, explained: 'If there was a single, undoubted goal of the committee, the energizing force which motivated the whole rule, it was the firm determination to create a class action system which could deal with civil rights and, explicitly, segregation.' Prepared Statement of John P. Frank, Hearings on S. 353 Before the Subcomm. on Administrative Oversight and the Courts of the Senate Comm. of the Judiciary, 106th Cong. (1999).

[6] For example, at the time '[t]he Advisory Committee … had suggested that a "mass accident … is ordinarily not appropriate for a class action" because of the presence in such cases of significant issues (including causation and possible defenses) that would impact upon the individual class members differently.' Coffee (1995, pp. 1356–57) (internal quotation marks omitted); *see also* Resnik (1991, pp. 9–11).

typical of the class; and d) representatives who would fairly and adequately protect the interests of the class.[7] These were rules that defined the need and the feasibility of a class action. But in addition there were policy requirements. That is, class actions were deemed appropriate when separate actions would risk inconsistent adjudication and hurt non-parties or when the defendant had acted against the interest of a class.[8] That is, if a defendant had acted badly, then there was a reason to have a class action in order to punish the defendant. But class actions were also justified when separate actions would hurt non-parties.

Think of the civil rights movement. The class could be certified because the targets were segregationists who had acted against the interest of a class, or because common issues prevailed so that it was better, more efficient, to try them all out together. And Rule 23 provided that it would be binding on every one, although it did preserve a right to opt out. Again this was a right to opt out, not a need to opt in. You are part of the class, but could opt out. According to John Frank – an old Yale professor, great lawyer in Arizona, former clerk of Justice Hugo Black, and member of the committee that gave rise to the class action lawsuit – the aim of this innovation was to vindicate civil rights claims and to combat segregation.[9] The Committee did not think at the time, insofar as class actions might spread beyond civil rights, that there would ever be a class of more than a hundred.[10] At most, they were thinking of a contemporaneous circus fire,[11] and airplane crashes.[12] (And these were crashes of planes that were not as big as planes today.) There was no mention, whatever, of business suits.

---

[7] Fed R. Civ. Pro. 23(a).

[8] Fed R. Civ. Pro. 23(b).

[9] *See supra* note 5.

[10] For instance, Committee member Judge Charles Wyzanski stressed the notice obligation as a barrier to an excessively large number of claims for a class action. In evaluating the 1966 changes to Rule 23, Judge Wyzanski observed: 'I think you would have to make a finding that the form of notice to be used would in all probability reach all persons in the proposed class. And I think it quite clear that in [an enormous case involving thousands] you could not make any such finding. I don't think that case is a class action except for those people who can be reached.' *See* Hearings Before Sen. Subcomm., Prepared Statement of John P. Frank, at 270; *see also id.* at 269 ('The concept of thousands of notices going ceremonially to persons with such small interests that they could not conceivably bring their own action was still in the future.').

[11] Professor J.W. Moore, a member of the Committee, contended that class actions should not reach a mass tort like the contemporaneous fire in the Ringling Bros. tent in Hartford. *See id.* at 268.

[12] *See id.* at 266 ('The basic idea of a big case with plaintiffs unified as to liability but disparate as to damages was the Grand Canyon airplane crash').

That was not in the antechamber of their minds. And rarely, if ever, was the concept of mass torts or modern products liability articulated in 1966 when Rule 23 was developed.[13]

In the 1970s and 1980s, a series of Supreme Court decisions came down, one after the other, favouring class actions, favouring the spreading of them. These are quite interesting decisions. They allowed the trial court to take an active role in creating the class, encouraging the trial court to bring classes together, to certify a class action where the trial court thought it was worthwhile.[14] They said that class actions saved resources and, therefore, nationwide class actions – even if brought in particular states – were desirable.[15] They found that avoiding multiplicity of actions was desirable both in view of the interests of the absentees and in order to spread the costs of litigation.[16] The Supreme Court said, and this is extraordinarily interesting, that the fact that the massiveness of these suits would encourage settlements was a good thing. The very fact that the defendants would settle quickly to avoid the suit was discussed as desirable. Thus, in the decisions of the Supreme Court in the 1970s and 1980s, class actions were favoured because they allowed people to bring suits that otherwise would not be economically feasible, because they enabled individuals who otherwise lacked effective strength or size of economic damages to bring such suits, and because they often would bring about settlements.

Not surprisingly with this kind of an open-ended statute and the encouragement from the Supreme Court, a huge expansion followed. Mass torts, asbestos, general product liability, shareholder derivative suits, corporate misbehaviours, breaches of fiduciary and credit duties (like my insurance agent), labour, and employment civil rights cases – involving people who are discriminated against on the job on the basis of race, sex, disability, and

---

[13] Resnik, *supra* note 6, at 9–11 (showing, based on comprehensive historical study, that Advisory Committee members 'did not see the class action as responsive to the problems of mass torts'); Coffee (1995, pp. 1345, 1357).

[14] *See, e.g.*, *Eisen* v. *Carlisle and Jacquelin*, 417 U.S. 156, 184 (1974) ('The purpose of Rule 23 is to provide flexibility in the management of class actions, with the trial court taking an active role in the conduct of the litigation.').

[15] *See, e.g.*, *Califano* v. *Yamasaki*, 442 U.S. 682, 701–702 (1979) ('[T]he class-action device saves the resources of both the courts and the parties by permitting an issue potentially affecting every [potential class member]… to be litigated in an economic fashion under Rule 23 … .'); *see also id.* ('[A] nationwide class [was not] inconsistent with the principles of equity jurisprudence.').

[16] *United States Parole Comm'n* v. *Geraghty*, 445 U.S. 388, 402–403 (1980) ('[J]ustifications that led to the development of the class action include … the protection of the interests of absentees, the provision of a convenient and economical means for disposing of similar lawsuits, and the facilitation of the spreading of litigation costs among numerous litigations with similar claims.').

age – all became subjects of class action suits. All of these were very different cases from the desegregation civil rights cases the framers of the class action had in mind when the modern Rule 23 was created in 1966.[17]

But while we know that the mix of cases is very different from what was foreseen in 1966, we do not know what the actual mix today is. Reliable figures, amazingly, are not available in the United States for the proportion of kinds of cases that have been brought. That is, there are figures available but they are contradictory. The Administrative Office of the Courts gives one set of figures of the proportion,[18] the Rand Corporation gives a very different set of figures,[19] and a third source, the Advisory Committee of the Civil Rules, gives a third set.[20]

2. CRITIQUES

All of these developments led to a variety of criticisms. Many of these criticisms focus on the interest of the poor plaintiff who is not being protected adequately.[21] But the people who are making the criticisms are not typically plaintiffs' groups. They are not the consumer unions. They are typically defence-oriented groups. And those in the legislature who have spoken most of poor plaintiffs are people like Representative Sensenbrenner, who for years was the Republican head of the House Judiciary Committee and who, in that role, was hardly known as a protector of the little injured plaintiff.[22] The criticisms were that there was inadequate

---

17 *See, e.g.*, Resnik, *supra* note 13, at 6–22;

18 *See* 26 Class Action Rep. 3 (2004).

19 *See* Hensler et al. (2000).

20 *See* Willging and Lee (2006).

21 *See, e.g.*, 151 Cong. Rec. H726 (statement of Rep. Sensenbrenner) (asserting the class action system produces 'outrageous settlements that benefit only lawyers and trample the rights of class members', and that today's class actions 'are too often used to efficiently transfer the large fees to a small number of trial lawyers, with little benefit to the plaintiffs'); 151 Cong. Rec. H735 (2005) (statement of Rep. Keller) ('In a nutshell, these out-of-control class action lawsuits are killing jobs, they are hurting small business people who cannot afford to defend themselves, they are hurting consumers who end up paying higher prices for goods and services.'); 151 Cong. Rec. H748 (2005) (statement of Rep. Blunt) ('In addition to unclogging certain overused courts, this bill ends the harassment of local businesses through forum shopping.').

22 *See* 151 Cong. Rec. H726 (statement of Rep. Sensenbrenner) ('The race to settle produces outcomes that favor expediency and profits for lawyers over justice and fairness for consumers. The losers in this race are the victims who often gain little or nothing through the settlement, yet are bound by it in perpetuity.').

protection of plaintiffs because the settlements were of limited benefit to the plaintiffs – only sixty dollars and ninety-eight cents, only six dollars and twelve cents – and covered a very small portion of the harm originally done to the plaintiffs.[23] There was confusion as to how one could opt out.[24] There was certification where the individual interest was not clear and, most of all (which I could keep repeating), class actions benefited the lawyers who brought these cases, who found a 'class representative,' and who did not truly help the members of the class.

There also were some broader policy criticisms that focused primarily on the federal-state question.[25] Multiple cases were brought on identical issues in different states, and that was undesirable because the same issue would be litigated several times.[26] Nationwide issues were decided locally.[27] A class could be established in a particular state that was especially favourable, both for easy certification and easy substantive law. And the results in that 'favourable' state decided questions affecting the whole nation.

The problems of the *defendant* were rarely discussed in the political criticism. They could be found in the academic literature and federal case law, in writings by Henry Friendly, Richard Posner, and others.[28] But that criticism was primarily a criticism of 'blackmail settlements,' settlements which people would pay because they could not afford to risk the very large

---

23 H.R. Rep. No. 109–14, pt. 1, at 14–20 (2005) (identifying a variety of examples of abusive settlements in which attorneys receive excessive fees 'with little or no recovery for the class members themselves'); *see, e.g.*, *Kamilewicz* v. *Bank of Boston*, 92 F.3d 506 (7th Cir. 1996).

24 *Id.* at 4 ('Often, the settlement notices ... are so confusing that the plaintiff class members do not understand what – if anything – the settlement offers or how they can opt out of it.'); *see also id.* at 21–22 (illustrating the dangers of 'drive-by class certifications').

25 *Id.* at 22 (describing the practice of some magnet state courts that too premissively certify national class actions).

26 H.R. Rep. No. 109–14, pt. 1, at 23 (2005) (describing the filing of 'copy cat' class actions across state courts).

27 *Id.* at 24 ('The effect of class action abuses in state courts is being exacerbated by the trend toward "nationwide" class actions, which invite one state court to dictate to 40 others what their laws should be on a particular issue, thereby undermining basic federalism principles.'); *see also id.* ('A recent study found that 77 percent of class actions brought in 2001 in a rural Illinois county known for its heavy class action docket sought to certify nationwide classes.') (citing Beisner and Miller (2003)).

28 *See, e.g.*, Friendly (1973); *In re Rhone-Poulenc Rorer, Inc.*, 51 F.3d 1293, 1299–1300 (7th Cir. 1995); Posner (1973); *see also* Posner (2001).

loss that a class action suit might entail.[29] (Now, I will say more about the economics of class actions a little bit later on. But one has to ask oneself, what is the meaning of a wrongful blackmail settlement. A person who determines that the odds of losing a suit are one in a hundred may choose to settle, therefore resolving the suit for one hundredth the value of what he or she might lose in litigation costs plus part of the administrative cost. That may seem like 'judicial blackmail'[30] but, in terms of social cost accounting, it is not a wrong decision. Only if you add in a significant likelihood of error in favour of plaintiffs in the one per cent of cases that actually would be won by the defendant, does the blackmail settlement become wrong from an economic point of view. The fact that somebody settles because he or she wants to avoid a hundred-to-one shot, or at least avoid the administrative costs of a hundred-to-one shot, is not in itself economically undesirable.)

In any event, all of this led to a turnaround in class actions in the United States, and specifically to the CAFA, the Class Action Fairness Act of 2005 introduced by Congressman Sensenbrenner.[31] CAFA changed the rules of diversity jurisdiction, so that while previously almost no class action suit could be removed from the state courts into federal courts, now almost any major class action suit can. Before there had to be total diversity, so among the victims a single plaintiff in the same state as the defendant would be enough to keep a case from being in the federal courts. Under CAFA, by contrast, so long as there is a single party who is not of the same jurisdiction as the defendant, there is federal jurisdiction if the amount in controversy is more than five million dollars.[32]

Notice that CAFA was limited to the *large* class action suit. The sponsors who professed their interest in protecting the plaintiff were apparently not interested in protecting all small plaintiffs. They were only interested in doing so in the class actions that had the potential for large losses for the defendants.

There certainly existed problems in such cases. Some states, perhaps in complicity with lawyers and class representatives, did allow class action suits in which individual class members were not protected. And there was the suggestion that *elected* state judges responded in this area to large

---

[29] *See, e.g.*, Friendly, *supra* note 28, at 120 (citing Handler (1971)); *In re Rhone-Poulenc Rorer, Inc.*, 51 F.3d at 1298 ('[Defendants] may not wish to roll these dice. That is putting it mildly. They will be under intense pressure to settle.').

[30] H.R. Rep. No. 109–14, pt. 1, at 20 (2005).

[31] Class Action Fairness Act of 2005, Pub. L. No. 109–2, 119 Stat. 4 (codified in scattered sections of 28 U.S.C.).

[32] 28 U.S.C. § 1332(d)(2).

electoral contributions by class action suers. Some states may very well have become homes for class action lawyers who knew these states had a legal culture which allowed lawyers to keep most of the money from class action settlements. But despite the rhetoric of CAFA advocates proclaiming an interest in targeting magnet state courts, that question was not really the one addressed in CAFA. The real reason for CAFA was that the Supreme Court and the federal courts by the year 2000 had turned around and had become very unfavourable to class actions. Increasingly, the federal courts interpreted Rule 23 against certification, while the state courts still were interpreting Rule 23 in favour of certification.[33]

There is, moreover, what is somewhat incorrectly called, pre-emption. As a result of CAFA, a suit may not be brought as a class action in the states. But federal law is such that there is either no liability, or no right to class certification for that suit in the federal courts. Damned if you do, damned if you don't. CAFA advocates denied they were trying to abolish class actions; they just structured a jurisdictional game that ended up with a zero result.

I don't mean that class actions have gone away since CAFA, but they have been significantly reduced. In part, this is not due to CAFA itself, but is because the lower federal courts have become unsympathetic to class actions. For example, just a few months ago the case *Miles* v. *Merrill Lynch* was heard in my own court by a panel on which I did not sit and, in fact, from which, for personal reasons, I would have had to recuse myself.[34] In that case the panel put the burden on the plaintiff to show that every single one of the Rule 23 requirements had been met, thereby breaking with the previously assumed interpretation that the burden was on the defendant to show that the requirements had not been satisfied. This is a very difficult burden for plaintiffs to meet. Other federal courts have said there isn't similarity of interests in cases like tobacco cases, because there are long-term smokers, short-term smokers, and smokers who have had this and smokers who have had that lung disease; therefore, the commonality of interest isn't as great as the difference and a class may not be certified.[35]

---

[33] *See e.g.*, H.R. Rep. No. 109–14, pt. 1, at 22 (2005) (observing that '[s]ome state courts with [a] permissive attitude have even certified classes that federal courts had already found uncertifiable').

[34] *Miles* v. *Merrill Lynch* (*In re Initial Public Offering Securities Litigation*), 471 F.3d 24 (2d Cir. 2006).

[35] *See, e.g.*, *Castano* v. *American Tobacco Co.*, 84 F.3d 734, 743 (5th Cir. 1996) ('The class members were exposed to nicotine through different products, for different amounts of time, and over different time periods. Each class member's knowledge about the effects of smoking differs, and each plaintiff began smoking for different reasons. Each of these factual differences impacts the application of

There is some truth to each of these points. But the question is whether that ends up meaning that the requisite commonality of interest can only very rarely be established.

CAFA has also had another important effect. By sending major class action cases to the federal courts, it created enormous problems of choice of law: which law will govern? There is no such thing as federal law for many of these things. Yes, in the securities cases there is, but in many of the others – in tort cases, and so on – it is supposed to be local law that governs. But whose local law? When there are many plaintiffs in the class, is it the local law of the class representatives/certifiers, or of someone else?

As a result of all this there is very much uncertainty now in the United States. Class actions have been expanded enormously. They are still very important. We see them all the time, particularly in business situations and in mass torts/products liability contexts. The business situation cases are almost entirely lawyer-driven, that is, someone puts together the class and then brings the suit.[36] The percentage of payment to lawyers in these cases ranges from 30 per cent of the recovery to as low as 14 per cent. The amounts range from as low as $600,000 in a case where the fee was 30 per cent to $117 million in an antitrust case where the fee was 25 per cent. Certainly the lawyers do very well. On the other hand, if we are concerned not so much with what the individual victims get, because without class actions they likely would not get anything at all, but rather with putting the cost on the defendants then these are not in themselves outrageous results.

There were abuses. Reforms, I think, have not really focused on the abuses but on reducing both good and bad class actions. The interest of class members in securing damages, as against the social interest in placing appropriate costs on the defendant – that is, the compensation and the deterrence goals – have not been sorted out. People haven't focused on the difference in these goals. The difference between aggregated and representative class actions also has not been sorted out much in the United States. And the federal-state problems are still totally there. You in Europe can deal with all of these, better than we have.

---

legal rules such as causation, reliance, comparative fault, and other affirmative defenses.'). *Cf. Barnes* v. *American Tobacco Co.*, 161 F.3d 127, 131 (3d Cir. 1998) ('Although there may be individual variations with respect to each class member's relationship with the defendants, the common questions of defendants' liability, which are intimately connected with their concerted conduct, support a finding that defendants have acted on grounds generally applicable to all members of the proposed class.').

36 *See* Coffee (1983a, pp. 669, 677).

3. REFORMS AND THE OBLIGATIONS OF SCHOLARS

Now I'll turn, if I may, briefly to the relationship between class actions and a form of punitive damages.

All of this background suggests there are problems that class actions address. The problems are: a) the failure of the defendant – the cost causer – to bear his or her full cost when individual victims may not know that they have a right to sue or may not have been damaged enough to make such a suit worthwhile because of the administrative costs of an individual suit; b) the failure of the victims to receive compensation in such situations; and c) even when individual suits are worthwhile, the existence of unnecessary administrative costs as a result of a multiplicity of suits. The first two clearly justify representative or lawyer-driven class actions, while the third perhaps justifies only aggregated types of class actions. (The abuses of each of these have been talked about.)

What is another way of dealing with these problems? Well, in the United States one can get punitive damages – extra-compensatory damages – in a variety of situations. There are many reasons for punitive damages. One reason is to make individuals into private attorneys-general, to go after people who have committed crimes as well as those who are so much at fault that they are like criminals. Punitive damages there serve as a bounty – an incentive for private law enforcement. There is also something of that in class actions.[37]

Another reason for punitive damages is to prevent defendants from making certain defences that we don't want to hear. The Ford Pinto case is a classic example of what I call 'tragic choices punitive damages', where Ford defended the placing of a gas tank in a place where it could rarely explode rather than in a place where never could explode. Perhaps tricked or forced by plaintiff, its defence seemed to become that the cost of burning babies is less than the cost of putting the gas tank in a place where it wouldn't ever explode.[38] Therefore, Ford seemed to claim, under the Learned Hand test for fault, that Ford's decision was not faulty and hence that Ford was not liable at all.[39] The court, in effect, said that it may look like a fault area, and you may be right to do a cost-benefit analysis and decide to put the tank where you did, but we will not have you telling us that burning babies is a

---

[37] *See generally* Coffee (1983b, pp. 215–217).

[38] *Grimshaw* v. *Ford Motor Co.*, 119 Cal. App. 3d 757, 174 Cal. Rptr. 348, 383 (1981).

[39] *Cf. United States* v. *Carroll Towing Co.*, 159 F.2d 169 (2d Cir. 1947).

socially desirable thing.[40] One hundred million dollars of punitive damages. Next time, shut up and pay. Now that's a very different function of punitive damages from the private attorney-general function previously mentioned. It is to keep people from telling us things that are too costly for us to know.

There is yet another form of punitive damages. And this is the one on which the U.S. Supreme Court has focused – the right of individuals to vengeance.[41] *Vendetta*. A great American right. The first thing the Puritans did when they arrived was to start suing each other for '*my rights*'. It is the reason the United States has so many good rights, constitutional rights. It probably is also the reason the United States has the death penalty, because the sense of *vendetta* is very much a part of American legal consciousness. It's *my right*, not as a matter of deterrence but just as *my right* to see that you are killed when you do that prohibited action. The Supreme Court, which is much concerned with that kind of thing – constitutional rights and capital cases – and doesn't deal much with tort law, not surprisingly thought of punitive damages in those terms and said, 'All right, but they cannot constitutionally be greater than a certain amount'.[42]

In this circumscribed view of punitive damages, however, the Supreme Court ignored all the other functions of punitive damages. One of the most important of these is what has been called 'the multiplier'.[43] And it's this function that is most closely related to class actions.

If a defendant is sued by a plaintiff and the damages to that particular plaintiff are ten, but there are fifty other plaintiffs who are unlikely to sue (or who, if they sue, may not win), then, if only compensatory damages are awarded, the defendant will not bear the social costs of his activities. He will bear ten, instead of five hundred. In that situation, what have been called punitive damages – but really should be called socially compensatory damages – should be awarded.[44] Although they are extra-compensatory as far as the particular plaintiff suing is concerned, these damages are meant not to punish but instead to assign costs. As such they are perfectly sensible. The differences between this type of punitive damages and some of the

---

40 *Grimshaw*, 119 Cal. App. 3d at 818–822.

41 *See, e.g.*, *Newport* v. *Fact Concerts, Inc.*, 453 U.S. 247, 266–67 (1981); *BMW of North America, Inc.* v. *Gore*, 517 U.S. 559 (1996).

42 *See Pacific Mut. Life Ins. Co.* v. *Haslip*, 499 U.S. 1 (1991); *TXO Prod. Corp.* v. *Alliance Resources Corp.*, 509 U.S. 443 (1993).

43 *See generally, e.g.*, Becker (1968); Polinsky and Shavell (1998); *Ciraolo* v. *City of New York*, 216 F.3d 236, 245 (2d Cir. 2000) (Calabresi, J., concurring).

44 Sharkey (2003a); Sharkey (2003b); *see also Ciraolo*, 216 F.3d at 245 (Calabresi, J., concurring).

others are notable. This type of punitive damages should be assigned, and has been assigned, even in the absence of any fault in the defendant, for there may be non-fault liability situations in which the defendant is held liable only one-in-ten times, or even one-in-fifty times. Defendants certainly don't need to have committed *willful* wrongdoing to be properly subject to this type of extra-compensatory damages. And, in contradistinction with some other types of punitive damages, there is every reason to allow, indeed to encourage, defendants to insure against this type of damages, thereby making them a part of the ordinary costs of doing business.

One could spend a great deal of time analysing what these 'multiplier' types of punitive damages entail, and I have written a little article which discusses when and how such damages are appropriate.[45] In the end, they are needed for reasons not very different from those Becker noted in his celebrated article that was in part the basis for his Nobel Memorial Prize in Economics.[46] Becker said that, in criminal law, if one simply charged the criminal with the amount of his theft there would be high incentive on the thief to keep stealing – perfectly obvious. But the same is true and more dramatically in the civil law area. If we want to assign costs – the real social costs – to the defendants, then we have to impose extra-compensatory costs of just this sort! This has been written about in an opinion by Posner, in an opinion of mine, and in a very long and thorough article by Shavell and Polinsky.[47]

Notice that what this form of punitive damages does is very similar to the class action in its social-allocation-of-cost function. One can take the place of the other. Both have problems, and the principal problem with both is: who gets the money? In the class action, it is the lawyers and class organizers, rather than the individual plaintiffs, who get the bulk of the money. In this form of punitive damages, it is the persons who sue first who get the money as against those who don't bother to sue or don't know enough to sue. And why should these 'early suers' get all of this extra money? Catherine Sharkey, in a very good article, has suggested that there ought to be enough of a bounty to encourage a person to bring such a suit, thereby getting these socially compensatory punitive damages assigned to the defendant. But that then the rest of the damages, which are nominally

---

45 *See* Calabresi (2005).

46 Becker (1968).

47 *See Kemezy* v. *Peters*, 79 F.3d 33, 35 (7th Cir. 1996) (Posner, J.) ('When a tortious act is concealable, a judgment equal to the harm done by the act will underdeter' because the tortfeasor 'will not be confronted by the full social cost of his activity'); *Ciraolo*, 216 F.3d at 245 (Calabresi, J., concurring); Polinsky and Shavell, *supra* note 43.

punitive but actually socially compensatory, should be assigned by the court to serve functions that benefit the class of people who usually do not sue.[48] In this way, such awards can be used for making highways safer, they can be used for reducing pollution, and they can be used for other such 'socially compensatory' actions. That would be one way of structuring recoveries if a legal system decided to permit this kind of punitive damages instead of, or along with, class actions.

There is not enough time today to go into any great detail as to the particular difficulties that this approach has in comparison to the class action approach. They both have their problems, and they both have their possibility of abuse. Do lawyers on contingent fees get more in the punitive damages case or do they get more in the class action case as against either plaintiffs or the class as a whole? Are these suits to be brought in states, or are these to be brought in federal courts? All of the questions discussed earlier with respect to class actions are also serious questions as to this form of extra-compensatory damages.

In closing, I would like you to think about a couple of things. At the moment Europe has neither, so you have a possibility of choosing. Thus, you don't need to call this type of extra-compensatory damages 'punitive damages,' which is a bad name. You can call them something else and see if you want to have them rather than certain types of class action. If you have them, you can decide what kinds of controls you want to put on them, with respect to lawyers fees, with respect to where the money goes, and all that. You can focus on how to deal with the possibility of blackmail, which is not simply proper settlement costs being allocated but actual blackmail in the sense of suits that ought not win. All of these are things which, looking at the issues *de novo*, you can deal with in a way that is much more difficult for us because both class actions and 'multiplier' damages are already part of our system of law and cannot be easily extricated from it. Extra-compensatory, socially compensatory damages are part of the whole punitive-damage pie and can't readily be separated from it in the United States, but in Europe they could be. How would one do it? We are trying, some people are trying in the United States, but it does not come easy.

Keep in mind that there will be here, as there is in the United States, fierce opposition from those who do not want to bear the costs of their activities. This is nothing new. Adam Smith suggested that every time business people get together, they try to find a way either to monopolise or to shift their costs onto somebody else. That hasn't changed. The pressure – from the right every bit as much as from the left – on government not to be free

---

48 Sharkey (2003a).

enterprise but instead to be mercantilistic, to benefit particular groups, is always there. That is a constant, constant theme. And so there is tremendous pressure, by those who want to avoid bearing the cost of their activities, in opposition both to class actions and to punitive damages of this 'multiplier' sort, precisely because of the good things that they may do. The opposition focuses, understandably, on the bad things, the dangers of these, in order to try to knock them down altogether.

In this circumstance, it is the role of scholars to come up with ways to ensure that socially compensatory damages – that is, these allocation costs – are properly placed by instituting legal devices that allow it to happen. You have to do the work on it because you will not find this pursued either by those who are seeking to avoid paying for the costs they cause or, for that matter, by those on the other side (the lawyers for the plaintiffs) who are going to argue that what is most desirable is whatever system gives them the largest percentage of the cake, that is, has the highest administrative cost from which they can draw their percentage. In this context, the victims themselves and the interest in properly allocating costs are not likely to be represented by anyone in the society if not by scholars. The victims are both too small and always a minority at the moment that they are victims. And before they become victims they are not going to be very interested in law reform. So, since realistically they are not there to say, 'I want law to protect me in case I have an injury at some point in the future,' the people who act as if they speak for victims are the plaintiffs' lawyers whose interests, instead, are very different. The people who speak on the injurer side have an interest that is very different too. The only ones who can speak for both the compensatory and proper deterrent rights are you. Not an easy task. I hope you take it on. Thank you.

REFERENCES

Becker, G.S. (1968), 'Crime and Punishment: An Economic Approach', *Journal of Political Economy*, **76**(2), 169–217.

Beisner, J.H. and J.D. Miller (2003), 'Class Action Magnet Courts: The Allure Intensifies', *BNA Class Action Litigation Report*, **4**(58).

Calabresi, G. (2005), 'The Complexity of Torts – The Case of Punitive Damages', in M.S. Madden (ed.), *Exploring Tort Law*, New York: Cambridge University Press.

Coffee, J.C. (1983a), 'Understanding the Plaintiff's Attorney: The Implications of Economic Theory for Private Enforcement of Law through Class and Derivative Actions', *Columbia Law Review*, **86**, 669–727.

Coffee, J.C. (1983b), 'Rescuing the Private Attorney General: Why the Model of the Lawyer as Bounty Hunter is Not Working', *Maryland Law Review*, **42**, 215–288.

Coffee, J.C. (1995), 'Class Wars: The Dilemma of the Mass Tort Class Action', *Columbia Law Review*, **95**, 1343–1465.

Conte, A. and H.B. Newberg (2002), *Newberg on Class Actions*, St. Paul, Minn.: Thomson/West.

Friendly, H.J. (1973), *Federal Jurisdiction: A General View*, New York: Columbia University Press.

Handler, M. (1971), 'The Shift from Substantive to Procedural Innovations in Antitrust Suits – The Twenty-Third Annual Antitrust Review', *Columbia Law Review*, **71**(1), 5–12.

Hensler, D. et al. (2000), *Class Action Dilemmas: Pursuing Public Goals for Private Gain*, Santa Monica: Rand Institute for Civil Justice.

Issacharoff, S. (2006), 'Settled Expectations in a World of Unsettled Law: Choice of Law After the Class Action Fairness Act', *Columbia Law Review*, **116**(7), 1839–71.

Issacharoff, S. and C.M. Sharkey (2006), 'Emerging Issues in Class Action Law: Backdoor Federalization', *UCLA Law Review*, **53**(6), 1353–1435.

Polinsky, M. and S. Shavell (1998), 'Punitive Damages: An Economic Analysis', *Harvard Law Review*, **111**, 869–962.

Posner, R.A. (1973), 'An Economic Approach to Legal Procedure and Judicial Administration', *Journal of Legal Studies*, **2**, 399–458.

Posner, R.A. (2001), 'Antitrust in the New Economy', *Antitrust Law Journal*, **68**, 925–43.

Resnik, J. (1991), 'From "Cases" to "Litigation"', *Law & Contemporary Problems*, **54,** 5–68.

Sharkey, C.M. (2003a), 'Punitive Damages as Societal Damages', *Yale Law Journal*, **113**, 347–453.

Sharkey, C.M. (2003b), 'Book Review: Punitive Damages: Should Juries Decide?', *Texas Law Review*, **82**, 381–411.

Subrin, S.N. (1988), 'David Dudley Field and the Field Code: A Historical Analysis of an Earlier Procedural Vision', *Law and History Review*, **6**, 311–374.

Subrin, S.N. (1989), 'Federal Rules, Local Rules, and State Rules: Uniformity, Divergence and Emerging Procedural Patterns', *University* of *Pennsylvania Law Review*, **137**(6), 1999–2051.

Willging, T.E. and E.G. Lee III (2006), *The Impact of the Class Action Fairness Act of 2005: Second Interim Report to the Judicial Conference Advisory Committee on Civil Rules*, Federal Judicial Center.

3. Class actions in the U.S. experience: an economist's perception

Frederic M. Scherer

My role in this book, addressing important changes being considered actively in Europe, is akin to what Augustine of Hippo did: confessing and distilling lessons from the sins of my youth. Specifically, how do class action suits work from the perspective of an economist who has participated as an expert witness in several? My focus has been mainly on antitrust suits, but I will recognize the relevance of other types.

1. THE RATIONALE OF CLASS ACTION LITIGATION

There are two main reasons for laws permitting class action litigation:

(1) To do justice, that is, to compensate a nation's citizens for harm that is done to them by powerful (usually industrial or medical) actors – e.g., through price fixing, selling defective and dangerous products or services, polluting the environment, polluting the information environment with false and misleading statements, and engaging in unwarranted discrimination – price or otherwise.

(2) To deter actions that might be illegal, but that might either escape the attention of law enforcement authorities, or be committed because the expectation of penalties administered by government agencies is insufficient, or to solve free-rider problems when no individual has a sufficient incentive to take corrective action that will benefit many fellow citizens.

Let us consider first the second of these explanations. Does deterrence from class action litigation actually work? In principle, the prospect of paying treble damages for violations of U.S. antitrust law ought to be a formidable deterrent. Whether it actually deters is questionable, given the plethora of large-scale price-fixing conspiracies brought to light in recent years, in both the United States and Europe. Examples include vitamins, carbon electrodes, airline fares, auction house fees, lysine, citric acid, dynamic random access memory chips, and most recently (January 2007, from a European Commission action), in electric power switchgear. (It was a 1950s case in electrical equipment, including switchgear, that precipitated some of the largest early damages awards under the U.S. antitrust laws.[1]) Similarly, much litigation against the U.S. cigarette manufacturers by private parties and state attorneys general has led to fines and punitive damages awards measured in the hundreds of millions of dollars, which, given inelastic demand for cigarettes, have been passed on to consumers in the form of greatly elevated prices. Despite the past history of litigation and damages, recent research has suggested that the cigarette makers have knowingly increased average nicotine levels by 10 to 11 per cent since 1998, presumably in the expectation of enhancing addiction effects for new smokers.[2]

Why does deterrence appear to be ineffective? There are two plausible reasons: a perceived low probability of being caught and assessed damages; and/or the insufficiency of the damages actually awarded when violation of the law is proven.[3] I find the latter explanation hard to believe, given the fact that class action plaintiffs under the U.S. antitrust laws can claim three times the actual amount of damages proven. Clearly, further analysis of what is happening is needed.

2. IS JUSTICE SERVED?

Closely related to the question of the sufficiency of damages is the question: is justice served? Are consumers in fact made whole as a result of class action suits? According to the preamble of the Class Action Fairness Act, which was passed by the U.S. Congress in 2005, justice is being served inadequately:[4]

> (3) Class members often receive little or no benefit from class actions, and are sometimes harmed, such as where:
>
> (A) Counsel are awarded large fees, while leaving class members with coupons or other awards of little value;

---

1 See Smith (1961a,1961b).

2 See Gladwell (2007).

3 See White (1988), for conference proceedings that thoroughly explore both the theory and evidence on class action suits under the U.S. antitrust laws.

4 Public Law 109–2, 119 Stat. 4 (February 2005). See also the roundtable discussion, Anonymous (2005, pp. 18–21).

(B) Unjustified awards are made to certain plaintiffs at the expense of other class members; and
(C) Confusing notices are published that prevent class members from being able to fully understand and effectively exercise their rights.

The coupon remedy is indeed a problem. What they often do is allow a discount on the purchase of another iteration of the same unsatisfactory product. And if I were a clever business manager forced to issue such coupons, I would try to offer a special product priced with such a high margin that I would profit even though I must grant what is purported to be a discount. My own experience is that I have been offered several such coupons and found it troublesome to obtain them and take advantage of them. Only once did I receive monetary damages from a class action settlement, and in that case, the amount was tiny.

The new Class Action Fairness Act attempts to create a process under which the adequacy of damages and the legitimacy of compensation to counsel are carefully considered by the federal courts, at least, in those nationwide cases where the federal courts assume jurisdiction from decentralized state courts.

3. BLACKMAIL?

Complementary to the problem of low damages actually accruing to the persons who have suffered from actionable conduct is the incentive for blackmail by entrepreneurial law firms. There are many such firms in the United States whose specialty is bringing class action suits in the expectation that the defendants will settle and pay substantial negotiated fees rather than incurring the costs and risks of protracted litigation. Steven Salop and Lawrence J. White found in an analysis of 1,959 U.S. class action antitrust suits that 88 per cent settled without a trial.[5] Only 106 cases, or 5.4 per cent of the sample, actually went to trial. For those that went into trial, the average trial length was 11.4 days. For cases that settled without a trial on which information was available, the attorneys initiating the actions realized on average 20.3 per cent of the total damages settlements as attorneys' fees.[6] However, the distribution of fees was highly skew. The *median* attorney's fee in cases ending through settlement was 110 per cent of

5 White (1988, pp. 10–11).
6 Ibid. p. 14.

the damages recovered by those named as plaintiffs (by the initiating attorneys) and hence those who were in principle injured.

Acknowledging that I have also participated in class action suits that I considered well-justified, let me illustrate this point with details on three actions that were either poorly based in facts or (I am unable to distinguish) brought for purposes of blackmail.

One was a class action alleging a price-fixing conspiracy by Canadian producers of potash, extensively used as fertilizer by farmers in the United States and elsewhere.[7] The Canadian province of Saskatchewan is the OPEC of world potash production, controlling roughly half of the world's minable potash reserves. The industry in Saskatchewan is tightly oligopolistic; six companies originated nearly all of the province's potash output. The suit was based upon evidence of abrupt and substantial price increases, shown in Figure 3.1 as occurring during mid-1987. But there was a simple and obvious non-collusive explanation for the price shock. Competing potash producers in the United States had achieved the initiation of an anti-dumping suit against the Canadians, and in March of 1987 (second dotted vertical line in Figure 3.1), the U.S. International Trade Commission ruled that the Canadian producers were likely to be subjected to substantial anti-dumping tariffs on future shipments. In fact, on August 21 (third vertical dotted line), the U.S. International Trade Administration announced preliminary anti-dumping margins, for which a bond had to be posted, averaging 37 per cent for all of the Canadian potash producers and 52 per cent for the largest seller. Anticipating that decision and hoping to minimize its future tariff liabilities, the leading firm announced a substantial price increase and then, two weeks after the preliminary dumping margin decision, added a further increase of $35 per ton. Other smaller members followed its price lead – not an actionable offense under U.S. law. A protracted and expensive legal process followed. But the Canadian potash producers refused to settle, and eventually, the suit was voided.

On my next example I must tread carefully, since parts of the litigation are still pending. In the so-called Branded Drug Litigation,[8] a group of law firms filed class action complaints against the leading U.S. pharmaceutical manufacturers, alleging that they conspired to deny discounts to drug

---

7 Potash Antitrust Litigation, MDL (multi-district litigation) Docket No. 981, U.S. District Court for the District of Minnesota. For more details, see Scherer (2000, pp. 364–7). I was a consultant for Kalium Ltd. and in my preparation visited the world's deepest potash mine.

8 MDL–997, Master File no 94 C 897 (U.S. Federal Court for the Northern District of Illinois). The case is described at greater length in Chapter 10 of Scherer (2000). I submitted testimony on behalf of Pfizer Inc.

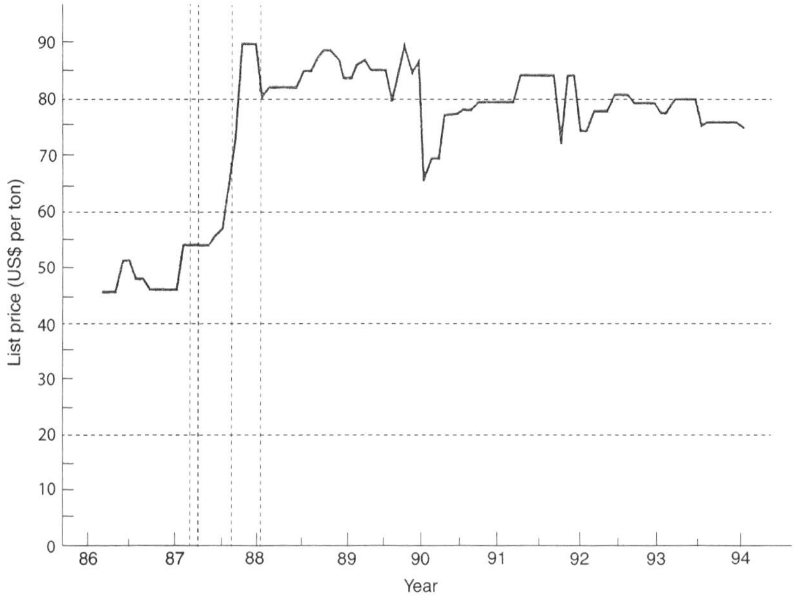

Figure 3.1 Movement of Saskatchewan potash prices, 1986–93

retailers even while they were offering large discounts to hospitals and health maintenance organizations. There were several flaws in the class action plaintiffs' claims. For one, they were not able to present direct evidence that the drug manufacturers actually conspired to orchestrate the discount structure. The most that could be proved is that the manufacturers cooperated with drug wholesalers on a computerized rebate system so that customers who had been granted discounts could be reimbursed promptly. The discounts themselves varied widely from case to case. Second, the hospitals and health care maintenance organizations had substantial bargaining power vis-à-vis the manufacturers, since they could deny a manufacturer's patented drug a place on their formulary of useable drugs unless acceptable discounts were offered. Retailers, on the other hand, had no such bargaining power. They were by law required to dispense a named patented compound if the patient arrived with a valid prescription. Thus, substitution was possible by the health care organizations but not by the retailers. Third, the drug retailers had a long history of advocating resale price maintenance (so-called 'fair trade') and shunning price competition among themselves. It was only when the U.S. laws supporting fair trade were abolished during the 1970s that retailers' gross margins declined from roughly 40 per cent to the 20 per cent value achieved under pressure from the U.S. government and so-called 'pharmacy benefit managers' bargaining over the margins they would reimburse.

A third such case accused the leading credit card companies of colluding to set the fees they charge for converting into dollars transactions consummated in non-U.S. currencies.[9] The principal alleged evidence of collusion turned on the participation of company attorneys at meetings whose principal subjects were government regulation of fee disclosures and the arbitration of disputes, and in which, the evidence showed, the magnitudes of conversion fees were mentioned only in passing. Persons present at the meetings denied under oath any attempt to agree on fees. Announcements of fee increases (from a 1 per cent base) extended over a period of several years, and by the end of 2004, when the suit was initiated, most Visa card providers were charging 3 per cent, one important Visa provider was charging 1 per cent, and American Express and Diner's Club were charging 2 per cent. The case continues.

4. IMPROVING THE LITIGATION PROCESS

The new U.S. Class Action Fairness Act seeks to correct some of the problems I have identified, but it will have little or no impact on cases such as the three I have described above that would be in federal courts rather than state courts. Even when jurisdiction is with federal courts, it is difficult for judges to sift through mounds of complex evidence and eliminate before a full trial is held the cases that are without merit. And even when a full trial is held – i.e., when the accused parties do not succumb to a settlement – judicial error is possible. One remedy that may place too much trust in the ability of economists is to have the court employ an expert economist as a clerk or expert advisor to the court. The first known instance of an economist serving in that role was not a class action, but a case litigated during the early 1950s by U.S. federal antitrust authorities against the United Shoe Machinery Corporation. In that case, Harvard University economist Carl Kaysen served as advisor to Judge Charles Wyzanski.[10] Since that time economists have served as court-appointed clerks or experts

[9] *Robert Ross et al.* v. *American Express Co. et al.*, Case No. 04 CV 05723 (WHP) (Southern District of New York). The author submitted evidence on behalf of American Express.

[10] *U.S.* v. *United Shoe Machinery Corporation* 110 F. Supp. 295 (1953). On his experience see Kaysen (1956).

in a handful of class action suits. Such service is no panacea. My own experience in two such cases reveals the difficulties.

For the damages phase of the folding carton litigation, I was retained by Judges Charles Robson and Hubert Will in Chicago to determine the reasonableness of the negotiated damages settlements.[11] (Shortly before, the U.S. Supreme Court had ruled that such consideration was necessary when class action suits were settled by negotiation.) Another economist had been retained by the Court to advise on the liability segment of the litigation. To the best of my knowledge, I received no information on the division of payments between attorneys and the carton users on whose behalf the suit was brought. Damages were computed for individual carton buyers. One thing that struck me was that the Pillsbury Company claimed by far the largest percentage elevation of prices as a result of the remarkably well-documented price-fixing conspiracy. The question was, why? Investigation revealed that Pillsbury, unlike other users of special, preprinted cartons, had required carton makers to bid on *all* of the 50 or so cartons it wanted in one annual competition. At the time there were more than 100 vendors of folding cartons, but only the 10 or 12 largest companies were party to the price-fixing conspiracy. By consolidating its bidding requirements, Pillsbury made it difficult for smaller, more specialized carton makers to bid, thereby rendering itself especially vulnerable to the relatively few large carton producers, who comprised the core of the conspiracy. I asked the judges whether a doctrine of contributory negligence was relevant to the assessment of damages. The answer was, no. But I believe there should be such a consideration when a buyer adopts a bidding system that is unusually well-suited for successful conspiracy by sellers.

Although I retain little documentation, I recall a similar issue in the treble damages suits that followed the 'great' electrical equipment conspiracy of the 1950s. Many of the products on which the conspiracy turned were sold to electric power producing utilities. At the time, those utilities were regulated, and their profits were established on the basis of a 'fair return on fair value' principle – the larger their asset base, the higher the profit they were allowed to retain. If the allowed rate of return on assets was higher than the cost of capital, as was commonly the case, the regulated firms had an incentive to increase their asset bases beyond the bounds of economic efficiency.[12] It was rumored at the time that at least some of the electric power companies knew about the conspiracy, but since it enhanced

---

11 MDL-250 (U.S. Federal Court for the Northern District of Illinois).
12 On the theory, see Scherer (1970, pp. 523–37).

their net profits under the regulated profit-setting formula, they did nothing to combat it. Again, a doctrine of contributory negligence would be appropriate to deal with such anomalies.

Similar negligence has been alleged in connection with the collapse of the Enron Corporation, harming many investors who had been misled by Enron's wildly optimistic financial reports. The accounting firm, Arthur Andersen, which had audited Enron's books and approved its financial reports, was held liable in part for the losses to Enron shareholders and had ceased operating as a result of the legal actions brought against it after the collapse. However, an article in the *New Yorker* magazine by Malcolm Gladwell revealed that a skilled and diligent analyst could see through Enron's accounting methods and realize that it was concealing substantial losses.[13] The indications of concealed trouble included the fact that Enron paid no U.S. income tax for several years, even though its financial reports claimed substantial profits, and that its cash flow was negative. Careful investors and the Wall Street analysts who advised them should have been wary, but hardly anyone did the necessary homework. Here too one might argue that damages claims should have been mitigated by the failure of prudent analysis.

In 1991 I participated again as advisor to Judge Will, this time in the Glass Bottles treble damages litigation.[14] With the benefit of previous experience, we established what appeared to be an ideal working arrangement. I was to be compensated half by attorneys for the plaintiffs and half by the defendants. At an intermediate stage of the proceedings, I met separately with counsel for plaintiffs and defendants, asking them to sharpen unclear points in their briefs and expert affidavits and suggesting statistical tests to focus the issues. When the actual trial began, I read the daily testimony transcript and prepared analytic summaries for Judge Will. My analysis confirmed testimonial evidence of a price-fixing conspiracy during the 1960s. An analysis of pricing revealed almost no deviation of actual transaction prices from list prices until roughly 1972, but after that time, transaction prices deviated by increasingly large percentages from list prices, suggesting that the conspiracy (of which there was no testimonial evidence for the 1970s) had indeed broken up. An expert economist witness for the defendants placed considerable stress on the transaction-list price deviations during the 1970s, but when asked on cross examination whether there was *ever* any price-fixing conspiracy, he denied its existence. Judge Will had planned to have me testify and be cross-examined by both parties after the testimony by

---

[13] Gladwell (2007).

[14] MDL 89C 5251 (U.S. Federal Court for the Northern District of Illinois).

plaintiffs and defendants was concluded. However, the proceedings lasted longer than anticipated, the Christmas recess was approaching, and my testimony would have meant that there would be a substantial interval between the completion of evidentiary proceedings and the time when the jurors would deliberate over their decision. Anxious to complete the case before the Christmas recess, Judge Will decided to forgo my testimony. Had I testified, I would have credibly contracted the defense witness's testimony alleging no conspiracy ever. However, I would have stated that the conspiracy broke up before the statute of limitations tolled, so plaintiffs would not be entitled to damages. Disbelieving the defendants' expert, the jury concluded that the conspiracy had continued into the 1980s, when it was not protected by the statute of limitations. As a result, recognizing that an injustice was being done, Judge Will stepped in and brokered a modest damages settlement. We were both left frustrated. Justice had gone astray because of an economist's refusal to concede his client's damages-free guilt.

5. THE PASS-ON PROBLEM

In 1977, the U.S. Supreme Court rendered an important decision in the *Illinois Brick* case, stating that only those who had directly purchased goods or services from conspirators to a price-fixing scheme were entitled to recover damages.[15] Awarding damages to 'downstream' purchasers – e.g., consumers who had bought the price-fixed product from a retailer, who in turn bought it from the manufacturer – was ruled out because of the difficulty of determining how much or how little of the conspiracy-induced price increase middlemen had passed on to ultimate consumers and because letting both middlemen and consumers sue for damages would unduly complicate class action litigation. But although the amount of pass-on depends upon the structure of the intermediate market, the degree of product differentiation, and other variables, it is highly probable that most of the burden of a price-fixing conspiracy falls upon ultimate consumers rather than the middlemen who are immediate purchasers from the conspirators.[16] Thus, justice is denied to the consumers. This problem was corrected in part as many states adopted their own antitrust damages laws without an *Illinois Brick* pass-on barrier. The asymmetry between state and federal laws encouraged litigation at the decentralized state level, among other things increasing the costs of damages recovery suits. How this

[15] *Illinois Brick Co.* v. *Illinois*, 431 U.S. 720 (1977). See also *Hanover Shoe Inc.* v. *United Shoe Machinery Corp.*, 392 U.S. 481 (1968).

[16] For a solidly-based predictive model, see Lynch (2004).

practice will be affected by passage of the federal Class Action Fairness Act, which seeks to reduce the amount of state-level litigation, remains to be seen. The implication for this conference is that if European nations develop their own class action procedures, they would be well advised to avoid the *Illinois Brick* pass-on precedent.

6. CONCLUSION

The U.S. experience with class action litigation reveals many difficulties that impair the working of the wheels of justice. The possibility of bringing class action suits does not appear to have deterred a substantial number of serious law violations, although increasing the damages multiple for serious offenses might have some deterrent effect. Entrepreneurship by specialist class action law firms often leads to opportunistic cases brought more for purposes of settlement blackmail than in the anticipation that a full trial will reveal the truth. Even when a full trial ensues, the decisions are not always in accord with either truth or justice. To be sure, some good is done. But in considering what kinds of class action laws they will enact, our European cousins are well advised to learn from the mistakes of the United States as well as from its positive experience.

BIBLIOGRAPHY

Anonymous, (2005), 'Class Action Fairness Act of 2005', *The National Law Journal*, May 16.

Gladwell, M. (2007), 'The Formula: Enron, Intelligence, and the Perils of Too Much Information', *The New Yorker*, January 8.

Harris, A. (2007), 'Study on Nicotine Levels Stirs Calls for New Controls', *New York Times*, January 19.

Kaysen, C. (1956), *United States v. United Shoe Machinery Corporation*, Cambridge: Harvard University Press.

Lynch, M.P. (2004), 'Why Economists Are Wrong to Neglect Retailing and How Steiner's Theory Provides an Explanation of Important Regularities', *Antitrust Bulletin*, **49**, 911–940.

Scherer, F.M. (1970), *Industrial Market Structure and Economic Performance*, Chicago: Rand McNally.

Scherer, F.M. (2000), *Competition Policy, Domestic and International*, Cheltenham: Edward Elgar.

Smith, R.A. (1961a), 'The Incredible Electrical Conspiracy', Part I, *Fortune*, **63**(4), 132–180.

Smith, R.A. (1961b), 'The Incredible Electrical Conspiracy', Part II, *Fortune*, **63**(5), 158–224.

White, L.J. (ed.) (1988), *Private Antitrust Litigation: New Evidence, New Learning*, Cambridge: MIT Press.

4. Will aggregate litigation come to Europe?

Samuel Issacharoff and Geoffrey P. Miller

The current wave of deregulation and market liberalization in Europe has had major repercussions for the prospect of litigated forms of collective redress. Once decried as the perversity of rapacious Americans, class actions are now the focus of significant reform efforts in many European countries and even at the level of the European Union. There are, no doubt, many reasons for the relatively sudden attention to means of collective redress. Some have to do with the need to create effective *ex post* accountability mechanisms to contain the potential adverse effects of goods and services freely entering the market. Others seek to create mechanisms for efficient resolution of the numerous intertwined claims that invariably arise from the mass production and delivery of goods and services across a broad market.

One should not gainsay the significance of these reform measures. All represent efforts to mobilize means of private enforcement to foster prevention through the prospect of civil litigation. For countries steeped in the civil law tradition, the move away from centralized public enforcement is a sea change in legal structures. The marriage of private enforcement mechanisms and relaxed barriers to entry into increasingly deregulated markets is a significant change as well. Add to that the diversity of litigation tools that are being developed and one would have to be almost churlish not to marvel at the liberalizing spirit sweeping the Continent.

And, yet, one need spend only a few minutes in conversations with European reformers before the proverbial 'but' enters the discourse, as in, 'But, of course, we shall not have American-style class actions'. At this point, all participants nod sagely, confident that collective actions, representative actions, group actions and a host of other aggregative arrangements can bring all the benefits of fair and efficient resolution to disputes without the dreaded world of American entrepreneurial lawyering. And no doubt the American entrepreneurial ways must be resisted and will be resisted fully, in much the same way that Europe has held off the unwelcome presence of McDonalds or Starbucks in its elegant piazzas. To this dignified and self-assured conversation we bring a simple but unwelcome question: Really?

We develop this chapter in two parts. First, we must acknowledge that the aversion to the American-style class action corresponds to sustained critiques of class actions in the U.S. as well. A number of American reforms, from revisions to the class action provisions of the Federal Rules of Civil Procedure to the Class Action Fairness Act, have taken aim at some of the misfirings of class actions. Some Supreme Court decisions, most notably Amchem[1] and Ortiz,[2] have burdened class actions with procedural strictures that have limited the class action as an effective vehicle for resolution of mass personal injuries. Thus, in the U.S., broad scale settlements of asbestos exposures or of pharmaceutical injuries are likely to take the form of bankruptcy workouts, or mass private aggregative settlements, as with the claims over harms caused by the anti-inflammatory drug, Vioxx.[3]

In this first section, we examine four sources of claimed dissatisfaction with the class action to assess which are meritorious, which are ill-founded, and which derive from a deeper contest over whether or not there should be private legal accountability for low value or negative value consumer claims.

We then move on to draw certain conclusions from the American experience with collective actions to ask whether the proper incentives and institutional arrangements exist in the European reform efforts. Our aim here is not to advocate that American processes need be adopted; neither of us sets foot in McDonalds or Starbucks when in Europe.[4] Rather, our inquiry is whether, based on some of the lessons that may be derived from both the American experience and the simple economics of incentive systems, the current European reforms are likely to be effective in realizing their stated aims. Our concern is that appears as an apparent cultural revulsion at accepting the reality of legal enforcement as entrepreneurial activity may leave the reforms without the necessary agents of implementation.

---

1 *Amchem Prods., Inc.* v. *Windsor*, 521 U.S. 591 (1997) (decertifying class settlement of asbestos claims).

2 *Ortiz* v. *Fibreboard Corp.*, 527 U.S. 815, 830 (1999) (also decertifying class settlement of asbestos claims).

3 The settlement is set out at http://www.merck.com/newsroom/vioxx/pdf/Settlement_Agreement.pdf.

4 One of us (Miller) confesses that he wishes to do so from time to time.

1. WHITHER AMERICA

At some level, the striking feature of current developments in aggregative practices is the apparent convergence between significantly different legal systems.[5] Increasingly, the concerns over efficient use of the courts, limits on anticipatory regulation, and the cost barriers to consumer claims have all pushed toward broader experimentation with various forms of collective law enforcement. At the same time, the extent of American liberalization of private enforcement remains a serious divide between the continents. So, as American commentators, it is perhaps best for us to begin by acknowledging the serious critiques leveled domestically against American class actions and to ground the European aversion to excess Americanism in those debates.

We will not rehash the basic arguments about why collective means of aggregating claims are necessary. We have both addressed these issues in many prior writings.[6] We both are deeply involved – one of us as a Reporter, the other as an Advisor – in the production of the Principles of the Law of Aggregate Litigation of the American Law Institute, which sets out the broader principles governing aggregate litigation. Instead, we want to address ourselves here to four distinct arguments raised in the American context over the further reaches, or perhaps excesses, of class-wide litigation.

Our focus will be on four features of class or aggregated litigation that are most at issue currently in the U.S.: first, the scope of settlement possible on a non-contractual basis; second, the limited nature of the recovery to potential class members; third, the uneasy relation between entrepreneurialism and avarice; and, finally, the manipulation of the judicial forum for litigation gain. We turn to each of these as an introduction to our assessment of European developments.

1.1 Mass Settlements

It is perhaps ironic that one of the features of American class actions that most appeals to foreign legal systems – the efficiency of mass resolution of

---

[5] Richard Nagareda discusses this convergence in Nagareda, Richard A. (2009).

[6] See, e.g., Miller, Geoffrey P. and Macey, Jonathan R. (1991, pp. 8–11, explaining the economic rationale for class actions); Miller, Geoffrey P. (1998, same); Issacharoff, Samuel (2007, pp. 380–81, highlighting the effectiveness of class actions in compensating victims of securities fraud); Issacharoff, Samuel (1999, p. 136, discussing mechanisms for aggregating consumer claims).

common disputes – is also a source of problems at home. Consider for example, the ongoing litigation of alleged securities improprieties involving Deutsche Telekom,[7] the first test of the German Capital Markets Model Case Act.[8] The German law is structured to give a representative case the authority to obtain controlling legal principles for all similar claims. But the statute provides no mechanism for enforcing the judgment for the non-represented parties, and does not have any mechanism to create and adjudge any proposed collective resolution. Thus, even were liability to be determined in the test cases, there is no mechanism for the expeditious resolution of the remaining 16,000 claims of fraud.[9] At the other pole, the Dutch legislation that provides for enforceable class-wide settlements[10] – an Act whose sweep was first tested in the proposed settlement of the non-U.S. claims in the Royal Dutch Shell securities fraud litigation[11] and is now the subject of increased judicial review – enables private parties to impose a settlement without providing any corresponding mechanism for collective trial. From the U.S. perspective, this appears to be an invitation for weak agents to step forward as purveyors of sub-optimal peace agreements.

In the U.S. context, however, the last three major Supreme Court decisions on class actions have all addressed the problematic further reaches of mass settlement. In *Matsushita Electrical Industrial Co.* v. *Epstein*, for example, the question was whether lawyers representing a state court class in a securities fraud case could agree to a classwide settlement of federal

---

[7] See Baetge, Dietmar (2007), 8–9 (summarizing the Deutsche Telekom case).

[8] Kapitalanleger-Musterverfahrensgesetz [Act on the Initiation of Model Case Proceedings in Respect of Investors in the Capital Markets], Aug. 16, 2005, BGBl. I at 2437, translated at http://www.bmj.bund.de/kapmug; see Baetge, Dietmar (2007, note 9, at pp. 12–13, describing procedures established by Model Case Act).

[9] See Baetge, Dietmar (2007), 13 (explaining that after an appellate court conducts the model case proceedings, a trial court decides all of the individual cases subject to the model ruling); Deutsch Telekom: Bad Connection, *Economist*, Apr. 12, 2008, at 74, available at http://www.economist.co.uk/business/display story.cfm?story_id=11021139 ('Even if the model plaintiffs are ultimately successful, all the other claimants must then sue separately in a lower court – a process which could take 20 years.'); Harbour, Laurel J. and Shelley, Marc E. (2007), 29 ('Under the Capital Markets Act, claimants must opt in and each must file an individual lawsuit.'). See also Baetge, Dietmar (2007, p. 20, noting that 'investors who have joined model proceedings at a later stage or have not brought a suit at all are not bound by the model decision').

[10] Burgerlijk Wetboek [BW] [Civil Code] arts. 3:305a-b; Tzankova, Ianika and Lunsingh Scheurleer, D.F. (2007, pp. 7–9, summarizing the main elements of the Dutch Act on Collective Settlements).

[11] See http://www.shellsettlement.com/ (providing information related to the proposed settlement); Harbour, Laurel J. and Shelley, Marc E. (2007, p. 28, discussing collective settlement actions in the Netherlands).

securities claims over which the state court had no jurisdiction – a mismatch between the scope of settlement authority and representation for litigation purposes much as now arises under the Dutch class action statute.[12] Then in *Amchem Products* v. *Windsor*, the Court struck down a sweeping asbestos settlement that would have exchanged compensation of current injured claimants for a structured workout of future claimants.[13] The latter group quite rightly exhibited 'rational apathy', as well put by Professor Jack Coffee,[14] for the prospects of settlement of claims were, for any particular individual at the time of settlement, a matter of remote discounted probabilities. Finally, in *Ortiz* v. *Fibreboard Corp.*, the Court refused to allow the limited assets of a litigation-crippled asbestos defendant to serve as the basis for a compelled workout of liabilities outside the formal structures of bankruptcy.[15]

The difficulty presented by each of these cases runs to the core of the American willingness to accept the notion of a private attorney general, a liberalized competition for the right to be an agent not selected by the principal. The difficulty in each of the three cases that reached the Supreme Court turned on the tension between principles of finality in settlement and the scope of the agency power of the class representative – in effect, of class counsel. None of the settlement arrangements under challenge would have raised an eyebrow if negotiated by the principals themselves, or by counsel who were directly retained by and contractually subject to oversight by their clients. Parties acting on their own behalf are free to settle their private disputes without the formalities of actually filing suit over claims (the issue in *Matsushita*) or agreeing to anticipated damages as against potential future claims (the stumbling blocks in the asbestos cases). The difficulty arises only when an unselected and effectively unsupervised agent handles this on the behalf of an absent class member.

American law responds to this tension in two ways, one formal and one a matter of intuition. The formal mechanism is to compel proposed class settlements into the strictures of the rules of procedure governing class actions. As recognized by the Court in *Amchem*, the fit is less than perfect.[16] The rules are structured to guide litigated disputes through the process of

---

[12] 516 U.S. 367, 369 (1996).

[13] 521 U.S. 591, 628 (1997).

[14] Coffee, John C. Jr. (2000).

[15] 527 U.S. 815, 864–65 (1999).

[16] 521 U.S. at p. 629 ('Rule 23, which must be interpreted with fidelity to the Rules Enabling Act and applied with the interests of absent class members in close view, cannot carry the large load [defendants], class counsel, and the District Court heaped upon it.').

pleading, discovery and trial. A consensual workout fits the formal rules structures poorly. Instead, in most class settlements, the Court retreats to what may be termed the 'due process minima' first identified in *Phillips Petroleum Co.* v. *Shutts*.[17] This requires individual notice, an opportunity (in the case of damages actions) to exclude oneself from the binding class resolution through the opt-out process, and a guarantee of unconflicted representation. Where the amounts at stake are small or the prospect of future injury is remote, courts and commentators are skeptical whether these procedural protections amount to much at all.[18]

Judicial intuition is a harder concept to formally define, but we believe it does some work. The key to the optimal class action is the principle of 'if as to one, then as to all'. No claimed broad-scale harm is likely to leave its victims in truly identical situations, but courts respond to the appearance of class members having basically fungible claims. In *Matsushita*, for example, there was no real difference between the shareholders who composed the class (except as to the quantum of their losses). The underlying claims all emerged from the same set of financial transactions, regardless of whether dressed up as state law or in their federal garb. A common settlement not only comported to a common sense or intuitive understanding of the case, it seemed inevitable, regardless of the forum in which the action might go forward.

By contrast, the sweeping asbestos settlements gave the impression of the bill of peace being stretched beyond its obvious role. In *Amchem*, most notably, the class was made up of claimants with substantially different diseases, with claims against different manufacturers and by extension insurers, with different future prognoses, and with wildly different sets of personal losses and suffering.[19] The integrity of mass resolution could neither be tested against a potential litigation of the claims (a poor test in any event given the paucity of trials generally in the American legal system[20]) or by a representational structure attuned to the more striking differences in the represented claimants, most critically the present injured and the unknowing future victims.

Apart from any intuitive sense of the propriety of any particular mass settlement practice, the fact remains that the class action settlement scene

---

[17] 472 U.S. 797, 803 (1985).

[18] See, e.g., Coffee, John C. Jr. (2006, p. 1535, discussing the shortcomings of class actions in achieving compensation for plaintiffs).

[19] 521 U.S. at 624 ('No settlement class called to our attention is as sprawling as this one.').

[20] See generally Galanter, Marc (2004, pp. 460–64, discussing the declining number of trials in the United States).

appears dominated by class counsel offering to settle claims of those they do not represent. *Amchem* and *Ortiz* really only touched on the core problem in the context of the manifestly variegated classes of far-flung personal injury victims. But the same process repeats itself across the spectrum of cases involving only economic harms in the consumer, antitrust and securities areas. Recent notable reforms to the role of the lead plaintiff under the Private Securities Reform Litigation Act as well as to Rule 23 have attended to the image of class counsel as itinerant purveyor of settlements.[21] But the issue remains very much alive in the American context.

1.2 Limited Recoveries

In virtually all class actions, the most significant recovery is by successful class counsel, not by any class member individually. Since attorneys are paid almost uniformly on a percentage of the common fund basis,[22] this is not only predictable, it is inevitable. Assume that attorney compensation in such common fund class actions runs in the range of 10 to 30 per cent of the total class recovery. Just as a matter of simple mathematics, the only way a class member could recover on the same basis as counsel would be if a single class member had suffered between 10 and 30 per cent of the harm. Assuming the underlying claim to be the malfunctioning of a $100 widget, there would have to be a consumer who repeatedly bought the same widget to discover again and again that it did not work before this level of harm could be reached. We confess that our impulse would be to take this woe-begotten consumer ungently by the shoulders and ask, 'Idiot, idiot, what were you thinking?'

Alternatively, it is argued that the recoveries in consumer cases are often sufficiently small that no rational person would ever pursue a claim for such amounts.[23] In such cases, class counsel are engaged in what the common law would have defined as the offense of barratry, the willful stirring up of

---

[21] See, e.g., Private Securities Litigation Reform Act of 1995, 15 U.S.C. § 78u-4(b) (2000) (establishing, inter alia, procedure for appointing lead plaintiff with most significant financial stake in the controversy); Fed. R. Civ. Pro. 23(g) (procedures for appointing class counsel); Fed. R. Civ. Pro. 23(h) (procedures for determining attorney fee awards).

[22] See Eisenberg, Theodore and Miller, Geoffrey P. (2004a, p. 28, showing that regardless of formal compensation system, size of fund is best predictor of attorney compensation); Eisenberg, Theodore and Miller, Geoffrey P. (2010, p. 248).

[23] See, e.g., Burch, Thomas (2004, p. 1027, acknowledging the tendency for potential plaintiffs in consumer cases to be deterred from bringing meritorious claims for small recoveries).

legal disputes for purposes of profiting thereby.[24] The smaller the actual harm visited on any individual consumer, the more apparent the fact that the driving force behind the litigation had to have been someone with an actual stake in its outcome, someone who stood to be paid from the overall amount in controversy rather than any individual's recovery. In such cases, the principal–agent relationship that normally characterizes the roles of client and attorney is disrupted since it is the agent who in effect creates the principal, or at least brings it into being by organizing the fact of collective representation.

To our mind, the only surprising thing about these related criticisms is that they are treated with any measure of surprise. The class action, as Judith Resnik aptly summarized it, is a state-created mechanism for subsidizing the litigation of claims that could not otherwise be justified.[25] The state in effect designates the agent, underwrites the cost of representation by removing the transactional barrier of having to contract with each client, and allows for a state-enforced taxation of the joint gains to compensate the agent. At least in the context of low-value claims, it is not only to be expected, it is necessary that the agent be paid much more than any individual might stand to recover and to do so because the transactional costs of litigation make every sane consumer unable to pursue an individual claim.

Consequently, the charge that class actions allow claims that would not otherwise be brought to come into the legal system is curious, to say the least. Of course they do; indeed, that is the prime justification for a class action in the first place.

The more serious issue is why a legal system would encourage the prosecution of low-value claims that are unlikely to lead to much recovery by the affected class members. This opens up a much broader discussion about the role of deterrence, the importance of *ex post* mechanisms of accountability,[26] and the general trade-offs between public and private

---

24 Barratry is traditionally defined as the 'offence of frequently exciting and stirring up suits and quarrels between [parties]'. William Blackstone, 4 Commentaries, *134. Some jurisdictions in the United States have entirely abandoned the common law claims of champerty, maintenance, and barratry, in favor of laws governing contingency fees, misconduct, and the bringing of frivolous suits. See, e.g., *Saladini* v. *Righellis*, 687 N.E.2d 1224, 1224, 1226–7 (Mass. 1997) (declining to recognize the doctrines of champerty, barratry, and maintenance); *Osprey, Inc.* v. *Cabana Ltd. P'ship*, 532 S.E.2d 269, 277–8 (S.C. 2000) (abolishing champerty as a defense).

25 Resnik, Judith (2000, pp. 2127–9).

26 For a more elaborate treatment of this issue, see Issacharoff, Samuel (2007).

enforcement. These are matters that have been extensively explored elsewhere, including in our prior writings. Our point here, however, is a more limited one. To the extent that the law wants to harness private enforcement to deter (and secondarily to compensate for) the harms that typify mass consumer markets, there must be procedures that make such conduct feasible but financially remunerative as well. And, yet, the less-than-platonic interests of class counsel in profiting from their representation are a constant source of disparagement of American class actions.

1.3 Corruption

In recent years, we have seen the fall from grace of several of the leading plaintiffs' counsel in class representations. Amid the guilty pleas of the leading figures of the securities bar,[27] and a similar plea by perhaps the most well-known figure in the mass tort bar,[28] have followed less high-profile but equally disturbing indictments of lawyers charged with criminal misconduct in mass actions.[29] The facts and the severity of the conduct vary from case to case. But the inescapable impression is of a deeply corrupt set of practitioners called to justice. If we may conclude that where there is smoke, there must be fire, then surely where there is fire, there must be conflagration. Does this not lend credence to the fundamental error of American practice? Licensing entrepreneurial activity in search of bounties must surely lead to this form of misconduct – or at least so goes the argument.

No one should countenance criminal misconduct and the breach of some of the most solemn obligations of all lawyers. And, surely, there is some connection between the American use of the private attorney general and the capacity for this kind of misconduct. Entrepreneurial enterprises seek to harness the desire for self-gain, and the line between invisible-hand style self-interest and avarice is a fine one indeed. The spate of current

---

[27] Glater, Jonathan D. (2008, at C3, discussing plea deals of Melvyn I. Weiss and William S. Lerach for their roles in 'concealing illegal kickbacks to plaintiffs').

[28] Bhattarai, Abha (2008, at C3, noting that Richard F. Scruggs, who gained fame for winning a multi-billion dollar settlement from the tobacco industry in the 1990s, was sentenced for attempting to bribe a Mississippi judge in a dispute over an insurance settlement arising out of Hurricane Katrina). Notably, the *New York Times* could not distinguish between court-supervised class actions, and private aggregations of individual cases – thus the reference to Richard Scruggs, a mass harm plaintiffs' lawyer, as a 'class-action lawyer'.

[29] See, e.g., Kay, Julie (2007, noting that Miami attorney Louis Robles was indicted for 'misappropriating $13.5 million in settlements').

scandals in the U.S. comports well with the European reluctance to license private lawyering in the service of collective redress.

Before becoming too enraptured with the perfidy of American love of self-interest as a motivator, however, a cautionary note: the question is always, compared to what? Most studies of regulatory behavior indicate that with the expansion of the centralized state sector comes an expansion of the gains to be had from political influence.[30] And with that expansion of state control comes a corresponding propensity toward corruption.[31] As one of the more comprehensive studies summarizes, '[w]e find that heavier regulation of entry is generally associated with greater corruption and a larger unofficial economy, but not with better quality of private or public goods'.[32] American entrepreneurial lawyering may yield misconduct; yet it is hardly as if the whiff of scandal has not reached countries more comfortably in the civil law tradition of state control. And, there can be no doubt that many of the more difficult features of American law turn on institutional arrangements such as the civil jury and elected judges that have nothing to do with the forms of private enforcement.

Nonetheless, here again European concerns over some of the excesses of American lawyer initiated mass actions correspond to concerns in the U.S. as well.

1.4 Magnets and Hellholes

The Shutts decision did more than simply set out the minimum due process constraints for the organization of a nationwide class action. In an opinion by then Justice Rehnquist, the Court looked to the class action as a quasi-administrative proceeding that could centralize comparably situated claims scattered across the country into one forum.[33] What Shutts did not address was the question of which was the proper forum for that centralization. That left open the possibility – soon realized – that cases of national scope, because of the undifferentiated movement of goods and services across the national market, could be brought anywhere that one aggrieved

---

30 Tanzi, Vito (1998, pp. 566–7); Ades, Alberto and Di Tella, Rafael (1997, p. 1025).

31 Djankov, Simeon et al. (2002, p. 35); Shleifer, Andrei and Vishny, Robert W. (1993, p. 600); Acemoglu, Daron and Verdier, Thierry (2000, pp. 194–5); La Porta, Rafael et al. (1999, p. 239); Adsera, Alicia et al. (2003, p. 450).

32 Djankov, Simeon et al. (2002, p. 35).

33 Shutts, 472 U.S. 797, 809 (1985).

potential class member could be found. In practice, this meant that plaintiffs, as the first movers in litigation, could select any desirable forum for the litigation of claims of nationwide sweep.

Cases of national scope quickly pointed to the frailty of a federal system.[34] The strength of a federal system is the diversity of responses to the common problems of social organization, what Justice Brandeis famously referred to as the 'laboratories of democracy'.[35] But the premise was that each unit of federalist experimentation would be an autonomous enterprise whose relative merits and demerits would be observable. The post-Shutts world, however, allowed each local jurisdiction to test its experimental regime not within its geographic boundaries, but wherever similarly situated claimants might happen to be found.

The effect of Shutts was to liberalize the ability to coordinate a case of national scope into one forum without providing any tools for resolving which forum that should be. Once we add differences in local rules governing aggregation, different legal cultures across the range of potential jurisdictions, the possibility for untoward influence with locally elected judges in some locales, and a range of other such experimental variables, the potential for strategic manipulation of forum becomes everpresent. The results were repeated claims, some no doubt well founded, of certain choice places being a 'magnet forum' or, less benignly, a 'judicial hellhole' for the ensnared defendant.[36]

Leaving aside the problem of potential undue local influence or even corruption, the broader problem is the inevitable mismatch between locally-based forms of judicial redress and markets that necessarily transcend local control. In the United States, the partial response has been to provide an expanded form of federal jurisdiction to allow nationwide cases

---

[34] This section is a pared down version of arguments more fully developed in Issacharoff, Samuel and Sharkey, Catherine M. (2006, p. 1353) and Issacharoff, Samuel and Nagareda, Richard A. (2008).

[35] *New State Ice Co.* v. *Liebmann*, 285 U.S. 262, 311 (1932) (Brandeis, J., dissenting).

[36] As expressed in the legislative history of the Class Action Fairness Act, '[t]he reason for th[e] dramatic increase in state court class actions cannot be found in variations in class actions rules; after all, the rules governing the decision whether cases may proceed as class actions are basically the same in federal and state courts – and of course, they are the same within states, i.e., the same in "magnet" jurisdictions such as Madison County and St. Clair County, Illinois, as they are in more easily accessible jurisdictions such as Cook County, Illinois.' S. Rep. No. 109–14, at 13 (2005), reprinted in 2005 U.S.C.C.A.N. 3, 13. See also id. at 21 (discussing the filing of frivolous class actions); Beisner, John H. and Davidson Miller, Jessica (2001, p. 155 'class action lawyers are bringing a large number of cases in a small number of state courts that have become "magnets" for interstate class actions').

to be brought into federal court[37] and, once there, to be consolidated for efficient pretrial development in one, suitable federal court.[38] These mechanisms leave unresolved conflicts in state laws governing the distribution of identical goods and services along a national supply chain.[39] But they are at least attentive to the problem of their being multiple potential venues for the same exact claimed misconduct.

It does not take great foresight to anticipate that the same problem of rival prospects for aggregation might take root in Europe as well. The European experiment with federalism begins with independent nation-states, rather than the more limited American states. But the problem is made more acute because of the absence of European-side courts of first instance, the equivalent of the American federal court system. Since claims of aggregate harm are necessarily tried in the national courts, with national procedures, the problem of the tension between the EU commitment to the free movement of goods and services and the local application of justice reproduces the American difficulties.

What unifies the four American controversies is precisely what most troubles Europeans about American class action practice: the role of private entrepreneurial lawyers. Each of the controversies in American practice returns to the issue of the incentives operating on lawyers who will predictably push the boundaries of the system. Yet, the simple fact is that lawyer initiative is the engine that fuels American aggregative practice. The question for reformers on both sides of the Atlantic is whether the endemic controversies that arise in a system built on self-interest can be mitigated without disabling the entire undertaking. In aphoristic terms, the question is very much one of throwing out the baby with the bathwater.

2. INCENTIVES, EUROPEAN-STYLE

Having looked at some of the flashpoints in American-style class actions, let us take a trip across the pond to Europe. Rules here are rapidly changing, and new proposals and recommendations are appearing at a dizzying rate. Analyzing European class actions is shooting at a moving target. Each

---

37 This is the effect of the Class Action Fairness Act of 2005 (CAFA), 28 U.S.C. §§ 1712–1715 (2006).

38 See 28 U.S.C. § 1407 (2006) (authorizing Judicial Panel for Multidistrict Litigation to consolidate actions in federal courts 'for the convenience of parties and witnesses and [to] promote the just and efficient conduct of such actions').

39 See Issacharoff, Samuel (2006, pp. 1840–4. examining conflicts of law in national market cases).

country is also unique, with its own legal culture, history, constitution, political system, court system, and rules governing the legal profession. It is risky, therefore, to attempt a detailed analysis of any particular country's venture into class actions, especially given our lack of detailed knowledge of any particular European system. What we can do is to examine certain features that commonly appear in the European setting without suggesting that these features appear in every country or that our stylized and general description of these features accurately reflects, at the level of detail, the law of any particular country.[40]

Three features in particular stand out: (1) the tendency to allow only organizations to represent consumers in class action cases; (2) the interaction between rules on litigation funding and class action procedures; and (3) the preference for 'opt-in' as opposed to 'opt-out' systems.

2.1 Organizational Standing

Class action procedures in Europe often restrict lead plaintiff rights to organizations which represent consumer interests.[41] This approach contrasts with that of the United States, where any class member can seek to represent the class. It is not necessary in the U.S. for the class representative to be an organization. All that is required is that the candidate must demonstrate that he will provide adequate representation and that his claims are typical of the claims of other class members.[42]

Rules limiting the lead plaintiff role to consumer organizations or similar groups appear designed to serve four objectives. First, like the requirements of typicality and adequacy under U.S. law, these rules select as the class representative a party who is expected to provide competent and loyal services to absent class members. Second, rules on organizational standing

---

[40] Class action procedures obviously vary across European countries. For a useful country-by-country table summarizing major recent developments in aggregate litigation in Europe, see Nagareda, Richard A. (2009). For more extensive comparative analysis of current European law, see Stuyck, Jules et al. (2007); Mulheron, Rachael (2008, pp. 79–120).

[41] Harbour, Laurel J. and Shelley, Marc E. (2007), 28 (discussing approaches of Spain and the Netherlands); Cafaggi, Fabrizio and Micklitz, Hans-W. (2008, p. 417, 'The majority of Member States in Europe start from the premise that consumer organizations should be given a role in administrative and/or in judicial enforcement.'). A recent exception is Spain, which does not restrict lead plaintiff rights solely to organizations – groups of individuals acting through a single lawyer can also maintain group actions.

[42] See Fed. R. Civ. P. 23(a) (listing the prerequisites for class actions). Additional requirements apply in securities fraud cases, as we will discuss below.

try to ensure that the class representative has the resources to pay the expenses of the case under prevailing rules on litigation funding. Third, these rules seek to thwart the emergence of American-style entrepreneurial class action attorneys. Fourth, and finally, there may be a jurisprudential element in organizational standing: the idea – often vaguely conceptualized – that the temporary authorization of a random individual to act as representative of a class is simply an insufficient basis for the court to take cognizance of the interest of absent parties. Something more substantial, such as a pre-existing relationship with an established group, may be needed. We will look at each of these justifications.

The last concern – jurisprudential problems with individual class members acting as lead plaintiffs – should not detain us long. All countries, as far as we know, recognize that people can be authorized to act on behalf of others. This is why the law of agency exists. There should be nothing in any well-developed legal system that prevents a court, if authorized by law and otherwise empowered to adjudicate a case, from appointing a party to act as a representative of the interests of others not present before the court.

The other three concerns, however, require more detailed investigation. In this section we will examine two of the justifications, deferring for the next section the investigation of whether organizations are better able to fund class action litigation.

So, will consumer organizations provide competent services to the class? The answer is probably a qualified 'yes'. Of course, merely having the status of a consumer organization does not mean that the people who work in the organization actually know how to manage lawsuits. Regardless of the title, an organization might be incompetent at the task, in which case the organization will not be a good class representative. But we can assume that organizations that purport to represent consumers usually have at least some expertise in enforcing consumers' legal rights. Moreover, the courts which appoint these organizations as lead plaintiffs should have discretion to assess whether the candidates for the position have the qualifications to do the work. On this score, organizational standing appears superior to the more liberal standing rules under U.S. class action practice, where the courts, in consumer cases, routinely accept class representatives whose understanding of the case can charitably be described as minimal.[43]

Even if they are competent, will consumer organizations provide loyal service to the class? Will they act as faithful fiduciaries of class interests?[44]

---

43 Miller, Geoffrey P. (2002–2003, p. 634, citing literature indicating that 'representative plaintiffs are usually mere eponyms').

44 For a perceptive analysis stressing the problems of accountability for consumer organizations, see Cafaggi, Fabrizio and Micklitz, Hans-W. (2008, p. 391,

Here the analysis is more qualified. We may assume that consumer organizations are staffed by people who conceive of themselves as dedicated to the cause of consumer protection. But even dedicated and idealistic people may not act as faithful champions when their guiding principles do not overlap with the interests of those they are assigned to represent.

The loyalty of consumer organizations to class member interests depends, to an extent, on a legal issue: are the organizations in question entitled under a given country's law to sue on behalf of all consumers, or is their representational status limited to their own membership?[45] If the organization can sue on behalf of all consumers, whether or not they are members of the organization, substantial agency problems can arise. The interests of non-profit consumer organizations may reflect ideological considerations that may not necessarily coincide with the economic interests of consumers. Suppose, for example, that an organization empowered to act as a class representative is committed to environmental protection – a noble aspiration, but not one necessarily consonant with the interests of a class of consumers who desire competitively-priced products that are fit for their intended purpose. If this organization selects cases and litigation strategy on the basis of environmental considerations – going easy, let's say, on companies that donate money to Greenpeace while vigorously pursuing companies that produce genetically modified crops – the enforcement of consumer interests would be skewed in ways that do not necessarily reflect the interests of consumers as a whole, who might prefer cheaper prices to greener products. This potential for distorted representation as a result of a distinct policy agenda is not as worrisome in U.S. class action litigation where the class is usually represented by attorneys whose interests are in obtaining a fee, not in changing the world.

This problem of ideological distortion is mitigated if many consumer organizations with different viewpoints are qualified to act as class representatives. When lots of organizations are available, the decision by one organization not to bring a case for ideological reasons doesn't prevent the case from being litigated by some other organization which may have different beliefs. The problem is not entirely solved, however. People with strong views tend to exercise disproportionate influence in voluntary organizations. Even when many organizations are qualified to act as class

---

'Consumer associations empowered with enforcement need to become more accountable towards members and the general public.').

[45] Harbour, Laurel J. and Shelley, Marc E. (2007, p. 28 noting that Spain permits consumer organizations to bring actions on behalf of both their membership and unidentified victims).

representatives, therefore, the consumer interest may not be fully represented. In such an environment, valid consumer cases may not be brought simply because no organization feels it desirable to do so.[46] Even when cases are brought, moreover, the organization given lead plaintiff status may elect to litigate the case through the perspective of its special concerns. For example, the class representative might settle a case in exchange, in part, for changes in business practices which address the organization's interests but which do not provide effective relief for consumers.

These concerns about ideological activities of consumer organizations are not as troubling if an organization is permitted only to represent its own members rather than all persons who have been injured by the challenged product or practice. People who join an organization usually endorse its stance on public issues. They are not prejudiced if the organization makes litigation decisions based on ideological factors with which they agree. But the problem of fidelity to consumer interests is only partially addressed when an organization is limited to representing its own members. If injunctive relief is permitted, for example, the organization may seek changes in the defendant's practices which serve the interests of the organization and its members, but which do not serve the interests of others. Moreover, if organizations represent only their own members, some consumers may receive no representation at all – an even worse outcome than if they receive representation that is only partially faithful to their interests.

Other problems of loyalty may be presented aside from ideological distortion of litigation decisions. There is always the risk, for example, that managers will not act as faithful agents of their organizations. Managers may misappropriate funds, pay themselves excessive salaries, appoint family or friends to jobs in the organization, or simply take too many holidays. These sorts of conflicts of interest may detract from the organization's ability to represent class members. The organization's role as lead counsel creates still other opportunities for managers to place personal gain over the interests of their institutions. If the organization has the power to allocate lucrative legal work, for example, there may be fruitful opportunities for referral fees from the law firms that receive these assignments.

---

[46] In the United States, for example, class actions have been brought against a company that manufactures chewing tobacco, claiming that the defendant illegally manipulated the market in this product. See, e.g., *In re Massachusetts Smokeless Tobacco Litigation*, No. 03–5038-BLS1 (Mass. Sup. Ct. Apr. 7, 2008). Because chewing tobacco is often considered to be a dangerous product, one could imagine that no consumer organization would take this case because the result, if the case succeeded, is that chewing tobacco would be cheaper and easier to obtain. One of us (Miller) has acted as an expert witness in a number of these cases.

These problems with organizational standing do not necessarily imply that European organizational standing rules are inferior to the American approach. All organizations face agency costs. The challenge for legal design is to find a structure of rights, duties and incentives that deliver the best package overall. If consumer organizations do manifest the problems described, moreover, the courts and legislatures will doubtless seek ways to deal with them. The question is whether organizational standing offers the best approach to protecting consumer interests, or whether some other approach would be superior.

The next issue is whether consumer organizations will be able to avoid being captured by entrepreneurial attorneys. Assuming for present purposes that entrepreneurial attorneys are bad for class action litigation – a topic investigated in Part I – the question is whether consumer organizations will prevent this blight from springing up in Europe? American experience is instructive here. The Private Securities Litigation Reform Act, a statute enacted in 1995, assigns lead plaintiff rights in federal securities fraud cases to the class member with the most significant stake in the controversy.[47] The purpose was to bring entrepreneurial attorneys to heel.[48] The lead plaintiff rules were intended to insert an active, sophisticated party with a genuine stake in the controversy as the champion of class interests, in order to counterbalance the power of self-interested plaintiffs' firms.[49]

These rules have changed securities litigation in the United States, in that the plaintiffs in such cases today are often institutional investors with significant amounts at stake. Institutional investors appear to exercise somewhat more control over class counsel than the individual plaintiffs who served as class representatives in the years before the PSLRA was enacted.[50] There is even evidence that attorneys' fees are lower when institutional investors act as lead plaintiffs.[51] Overall, however, the lead plaintiff rules have not significantly changed the environment. The same firms that dominated class action litigation prior to 1995 control it today

---

47 15 U.S.C. § 78u-4 (2008).

48 H.R. Rep. No. 104–369, at 31 (1995) (Conf. Rep.) (noting 'abusive practices committed in private securities litigation,' including 'routine filing of lawsuits against issuers of securities and others whenever there is a significant change in an issuer's stock price, without regard to any underlying culpability of the issuer'). Perino, Michael A. (2006).

49 Id. at 34–35.

50 See Perino, Michael A. (2006).

51 Id.

(although some attorneys have departed for other reasons).[52] Entrepreneurial attorneys continue to dominate securities class action practice today as they did in prior years.[53]

The U.S. experience suggests that the selection of consumer organizations to act as class champions may not, in and of itself, prevent such litigation from being dominated by attorneys. It is possible that attorneys may themselves form consumer organizations with a view towards awarding themselves the right to litigate cases entrusted to these entities. Even if the organization is formally independent, attorneys interested in obtaining fees may find many ways to obtain influence. The allocation of control over cases under European organizational standing rules will predictably depend on matters such as the stature and funding of the organization, its financial stake in the litigation, the source of funding for class counsel, the power, prestige and qualifications of counsel, and the relationship between counsel and the management of the organization.

2.2 Litigation Funding

In law as in life it is dangerous to make an unqualified statement for fear of immediate refutation. But one thing seems certain: there are no societies where lawyers work for free. As the fool puts it in King Lear, worthless words are 'like the breath of an unfeed lawyer – you gave me nothing for't'.[54] It can safely be said that none of the class action procedures adopted or proposed across Europe in recent years will succeed if it fails to adequately compensate counsel. This is not a controversial point. Others more familiar with the European legal landscape have made the same observation.[55] But carrying that recommendation into reality, in the context of European legal systems, can be a challenging task.

Two rules commonly found in European procedure present problems for class actions. First is the prohibition on contingency fees. This rule is beginning to break down; recently, for example, the German Constitutional Court ruled that the ban on contingency fees unconstitutionally burdens

---

52 See Choi, Stephen J. and Thompson, Robert B. (2006, p. 1489 finding that 'individual law firms' market shares … suffered no appreciable change in the wake of the PSLRA').

53 See id. (finding that 'few plaintiff law firms either entered or exited the market after the enactment of the PSLRA').

54 William Shakespeare, King Lear, Act I, Scene 4.

55 See Cafaggi, Fabrizio and Micklitz, Hans-W. (2008, p. 391 'Pecuniary and non-pecuniary incentives need to be provided for plaintiffs' lawyers. These may not be only market driven, but also public policy oriented, thus affecting the selection of claims to be litigated.').

clients' rights of access to the courts and attorneys' rights to practice their profession.[56] England and Wales also permit a form of contingency fees and the concept appears to be gaining momentum elsewhere.[57] But to the extent the ban on contingency fees remains in effect – and this seems to be many places – the consequences for class action litigation are significant.

The contingency fee permits the attorney to fund the litigation, and thus overcomes problems of liquidity that may make it impossible for an individual to pursue his rights. Attorneys are good litigation funders. As legal specialists, they have the ability to assess the value of suits. They will thus tend to direct valuable resources (their time and energy) to cases which offer the largest expected benefit for class members and society as a whole. Because attorneys handle numerous lawsuits, moreover, they can achieve portfolio diversification in ways not possible for ordinary clients, who are usually involved in only one. And attorneys tend to have better liquidity than consumers. They finance cases through their own efforts. If bank financing is required, they are probably better than their clients at obtaining loans at favorable rates. Accordingly the contingent fee can generate effective funding of class action litigation. Essentially all U.S. class actions are funded with contingent fees.

It is difficult, however, to design an effective class action procedure in the absence of a contingent fee. Consider the case where the law imposes on an individual plaintiff the responsibility to pay the expenses of litigation with no right of contribution from other class members, as under the German representative action for securities improprieties. Under these conditions the plaintiff faces the following payoffs: if the case succeeds, receive his or her share of the class recovery (which may be only a few Euros); if the case fails, pay not only the class attorneys' fee, but the defendant's fee as well. No rational individual would be willing to serve as class representative in these conditions.

---

56 See Bundesverfassungsgericht [BVerfG] [Federal Constitutional Court] Dec. 12, 2006, Entscheidungen des Bundesverfassungsgerichts [BverfGE] 1 BvR 2576/04, 1–115 (F.R.G.), available at http://www.bverfg.de/entscheidungen/rs20061212_1bvr257604.html.

57 Since the 1990s, England and Wales have allowed the conditional fee model, which takes two forms: a 'no win no fee' agreement and an uplifted fee if the case is successful. In either case, the size of the increased fee is independent of the award or settlement in the case. Hodges, Christopher (2007), 27–8. Other European nations have experimented with, or are considering, introducing this system of financing litigation. Emons, Winand (2007), 89–90. For a detailed history of the adoption of the conditional fee system in England, see Abel, Richard L. (2001), 253–7 (outlining the history of and policy behind the adoption of contingent fees in England).

A few jurisdictions have allowed experimentation with litigation-funding corporations as means for capitalizing class action litigation. The concept is perhaps best developed in Australia, where several such firms are in operation; with such firms now even being listed on the Australian Stock Exchange.[58] These organizations, which also operate in Canada, advance funds for the litigation and provide indemnities against possible liability for fees, in exchange for a cut of the proceeds if the plaintiffs succeed.[59] Such organizations do not appear to have caught on yet to any substantial extent in Europe. Litigation funding companies are an innovative solution to the funding problem. At bottom, however, they appear to rely on rules for allocating litigation proceeds that are functionally similar to the contingent fee.

Another alternative to the litigation funding dilemma is to use organizations as representative plaintiffs. The advantage of these parties is that they may have a budget to cover the costs of consumer suits, and therefore may not be as liquidity-constrained as the average consumer. Even so, organizations are likely to face difficulty in funding class action litigation in the absence of a contingent fee. Money does not materialize out of the sky. Who will fund the organizations?

Under traditional rules it appears that an organization could not get funding from the case itself.[60] If a case succeeds, the benefits of the judgment go to class members rather than to the organization. If a case fails, a representative organization has to pay both its attorney's fees and the defendants' attorney's fees. This is a losing proposition overall; the organization either gains nothing or loses a lot. The rules could of course be adjusted to allow organizations to collect a share of the proceeds of successful cases prior to the payments to class members. If these payments are large enough to compensate for the costs of cases that fail, they can make these organizations financially viable without other funding. But

---

58 See IMF (Australia) Ltd Home Page, http://www.imf.com.au/ ('IMF is a publicly listed company providing funding of legal claims and other related services where the claim size is over $2 million.') (last visited Oct. 10, 2008).

59 The Australian Supreme Court upheld such arrangements against the claim that they violate rules against champerty and maintenance. See *Campbells Cash & Carry Pty Ltd* v. *Fostif Pty Ltd.*, 229 A.L.R. 58, 1–211 (2006), available at http://www.austlii.edu.au/au/cases/cth/HCA/2006/41.html ('By 'organising' persons into a legal action for the vindication of their legal rights, representative proceedings are not creating controversies that did not exist.').

60 See Sullivan, Kathleen M. and Gunther, Gerald (2004) ('Third-party standing is thus more likely to be allowed the closer the relationship and the greater the identity of interest with the rightholder…').

allowing the organizations to take a share of the class recovery is nothing other than a contingent fee by another name.

If organizations are not funded from the proceeds of successful cases they must find other sources of support. Class members are an obvious possibility. But obtaining payment from class members is fraught with difficulty.

Obtaining payment after the fact, in the absence of a prior agreement, would appear all but impossible. Many class members would probably refuse an organization's request that they share the benefits of a judgment if the case succeeds. They are even less likely to want to share the costs if the case fails.[61] Even if, under applicable law, a class member's decision to opt-in to a case obligates him to pay his share of the expenses if the case fails, an organization that fronts such expenditures may face claims that they did not properly inform class members of the risks of opting-in. It could be difficult for the representative plaintiff to pursue class members for payment in this situation.

Perhaps such organizations could condition membership on payment of dues. With the money in hand, the organizations would not face the challenge of collecting it post hoc. But dues paid in advance also present difficulties. If the consumer organizations represent everyone who is harmed by a defendant's conduct, rather than just its membership, severe free-rider problems would be created. Consumers would be better off not joining the organization and getting its services for free. Even if the consumer organizations represent only their members, they would have to charge dues sufficiently high to compensate it for anticipated litigation expenses. It is not clear that consumers would be willing to pay these costs in advance when the return on their investment is only the hope that they might someday share in the recovery from a lawsuit. Consumer resistance to paying dues in advance could be avoided if organizations conditioned

---

[61] One such case famously occurred in the United States. See *Kamilewicz* v. *Bank of Boston Corp.*, 100 F.3d 1348, 1349 (7th Cir. 1996) (a class action settlement case in which class members were paid a settlement award, but after the attorneys fees for obtaining the settlement were deducted from their award, many class members yielded a net loss). Subsequently Congress banned the practice under the Class Action Fairness Act. See 28 U.S.C. § 1713 (2008) ('the court may approve a proposed settlement under which any class member is obligated to pay sums to class counsel that would result in a net loss to the class member only if the court makes a written finding that nonmonetary benefits to the class member substantially outweigh the monetary loss.').

membership on taking a cut of the recovery if the case succeeds. But this strategy is nothing more than a contingent fee under another name.[62]

The other alternative for funding class action litigation appears to be the government. Certainly the government has the necessary resources. And because consumer class actions are brought on behalf of large segments of the public, the argument in favor of public funding is substantial. Yet government funding is not a panacea. If organizations are funded by public authorities, their survival becomes captive to politics. Funding is never certain, and in times of austerity consumer organizations may find that their budgets are among the first to be slashed. Moreover, the principle of 'he who pays the piper calls the tune' is likely to operate in the case of government funding. Politicians may seek to influence the organization's behavior. Prosecution of particular cases may be encouraged or discouraged by politicians who wish to punish enemies or reward friends. In short, the independence of consumer groups cannot be guaranteed if they rely on public funding for their operations.[63]

Some of the funding problems associated with the lack of a contingent fee could be alleviated if the 'loser-pays' rules are reformed to make the consequences less draconian. For example, in consumer cases, the rule could be transformed into a 'one-way' fee shifting system, under which the defendant must pay counsel fees if the class succeeds but the class does not have to pay the defendant's fees if the case fails.[64] Eliminating class members' risk of liability could enhance their willingness to participate in cases. Such proposals, however, can be expected to be resisted by business interests who may perceive them as unfairly one-sided. Even if adopted, moreover, they would not fully address the funding problem. Although they eliminate one cost of litigation – the obligation to pay the defendant's fee if the case fails – they do not eliminate another cost, namely the obligation to pay class counsel if the case fails. Unless a practicable means

---

62 Free-rider problems can also be problematic. If the consumer organization is allowed to seek compensation for all injured consumers, not just those who are members of the organization, then consumers would lose the incentive to join the organization in the first place because by doing so they would be subsidizing class members who did not join.

63 The opposite problem may also be present. If an organization has strong views on controversial topics, the provision of government funding could represent a potentially troublesome subsidy by the government of private ideological activism.

64 Quebec has apparently come close to this approach by limiting class members' liability to nominal costs. Watson, Garry D. (2001, p. 274). Ontario has established a public corporation charged with reimbursing unsuccessful lead plaintiffs for cost obligations. Id. at pp. 274–5.

is found to pay this cost, one-way attorneys' fee rules will not fully address the funding problem for class action litigation.

2.3 Opt-in versus Opt-out Procedures

A third notable feature of several European class action procedures is that they utilize opt-in rather than opt-out mechanisms (the recent Italian statute is an example[65]). No doubt, such opt-in procedures have advantages. They ensure that class members who join litigation do so voluntarily and out of their own free will – in marked contrast with the opt-out process under which it is possible for a class member to be a part of a lawsuit and suffer a preclusive judgment without even realizing that fact. Opt-in procedures also respect the jurisprudential idea that litigation cannot be legitimate, as regards an innocent party, unless he has voluntarily agreed to join the action.

But opt-in procedures also pose problems. We will discuss three of these difficulties: problems with incentivizing a named plaintiff under an opt-in regime; difficulties in attracting adequate participation rates, and the challenge of offering defendants the opportunity to achieve global peace through the class procedure. We then turn to the relationship between the choice of opt-in or opt-out rules on the objectives of deterrence and risk internalization that underlie a system of after-the-fact liability for wrongful conduct.

2.3.1 Who will step forward?

Opt-in procedures can create complicated strategic dynamics that can impede or prevent the successful prosecution of consumer rights. In particular, they can create a reluctance for anyone to step forward as the representative plaintiff – a feature that has hampered the application of the new Capital Markets Model Case Act in Germany, for example.[66] So long as there are collective gains to be had from being a passive party in a representative action, and so long as that is coupled with the risk of suffering losses if one is the representative party, the overwhelming temptation will be to remain a passive free-rider. The losses are of two forms. The simpler is the loss that comes from actually being a party to losing litigation. The disparity between the loss that the representative party may face and the risks of the other potential claimants can be mitigated by an

---

[65] See Legislative Decree 6 September 2005 no. 206, art. 139 (in Ordinary Supplement no. 162 to the Official Journal 8 October, no. 235) (on file with the authors); Capiello, Stefano (2006, pp. 21–5).

[66] Baetge, Dietmar (2007, p. 31).

expansion of the preclusive effect of a representative judgment that the individual may realize – a practice that appears to be gaining favor in England and Wales under Group Litigation Orders. But the deeper problem is that, so long as there is a loser-pays rule, the named claimant in the representative action is being asked to assume the entirety of the risks associated with a failed venture, while delivering a common good to the other claimants if successful. Whenever there is such a marked disparity between concentrated risks and diffuse benefits, the temptation to free-ride is dramatic. And, in the absence of a coordination mechanism on cost exposure, one would expect the classic form of failure associated with collective action problems.

2.3.2 Insufficient participation

American experience suggests that the opt-in procedure will face difficulty in attracting widespread participation. The reason is inertia. Experience under American opt-out rules confirms that class members usually do nothing. They almost never opt out. In consumer cases, on average, less than 0.2 per cent – two in a thousand – exercise the right to exclude themselves from the case.[67]

While opt-out rates are somewhat informative about probable participation under European opt-in procedures, but they need to be evaluated with caution because of a significant difference between the contexts. In the case of opt-outs, the path of inertia – doing nothing – also is the path of rationality. It is nearly always in the class member's interest not to opt-out of class cases. If the class member opts out he gains virtually nothing but loses the right to participate in whatever benefit the class litigation may generate – a small benefit, perhaps, but still one that confers some value. Conversely, if the class member does nothing, he loses nothing other than an essentially worthless right to bring his own lawsuit, but gains the right to participate in the proceeds of the class litigation. A rational class member will not opt-out.

The incentives are otherwise with the opt-in decision. Here, rationality counsels class members to opt-in. If the class member opts-in, he gets to participate in whatever value the class action may generate, whereas if he fails to opt-in, he forfeits the right to participate in the class case and gains only the essentially worthless right to bring his own individual action. In opt-in cases the path of rationality is to act rather than to do nothing. Thus

---

[67] See Eisenberg, Theodore and Miller, Geoffrey P. (2004b, p. 1532, this figure was derived from a study examining several thousand class action decisions between 1993 and 2003).

the behavior of class members in opt-out cases, where inertia and rationality coincide, will not necessarily carry over to opt-out cases, where they conflict.

A more direct analogue to European opt-in statutes is found in three American statutes that use opt-in rather than opt-out procedures (the Age Discrimination in Employment Act,[68] the Fair Labor Standards Act,[69] and the Equal Pay Act[70]). Evidence from reported cases suggests that participation rates under these statutes are around 50 per cent.[71] Although not as high as they might be if class members behaved rationally, such participation rates are not at all bad. But we should not readily conclude that consumer class actions in European opt-in regimes will have similar participation rates. American opt-in statutes apply in the specialized context of workplace litigation. Cases brought under these laws typically involve only a small number of plaintiffs; the class members have many opportunities to communicate with one another about the litigation, both at the workplace and via electronic means such as the Internet; and the amounts recovered are often substantial – all factors tending to increase participation rates. Where these factors are absent – as in the typical consumer case, where class members have nothing in common other than that they purchased a particular product – participation rates can be expected to be considerably lower.

An even closer American analogue to European opt-in procedures might be found in class action settlements. U.S. class action cases often settle, and when they do, class members who have not opted out are often required to submit claim forms establishing their entitlement to relief. If they do not file claims they get nothing. The claiming process after settlement of an opt-out case is thus functionally similar to the opt-in process under European statutes. If anything, in fact, the incentive to claim, post-settlement, is greater in opt-out cases than in opt-in cases because failing to file a claim forfeits all right to recovery whereas failing to opt-in only forfeits the right to participate in the action before the court.

---

[68] Age Discrimination in Employment Act of 1967, 29 U.S.C. § 626(b) (2008) (opt-in requirement for ADEA).

[69] Fair Labor Standards Act of 1938, 29 U.S.C. § 216(b) (2008) (opt in requirement for FLSA).

[70] Equal Pay Act of 1963, 29 U.S.C. § 206(d) (2008) (codified along with the FLSA, the EPA is therefore subject to the opt-in provisions of 29 U.S.C. § 216(b)).

[71] See, e.g., *Su* v. *Electronic Arts, Inc.*, 2006 WL 4792780 (MDFL 2006) (76 members of 110-member class joined FLSA class action); *Lenahan* v. *Sears, Roebuck & Co.*, 2006 WL 2085282 (DNJ 2006) (1700 of 16 252 class members joined FLSA class action).

Claim rates depend on factors such as the size of per capita recovery, the extent of the notice program, the ease of filing a claim, and the degree of outreach undertaken by class counsel. Overall, however, the American experience is mixed. Cox and Thomas studied claiming rates in securities cases and found that even highly sophisticated institutional investors often fail to claim the settlement benefits. Less than 30 per cent of the institutional investors with demonstrated entitlement to relief filed claims, even though failing to do so left billions of dollars on the table.[72] This study, moreover, dealt with securities cases with sophisticated parties and significant amounts at stake. Claiming rates in consumer cases are often even lower – not a surprising fact given that the parties are less sophisticated and the recoveries tend to be small. Some documented consumer claim rates have been in the single digits, and in one case not a single class member filed a claim even though the class consisted of more than a million people.[73]

Based on this experience, what levels of participation can be expected in European opt-in cases? An important factor here will be the scope of consumer organization standing. If the scope of representation is limited to the organization's members, opt-in rates can be anticipated to be relatively high, because by joining an organization people signal their willingness to participate in its activities. Moreover, it might be possible, under the law of some jurisdictions, for the consumer organizations to obtain advance agreements from their members to participate in all applicable class action litigation brought by such organization in the future. If such agreements were respected, participation rates could come to resemble the U.S. style opt-out procedure, although all the opt-ins would be members of the organization. If the scope of representation extends more broadly to all consumers damaged by the defendant's conduct, however, opt-in rates are likely to be much lower, and probably in line with U.S. experience for claiming rates in settlements.

Overall, for the opt-in process to render effective relief, it will be crucial for jurisdictions implementing it to provide effective means for participation, in the form, for example, of clear notice (ideally, in consumer cases, including telephone information lines and Web Pages as well as written and/or publication notice), cheap and easy opt-in forms (again including Web-based sign-up facilities), and outreach by the representative plaintiff coupled with suitable incentives for that party to maximize participation rates.

---

72 Cox, James D. and Thomas, Randall S. (2005, p. 412).

73 *Nienaber* v. *Citibank* (South Dakota) N.A., No. Civ. 04–4054, 2007 WL 752297, at *2 (D. S.D. Mar. 7, 2007).

2.3.3 Insufficient finality

Let's turn now to the question whether opt-in procedures can accomplish global peace (global, that is, in the small world of a consumer dispute). U.S. experience indicates that defendants desire to extinguish all liability when they settle a class action. That desire is expressed in clauses, demanded by defendants, which declare the entire agreement to be null and void if more than a specified number of plaintiffs opt-out of the litigation. The goal of global peace is also indirectly beneficial to members of the class because defendants will pay more for settlements that offer assurances against future litigation.

Compared with opt-out procedures, the opt-in requirement offers significantly less assurances against continued litigation. In an opt-out environment, anyone who doesn't exclude himself is bound by the outcome and cannot participate in future litigation within the scope of the release or judgment. In an opt-in environment, only those who affirmatively join the litigation are bound by the outcome; everyone else is free to bring additional lawsuits. The defendant obtains no protection against these claims. Moreover, the threat of additional lawsuits is not merely theoretical. If only a small percentage of the class opt-in to a class action, it may be possible for another class action to be brought on behalf of those who did not opt-in.[74] This problem with lack of global peace is illustrated in the Deutsch Telekom litigation in Germany. Even if a model litigation were able to determine that Deutsch Telekom should lose on the issue of liability, there would still be 16,000 pending cases without an organizational vehicle for an efficient collective resolution.[75]

It would appear possible, even within the constraints of an opt-in procedure, to implement rules that provide protections against future litigation similar to those that can be obtained in an opt-out regime. Jurisdictions could provide that class members who do not opt-in are free to bring later individual actions but cannot thereafter participate in other class actions. A rule that allows only one opportunity to participate in a class action would accomplish effective global peace. Although class members who do not opt-in can bring later individual actions, few will do so because it is not economically viable to litigate consumer cases on an individual basis.

---

[74] Defendants apparently prefer the opt-in rule, notwithstanding its impact on their ability to obtain a comprehensive settlement, because of the substantially lower damages they expect to pay under this procedure, a point we address below.

[75] Baetge, Dietmar (2007).

2.3.4 Deterrence

Finally, let's consider the deterrent effect of opt-out and opt-in procedures. Here, the opt-out approach offers advantages, although these are not always realized in actual cases. With an opt-out procedure the class consists of everyone who has not opted out, which will be the vast majority of class members given consumer inertia. To persuade a court that a settlement is 'fair, reasonable, and adequate',[76] therefore, a plaintiffs' attorney must argue that the benefits of the litigation are sufficient for everyone who remains in the class. With an opt-in procedure, in contrast, the settlement need only provide benefits that are adequate for the (usually much smaller) set of plaintiffs who have joined the litigation. Therefore, as a general matter, opt-out procedures offer better deterrence because they impose on the defendants more of the social cost of the defendant's wrongful behavior.

However, here as elsewhere, the analysis is not quite that simple. Attorneys in U.S. cases have found ways to make class action settlements resemble outcomes under an opt-in rule. When a common fund is created, some settlements contain 'reverter' clauses providing that any amounts not claimed revert to the defendant.[77] Reverter settlements are no longer seen in securities class actions,[78] but are occasionally found in other contexts. Much more common, these days, is the consumer class action settlement where the defendant promises to provide relief in a defined amount to every class member who files a claim. These settlements, as a practical matter, are similar to settlements under opt-in class actions because the defendant ends up having to pay out only to those class members who file claims – usually only a fraction of the class.

It might be possible, under European systems, to combine an opt-in procedure with the assessment of damages to the entire class, thus achieving better deterrence. Courts could order undifferentiated relief for classes and apportion it on a pro rata basis to class members who opt-in and claim.

---

[76] Fed. R. Civ. P. 23(e)(2).

[77] See Miller, Geoffrey P. and Singer, Lori S. (1997, p. 106, examining reverter clauses). Reverter clauses offer the benefit that they may be valued, for purposes of calculating percentage attorneys fees, as if the entire benefit had gone to the class, even though the defendant expects to receive some of the settlement consideration back. See *Boeing Co.* v. *Van Gemert*, 444 U.S. 472, 481–82 (1980) (ruling that class counsel attorneys' fees may be calculated based on the total funds potentially available for relief rather than the actual payout).

[78] This is probably due to the fact that the PSLRA requires that percentage fees be based on the amount of any damages 'actually paid to the class.' 15 U.S.C. § 78u-4(a)(6) (2008). This provision reverses the presumption in *Boeing Co.* v. *Van Gemert* that fees can be based on the full amount that would be paid if all class members filed claims. 444 U.S. at 481–2.

This is the way many class action settlements are handled in the United States. The settlement administrator holds the claim forms until the claim period has expired and then distributes the settlement proceeds to the claiming members in proportion to their claims. Alternatively, claims administrators pay out proven claims as they come in and then make a second distribution of unclaimed amounts to class members who have filed claims. If distribution to claiming class members is considered problematic because some would receive more than their actual damages, jurisdictions could consider alternative recipients of the excess damages, such as escheats to the government. Strategies such as these, if permissible under governing law, could go far towards improving the deterrent effect of opt-in class actions.

3. CONCLUSION

At bottom, the gulf between the European and American developments in class actions and other forms of aggregation reflect a deeper divide than doctrines and formal laws alone would reveal. For the civil law countries of continental Europe, the resistance to collectivist measures of adjudication is in part a continuation of what Hayek has termed a 'constructivist rationalism' – a deep-seated belief in the importance of rationalist expertise in top-down administrative decision-making.[79] What characterizes the American legal tradition – what Hayek in turn would term 'spontaneous order'[80] – is the common law attachment to the bottom-up competitive evolution of legal rules.[81] One need not fully endorse Hayek's further claim about the inherent superiority of the less intrusive forms of common law regulation[82] to recognize that class actions allow non-state actors to assume the collective responsibility that civil law systems have traditionally reserved exclusively for the state.

Thus, when the evolving laws of aggregate procedure in the U.S. and Europe are held up for comparison, what seems to jump out is a core

[79] The term itself is formulated in Hayek, Friedrich A. (1973, p. 95). Hayek attributed this view to a Cartesian belief that all advances in human society and knowledge were the product of reasoned design. Id. at 10–12.

[80] Id. at 118–122.

[81] See Posner, Richard A. (2003, pp. 275–6, analogizing Hayek's 'spontaneous order' theory to Darwin's theory of natural selection).

[82] Mahoney, Paul G. (2001, p. 504, '[Friedrich Hayek] argues vigorously that the English legal tradition (the common law) is superior to the French (the civil law), not because of substantive differences in legal rules, but because of differing assumptions about the roles of the individual and the State.').

question: who will organize, fund, and lead the collective efforts? We focus on these issues to highlight our – admittedly American – reaction to the emerging trends in Europe. Both the strengths and the weaknesses of American collective procedures have been the willingness to entrust a great deal of social regulation to private initiative and common law forms of adjudication. Once unleashed in the U.S., private actors found ways to harness aggregative procedural devices, most notably class actions, to create powerful litigation tools and, by extension, a new source of common law decision-making. The evolving European law attempts to realize some of the benefits of collective dispute resolution, but is conspicuously limited in its conception of how these processes will come to be realized. From the American vantage point, we look at the European experiments with a concern that law without the institutional framework for its enforcement is necessarily lacking.

At the end of the day, it is all well and good to lay down railroad track and invest in a stock of modern trains. But someone has to drive the train. The U.S. has a creaky rail network and trains that are the envy of no one. Compared to the rail systems of Europe, it is difficult to believe that a wealthy country cannot connect its major cities efficiently. But, in our legal analogue, we do have trained engineers quite willing to drive class action cases forward. This may not be much; it may not be sufficient; it may at times prove problematic; but it may also prove to be necessary.

REFERENCES

Abel, Richard L. (2001), 'An American Hamburger Stand in St. Paul's Cathedral: Replacing Legal Aid with Conditional Fees in English Personal Injury Litigation', *DePaul Law Review*, **51**, 253–313.

Acemoglu, Daron and Thierry Verdier (2000), 'The Choice between Market Failures and Corruption', *American Economic Review*, **90**, 194–211.

Ades, Alberto and Rafael Di Tella (1997), 'National Champions and Corruption: Some Unpleasant Interventionist Arithmetic', *Economic Journal*, **107**, 1023–42.

Adsera, Alicia et al. (2003), 'Are You Being Served? Political Accountability and Quality of Government', *Journal of Law, Economics and Organization*, **19**, 445–90.

Baetge, Dietmar (2007), Class Actions, Group Litigation And Other Forms of Collective Litigation – Germany, available at http://www.law.stanford.edu/display/images/dynamic/events_media/Germany_National_Report.pdf

Beisner, John H. and Jessica Davidson Miller (2001), 'They're Making a Federal Case Out of It ... in State Court', *Harvard Journal of Law & Public Policy*, **25**, 143–208.

Bhattarai, Abha (2008), 'Class-Action Lawyer Given 5 Years in a Bribery Case', *New York Times*, June 28.

Burch, Thomas (2004), 'Necessity Never Made a Good Bargain: When Consumer Arbitration Agreements Prohibit Class Relief', *Florida State University Law Review*, **31**, 1005–1040.

Cafaggi, Fabrizio and Hans-W. Micklitz (2008), 'Collective Enforcement of Consumer Law: A Framework for Comparative Assessment', *European Review of Private Law*, **16**, 391–417.

Capiello, Stefano (2006), 'Supervision and Class Action Against Conflicts of Interest in Universal Banking: The U.S. Experience vis-à-vis Recent Italian Initiatives', NYU Hauser Global Law Working Paper, No. 03/07, 21–25, available at http://papers.ssrn.com/sol3/papers.cfm?abstract_id=949896.

Choi, Stephen J. and Robert B. Thompson (2006), 'Securities Litigation and Its Lawyers: Changes During the First Decade After the PSLRA', *Columbia Law Review*,**106**, 1489–1533.

Coffee, John C. Jr. (2000), 'Class Action Accountability: Reconciling Exit, Voice, and Loyalty in Representative Litigation', *Columbia Law Review*, **100**, 370–422.

Coffee, John C. Jr. (2006), 'Reforming the Securities Class Action: An Essay on Deterrence and Its Implementation', *Columbia Law Review*, **106**, 1534–86.

Cox, James D. and Randall S. Thomas (2005), 'Letting Billions Slip Through Your Fingers: Empirical Evidence and Legal Implications of the Failure of Financial Institutions to Participate in Securities Class Action Settlements', *Stanford Law Review*, **58**, 411–454.

Djankov, Simeon et al. (2002), 'The Regulation of Entry', *Quarterly Journal of Economics*, **117**, 1–35.

Eisenberg, Theodore and Geoffrey P. Miller (2004a), 'Attorney Fees in Class Action Settlements: An Empirical Study', *Journal of Empirical Legal Studies*, **1**, 27–78.

Eisenberg, Theodore and Geoffrey P. Miller (2004b), 'The Role of Opt-Outs and Objectors in Class Action Litigation: Theoretical and Empirical Issues', *Vanderbilt Law Review*, **57**, 1529–67.

Eisenberg, Theodore and Geoffrey P. Miller (2010), 'Attorneys' Fees and Expenses in Class Action Settlements: 1993–2008', *Journal of Empirical Legal Studies*, **7**, 248–81.

Emons, Winand (2007), 'Conditional Versus Contingent Fees', *Oxford Economic Papers*, **59**, 89–101.

Galanter, Marc (2004), 'The Vanishing Trial: An Examination of Trials and Related Matters in Federal and State Courts', *Journal of Empirical Legal Studies*, **1**, 459–570.

Glater, Jonathan D. (2008), 'Class-Action Lawyer Gets 30 Months in Prison', *New York Times*, June 3.

Harbour, Laurel J. and Marc E. Shelley (2007), 'The Emerging European Class Action: Expanding Multi-Party Litigation to a Shrinking World', *Practical Litigator*, **18**, 23–36.

Hayek, Friedrich A. (1973), Law, Legislation and Liberty, 1 Rules and Order, Chicago, University of Chicago Press.

Hodges, Christopher (2007), 'Global Class Actions Project Country Report: England and Wales', available at http://globalclassactions.stanford.edu/sites/default/files/documents/England_Country%20Report.pdf

Issacharoff, Samuel (1999), 'Group Litigation of Consumer Claims: Lessons of the American Experience', *Texas International Law Journal*, **34**(135), 139–43.

Issacharoff, Samuel (2006), 'Settled Expectation in a World of Unsettled Law: Choice of Law after the Class Action Fairness Act', *Columbia Law Review*, **106**, 1839–71.

Issacharoff, Samuel (2007), 'Regulating After the Fact', *DePaul Law Review*, **56**, 375–387.

Issacharoff, Samuel and Richard A. Nagareda (2008), 'Class Settlements Under Attack', *University of Pennsylvania Law Review*, **156**, 1649–1722.

Issacharoff, Samuel and Catherine M. Sharkey (2006), 'Backdoor Federalization', *UCLA Law Review*, **53**, 1353–1434.

Kay, Julie (2007), 'Asbestos Attorney Accepts 10-Year Term in Plea Deal', *Daily Business Review*, Apr. 19, available at http://www.law.com/jsp/article.jsp?id=1176887061450.

La Porta, Rafael et al. (1999), 'The Quality of Government', *Journal of Law, Economics and Organization*, **15**, 222–79.

Mahoney, Paul G. (2001), 'The Common Law and Economic Growth: Hayek Might Be Right', *The Journal of Legal Studies*, **30**, 503–525.

Miller, Geoffrey P. (1998), 'Class Actions', in Newman, Peter (ed.), *New Palgrave Dictionary of Economics and the Law*, I , London: Macmillan Press, pp. 257–62.

Miller, Geoffrey P. (2002–2003), 'Competing Bids in Class Action Settlements', *Hofstra Law Review*, **31**, 633–50.

Miller, Geoffrey P. and Jonathan R. Macey (1991), 'The Plaintiffs' Attorney's Role in Class Action and Derivative Litigation: Economic Analysis and Recommendations for Reform', *The University of Chicago Law Review*, **58**, 1–44.

Miller, Geoffrey P. and Lori S. Singer (1997), 'Nonpecuniary Class Action Settlements', *Law and Contemporary Problems*, **60**, 97–154.

Mulheron, Rachael (2008), 'Reform of collective redress: A perspective of need', http://www.civiljusticecouncil.gov.uk/files/collective_redress.pdf.

Nagareda, Richard A. (2009), 'Aggregate Litigation across the Atlantic and the Future of American Exceptionalism', *Vanderbilt Law Review*, **62**, 1–52.

Perino, Michael A. (2006), 'Institutional Activism through Litigation: An Empirical Assessment of Public Pension Fund Participation in Securities Class Actions', St. John's University School of Law Legal Studies Research Paper Series, 1, Paper No. 06–0055, available at http://papers.ssrn.com/abstract=938722.

Posner, Richard A. (2003), *Law, Pragmatism, and Democracy*, Cambridge, MA, Harvard University Press.

Resnik, Judith (2000), 'Money Matters: Judicial Market Interventions Creating Subsidies and Awarding Fees and Costs in Individual and Aggregate Litigation', *University of Pennsylvania Law Review*, **148**, 2119–2195.

Shleifer, Andrei and Robert W. Vishny (1993), 'Corruption', *The Quarterly Journal of Economics*, **108**, 599–617.

Stuyck, Jules et al. (2007), *An analysis and evaluation of alternative means of consumer redress other than redress through ordinary judicial proceedings*, http://ec.europa.eu/consumers/redress/reports_studies/comparative_report_en.pdf.

Sullivan, Kathleen M. and Gerald Gunther (2004), *Constitutional Law*, New York, NY: Foundation Press.

Tanzi, Vito (1998), 'Corruption Around the World: Causes, Consequences, Scope, and Cures', International Monetary Fund Staff Papers, **45**, 559–94.

Tzankova, Ianika and D.F. Lunsingh Scheurleer (2007), *Class Action, Group Litigation and Other Forms of Collective Litigation*, Dutch Report, available at http://www.law.stanford.edu/display/images/dynamic/events_media/Netherlands_National_Report.pdf

Watson, Garry D. (2001), 'Class Actions: The Canadian Experience', *Duke Journal of Comparative & International Law*, **11**, 269–87.

5. Class action as a remedy for market failure

Jürgen G. Backhaus

INTRODUCTION

Recently and only after the turn of the century, we have been able to witness a remarkable phenomenon in Europe which had long been important to the United States. In fact, class actions in Europe do not even belong to the curriculum of the study of jurisprudence of a typical German Law School.

In this chapter, I briefly identify the recent development of class actions in Europe and then try to explain its significance. (I) In doing so, we begin with a definition of class actions. (II) This definition does not include the considerations of forensic symmetry. The need for such a more inclusive analysis becomes particularly urgent when issues of market failure and forensic dynamics are to be considered. (III) While the class action as an institution is significant for overcoming market failure in the context of forensic symmetry, it is marred by principal–agency problems and cannot be relied upon as a perfect remedy. The Rosenfield[1] effect indicates the extent to which it fails to overcome market failure and the extent to which it may have to be complemented by other forensic institutes.

1. SECTION I

Originally, the class action is a product of English common law, which has no counterpart in either Roman law or the Germanic legal culture. It did, however, also occur in the United States through the federal rule of civil procedure and variously in state law. In the United States the class action had its greatest triumphs, as it lends itself to remedy market failure of the form of what may be called a Phillipian relation. Phillip of Macedonia had

1 Rosenfield (1976).

organized a treaty system with the Greek city states so as to be predominant, while the city states taken together were by far more powerful than the King of Macedonia. The King, however, was by far more powerful than any individual city state on its own. So he organized a treaty system by having individual contracts with each city and preventing them from banding together against him. This is the situation in modern industrial society with mass production, when a producer of a good or service has individual relations with millions of customers. There is an incentive to imperceptibly cheat on each of these customers to a relatively small extent, when the damage caused is not worth bringing a suit against the company on an individual basis. However, the damage taken together over all the parties affected may very well warrant an action. This is the situation where the class action can serve its function. The class in order to be certified must be held together by a common characteristic which allows a clear decision as to who is a member of the class and who is not. For the class to be certified it need not organize itself, however, as the *ex ante* costs of organization may outweigh the damage incurred. This is particularly likely before the suit is taken up, as the damage incurred needs to be weighed with the probability of court error, thus resulting in an *ex ante* settlement that is smaller than the damage incurred, if the probability of court error is positive. After the judgment has been made or a settlement negotiated, the amount resulting from the judgment or the settlement will certainly exceed the cost of organizing the class. For this reason, it is important that the costs of organization be postponed until after the settlement or judgment. This requirement raises serious difficulties in continental and Roman civil procedure that do not occur in American civil procedure.

A related problem refers to the homogeneity of the class. For the class to be certified, the damage incurred must be identical or similar by nature, not by extent. An individual customer may however have multiple relations with one and the same firm and hence also incur different kinds of damages. If they all come about in the same way, there is no legal problem, but if different kinds of damages coming about differently lead to different legal constellations, the class may be too heterogeneous to be certified. The certification occurs by the judge before whom the attorney accompanied by selected class members brings the suit. Since the class has not yet been organized, the attorney acts for the class and on behalf of it.

From the point of view of the defendant, the plaintiffs' claim may appear frivolous, only made so as to extract a payment. For this reason, the certification is really the crucial step in the whole class action and needs to be carefully prepared by the attorney who brings the action. Since the attorney plays such a crucial role, and since the class has not yet formed, the relationship between class and attorney is potentially plagued by principal–

agency problems. This can be illustrated by referring to the Conference on Jewish Claims against Germany, Inc., a New York based organization pressing claims as the name indicates.

This organization has accumulated reserves of more than sixty billion US $, which it keeps as a war chest instead of dispersing it to the presumed victims. The organization has an interest to do so, since the victims are necessarily all of an advanced age and may soon die before receiving any compensation. Since presumably the organization has an endless life while the victims are mortal, the principal–agency problem is inescapable.

2. SECTION II

In his anatomy of market failure, Francis Bator[2] does not mention the systematic nuisance that Phillipian relations invite. For this reason, there has not been a discussion of this type of contract externalities.

With this influential article, Bator set off a strange development. Market failure became something like an agenda for good government. A government has its main purpose in correcting market failure. This is the central agenda for many textbooks in public finance, which with this narrow focus is often called public economics. What is not taught is how a government can be expected to correct such market failure with which instruments and with which motivation. Public economics steers into a stark contrast with public choice. Instead, the emphasis should be on finding self-correcting institutions of market failure. Class actions can be viewed as such a self-correcting institution overcoming market failure.

Externalities stemming from Phillipian relations, although not mentioned by Bator, are market instances of market failure nevertheless, and there is always a contractional relation between malfeasor and victim. The externality cannot be internalized or remedied, however, because the cost of doing so exceeds the harm, which is why the harm would rest with the victim if it were not for the option of a class action, which works like an automatic remedy. The automatism comes about, if an attorney has discovered the niche of organizing these class actions and of bringing the suits. It takes a specialized organization to discover and document the potential actions, and it also takes a hospitable legal system to certify the classes. This is why class actions tend to occur in some districts more often than in others. In Europe, where class actions so far have been only available in

2 Bator (1958).

England, it is likely that substantial differences will result minutely reflecting the procedural differences that are likely to come about when different member states and perhaps even the European Union itself start legislation enabling such actions.

The self-correction of market failure that class actions bring about is typically overlooked in legal discourse, although from an economic point of view it is the primary purpose of class actions. Here is an important bridge that law and economics research can provide between economic analysis and legal discourse.

Although they are self-correcting, class actions do not completely remedy the market failure. This is due to the specifics of organizing class actions. The extent to which the remedy is incomplete is called the Rosenfield effect, to which we now turn.

3. SECTION III

England has a differentiated organization of its legal profession and makes the distinction between attorneys and solicitors. Only solicitors are accredited at the higher courts where class actions have to be brought. Due to this organization, the initial burden of bringing a class action is relatively higher in the country where they originated than in the United States, where no distinction between attorneys at law and solicitors exist.

In the United States, however, legal fees are born indirectly through a kind of sharecropping[3] system called contingency fees. If the attorney is successful in court, he charges a fee contingent upon the extent of his success; if he fails to succeed, he has worked for nothing. This fee arrangement has a dual effect from the point of view of an optimal internalization of externalities. First of all, if there is poor precedent or the attorney is inexperienced in the area, he will be reluctant to take the case on. Hence, the self-enforcing mechanism of repairing market failure may take some time to catch on, giving criminal entrepreneurs[4] an innovator's (Schumpeterian) chance. The characteristic of the contingency fee arrangement is akin to what occurs in sharecropping. The sharecropper plants less than the farmer who owns his farm, as he can only harvest for his own gain a part of the crop and has to pay the rent with the remainder. If as it is common in contingency fee arrangements, the fee amounts to forty per cent, the attorney will set out to maximize the expected sum of his fee payment and not the expected sum of the damages. For this reason, he will settle before

---

3 Compare Cheung (1968 and 1969).

4 Schumpeter (1912 (1), 1926 (2)).

the maximum damages have been reached, as the curve of his expected fees peaks before and, of course, lower than the curve of expected damages to be recovered. In this sense, the self-correction of market failure due to the Phillipian relation is incomplete.

Different remedies have been suggested in the literature to take account of this incompleteness. As Coase[5] has pointed out, the market solution is hard to reproduce precisely through a legal solution, and for this reason these remedies have to be taken with a grain of salt. The first and the most obvious remedy is the award of multiple or punitive damages. From a legal point of view, this route is hard to navigate because civil law and penal law with their different dogmatic and legal procedures are being intertwined, leaving a lot of room for skilled attorneys' maneuvering. If in addition juries are involved, the judge may be well advised to leave this route unexplored.

Sometimes, the damage is not easy to put down in figures and may have repercussions going far beyond the original class. For this type of case, American jurisprudence has developed the doctrine of fluid recovery requiring the malfeasor to undertake some highly visible positive action with wide repercussions. Whether this type of creative adjudication would be acceptable to the European legal profession is a matter of speculation.

Finally, in the country where they originated, class actions are really a matter of class, excluding the poorer pockets of the population from access to the legal system. This is because the solicitors have to be paid up front. As a remedy, Labour governments have toyed with the idea of legal expense insurance. These forms of insurance are fraught with multiple occurrences of moral hazard and tend to work only in clearly circumscribed cases, typically as an add-on to the membership fee of a professional organization. For this reason, due to legal expense insurance, large class actions may indeed be brought about in fairly rare cases of professional disputes and can therefore not be considered as a general remedy for the deficiency of the self-correcting mechanism of class actions.

4. SUMMARY

The chapter offers an introduction into the basic economics of class actions emphasizing their function as self enforcing remedies to market failure. Their shortcomings, however, are likewise discussed.

---

5 Coase (1960).

REFERENCES

Backhaus, J. (1977), *Forensische Symmetrie*, Book Manuscript, University of Constance.

Bator, F. (1958), 'The Anatomy of Market Failure', *The Quarterly Journal of Economics*, **72**(3), 359–79.

Cheung, S.N.S. (1968), 'Private Property Rights and Sharecropping', *The Journal of Political Economy*, **76**(6), 1107–1122.

Cheung, S.N.S. (1969), *The Theory of Share Tenancy. With Special Application to Asian Agriculture and the First Phase of Taiwan Land Reform*, Chicago, London: The University of Chicago Press.

Coase, R.H. (1960), 'The Problem of Social Cost', *Journal of Law and Economics*, **3**, 1–44.

Rosenfield, A. (1976), 'An Empirical Test of Class-Action Settlement', *Journal of Legal Studies*, **5**(1), 113–120.

Schumpeter, J.A. (1912(1)), (1926(2)), *Theorie der wirtschaftlichen Entwicklung*. Leipzig: Duncker & Humblot. English translation of the second edition published in 1934 as *The Theory of Economic Development*. Cambridge, MA: Harvard University Press.

Tullock, G. (1967), 'The Welfare Costs of Monopolies, Tariffs and Theft', *Western Economic Journal,* **5**(3), 224–32.

6. The economics of class action litigation

Thomas S. Ulen[1]

1. INTRODUCTION

The United States is almost unique in many aspects of its legal system – for example, in allowing contingent fee contracts between lawyers and clients and in making legal education exclusively graduate education, in using juries in civil disputes, and allowing class action litigation. This last practice – facilitating and regulating the consolidation of numerous similar lawsuits into a single action – is practiced elsewhere, but it has reached its most extensive use in the highly competitive U.S. legal market. The principal argument in favor of class action litigation is straightforward: it is likely to be more efficient to litigate the same general complaint once rather than to do so in a series – perhaps a large number – of similar complaints. To put the matter in economic parlance, there are likely to be economies of scale for both plaintiffs and defendant or defendants in having one large trial than in having individual trials.

However compelling this simple argument in favor of class action litigation may be, the practice of class action litigation in the modern United States' legal system has not commanded universal approval. While there are those who see it as a socially beneficial practice that allows, for example, appropriate redress to small claimants against major corporations, there are those who see class action litigation as socially costly in that it fosters frivolous litigation that threatens to erode business confidence and competitiveness. The public debate between these opposing views has been

[1] I owe great thanks to Amber Evans, University of Illinois College of Law, Class of 2008, for her excellent assistance, and to Theodore L. Ulen and Timothy B. Ulen for comments on an earlier draft. I also want to thank Professor Giovanni Ramello of the Department of Public Policy and Collective Choices, University of Eastern Piedmont, Italy, for organizing the conference and volume of contributions of which this chapter is a part.

heated and has resulted in numerous attempts to regulate class actions. The debate is far from resolved, and much scholarly investigation of these matters remains to be done.

At the same time that the United States is wrestling with how to regulate class actions, the European Union is considering creating a union-wide action for 'collective redress', a proposal that seems to take strength from the arguments made by supporters of class actions in the U.S.

The conjunction of a U.S. debate on the desirability of class action litigation and the EU's consideration of a proposal to broaden collective actions for compensation seems an appropriate time to take stock of class actions. Perhaps the U.S. experience can help to guide the EU proposal so that it creates an action that creates the greatest net social benefits of collective redress and avoids some of the pitfalls that have plagued the U.S.

In this chapter I shall use economics to examine the theory and practice of class action litigation in the U.S. Although I am deeply convinced that economics is a crucially important tool in understanding almost any legal topic, I am also aware that there are deep and vexing legal issues that attend the creation and furtherance of class actions. I will leave a consideration of those legal issues to others in order to focus on the economics of class actions. I shall proceed as follows: Part 2 will consider the economics of class action litigation. The argument will be at a very general level, without consideration of the costs and benefits of class actions in particular forms of litigation, such as securities fraud and antitrust. Part 3 will consider some recent commentary on class action litigation, attempts at reform in the U.S., and other practical matters. A brief concluding section summarizes.

2. THE ECONOMICS OF CLASS ACTION LITIGATION

Like almost everything in life, class action litigation has social costs and social benefits. The purpose of this section of the chapter is to identify those costs and benefits and to speculate on what role law can play in securing the greatest net social benefit from the consolidation of similar claims into a single action. I shall begin with a brief consideration of the social benefits, then turn to a brief discussion of the social costs, and, finally, consider reforms that may lead to greater net social benefit of class action litigation.[2]

[2] I have relied heavily on two wonderful scholarly treatments of the economics of class actions for much of the material in this section: Bone (2003, pp. 269–98) and Miller (1998).

I shall not here discuss the phenomenon of 'mass torts', in which a single event gives rise to injuries to a large number of claimants and whose claims might be consolidated into a single action. The claims against Union Carbide for the chemical leak at its Bhopal, India, plant in 1984 and those against asbestos manufacturers are interesting examples.

2.1 The Social Benefits of Class Action Litigation

The potential economic benefits of class actions are clear: they allow a group of similarly situated plaintiffs, all of whom claim to have been injured by the same action or actions of the defendant or defendants, to consolidate their individual claims into a single group action. The simple economic argument in favor of a group action (to which we shall soon see many nuances) is that there are economies of scale to be realized from consolidation. Imagine that 10,000 patients claim to have been harmed from having taken a pharmaceutical produced by the defendant company. Rather than have a series of 10,000 independent individual actions against the defendant – each of which actions might require a new set of motions, empanelling of and deliberation by a jury, and presentation of substantially identical evidence – consolidation allows one jury, one set of witnesses, and one deliberation on liability and damages. The situations, ages, medical conditions, losses, and other facts about the plaintiffs may be very different, but the demonstration that they took the defendant's drug and that the taking of the drug led to the common (adverse) reactions among the plaintiffs need not be made 10,000 different times in order for justice to be done.[3]

---

[3] Of course, this is a stylized version of the litigation. There may be, as we shall see, a bifurcated trial in the first phase of which the common facts of liability are brought out and separate later proceedings in which individual losses are calculated. Even in the instance of bifurcation, there still may be significant cost savings from consolidating the liability phase of the proceedings. In point of fact, it is more common – and more productive of problems, as we shall see – to dispense with the separate proceedings on individual damages and, instead, to award the class a lump-sum with each plaintiff getting a pro rata share.

There is another stylization to the example: I have assumed that one large trial replaces 10,000 individual trials. That is extremely unlikely. Even if class actions were illegal, there would almost certainly not be 10,000 individual trials. Rather, there would probably be a series of enough individual trials for the other plaintiffs and the defendant to form a strong belief about how the future trials would be likely to go – that is, whether plaintiffs or the defendant would be likely to win. In light of those beliefs, settlements or dropped complaints will account for the largest percentage of the 10,000 possible trials.

We may grasp some further benefits of the class action if we consider the difference between two very different groups of litigants: first, those for each of whom litigation has a positive expected value, and second, those for each of whom litigation has a negative expected value.[4]

2.1.1 Classes with positive-expected-value litigants

For the members of this class an individual case against the defendant makes economic sense. Nonetheless, there are two strong economic reasons for consolidating their claims against the same defendant for, essentially, the same wrongs: first, consolidation saves litigation costs through economies of scale (and has some other associated efficiencies), and second, consolidation attenuates external costs associated with a series of individual litigations on the same matters.[5]

First, class actions allow the realization of economies of scale, in that the total resource cost of litigating all the claims is less in a consolidated proceeding than in a series of individual trials or settlement negotiations. Obviously, there are no duplicative requests in pre-trial discovery or in the presentation of evidence at trial.

The savings in litigation costs (including discovery) may allow the plaintiffs to invest in a more efficacious case (in the forms, say, of a better lawyer, more discovery, and better and more expert testimony) than they would do in a series of individual cases.[6] To the extent that this leads to a heightened chance of recovery of meritorious claims, this is a social benefit.

Relatedly, class consolidation may even the playing field as between plaintiffs and the defendant or defendants. This may be a benefit in that the field may be tilted in favor of defendants where there may be a series of individual plaintiffs alleging the same injuries. Why would that be the case? If the defendant anticipates a series of trials against individuals, all of whom have the same general claim, then the defendant, as a repeat player with much to lose from this series of trials, has a strong incentive to invest heavily in winning the early cases. The point is that the defendant may be willing to expend much more on each early case than would each individual plaintiff. All other things equal, this would give the defendant an increased

---

4 If a litigant has a 'positive expected value of litigation', then the amount that he anticipates recovering if his case is successful, multiplied by the probability of success, exceeds the anticipated cost of litigation. For someone who has a 'negative expected value of litigation,' the amount that she anticipates recovering times the probability of success is less than her anticipated costs of litigation. I shall make a further distinction within the class of negative expected value litigants shortly.

5 See Bone (2003, pp. 261–5).

6 See Hay and Rosenberg (2000a).

likelihood of prevailing in the early cases to his great advantage in that these successes may discourage later litigation. Allowing the plaintiffs to consolidate may remove the advantage that the defendant would otherwise have.

Note that all of these benefits could have been achieved through voluntary agreement among the individual litigants (without any formal legal mechanism for creating and certifying a class, as in Rule 23 of the *Federal Rules of Civil Procedure*). For example, they might have met and agreed to a strategy of litigation that would, in essence, achieve the economies of scale by developing a common plan for pre-trial discovery and litigation, organizing an order of presentation of the claims (with, perhaps, the strongest claims going to trial first), agreeing on a plan to apportion any damages or settlements among members of the group, and so on.

The transaction costs, however, of achieving this voluntary agreement are likely to be prohibitive. As a result, voluntary organization of a class of similarly situated claimants with positive-expected-value cases seems unlikely. So, the individual claims might proceed, but at higher total cost of social resources than would be the case if there were a method of overcoming the transaction costs of class organization. This is precisely the case for the state's creating a procedure for lowering the transaction costs of claim consolidation through a class certification procedure. Doing so allows those with positive-expected-value claims against the same defendant or defendants for similar injuries to make their cases at relatively low private and social cost. And that has the further social benefit of deterring wrongdoing.

Second, consolidation of positive-expected-value individual claims into a single class may avoid external costs that might arise in a series of individual trials. Professor Bone gives this revealing example:

> Suppose that 100,000 persons claim injuries from taking a drug manufactured by the defendant drug company (D). Each of the injured parties brings an individual suit, and each seeks $6 million in compensatory and punitive damages. Suppose each suit has a 60 per cent chance of success. Also, suppose that D's liability insurance is capped at $50 million, and its corporate assets are worth another $50 million.
>
> The total expected [value] of all 100,000 injured parties is 0.6 × 100,000 × $6 million = $360 billion. The total amount available to satisfy all the judgments is $100 million, which is nowhere near the $360 billion expected liability, even allowing for individual judgments to be spaced out over time. Under these

> circumstances, the first few plaintiffs are likely to exhaust all the available resources, leaving the rest with nothing to satisfy their judgments.[7]

A class action consolidation of all 100,000 claims can avoid this situation, which is known as a 'limited fund'. For example, the class could agree to apportion the expected value of the claims – $360 billion – among the members of the class according to some formula. Note that where there may be a limited-fund situation, the possibility of certifying a class can forestall the problems that would arise if the class members realized that there might be little or no satisfaction available to late arrivals and began a stampede to be the first to litigate.[8]

2.1.2 Classes with negative-expected-value litigants

Now turn to the second situation, one in which there are a large number of plaintiffs, each of whom has a negative-expected-value claim.

It is important to note that there are two very different ways in which the members of this group have negative-expected-value claims. The first is one in which the negative-expected-value of each claim arises from the fact that each of the plaintiffs has suffered no injury (or no compensable injury). Even if the cost of litigation were trivial, these claims would have no merit. These are 'frivolous' claims, which any well-functioning legal system ought to be able to filter out. In the following section I shall turn to the possibility that the class action mechanism does not do a very good job of performing this filtering function and may, in fact, encourage frivolous claims.

The second way in which there might be negative-expected-value claims is that each member has truly suffered a wrong but the extent of the wrong is relatively small. As a result, the expected value of the claim (the anticipated recovery times the likelihood of prevailing at trial), even if the likelihood of success is very high, is less than the cost of bringing the claim. This sort of class is frequently referred to as a 'small claim' class and typically arises in securities fraud, antitrust, and consumer protection litigation.

Professor Bone gives this example of a small claim class:

> Suppose each member of a securities fraud class suffers an average loss of $100, and suppose the expected cost of litigating the securities fraud claims through [to judgment] is $1 million. Suppose as well that the likelihood of success on liability is 60 per cent. Obviously, no one in the class would bring an individual suit for

---

7 Bone (2003, pp. 263–4).

8 In this regard, the class certification procedures avoid the same problems that might arise in a bankruptcy proceeding in which the total claims of the creditors exceeded the assets of the debtor.

> $100. But if there are 100,000 class members, the expected class recovery is $6 million [0.6 × 100,000 × $100 = $6 million], which is large enough to interest an attorney who expects to get, say, 20 per cent of the total recover (or $1.2 million) as his fee.[9]

The legal system can assist these claimants by making it possible for them to form a class. Why should it do so? There are two related reasons. First, the costs to the members of the small claim class of organizing themselves so as to recover from the defendant or defendants are prohibitively high. Second, without the assistance of the law to organize a class, thereby allowing the plaintiffs to proceed against the defendant or defendants, the wrong that the defendant or defendants have inflicted on the members of the group may not be deterred. Allowing for a relatively low-cost method of certifying a small-claim class can, therefore, realize a significant social benefit.[10]

I have, following Professor Bone's and Professor Miller's superb lead, divided the world of class action litigation into groups of positive-expected-value and negative-expected-value claimants. A moment's reflection will have shown, however, that the categorization is not exact. There are, of course, actual examples of both types of class. But there are also numerous examples of classes that consist of a mixture of positive- and negative-expected-value claimants. Those mixed groups present some special issues, which will concern us in the next section.

2.2 The Social Costs of Class Action Litigation

To this point I have tried to demonstrate the social benefits of group litigation. But there are social costs, too. In this section I shall identify four sources of social costs in class action litigation: (1) litigation costs (again),

---

[9] Bone (2003, pp. 266).

[10] Bone notes, *id.* at 267–8, that there are alternatives to the class action for deterring defendants from inflicting small injuries on a large-number of individuals. For example, treble damages for successful plaintiffs, as are allowed in the U.S. federal antitrust statute, may create a strong incentive to litigate and a strong deterrent on wrongful action. Note, however, that in the example given above treble damages would not have converted any individual's negative-expected-value claim into a positive-expected-value claim. There may be other public enforcement mechanisms beside individual causes of action. In securities fraud, for instance, the U.S. Securities Exchange Commission can bring actions against firms for violations of the securities regulations, including seeking criminal penalties. Nonetheless, it is almost certainly the case that the appropriate policy is one of *both* private causes of action (including class actions) and public enforcement (through *ex ante* regulation and *ex post* public enforcement). See Kolstad, Johnson and Ulen (1990).

(2) agency costs, (3) costs associated with adverse selection and opt outs, and (4) the strategic use of class actions for blackmail settlements.

2.2.1 Litigation costs

Although I have suggested that the costs per litigant are less in a class action than in the individual cases of the litigants, that is not to say that the costs of a class action are inconsiderable. In fact, they can be substantial. Simply managing communication among the class members (such as giving all potential members a chance to opt out of the class) is a considerable expense and administrative burden. Because individuals and subgroups within the class may have their own attorneys, there typically must be a litigation steering committee and a lead counsel. These committees can be fractious.

In some instances, there are overlapping class actions proceeding against the same defendant or defendants for similar injuries at the same time, and the attorneys for those various actions will want to coordinate among the cases. And coordination costs can be substantial.

Finally, once a class has been certified, the trial strategy must be developed and approved with the help of the judge. Among the issues that arise in this regard are whether to adjudicate liability jointly for all members of the class and damages individually or all matters jointly.

Even though one suspects that the total litigation costs (and the costs per claim) will be less in a class action than in a series of individual actions, the three factors noted in the previous paragraphs are expensive and arise because of the consolidation of claims.

2.2.2 Agency costs

A source of significant social cost in class action litigation is the relationship between the class counsel and the members of the class. In the parlance of economics, there are 'agency costs' in that the desires of the principal (the members of the class) are not perfectly consonant with those of the agent (the class counsel). When a principal suspects that there are agency costs, he or she can incur monitoring costs to observe the agent's behavior or institute a compensation scheme that better aligns the agent's interests with those of the principal (as when the agent is given a share of the enterprise's profits, which the principals would like to have maximized).

In a small claim class, none of the individuals has enough at stake to warrant incurring monitoring costs. In a class in which there are large claims (positive-expected-value claims), there may also be an agency-cost problem in that the members of the class may try to free ride on the monitoring efforts of others. And, of course, if each member of the class wants others to bear the costs of monitoring the lead counsel, then each of them will hang back waiting for someone else to undertake the monitoring function.

Unless these agency problems are solved, class counsel can seek to maximize its own interests – typically, its fee – rather than the interests of the class members. In an effort to minimize this problem, most class action litigation requires the court to approve the fee awarded after a litigated result for the class or as part of a settlement.

There are two common methods of calculating the attorneys' fees in class action litigation. In the 'lodestar method', the class counsel files a report of the number of hours that he or she has worked on the cases. The court then generates what is called a 'lodestar' compensation figure by multiplying those hours by a reasonable hourly fee. The judge then adjusts the actual compensation awarded up or down from that lodestar figure depending on his or her assessment of the particularities of the case, such as the number of parties involved, the complexity of the legal issues involved, and the like.

The alternative method is the 'percentage of the recovery' method, under which the judge decides what share of the recovery to award to the attorney or attorneys based on his or her assessment of the same kinds of factors that lead to adjustments away from the lodestar method.

The incentive effects of attorney behavior of these two methods of compensation are straightforward. Under the lodestar method, class counsel has an incentive to put in for compensation of as many hours as possible. He or she may, therefore, have an incentive to prolong the litigation. Under the percentage-of-recovery method, the attorney has the same incentives as under a contingent-fee arrangement – namely, to settle early and for as large amount as possible (but surely for less than the expected value of the class claims).

Even worse, class counsel may have an incentive to arrange a 'sweetheart settlement', under which counsel agrees with the defendant to settle the claim for a high attorney's fee and a low class recovery.[11] In the same vein

[11] Professor Bone cites *Kamilewicz* v. *Bank of Boston Corp.*, 100 F.3d 1348 (7th Cir. 1996), as an example. 'In [that case], a class of 715,000 mortgagees, whose mortgages were serviced by BankBoston Mortgage Corp., sued for damages in an Alabama state court, alleging that the bank improperly calculated the surplus that the mortgagees had to maintain in their escrow accounts. The parties settled, with the class attorneys receiving somewhere between $8.5 and $14 million in fees and class members receiving one-time interest payments between $0 and $8.76. The settlement provided that BankBoston could deduct the attorney's fees from each mortgagee's escrow account, and in most cases this deduction exceeded the interest payment, with the result that most class members suffered a net loss from the litigation.' Bone (2003, p. 277).

(but distinguishably) class counsel may agree to a high fee for itself and something less than complete compensation for the class members. For example, defendants in class action litigation frequently offer in-kind, nonmonetary compensation for the members of the class, such as coupons good for discounts on future purchases from the defendant. Or the defendant may propose the creation of a 'reversionary fund', on the basis of which the attorney's fees are awarded (perhaps on a percentage basis) and any amounts unclaimed from the fund after a fixed period of time revert to the defendant. In both instances it is very difficult for anyone to estimate the true value of the class's recovery, but one may be fairly confident that the extent of the compensation for the attorneys involved is handsome and that for the class members, less so.

The judge, in his or her capacity to review settlements, should identify and prevent abusive outcomes. But judicial review of class settlements is imperfect. Sweetheart and difficult-to-evaluate settlements – both of which are likely to run in favor of the class attorney's and defendant's interests and against those of the class members – surely undermine the deterrence effect of class action litigation by making the cost of the defendant's wrongdoing less than it ought to be. To that extent, these abuses impose substantial social costs.[12]

While there is a general consensus among commentators that the percentage-of-recovery method is the more efficient method of calculating attorney's fees in class action litigation, there have been some additional attempts to find superior compensation methods. One of these has recently been tried with regard to some small claim class actions – auctioning the position of lead counsel. The court oversees the auction, inviting bids from the various attorneys in which the attorneys specify a fee schedule and

[12] Two recent empirical studies of attorney's fees in class action litigation throw light on the actual practices in recent litigation. Ted Eisenberg and Geoff Miller examined two extensive data bases of class action data spanning the period 1993–2002. Their findings are that the size of the class's recovery is the principal determinant of the attorney's fees. Even in cases in which the court performed the lodestar calculation, the size of the recovery (whether in money or in coupons or other forms of soft relief) was the principal determinant of the attorney's fees. 'The mean fee award in common fund cases is well below the widely quoted one-third figure, constituting 21.9 per cent of the recovery across all cases [].' Eisenberg and Miller also found a positive correlation between the degree of risk in the litigation and the attorney's fees. See Eisenberg and Miller (2004). Eric Helland and Jon Klick also studied factors affecting the size of attorney's fees in class actions. They find that judges who face crowded dockets are more likely to approve higher attorney's fees, all other case characteristics held constant. See Helland and Klick (2007).

other quality controls. The court then chooses the lowest bid, subject to quality minima.

Yet another method of minimizing the agency-cost problem is to address the effectiveness with which the class members monitor the lead counsel and litigation committee. For example, the Private Securities Litigation Reform Act of 1995 (PSLRA), about which I shall say more in the next section, requires that the 'party filing a securities fraud action in federal court publish notice inviting members to apply for appointment as representatives' of class members. The representatives will then select the lead counsel for the class. The court selects the representatives from those nominated and tends to choose those with the largest stake in the litigation outcome, such as institutional investors, on the theory that they will have the greatest incentive to choose an able lead counsel and then monitor him or her carefully.

2.2.3 Adverse selection and opt-outs

The class counsel has an incentive to maximize the size of the class that he or she represents. More class members typically means more hours of work or a greater total recovery, so that under either of the typical methods of attorney fee calculation the class attorney does better with a bigger than with a small class.

This incentive to increase the size of the class inevitably leads to a problem of adverse selection. Because they anticipate receiving more than their claims are worth, weak claims are more likely to opt into the class than are strong claims, which could, perhaps, recover more in an individual claim than they can anticipate receiving as a pro rata member of the class.

The problem is exacerbated by the fact that the defendant may anticipate the fact that weak claims are likely to predominate the class and may, as a result, offer a lower settlement amount to the whole class than they otherwise would. If there is a settlement on these terms, then there is a transfer of wealth from those with strong claims to those with weak claims. In the extreme, it may be the case that this adverse selection sets off a 'death spiral': the defendant offers a lower amount than the strong claims believe they are entitled to, leading the strong claims to opt out of the class, leading the defendant to offer a lower settlement amount, causing more strong claims to exit the class, leading the defendant to offer still less, and so on.

In practice this unraveling is unlikely to happen because there are some (perhaps, many) strong claims who are unaware of how strong their claims are. As a result, some of the strong claims are likely to remain in the class, even though they might do better through individual litigation. Nonetheless, even if the end result is not that *all* remaining claims in a class are weak, the adverse selection effect is likely to lead to either a significant number of weak claims and possibly even to a dominance of weak claims over strong claims.

Where there is great concern about this adverse selection problem (as, for example, might be the case where there is a large variance in the size or quality of the claims) but where class litigation is likely to be, on net, socially beneficial, the appropriate remedy is to remove the right to opt out of the class.[13]

2.2.4 The strategic use of class action litigation for blackmail settlements

An increasingly common complaint about class action litigation is that it lends itself not to the benign purposes upon which we have focused but to malign purposes – specifically, for the purpose of extracting unwarranted payments (in that these are negative-expected value claims) from vulnerable defendants. Rather than chance losing substantial sums of money in uncertain litigation, defendants may make 'blackmail settlements'.

Professor Bone gives this example of how the large stakes in a class action litigation can lead to an unwarranted settlement:

> Suppose that a class includes 10,000 members, each of whom has a frivolous suit but could prove \$500,000 in damages if the court mistakenly found liability. Also suppose that the attorney's fee is 20 per cent of the class recovery. Under these circumstances, an attorney will expect a fee of \$20 million [$0.20 \times 10{,}000 \times 0.02 \times$ \$500,000 = \$20 million], and, therefore, should be willing to litigate the class action even if the expected cost is in the millions.[14]

These are precisely the arguments made by Judge Richard A. Posner in *In the Matter of Rhone-Poulenc Rorer, Inc.*, 51 F.3d 1293 (7th Cir. 1995). The litigation in that case involved a group of about 300 hemophiliacs who alleged that they had become HIV-positive as a result of taking AHF, a clotting agent made by Rhone-Poulenc Rorer, Inc., in the early 1980s. The 300 plaintiffs all had similar enough claims that they sought and received certification as a class from the federal district court. Judge Posner was reluctant to certify the class.[15] Of the 13 individual cases that had been brought at the time of this appeal, 12 had been won by the defendant, and Judge Posner speculated that the defendant would have probably won the vast majority of the remaining individual cases. Nonetheless, he suggested that if the class were to be certified, many more plaintiffs would present

13 Bone (2003, pp. 282–5).

14 Id. at 291.

15 The case also involved some complicated procedural issues. For the purposes of focusing on the class-action-litigation aspects of the controversy, I shall ignore those issues.

themselves, perhaps in the thousands. And in that circumstance Rhone-Poulenc Rorer might be facing $25 billion in potential liability and, as a result, bankruptcy. 'They may not wish to roll these dice. That is putting it mildly. They will be under intense pressure to settle.' Judge Posner quotes Judge Henry Friendly as saying, 'settlements induced by a small probability of an immense judgment in a class action [are] "blackmail settlements"'.[16] The implication is that there are circumstances in which the mere act of certifying a class may be enough to convert low-merit claims into such a high risk of catastrophic failure that the defendant will be impelled to settle.[17] Judges might, therefore, exercise discretion in class certification proceedings so as to weed out the unmeritorious individual claims that might be converted into formidable class actions that rational defendants will buy off.[18]

There has been some recent scholarly support for tying class certification to the underlying merits of the actions.[19]

2.3 'Settlement Class Actions'

The most controversial use of settlements in class actions are those that cover not only those who already claim to have been injured but also future claimants. The category of 'future claimants' includes those who might discover later that they were injured by the same actions of the defendant that have given rise to the current settlement offer. Typically, the 'settlement class action' occurs before suit is filed. The defendant or defendants and the

---

16 *Rhone-Poulenc Rorer*, at 1298, citing Friendly (1973).

17 But see Schwartz (2002). Professor Schwartz seeks to articulate why it is thought to be normatively undesirable for a class action to result in a settlement if the underlying individual claims had little chance of success. 'I speculate that what really moved Judge Posner was a belief that too much power has been conferred on juries and that juries are using that power systematically to discriminate against defendants.' Id. at 309. 'The opinion is an unhappy mixture of expediency (do anything to reduce the harm inflicted by irresponsible juries), obfuscation (what, exactly, is the theory of the case?), and disingenuousness (tears for defendants settling to avoid bankruptcy but apparent indifference to victims settling to avoid destitution).' Id. at 310.

18 For the case in favor of aggregating some NEV claims and for worrying less about blackmail settlements, see Silver (2003). Silver notes that '[a] year and a half after Posner decertified the *Rhone-Poulenc* class and seemingly in deliberate defiance of his opinion, the parties negotiated a class-based settlement that paid $100,000 per "case" infection, exclusive of attorneys' fees and costs, which were provided for separately.' Id. at 1376.

19 See Bone and Evans (2002).

lawyers who represent the class members agree to the settlement and then proceed to court, where they ask for class certification and approval of the settlement.

Defendants obviously like this form of settlement because it relieves them of all future liability. But the practice is highly controversial because it seems to deny recovery to deserving parties.

3. RECENT U.S. EXPERIENCE WITH CLASS ACTION LITIGATION

Class action litigation has been an important public policy issue in the United States for the last 15 years – so much so that Congress has passed important legislation on these matters, and the United States Supreme Court has handed down noteworthy opinions in cases involving class actions. In this section, I shall briefly describe the public policy debate, the legislation that has been passed and its effects, and some recent decisions on aspects of class action litigation.

3.1 Legislative Attempts at Reform

A principal source of dissatisfaction in the U.S. with class action litigation has been private actions for securities fraud. That litigation, which had grown in volume through the late 1980s and early 1990s, takes much of its force from a theory that is almost unique in the world to the U.S. legal system – the 'fraud on the market' theory.

The gist of that theory is that misrepresentations, deceptive practices, and withholding information are fraudulent to purchasers and sellers generally – that is, without any allegations of those behaviors having adversely affected particular individuals. As a result, investors who have suffered losses because of a decline in the value of the shares that they hold may premise an action for recovery of some or all of those losses on misbehaviour by the issuers of the shares – for example, by officers of the firm – regardless of whether the investor explicitly relied upon, say, misrepresentations and misleading statements from the firm.[20]

The U.S. Supreme Court endorsed this theory in *Basic* v. *Levinson*, 485 U.S. 224 (1988), on the ground that 'in an open and developed securities market, the price of a company's stock is determined by the available

[20] For an excellent summary of the fraud-on-the-market theory, including criticisms of the theory, see Macey (1998).

material information regarding the company and its business. ... Misleading statements will therefore defraud purchasers of stock even if the purchasers do not directly rely on the misstatements'.[21]

Many observers of the stock exchanges, capital markets, and of general business believed that the combination of the fraud-on-the-market theory, the certification of large classes of shareholders who had owned shares of firms whose value had tumbled, and the possibility of 'blackmail' settlements was highly detrimental to the U.S. economy. And some of those observers began to argue in favor of reform of securities fraud class action litigation so as to make those causes of action far less common or, at least, less damaging.[22]

The initial result was the Private Securities Litigation Reform Act (PSLRA) of 1995.[23] The Act made it more difficult to bring securities fraud allegations in three respects: (1) the plaintiff must plead misleading statements 'with particularity' – that is, the plaintiff must say which statements were misleading and the reasons the statements were misleading; (2) the plaintiff must plead that the defendant knew (*scienter*) that the statement was misleading or was reckless in making the statement;[24] and (3) the plaintiff must prove loss causation – that is, that the misleading statement, knowingly made, was the cause of his or her loss.

This was not the end of the matter. There was a perception that those intent on filing private class actions against companies for securities fraud were evading the Act by filing actions in state courts. Congress dealt with this perceived evasion by enacting the Securities Litigation Uniform Standards Act of 1998 (SLUSA), which allowed the removal to federal court of any act covered by PSLRA.[25]

---

21 *Basic* v. *Levinson*, at 241–42.

22 Some of the professional literature on this includes Alexander (1991) (arguing that almost all securities fraud class actions are without merit); Bohn and Choi (1996) (a large number, but not all, are meritless); and Seligman (1994) (arguing that the literature on the merits of securities fraud class action litigation is far from conclusive). A marvelous study and summary of the literature on class actions is Hensler, Pace, Dombey-Moore, Giddens, Gross and Muller (2000).

23 The Act was passed by Congress over President Clinton's veto. One of the principal House sponsors of the bill was Chris Cox, Republican of California, who has since become the head of the Securities and Exchange Commission.

24 This has proved a tough hurdle for plaintiffs to get over; they cannot simply cite a misleading or false statement and say that the defendant 'must have known' that it was false or misleading, as they could have before passage of the PSLRA.

25 See Helland (2006). The focus of Professor Helland's article is whether directors at a company that has been the subject of a successful securities fraud action pay a reputational price. He finds very little evidence of a decline in

Finally, the Class Action Fairness Act of 2005 (CAFA) attempted to address some of the apparent shortcomings of the earlier legislation. Specifically, the Act expanded the diversity jurisdiction of the federal courts to deal with class actions.[26] And secondly, the Act addressed the issue of attorney compensation, reducing the acceptability of 'coupon' settlements and allowing for the expanded judicial scrutiny of the class's attorney fees.[27]

3.2 Some Empirical Evidence

The legislation reviewed in the previous section and the commentary reviewed earlier has been informed by extensive empirical investigations of class action litigation. The details of those investigations are beyond the scope of this chapter, but we can present at least a bare summary of the trends.[28]

There is somewhat mixed evidence on the extent to which the various attempts to reform private class action litigation – both legislative and judicial and particularly in the area of securities fraud – has been successful. Some investigators suggest that 'the class action securities fraud litigation business [ ] is shrinking faster than a polar ice cap'.[29] Professor Grundfest argues that this decline in the absolute number of private securities fraud class actions is significant but that even more significant is the decline in the dollar amounts at issue. 'From 1996 to 2005 the maximum dollar loss (the decline in the company's stock market valuation) average $683 billion per year. The peak was $2.07 trillion in 2002. The maximum dollar loss in 2006 was $294 billion (or only $198 billion if one excludes the option backdating cases)'.[30]

What might account for these trends? Grundfest imagines several. First, there may be less fraud. That is, the effect of the spate of securities fraud

---

reputation and wonders, therefore, whether private class action litigation for securities fraud has desirable effects.

[26] The 'diversity jurisdiction' refers to the fact that any party can remove a case to a federal court if the other side is domiciled in a different state.

[27] This provision reflects the widespread revulsion that greeted the facts in *Kamilewicz* v. *Bank of Boston Corp*., 100 F.3d 1348 (7th Cir. 1996), discussed in n. 11 supra.

[28] For more extensive discussion, see Willging, Hooper and Niemic (1996); Hensler, Pace, Dombey-Moore, Giddens, Gross and Muller (2000); Simmons and Ryan (2006); Willging and Wheatman (2005); and Willging and Lee (2007).

[29] Grundfest (2007). Professor Grundfest, now at Stanford Law School, previously served as a commissioner of the Securities and Exchange Commission.

[30] Id.

class action litigation in the 1990s might have got the attention of the business community so that they actually engage in less fraudulent behavior. The spectacular failures of Enron and WorldCom and the lengthy prison sentences for several of their officers may have underscored the message of the successful litigation of the previous decade.

Second, the criminal prosecution of the Milberg Weiss law firm, the leader in securities fraud class action litigation (about which more shortly), may have dissuaded other firms from entering this area of litigation.

Third, the very strong performance of the equity markets in 2005 may have meant that there were very few instances of share price falls that would have been candidates for securities fraud actions.

Finally, Grundfest says that there is a new method of dealing with securities fraud that investors find to be superior to private class actions. 'The SEC and the Department of Justice now insist that any corporation suspected of a sufficiently serious fraud conduct an internal investigation that will finger the executives responsible. The corporation must also cooperate in prosecuting these executives'.[31] Additionally, under the Sarbanes-Oxley Act, the Securities Exchange Commission has the power to 'collect funds that can be distributed to shareholders who have been harmed by fraud'.[32] The net amount that the average defrauded investor might collect in this fashion may be greater than if she were to participate in a class action in which the class attorneys take one-third of the judgment in the form of a contingency fee.

It is also possible that the effects of the recent legislation, judicial holdings, and factors identified by Grundfest have dissuaded pursuing some class action complaints through to judgment. But they may not have dissuaded complaints that settle short of a full trial. In a recent AEI-Brookings Conference on the Interim Report of the Committee on Capital Market, held in Washington, DC, on 20 April 2007, Robert E. Litan suggested that the figures on class action settlements suggest that settlements in these forms of complaint have increased continuously since 1999. He cited the following chart from Laura E. Simmons and Ellen M. Ryan:

31 Id.

32 Id.

Table 6.1 Securities class action settlement trends

Year	Number of settlements	Total settlement amounts (in $million)
1997	14	150
1998	29	444
1999	65	1123
2000	90	1601
2001	96	2238
2002	111	2688
2003	93	2071
2004	113	2983
2005	124	3511

Source: Laura E. Simmons and Ellen M. Ryan, 'Post-Reform Act Securities Settlements: 2005 Review and Analysis' (Cornerstone Research, 2006).

Finally, in a careful study of the effects that followed the passage of the Class Action Fairness Act (CAFA) of 2005, Thomas Willging and Emery G. Lee III find 'a substantial increase in class action activity during the period from January 1, 2001, through June 30, 2005, a time that spans the February 18, 2005, effective date of CAFA'.[33] Most particularly, they found 'a substantial increase in class action activity during the months following CAFA's effective date'.[34] They try to disentangle longer-term trends from short-term fluctuations but still conclude that there was a statistically significant increase in class action filings after the passage of CAFA.

As one can see, the empirical evidence on private class action litigation and on the effects of recent legislation does not tell a clear story. The weight of the evidence seems to me to suggest that for a confluence of reasons, private class actions for securities fraud are on the decline. But confidence in that judgment will have to wait for further empirical work and for more time to pass.

[33] Willging and Lee (2007).

[34] Id.

3.3 The Milberg Weiss Indictments

One indication of the unhappiness with class-action litigation in the United States is the indictment handed down in May, 2006, against one of the most prominent class-action securities law firms, Milberg Weiss Bershad & Schulman and two of its partners, David J. Bershad, 66, and Steven G. Schulman, 54.[35] The indictment alleges that the firm and those two partners made more than $11 million in secret payments (called 'referral fees') to three individuals in order to induce them to serve as plaintiffs in more than 150 class action lawsuits. The lawsuits took place over a 20-year period and generated more than $216 million in fees for Milberg Weiss.

The 20-count indictment, handed down by a Los Angeles federal grand jury, accuses the firm and the two partners of, among other things, engaging in a 'racketeering conspiracy, mail fraud, a money laundering conspiracy, and obstruction of justice'. Prosecutors seek the disgorgement of the legal fees earned by the firm and the partners who were named as well as prison terms for the two partners (up to 20 years, for example, in the case of the racketeering-conspiracy allegation). William W. Taylor, a lawyer at Zuckerman Spaeder who is representing Milberg Weiss, said, 'The people who are going to be happy about this indictment are the hundreds and hundreds of companies that Milberg Weiss successfully sued and the political demagogues who rail about trial lawyers' running up the price of eggs. You could hear the cheering from Wall Street to Pennsylvania Avenue, and it feeds right into the hands of people who want to prevent victims from being able to get the justice from big companies that they deserve'. Milberg Weiss is thought to have won about $45 billion in judgments or settlements from corporations in class-action securities fraud actions over the past several decades.[36]

The indictment might have profound effects on the class action market. It might lead, for example, to litigation to reopen judgments and settlements in the past and, also, attempts to remove Milberg Weiss as lead counsel in pending class-action litigation. Shareholders may also bring actions against the firm for recovery of judgments or settlements made in the past. In a story on 1 June 2007 *The New York Times* reported that Milberg Weiss has lost prominent institutional clients and some top partners as a result of the May 2006 indictment.

Milberg Weiss has 125 partners in the firm and an additional 240 employees, and the firm's website says that the vast majority of the partners

---

[35] See Creswell (2006).

[36] See www.milbergweiss.com. See also www.milbergweissjustice.com. The last statement on the indictment on that website is dated 17 July 2006.

and employees did not participate in or know nothing at all about the alleged abuses. The government wanted the firm to waive the attorney-client privilege as a condition of not being indicted. The firm considers that privilege so important that it refused to agree.[37]

Also named in the indictment is a retired California lawyer and former Milberg Weiss client named Seymour M. Lazar, 78. Mr. Lazar or members of his family have been plaintiffs in over 70 lawsuits for Milberg Weiss. The indictment alleges that the Lazars received approximately $2.4 million in 'secret and illegal kickback payments'. 'Plaintiffs would buy securities anticipating that they would decline in value, hence positioning themselves to be named plaintiffs in the class actions'. The payments created a conflict of interest in that the plaintiffs had, after receiving the payments, a 'greater interest in maximizing the amount of attorneys' fees awarded to Milberg Weiss than in maximizing the net recovery' to others in the class, according to the indictment.

Another unindicted co-conspirator is a Beverly Hills ophthalmologist named Dr. Steven G. Cooperman. He or members of his family were plaintiffs in nearly 70 class-action lawsuits filed by Milberg Weiss and received about $6.5 million in payments. Apparently, Dr. Cooperman was eager to testify in the Milberg Weiss matter in exchange for a reduction in sentencing for art insurance fraud. (Cooperman faked the theft of two pieces of fine art from his home. He was serving a 30-month prison sentence.) The indictment alleges that a partner at Milberg Weiss disguised the payments to Dr. Cooperman as an option payment on Picasso's 'Nude Before a Mirror'.

In July, 2007, David Bershad pled guilty to one charge of conspiracy against him. In response, the firm fired him and changed its name to Milberg Weiss.[38]

In September, 2007, Melvyn Weiss, one of the named partners at Milberg Weiss, was indicted on charges of conspiracy, racketeering, obstruction of justice, and making false statements to a federal grand jury.[39] If convicted, Mr. Weiss, who is 72 years old, could face up to 40 years in prison. At the same time Steven Schulman, a former named partner of the Milberg Weiss firm, agreed to plead guilty to a conspiracy charge, agreed to cooperate with prosecutors, to disgorge $1.85 million in profits, to accept a prison

---

37 See http://www.milbergweiss.com/newsevents/publicationsdetail.aspx?pubtype=5280&pubid=774.

38 Creswell (2007). As part of the plea agreement, Mr. Bershad agreed to give back $7.75 million, to pay a $250,000 fine, and to cooperate with the prosecution in further matters having to do with the conspiracy.

39 Meier (2007).

sentence of between two and three years, and to pay a $250,000 fine. Finally, William S. Lerach, formerly of Milberg Weiss, pled guilty to a federal conspiracy charge associated with the plaintiff kickback scheme. He will spend time in prison but has declined to cooperate with federal prosecutors.

3.4 *Tellabs* v. *Makor Issues & Rights, Ltd.*

Tellabs is the manufacturer of equipment for fiber-optic cable telecommunications networks. Certain shareholders, the original plaintiffs in the case, had purchased shares of the company's stock in 2000 and 2001. Tellabs' shares subsequently lost substantial value, falling from a high during the period of $67 to just below $16. Those shareholders then brought a class action on behalf of all Tellabs shareholders, contending that the company and two of its officers – Robert C. Notebaert and Michael J. Birck, CEO and chairman respectively – engaged in securities fraud in violation of §10(b) of the Securities Exchange Act of 1934 and Securities and Exchange Commission Rule 10b-5. The company and the officers, the complaint maintained, had misled shareholders about the demand for the company's products, misstated financial results, and knowingly exaggerated expected future performance and profits.

Tellabs moved to dismiss the class action complaint on the ground that it did not comply with the requirements of the PSLRA, particularly in that the complaint failed to plead with the particularity that the PSLRA requires. The District Court dismissed the complaint.

The class then amended the complaint to refer to specific incidents and statements. The District Court felt that the amended complaint adequately demonstrated that some of CEO Notebaert's statements had been misleading but that he had not acted with the degree of scienter required by the PSLRA. So, the Court dismissed the complaint, this time with prejudice.

The U.S. Court of Appeals for the Seventh Circuit reversed, holding that 'courts should examine all of the complaint's allegation to decide whether collectively they establish an inference of scienter'. The complaint would survive, the court stated, if a reasonable person could infer from the complaint's allegations that the defendant acted with the requisite state of mind.[40]

The U.S. Supreme Court decided the case 8–1 in favor of Tellabs.[41] The majority held that the Seventh Circuit's criterion for requisite scienter – that

---

40 *Tellabs, Inc.* v. *Makor Issues & Rights, Ltd.*, 437 F.3d 588 (2005).
41 *Tellabs, Inc.* v. *Makor Issues & Rights, Ltd.*, 551 U.S. 308 (2007).

to proceed the plaintiffs must show that it was 'reasonable and plausible' that the speaker knew that the statements were false or misleading – was inadequate. Rather, the Court held that the PSLRA requires that the scienter allegation of the intent to defraud be 'cogent and compelling'.

This interpretation of a crucial requirement of the 1995 PSLRA makes it even more difficult for a private securities fraud class action to proceed.[42]

4. CONCLUSION

In this brief introduction to the law and economics of private class action litigation these forms of 'collective redress' have much (in terms of efficiency) to be said for them and something to be said against them. The key for policymakers, like those in the EU who are contemplating making class actions more easily available to litigants, is to structure procedural and

---

[42] In another case from the October, 2006, term, *Bell Atlantic Corp* v. *Twombly*, 550 U.S. 544 (2007), the U.S. Supreme Court handed down an opinion that, although not strictly about class action litigation, has implications for class action litigation. At the heart of the litigation was an antitrust claim arising from behavior having to do with the Telecommunications Act of 1996. In relevant part, the Act ended the local exchange monopoly that the regional Bell operating companies (RBOCs) had maintained since the Modified Final Judgment of 1982 had broken up the national monopoly of American Telephone and Telegraph and created the regional companies. Twombly, on behalf of all relevant telecommunications consumers, brought an action against various RBOCs on the ground that they had been conspiring since the passage of the 1996 Act not to compete by not extending their service into one another's territories. If that allegation were true, the actions would constitute a violation of the Sherman Antitrust Act.

Under previous interpretations of the 1938 *Federal Rules of Civil Procedure*, a complainant need only provide the defendant 'a short and plain statement of the claim showing that the pleader is entitled to relief.' And having done that, the plaintiff may then proceed to engage in extensive pretrial discovery. Complying with that discovery can be so expensive that some defendants may be moved to settle the complaint rather than litigate, even if they do not concede the truth of the underlying complaint. After he filed his complaint, Twombly had begun to interview RBOC employees.

The U.S. Supreme Court held that a §1 Sherman Antitrust claim 'requires a complaint with enough matter (taken as true) to suggest that an agreement was made. An allegation of parallel conduct and a bare assertion of conspiracy will not suffice.'

The holding applies only to antitrust claims, but it is in line with the spirit of the PSLRA that we just reviewed in raising the bar for those who would come to court, including those asserting a claim on behalf of a class of plaintiffs, for relief. See Epstein (2007).

substantive safeguards so as to realize the greatest net benefits from consolidated litigation.

REFERENCES

Alexander, J. (1991), 'Do the Merits Matter?: A Study of Settlement in Securities Class Actions', *Stanford Law Review*, **43**, 497–598.

Bohn, J. and S. Choi (1996), 'Fraud in the New Issue Market: Empirical Evidence on Securities Class Actions', *University of Pennsylvania Law Review*, **144,** 903–982.

Bone, R.G. (2003), *The Economics of Civil Procedure*, New York: Foundation Press.

Bone, R.G. and D.S. Evans (2002), 'Class Certification and the Substantive Merits', *Duke Law Journal*, **51**(4), 1251–1332.

Creswell, J. (2006), 'U.S. Indictment for Big Law Firm in Class Actions', *The New York Times*, May 19.

Creswell, J. (2007), 'Ex-Partner at Milberg Weiss Pleads Guilty to Conspiracy', *The New York Times*, July 10.

Eisenberg, T. and G. Miller (2004), 'Attorney Fees in Class Action Settlements: An Empirical Study', *Journal of Empirical Legal Studies*, **1**, 27–78.

Epstein, R. (2007), 'Legal Sanity Discovered', *Wall Street Journal*, May 24.

Friendly, H.J. (1973), *Federal Jurisdiction: A General View*, New York: Columbia University Press.

Grundfest, J.A. (2007), 'The Class Action Market', *The Wall Street Journal*, February 7.

Hay, B. and D. Rosenberg (2000a), *The Individual Justice of Averaging*, Discussion Paper No. 285.

Hay, B. and D. Rosenberg (2000b), '"Sweetheart" and "Blackmail" Settlements in Class Actions: Reality and Remedy', *Notre Dame Law Review*, **75**, 1377–1408.

Helland, E. (2006), 'Reputational Penalties and the Merits of Class-Action Securities Litigation', *Journal of Law & Economics*, **49**(2), 365–95.

Helland, E. and J. Klick (2007), 'The Effect of Judicial Expedience on Attorney Fees in Class Actions', *Journal of. Legal Studies*, **36**, 171–87.

Hensler, D.R., N.M. Pace, B. Dombey-Moore, B. Giddens, J. Gross and E.K. Muller (2000), *Class action dilemmas: Pursuing public goals for private gain*, Santa Monica: Rand Corporation.

Kolstad, C., G. Johnson and T.S. Ulen (1990), 'Ex Ante and Ex Post Regulations: Complements or Substitutes?', *The American Economic Review*, **80**, 888–901.

Macey, J.R. (1998), 'Fraud-on-the-Market', in P. Newman (ed.), *The New Palgrave Dictionary of Economics and the Law*, vol. 1, New York: Stockton Press, pp.159ff.

Meier, B. (2007), 'Top Class-Action Lawyer Faces Federal Charges', *New York Times*, September 21.

Miller, G.P. (1998), 'Class Actions', in P. Newman (ed.), *The New Palgrave Dictionary of Economics and the Law*, vol. 1, New York: Stockton Press, pp. 257–62.

Schwartz, W.F. (2002), 'Long-Shot Class Actions: Toward a Normative Theory of Legal Uncertainty', *Legal Theory*, **8**, 297–311.

Seligman, J. (1994), 'The Merits Do Matter: A Comment on Professor Grundfest's "Disimplying Private Rights of Action under the Federal Securities Law: the Commission's Authority"', *Harvard Law Review*, **108**, 438–537.

Silver, C. (2003), 'We're Scared to Death: Class Certification and Blackmail', *New York University Law Review*, **78**, 1357–1430.

Simmons, L.E. and E.M. Ryan (2006), *Post-Reform Act Securities Settlements: 2005 Review and Analysis*, Cornerstone Research.

Willging, T.E. and E.G. Lee III (2007), *The Impact of the Class Action Fairness Act of 2005 on the Federal Courts, Third Interim Report to the Judicial, Conference Advisory Committee on Civil Rules*, Washington, D.C.: Federal Judicial Center.

Willging, T.E. and S.R. Wheatman (2005), *An Empirical Examination of Attorneys' Choice of Forum in Class Action Litigation*, Washington, D.C.: Federal Judicial Center.

Willging, T.E., L.L. Hooper and R.J. Niemic (1996), *Empirical Study of Class Actions in Four Federal District Courts: Final Report to the Advisory Committee on Civil Rules*, Washington, D.C.: Federal Judicial Center.

PART 2

Disentangling the law and economics of class action

7. Private, club and public goods: the economic boundaries of class action litigation

Alberto Cassone and Giovanni B. Ramello*

1. INTRODUCTION

In recent decades, class action litigation has attracted growing attention from citizens and legislators around the world, by virtue of its ability to extend the protection of victims where traditional methods – i.e. individual civil action and regulation – have proven vulnerable.

First introduced in the US legal system in 1938, through Rule 23 of the Federal Rules of Civil Procedure, it then took nearly three decades for class action to be fully implemented into US civil procedure, with the 1966 issuing of the new version of Rule 23 by the Supreme Court.[1] Since then, class action has been fiercely criticised by a number of opponents, to the point of starting, in the 1970s, what has been described as a 'holy war' (Hensler et al., 2000).[2] However, despite these negative stances, it has over the years become 'one of the most ubiquitous topics in modern civil law' in the US, and nowadays one of '[t]he reason for the omnipresence of class actions lies in [its] versatility' (Epstein, 2003, p. 475) which, according to a great many commentators, can make it an effective means for serving justice and efficiency in a broad sense.

* This material substantially refers to Cassone and Ramello (2011).

1 Some authors have detected a precursor to class action in the Medieval group litigation of England. (Yeazell, 1987). Though not questioning the legacy owed by class action to previous regulations, we shall focus here on modern class action, which is essentially rooted in US civil procedure.

2 Of course class action, like all juridical tools, is not per se a panacea for every possible situation. Critical concerns have been repeatedly addressed by scholars; among others, see Klement and Neeman (2004).

The collective litigation system thus continues to operate, and its utility remains undisputed in the North American judicial system. The most recent amendment, brought by the Class Action Fairness Act (CAFA, 2005), though aimed according to some authors at curbing some of its pernicious features (Lee and Willging, 2007), carefully avoided criticising collective litigation as a whole, and in fact reaffirmed its substantive validity, strongly asserting that 'class-action law suits are an important and valuable part of the legal system when they permit the fair and efficient resolution of legitimate claims of numerous parties by allowing the claims to be aggregated into a single action against a defendant that has allegedly caused harm' (CAFA, 2005, sect.2).[3]

The purpose of this chapter is to examine the productive nature of class action as a litigation technology, identifying its peculiarities and the conditions under which this 'legal machinery' can produce a socially efficient outcome, and highlighting any critical aspects.

In particular, the traditional tools of economic analysis enable us to identify the characteristics and 'productive' conditions under which this judicial mechanism can create a specific risk market aimed at producing two instrumental goods, a profit for the attorney and protection of the victims, and one objective good consisting of deterrence, serving to promote efficiency.

Adopting this perspective, we find not only that the ultimate goal of efficiency can be attained even without full compensation of victims, but also that this eventuality, coupled with the attorney's appropriation of expected benefits, is in fact the currency that permits reallocation of the risk associated with the legal action.

The chapter is organised as follows: Section 2 sets out the principal features of class action, and discusses its idiosyncrasies with respect to standard civil procedure. Section 3 reinterprets these features through the lens of economic theory, also with references to analogous situations that have led to the emergence of ad hoc institutions; this is followed in Section 4 by an examination of the economics of this particular juridical technology that successively produces private, club and public goods. Section 5 discusses possible alternative solutions to class action for extending liability and protection of victims. Section 6 sets out the conclusions.

---

[3] Pub. L. No. 109–2, 119 Stat. 4, 2005.

2. PROCEDURAL FEATURES OF CLASS ACTION LITIGATION

The first effect of class action is to permit the adjudication of meritorious claims that would otherwise not be litigated due to imperfections in the legal systems (Rodhe, 2004). In fact, class action is a legal device employed today for tackling torts in a wide array of cases, including financial market and securities fraud in recent times (Porrini and Ramello, 2005; Chapter 6 of this book).[4] However, from its inception class action was infused with a broader political agenda, extending beyond the tort domain to embrace matters such as civil rights (in particular segregation), health protection, consumer protection, environmental questions and many others (Hensler et al., 2000).

As a whole, class action has the effect of altering the balance of power and the distribution of wealth among the various social actors – e.g. firms vs. consumers – thereby extending its scope in terms of overall impact on society. All the above elements, taken together, thus play an important role in guiding the legislator's decision of whether (or not) to adopt class action and, ultimately, the battle in favour of or against the introduction of class action into the different legal systems is played out on a purely political terrain (Porrini and Ramello, 2011).[5]

Nonetheless, it is the procedural technicalities that have for the most part given sceptics grounds for criticising class action, and questioning its ability to be implemented in legal systems different from those where it arose. These are often specious arguments which disregard the simple fact that any 'juridical technology' intended to achieve certain outcomes must be adapted, in its design, to the constraints of the target legal system, if it is to

---

4 These were formerly litigated under Section 10(b) of the Securities Exchange Act of 1934 and under Rules 10–5 and 23 of the Federal Rules of Civil Procedure. However, the idiosyncratic nature of securities class actions and the particular features of these kinds of lawsuits called for a dedicated statute, issued in 1995 as the Private Securities Litigation Reform Act, designed to reduce the risk of 'frivolous' litigation and therefore to make securities class actions more efficient. In 1998 the Securities Litigation Uniform Standards Act was then amended in order to further fine tune class action in securities litigations. On class action in financial markets in general ref. Porrini and Ramello (2011).

5 For example, the introduction of class action has generally been opposed by mass production firms as it would substantially increase their costs and likelihood of being prosecuted, as also by the insurance firms who would have to settle high claims (Hensler et al., 2000). In general '[g]iven their potential to transfer massive amounts of wealth and to reorganise important institutions, it should surprise no one that class actions are politically controversial' (Silver, 1999, p. 195).

provide regulatory solutions that are effective and compatible with its context. The heart of the problem, therefore, consists in opportunely adapting the 'legal machinery' to each jurisdictional setting in a manner that obtains the desired results without prejudicing its essential features.[6] In the case of class actions, these characterising features are:

(i) The aggregation of separate but essentially cognate claims, united by design and not by substantive theory.
(ii) The indirect representation of absent parties.
(iii) The provision of entrepreneurial opportunity to an attorney, who thus becomes the main engine of the civil action.

If we combine the three above elements, class action can essentially be described as a form of representational lawsuit that eliminates duplications in related claims, by aggregating all the potential claimants into a group – the class – and by giving a lawyer – the class counsel – control over all of them. In other words, what makes class action a special legal device within civil procedure is the unusual feature of binding individuals with related claims, even if they were not originally named parties in the proceedings. As a result, once a judgment is handed down, it extinguishes all claims included in the class, and not just those of the named parties. This means that everyone falling within the class is considered an absent class member and thus included *de jure* in the lawsuit, unless there is a specific opt-out request, as will be discussed below (Dam, 1975).

The obvious main consequence is that, by aggregating similar claims, class action increases the possibility of litigation, and so also the liability of wrongdoers who would otherwise not be sued by victims; hence, it may redress the imbalance which exists between plaintiffs and defendants in several areas of litigation.

The indirect representation stems from the fact that the attorney is not appointed directly by each individual claimant, but rather through a specific set of procedures established by law, which essentially rely upon the initiative of a minority among them, and the subsequent acceptance by the judge, to start the trial (Hensler et al., 2000). In fact, the civil action is filed by an individual or a small group of victims assisted by an attorney. The

[6] The efficacy of legal transplant has been widely debated, here again with advocates and detractors, starting from the seminal contributions of Watson (1974). The practice is however current, and there are many instances – beginning with antitrust law – showing that, with the needed adjustments, legal institutions can be transferred from one system to another.

class is then certified by the judge who consequently also 'appoints' the attorney as a representative of all the class members (Dam, 1975).

It is worth noting that the mere appointment of a class counsel does not, of course, per se assure attainment of any efficient outcome, nor does it rule out opportunistic behaviours (see Chapter 12 of this book). It is only a first step for making the desired outcomes possible and, as usual in tort litigation, demands a well designed set of incentives for the lawyer in order to work properly (Klement and Neeman, 2004; Chapter 11 of this book). On the other hand, indirect representation and the need for proper incentives are likewise found in regulation, where the public agency acts as a *parens patriae* on behalf of interested parties, and is charged with pursuing the public (rather than the individual) interest by means of a specialised bureaucracy (Glaeser and Shleifer, 2003).[7] Accordingly, the puzzle cannot be solved by fostering regulation as a substitute for litigation.

This last is a significant point because class action does bear some similarities – albeit limited to the civil procedure domain – to regulation: in fact, where the judge determines that individual actions may not be sufficiently effective, yet the litigation is in the collective interest, on request of a representation of victims she reallocates the individual rights over that particular prospective litigation. Thus, also in this case, an agent is nominated to represent the interests of a group, but with a narrower scope compared to fully fledged regulation. Here, the indirect representation serves merely to exploit the possibility of aggregating related claims without bearing the costs of searching for and coordinating a huge number – often a 'mass' – of potential plaintiffs, that would otherwise make bringing the lawsuit unaffordable.

Finally, there is one last feature that makes collective action possible: it is the creation of a specific entrepreneurial space for the class counsel, who undertakes to identify an unmet demand for justice and, acting self-interestedly, restores access to legal action for the victims. The class counsel is generally driven by the purely utilitarian motives of a 'bounty hunter', who offers a service in exchange for recompense. It is thus a behaviour consistent with the paradigm of methodological individualism, and which

[7] Moreover, indirect representation is not a novelty in lawsuits under either civil law or common law systems, since it arises whenever there is the risk of systematically preventing specific categories of individuals from protecting their own rights. In other words, indirect representation occurs when a party is unable to personally file a lawsuit due to incompetence, lack of money, or for other reasons. This is the case, for example, with children or the mentally ill, but it also applies to consumers who cannot afford law enforcement on their own.

is sometimes regarded with suspicion by those who consider private interests unsuitable for representing the collective interest. Such misgivings have, moreover, helped give support to regulation over individual civil action on the grounds that, as Justice Robert Young suggests (2001, p. 3) 'in the judiciary, the process, though public in name, is private in essence'.[8] Yet this mechanism, endorsed by economic theory starting from the paradigm of the invisible hand, also underpins the economic analysis of law, given that many institutions, beginning with property rights, are designed to promote the collective interest through individual initiative (Ramello, 2011).

Hence, the reluctance to pursue collective welfare through private interest is not only theoretically unfounded (and in fact contradicts decades of scientific investigation), but also assumes the peculiar and unproven hypothesis that it is possible to select for particular roles – such as regulators or public prosecutors – special human beings entirely unmoved by individual utility, and who are on the contrary able to exclusively promote the collective interest without any eye to their private benefit. The reality appears to be greatly different.[9]

Class action thus has the particular merit of aligning the private interest of the case attorney, who seeks to obtain a profit, with that of the victims, who seek redress of the harm and promotion of justice, and with that of society which instead benefits from a system that internalises the externality. This in fact creates a deterrent to wrongdoing and ultimately works to minimise the social costs, in accordance with Hand's rule. In this light, therefore, the miracle of the invisible hand is again renewed, and the self-interest of the victims and class counsel can play a role of public relevance.

3. LAW AND ECONOMICS INSIGHTS

The tools of economic analysis and efficiency are further brought into play when we consider the wider effects of class action on the judicial system and on the economic system. In particular, economic science offers two

---

[8] This is in fact an old debate that has for at least one hundred years pitted the administrative against the judiciary, and helped trigger what has been termed the 'rise of the regulatory state' (Glaeser and Shleifer, 2003).

[9] Judges, public prosecutors and regulators are individuals who have the same motivations and behaviours as other economic actors. Therefore, there is no solution in which the methodological individualism assumed by economic theory can be eliminated. For example, with respect to judges, the scholar and 'judge' Posner (1994) notes that not only is this a mythological category populated by heroes, titans and saints, but also that all its members, as the title of his essay states, 'maximise the same thing everybody else does'.

complementary routes for conducting such an analysis. The first concerns the manner in which class action can serve efficiency and collective welfare; the second provides the analytical framework for representing the legal machinery and studying its workings, thus determining under what conditions and in what way class action promotes social welfare.

However, for the investigation to be fruitful, we have to specify the initial conditions, i.e. the circumstances under which regulation and individual action are not effective. In other words, we must define the context that gives rise to a failure to protect victims, which is the prerequisite for introducing a new legal device (Silver, 1999; Porrini and Ramello, 2005). The conditions surrounding the failure and making class action valuable for the solution are the following:

- Existence of *fragmented claims*, very often worth less to each plaintiff than the individual litigation cost, or which in any case entail a prohibitively costly individual litigation.
- Sufficient *homogeneity of claims* for the court to issue a 'one size fits all' decision, and for the victims to be able to adhere to the collective action.
- A *judicial market failure*, as a result of which some claims, no matter how meritorious, are not brought, so that certain individuals are unable to exercise their rights.
- A *failure of regulation* which thus does not offer a practicable alternative for resolving the preceding issues.

The conditions under which class action is potentially useful are those where certain rights established by law are not exercised, or only imperfectly exercised, due to a misalignment between what is theoretically asserted by the law and the concrete incentives provided to individuals. Such a circumstance is by no means new to the law and economics literature and, for example, also emerges in the case of property rights: the mere possession of the right does not necessarily result in its being exercised, even when this would be opportune and socially efficient. This condition creates a discontinuity in the laws, and renders them incomplete (Barzel, 1997). In the case of property, for example, the described situation occurs where there is excessive fragmentation of rights, or in the presence of market imperfections which push up the costs of the exchange, resulting in a market failure.[10]

---

[10] The example here essentially refers to situations such as the anticommons, where a lack of coordination connected with the cost of using the market for

The solution involves an institutional reorganisation to produce a lowering of these costs and/or promote the – sometimes forced – reallocation of the rights. Examples of this are the aggregation of rights in the case of patent pools (Gallini, 2011), and the compulsory licensing systems established for intellectual property, or for essential facilities in antitrust, as also the takings of private land (Nicita and Ramello, 2007; Mercuro, 1992).[11]

By thus regarding victims as owners of 'property rights' over a specific litigation, whose enforcement may incur costs exceeding the expected individual benefits, we can interpret class action as a system that follows a comparable judicial path to that described for property, aggregating the individuals' rights when their exercise on the judicial market is precluded (or limited) by contingencies which make the net benefit of the action negative.

In general, these contingencies arise from the aforesaid fragmentation and its attendant coordination costs, from the limited size of the individual damages (so-called 'small claims'), and also from the existence of asymmetries between the would-be plaintiffs and defendant (i.e. availability of information, capacity to manage the litigation risk, access to financial resources, and more).

Creating a pool of rights thus enables victims to access a less costly litigation technology, and thereby pursue justice. The productive efficiency of a static character concerns the overall production of 'justice', on the demand and supply sides, since on the judicial market both jointly concur to its production, albeit for different reasons. Class action in fact allows a so-called 'judicial economy' to emerge, which on the demand side, through aggregation of small claims, produces economies of scale in litigation that cause individual costs to decrease with increasing number of plaintiffs (Bernstein, 1977). On the supply side, there is likewise a reduction in costs if the aggregation permits overall savings in resources compared to multiple individual actions, provided though that the savings afforded by aggregation are not offset by an increase in the number of lawsuits.[12]

---

excessively fragmented rights, or the strategic use of property by some right holders in order to extract all the surplus created by the exchange – the so called 'holdout problem' – frustrates achievement of a socially desirable outcome (Heller, 2008).

[11] The law and economics literature shows, for example, how property laws are designed to smooth the workings of the market, restoring rights to their legitimate holders where possible, or reallocating them to new actors when the previous solution is not practicable.

[12] This aspect is naturally ambiguous with respect to the supply side, due to the need to balance the judicial costs with the social costs. Thus class action brings about a net saving if it reduces the number of lawsuits, but may also increase their number if it makes possible suits that would otherwise not have been brought. Even

There is, then, a second level of efficiency connected with the economic nature of class action, and which has the purpose of aligning different interests to achieve the previously stated goal. In effect, the system, if properly applied, has to introduce a set of distinct incentives which together concur to produce three different outputs: a profit for the attorney, redress of the harm for the victims, and deterrence of wrongdoing (thereby minimising the social cost) for society.

In other words, the role of class action is to reconcile the conjoined individual interests of victims with the collective interest of society, by passing through the private interest of the class counsel. It thus has the nature of a *private good* for the attorney, who takes on the entrepreneurial role of setting in motion the collective action, which is in its turn aimed at obtaining redress of the harm (Dam, 1975). Though this ultimately has an effect on each victim, it can only be produced as a local public good for the cohort of all victims, and thus takes the form of a *club good*. Finally, the transfer of the cost of the wrongdoing from the victims to the injurer has the consequence of re-establishing a higher level of deterrence, thereby resulting in production of a *public good*. This deterrence, it is worth noting, pertains to what is generally termed dynamic efficiency, since its production in a given time frame is also instrumental to the intertemporal optimal production of other goods.

The described mechanism thus works to promote various economic interests, and at the same time enhances efficiency by favouring the internalisation of externalities, reconfirming the instrumental role of tort law in reducing the risk of accidents (Calabresi, 1970).[13]

Therefore, the points discussed thus far can fully account for the economic role of class action, whose characteristics and workings can be investigated through the customary analysis tools provided by the theory.

---

so, however, it can still produce a net saving if the deterrence effect, as we shall discuss, reduces the social cost. Naturally this requires that it doesn't produce another externality, connected with court congestion (Chappe, 2011).

[13] The production of deterrence, in particular, becomes crucial to the extent that the consequences of wrongful behaviour extend beyond the private sphere of pure transfer of wealth (pure economic loss) to also influence the level of precaution taken, determining the overall allocation of resources in the economic system (Porrini and Ramello, 2005).

4. PRODUCING GOODS: CLASS ACTION AS TECHNOLOGY

As discussed above, class action works by rearranging property rights over a specific claim, to promote the attainment of an efficient organisation in litigation. Through the attorney, it restores the incentive for claimants to bring the suit, thereby reinstating access to justice and, in consequence, enhancing deterrence.

Using the traditional categories of economic analysis, we can represent the described situation and interpret the 'productive' roles of the various actors taking part in the class action. For simplicity, let us image a scenario where the injurer has unilateral control over the level of care, and the level of activity is extensive, thus better handled by a strict liability regime in which the cost of the accident is borne by the defendant, irrespective of the level of precaution taken.[14] According to law and economics theory, the rule of strict liability with perfect compensation thus causes the injurer to internalise the costs and benefits of precaution, which gives the injurer an incentive for efficient care. Full internalisation of the damage by the tortfeasor fulfils Hand's condition, under which the social marginal cost of care equals its social marginal benefit, and so makes it possible to minimise the expected social cost of accidents (Calabresi, 1970; Brown, 1973).

4.1 Class Action and Club Theory

The organisation of plaintiffs into a 'class' corresponds to what in economic theory is termed a 'club', that is to say a 'group of individuals who derive mutual benefit from sharing one or more of the following: production costs, attributes of the members, or goods characterised by excludable benefits' (Cornes and Sandler, 1996, p. 347).

This results in the production and ensuing consumption of specific goods that would not otherwise be produced: the club good is an excludable but non-rivalrous public good for the club members. Therefore it is congestible, in the sense that an increase in the number of members will at some point negatively affect their benefits.

In the case of class action, the club good is the reinstated access to justice and the resultant redress of the wrong, which is then naturally shared out

[14] Given the broad nature of the class, it would be difficult to coordinate the action of victims to contribute to precautions. Also, if this were not the case, there would be no failure of individual action since the victims would be able to coordinate and bring the suit also at some later time.

among the individual members. Though the compensation is ultimately private, its collective production is a club good. In accordance with the literature on clubs, collective litigation and damages are non rivalrous for the victims once the lawsuit has been started, but excludable through certification by the judge (Silver, 1999). The role of excludability here is twofold: on the one hand, in accordance with club theory, it is needed in order to provide the proper incentive to the club members, as otherwise free-riding would be possible (Cornes and Sandler, 1996); and on the other hand, excludability is the element which distinguishes the judiciary from regulation, since in the absence of exclusion the class could conceivably include everyone, making it no different from regulation. It is worth noting that we are assuming here a failure of regulation, so that any equivalence between regulation and litigation cannot be envisaged without necessarily implying a negative outcome also for the latter.

Compared to traditional clubs, opt-in for class action is partly determined by the injurer, who 'creates' the category of potential victims, and subsequently refined by the judge who certifies the class, i.e. defines those who have the right to take part in the litigation (Issacharoff, 1997).[15] This peculiar situation places a limit on the number of members, and is consequently useful for remedying the potential congestion that is a typical problem of clubs. Opt-out then permits a further fine-tuning, also benefiting the victims' choices. In fact, each member of the class has the residual right to express his or her will by opting out, and thereby exiting the collective litigation. This solution thus preserves the voluntariness requirement which generally characterises membership of a club, and would otherwise be of necessity violated (Cornes and Sandler, 1996).

What is more, opt-out provides a sanity check for the undemonstrated assertion that the class action is the proper solution for protecting individual rights. In fact, if the class action were not the optimal solution for safeguarding the individual victims (or if the certification of the class were incorrect, which is an equivalent situation) the members of the class would still have the opportunity to opt out and choose individual litigation instead. This solution therefore introduces a sort of competition between different litigation technologies, and hence assures optimality – i.e. maximising of the expected net benefit – to the individual members.[16]

---

[15] 'The defendant must have subjected all class members to a common practice or course of conduct, justifying a class-wide grant of declaratory or injunctive relief. Or, questions of law or fact common to all class members' claims must predominate over any individual questions that may arise' (Silver, 1999, p. 197)

[16] A similar evaluation of whether the class action is superior to individual litigation is also made by the judge at the time of certification.

It is interesting to note that, compared to the difficulties highlighted by club theory, class action presents a fairly manageable case since it groups together homogeneous members – victims who have suffered a comparable harm. Legal practice bears out this assertion, since in cases of significant dissimilarity of victims and harms the judges do not certify the class, or have the possibility of invalidating the action in progress.[17]

Thus, given a population of $N = \{1,\ldots,m\}$ individuals – i.e. all of humanity – only a part of these will possess the characteristics for being included in the subset of victims V, that is to say $V \subset N$. Formation of the club, from a legal standpoint, in fact, requires certification of a class of size n, which may of course be smaller or greater than the actual number of victims. The judge's discretionary power stems from the need to define a group of claimants that is sufficiently homogenous to make collective action possible. For each victim, the alternative options are to file an individual suit against the injurer, or to do nothing. The cost of the litigation $c(n)$ is zero if no lawsuit is brought, and otherwise generally increases with the number of individuals for values $n \geq 1$. The representation can thus be expressed as the following dichotomic formula, which assumes a linear relation between costs and number of victims:

$$c(n) = \begin{cases} 0 & n=0 \\ f+nz & n \geq 1 \end{cases} \tag{7.1}$$

Where f is the fixed cost for embarking on the litigation, and z is the marginal cost for each individual member of the group. The fixed cost can be regarded as the price of admission to the judicial market, which must be paid whenever a legal action is brought; it might, for example, include expenses such as expert surveys or other technicalities specific to the litigation, and is essentially a set-up cost for establishing a club of any size, having 1 or more members. Therefore, if each victim n pursues the route of individual litigation, f will be incurred n times.

The described cost function therefore exhibits increasing returns to scale for the number of joint plaintiffs, that is to say $AC(n) = \frac{f}{n} + z$ with $AC'(n) < 0$. This hypothesis is consistent with the literature, which in fact interprets clubs as a method for pursuing cost-sharing arrangements and producing economies of scale (Cornes and Sandler, 1996).

[17] This is, for example, what happened for two proposed class action settlements for asbestos litigation that were invalidated by the US Supreme Court on these grounds, in *Amchem Products Inc.* v. *Windsor* 521 U.S. 591, 1997, and in *Ortiz* v. *Fibreboard Corp.* 527 U.S. 815, 1999, and which nevertheless were able to benefit from consolidated litigations.

The described situation thus qualifies efficiency from the standpoint of demand, since it makes individual participation more accessible with increasing number of club members. According to the literature, economies of scale legitimately arise from the presence of significant indivisibilities in production, resolvable only through the creation of extensive productive hierarchies that can, in the case under study, take the form of a class (Edwards and Starr, 1984). What is more, the nature of a club, as a more efficient instrument for providing members with an excludable but non-rivalrous good, equally presupposes the existence of indivisibilities in production (as otherwise individual production would be more efficient).

The harm h, once it has taken place, has a finite value and is uniformly distributed among the victims; a substantial homogeneity of the victims, as noted above, is a prerequisite for certifying the class, without which the litigation is invalidated. This likewise strengthens recourse to the club as an instrument for redressing a harm common to all the members.

For simplicity, let us hypothesise also that the claimants are neutral to risk and that their utility is therefore described by the expected total gross benefit $b(n)$, concave and twice differentiable. This simplification merely assumes that enlargement of the class will at some point negatively affect the expected gross benefit, so that the potential profits for the class members do not increase with increasing class size, in line with the congestible nature of clubs. The function thus described represents a sort of gross return, before payment of litigation costs, that is hypothesised to be non-negative at least for a wide range of values of n. These returns, net of the costs (and of any top up for the attorney, as we shall discuss) are then divided equally among the members of the club.

4.2 Victims and Cost-Benefit Analysis

The condition which determines the failure of individual litigation is when $b(n) < c(n)$ for values of $n \geq 1$. It is of course intuitively apparent that such a situation depends both on the size of the expected return and on the cost: for very small values of f, that is to say when the price of admission to the litigation is low, it is easier for the failure condition to be averted. Likewise, if $b(n)$ is small – the typical example being that of small claims – the failure of the individual action is more probable.

In particular, for a judicial market failure of individual litigation to occur, the condition $b(1) < c(1)$ must be met, and the condition which remedies the failure is the definition of a class of size n such that:

$$b(n) - c(n) \geq 0 \tag{7.2}$$

The above condition thus has the nature of a participation constraint, which justifies the introduction of class action to reinstate the efficacy of tort law. However, if due to some error individual action is able to produce a greater net benefit than collective action, each class member – as we have seen – has the opportunity of opting out, which also yields the incentive compatibility constraint, according to the condition:

$$b(n) - c(n) > b(1) - c(1) \tag{7.3}$$

The above thus confirms the possibility of certifying a class of size $\bar{n} \leq n \leq \hat{n}$, for which the collective action produces a non-negative net benefit, representing the set of all values for which class action is a solution.

At the endpoints of the range, the expected net benefit for claimants is zero, since the gross benefits are equal to the costs, while for intermediate values there is a profit to the class for litigating the claim. Figure 7.1 shows a graphical representation of the case where the conditions for failure of individual litigation apply, while it is possible to define a population $n \in]\bar{n},\hat{n}[$ for which the collective action is profitable. For convenience, given the cost function, the origin of the abscissa corresponds to the case of one victim.

Minimising the social cost of accidents requires applying the criterion of full internalisation derived from the strict liability rule (Brown, 1973). Such an outcome depends essentially on the determination of the external cost, and then of the damages d, which are not univocally defined, but rather contingent on specific evaluations and, in part, on the prevailing judicial system. In particular, the level of damages established by the judge or jury reflects the concept of harm that is adopted, and the number of identified victims.

Let us for now hypothesise a strictly cost-based compensation for the class counsel (i.e. no positive profits are possible for the attorney): technically, the damages awarded should be equal to h if the American Rule is applied, as usually happens for US class actions.[18] This definition stems from a specific interpretation of 'external cost' that focuses exclusively on the specific harm, without, for example, including the externality of the

[18] The English Rule, adopted in many jurisdictions, provides that the losing party must pay the winner's reasonable fees, while the American Rule requires each party litigating the dispute to be responsible for paying its own attorney's fees. Whether the former or the latter is better suited for promoting efficiency is outside the scope of the present chapter (ref. e. g. Eisenberg and Miller, 2010).

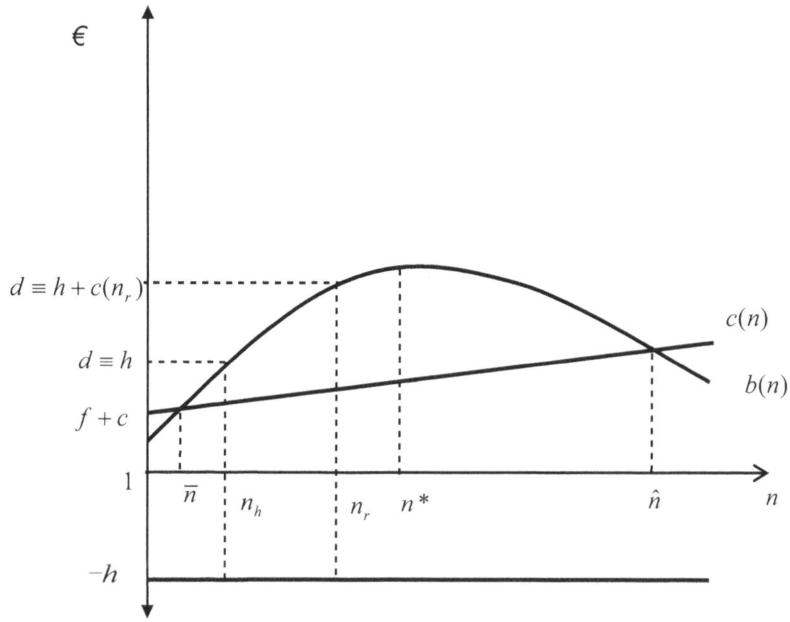

Figure 7.1 Class action litigation: the simple economics

litigation. In such a case, full compensation of the victims can never be achieved, since by definition $b(n_h) - c(n_h) < h$; such a situation also frequently arises in individual litigation, and is unrelated to full internalisation of the damage by the injurer.

Some legal systems seek to partly overcome this problem by adopting the English Rule, which is a mechanism for cost-shifting to the losing party. This system thus enables plaintiffs who win the dispute to obtain greater benefits, but also renders the nature of the costs probabilistic, with a probability distribution that can significantly impact upon the constraints (7.2) and (7.3) which determine the choices of the would-be plaintiffs. In any case, there is a wide range of values for which the expected net benefit for victims (and, as we shall see, the net compensation expected by the class counsel) remain unaltered, preserving the favourable outcome of the collective litigation.[19] The consequences can in fact be more onerous for the defendant, who in the event of losing is forced to pay damages equal to $h + c(n)$.

---

[19] Intuitively, the cost function will be zero with a certain probability $0 < \phi < 1$ if the suit is won (increasing the net benefit), or will increase by a coefficient $\mu > 1$ if the

Yet this last-mentioned situation is still compatible with the American Rule if we consider the possibility, in the US system, of introducing punitive damages. These can be considered, in whole or in part, as a way to internalise the litigation cost imposed on the class, thereby reconciling the system with a broader definition of external cost.[20] In this situation the model requires defining a class of size n_r such that $b(n_r) - c(n_r) = h$ which in Figure 7.1 makes it possible to cover all external costs. Therefore punitive damages (as also application of the English Rule under certain conditions) can lead to the definition of a larger class, compared to the case without this remedy. Yet if we consider the bounded rationality that generally impinges on legal action, the risk of defining an overly large club is less than that of underestimating its size, which would make the legal action as a whole inefficient, as we shall discuss below.

Consider, furthermore, the following different scenarios for punitive damages (or English Rule), in which maximising of the net benefit occurs with a class of size n^* for which the condition $b'(n^*) = z$ is met. It is possible that this class corresponds to that which fully internalises the overall harm $h + c(n)$, in which case it represents the optimal and maximum size of the class. When this is not true, for example because full internalisation is not possible in any case (imagine a downward shift of the curve $b(n)$ in Figure 7.1) the class of size n^* will nevertheless still represent a second best. Finally, there is the case where the damages granted either produce full internalisation of the harm before maximising of the net benefit takes place, or follow the American Rule: the class certified by the judge will in any case be of size $n < n^*$, for example in the figure for n_r or n_h.

With respect to the three possible scenarios, n^* represents the upper limit for certification of the class by the judge, irrespective of the criteria followed for internalising the damage.[21]

The above reasoning applies equally to the case of settlement, if the value agreed between the parties reflects what has been discussed previously; it is thus possible to imagine an equation for the expected net benefits that incorporates a possibility of paying 'discounted' costs in the case of early

suit is lost. Therefore, there exist values for which the two components cancel each other out. For example a plausible relation is $\phi = 1 - 1 / \mu$, which implies, for instance, that with a 50% probability of winning, the costs in case of losing will be double those directly incurred.

20 For an in depth discussion of punitive damages ref. Cenini, Luppi and Parisi (2010).

21 Naturally, it is assumed that in case of punitive damages the plaintiffs will be able to include these in the function $b(n)$ which will have a higher or lower maximum depending on the criterion used.

settlement. Under certain conditions, similar to those discussed for the English Rule, the outcome may produce an expected net benefit comparable to what has been described. Though the transactions will generally be for lower sums than the potential damages, the costs will also be correspondingly reduced. This, of course, provided that the settlement does not lead the class counsel to act opportunistically toward victims, in collusion with the defendant. However, settlements, too, are generally scrutinised in detail and approved by the judge only after submitting the proposal to the victims and considering any objections, in order to minimise the likelihood of adverse outcomes, which as a consequence are not the norm (Koniak and Cohen, 1996).

4.3 The Animal Spirit of the Attorney

The hypothesis of a strictly cost-based compensation for the class counsel, though convenient for the discussion thus far, is not consistent with the rationale of class action, which relies on the attorney's animal spirits as an instrument for triggering the litigation (Dam, 1975).

In fact, the notion of transferring the initiative to the class counsel requires creating sufficient economic incentives to motivate the counsel to act. It is naturally crucial, in this context, to define a suitable mechanism for appropriating part of the benefits of the legal action on the one hand, and for reallocating the risk and, subsequently, the expected benefits/costs on the other hand (see Chapter 5 of this book). In effect, the failure of individual action depends on a negative balance between expected costs and benefits for individual victims, and the same thing can also happen in the case of a collective action, if the costs are known but the benefits highly uncertain. In such a case, the victims' decision to bring the civil action is also dependent on their combined capacity (generally rather limited) to manage the risk.

Class action has developed a system for managing risk which, similarly to what happens with productive organisations, shifts it to those actors who are best able to manage it (Porrini and Ramello, 2011). This aspect clearly emerges if we consider the scheme for compensating the class counsel. In effect, the traditional fee-for-service determination here appears somewhat problematic, due to certain inherent features of collective litigation: the victims are dispersed and the class action, to circumvent the insurmountable costs of finding and coordinating all the class members (most of whom are absent), relies on indirect representation. Therefore, it is not possible to collect a per-capita fee *ex ante*; and if it were possible to do so *ex post*, the absent club members, once identified, could in case of failure of the litigation avoid payment by choosing to opt out.

The only practicable solution thus appears to be to grant a right to appropriate potential returns in exchange for known costs; this solution is called a contingent fee reward scheme, because it sets benefits discounted by a probability of less than 1 against known costs, and in order to be economically acceptable to the attorney requires the attribution of profits far exceeding the costs in case of success.

Now, considering that the damages must cover the costs, remunerate the class counsel and provide at least a minimal compensation for the victims, they will generally need to be considerably high.

If, for example, the expected gross benefit of the class counsel $x(n)$ is a probabilistic value that permits appropriation of a share $0 < \theta < 1$ of the expected benefits, the following condition must be met:

$$x(n) = \theta b(n) \geq c(n) \tag{7.4}$$

That is to say, the amount must be non negative, and thus its minimum value corresponds precisely to the expected cost-based fee. Jurisprudence shows that appropriation occurs for a positive coefficient θ, defined in consultation with the judge, having a value 0.2 – 0.3 (Klement and Neeman, 2004; Eisenberg and Miller, 2004).

Therefore, rewriting equation (7.4) as $b(n) \geq \frac{c(n)}{\theta}$ and considering the values indicated by legal practice, we obtain a sort of 'golden rule' showing that class actions generally require an expected gross benefit for the class of at least 3 times the litigation cost; in other words, the class action must generally produce an amply positive surplus.

This result first of all shows that the requirement of a non-negative profit for the counsel forces overly costly and unprofitable class actions out of the market. We can thus formulate a first efficiency criterion, and namely that class action litigation technology is not a panacea for every harm.[22]

A second criterion is the de facto requirement for total returns that amply exceed costs, and which serve partly to cover the costs and partly to compensate victims, whilst leaving a further reserve of appropriability for the entrepreneurial attorney, who is the trigger that makes class action effective where individual action fails.

In effect, the logic of class action presupposes the creation of a sort of legal monopoly for the counsel over the specific collective litigation. Now, even though such a monopoly is regulated by the judge's intervention in

---

22 Class litigation moreover has limits, as do individual action and regulation. It could in fact be objected that, in such a case, class action might leave unmet some parts of the demand for justice: this is naturally acceptable if their social cost makes them inefficient.

defining the coefficient θ, the very structure of litigation leads the class counsel to extract a substantial quasi-rent. Given that there is an opportunity cost of foregoing other profitable activities, potentially having a higher likelihood of yielding benefits, the attorney must not only fulfil (7.4), which represents his participation constraint, but also secure a return such that:

$$x(n) - c(n) \geq \bar{x} \tag{7.5}$$

Where $\bar{x}$ corresponds to the foregone profit of alternative activities. Equation (7.5) is the incentive compatibility constraint for the attorney.

Without loss of generality, assume for example that the alternative activity is paid through a fixed fee established *ex ante* (for example a standard legal action with no contingent fee), and rewrite equation (7.4) expressing the probability, i.e.

$$x(n) = px^* \tag{7.6}$$

Where the probability is $0 < p < 1$ and x^* is the fee effectively received if the case is won. We can now substitute (7.6) into (7.5) and rewrite it as $x^* \geq \frac{\bar{x} + c(n)}{p}$. This shows not only that the effective fee received by the class counsel in case of winning must be sufficiently large to cover costs and foregone alternative profits, but also that, to take into account the risk that is borne, this amount must be multiplied by a factor $\frac{1}{p}$ which is by definition always greater than 1, and increases with diminishing probability of winning.[23]

The class counsel in effect takes on the claimant's risk in exchange for the right to appropriate a share of the returns that is far greater than the costs. This mechanism, which transforms the attorney into a bounty hunter, should not be considered suspect and is in fact the second strong point of class action, because it creates a market for allocating the risk to the actor best equipped to manage it. The standard equation here is that the entrepreneurial attorney fosters the protection of the victims' rights in exchange for a share of the awarded damages, as a reward for the risk. On the whole, this possibility – which in general works better with contingent fees – alters the cost-benefit ratio for the individual and provides the incentive to proceed (Dam, 1975; Eisenberg and Miller, 2004).

The reasons for the class counsel's superior capacity to manage the risk stem from a number of factors, the most significant being specialisation,

---

[23] It is easy to see that the external lower bound is $\lim_{p \to 1} \frac{1}{p} = 1$. Now, since by definition $p < 0$, the multiplier is consequently always greater than 1.

and the ability to create a portfolio of diversified risks which, taken together, lower the average risk.

The described solution has a secondary consequence that is equally useful for realigning risk and its management among the parties to the proceeding, since class counsel and defendant are placed on a more equal footing, also in this respect, compared to the relation between victim and wrongdoer.

What is more, the imperfection of capital markets generally make access to external financing impracticable for the victim, who likewise has limited personal liquidity, whereas here again the class counsel is better placed and can more easily secure or obtain the resources required for the legal action (Dana and Spier, 1993).

Overall, we thus see the emergence of a new organisational configuration, indispensable for making the civil action possible, which recreates in the judicial sphere a sort of financial market provided with all its own instruments: in the final analysis, therefore, the contingent fee, with its attendant uncertainty, can be interpreted as a stock option that makes it possible to align the interests of the attorney with those of the represented clients, who here become stock holders of the legal action (Dam 1975; Chapter 5 of this book).[24]

The above discussion therefore shows that: (a) partial compensation for victims can still be consistent with the efficiency paradigm, if defined as an equilibrium on the risk market, and (b) even where there is only partial compensation, the public good of deterrence can still be produced. In this case, the club good becomes merely instrumental to the existence of the legal action, and so long as the victims express at least a minimum of satisfaction, even if only because 'justice is done', and thus do not choose to opt-out en masse, the mechanism works perfectly and the injurer is forced to internalise the social costs, even if a significant portion of the damages are in practice appropriated by the class counsel.

In the worst case there will be a pure economic loss which, in accordance with what has been discussed in the law and economics literature, pertains strictly to the distribution of wealth without detrimental consequences on collective welfare (Porrini and Ramello, 2005).[25]

---

[24] The literature concurs on the fact that 'if the attorney were paid either a fixed fee or an hourly fee, then she would have little financial incentive to reveal to her client that the case had a low expected return. Instead she might lead the plaintiff blindly into litigation regardless of the case's merit' (Dana and Spier, 1993, p. 350).

[25] What is more, full compensation is also often not achieved even in individual actions, where the attorney in any case always has an incentive to appropriate part of any benefits.

Obviously, this consequence is somewhat puzzling for those who maintain that tort law should be first and foremost concerned with compensation, to restore the original utility of the victim; instead, what emerges here once again is the pro-efficiency function of tort law, even in the absence of full compensation.

That said, it is worth noting that when the victims' compensation is zero, class action again comes to resemble regulation, with the class counsel acting on behalf of claimants in a manner comparable to regulators, and the victims receiving nothing more than protection.

5. EFFECTIVENESS OF ALTERNATIVE PRODUCTIVE ORGANIZATIONS IN LITIGATION

The criticisms of class action presuppose that there exist better alternatives for pursuing social welfare through internalisation of the damage. By definition, the existence of class action stems from a failure of both regulation and individual litigation. The practicable alternatives which remain are therefore suing for damages in a criminal court, or successive civil actions to create a sort of intertemporal club that brings together all the victims under the aegis of a precedent.

In the alternative of criminal proceedings, the principal actor is the public prosecutor, who plays a similar role to that of the class counsel, by bringing the action on behalf of the victims, even if absent. The public prosecutor therefore bears the fixed costs, and makes civil protection more practicable for the individual plaintiffs, who will pay a value closer to the marginal cost z. This situation can effectively reinstate the cost-benefit balance.

However, there are certain caveats which make this a weaker solution than class action: first of all, the objective function of the public prosecutor may differ from that of the victims, in the absence of those mechanisms for realignment of interests which class action instead incorporates. After all, we are dealing with a criminal proceeding that has the civil remedy as its externality, which leaves optimal choices very much to chance. For example, the choice of which offences to pursue (albeit in accordance with guidelines), and the amount of effort devoted to the lawsuit, are decisions taken by the public prosecutor independently of the wishes of the victims.[26]

---

[26] This would also apply in those few systems, such as Italy, where criminal proceedings are obligatory, but where rules prescribing the effort devoted by public prosecutors to different offences produce a de facto selection (Peri, 2010).

Secondarily, the actions of the public prosecutor are necessarily restricted to offences pursuable in a criminal court, and so do not cover those wrongdoings which, though not classed as criminal offences, are nevertheless significant and punishable through tort law. In consequence, the route of criminal prosecution cannot be a substitute for class action, and at best can only serve to complement it.

Furthermore, considering the starting hypothesis of a regulation failure, and given that public prosecutors have many elements in common with regulators, it is likely that the criminal action will also suffer from the same problems.

The second available option is that of successive civil actions, forming a kind of intertemporal litigation pool, in which an attorney launches a pilot action and, if successful, follows it up with a series of individual actions. Also in this case, the subsequent actions need only pay the marginal cost, benefiting from the precedent which provides greater assurance of success. However, this scheme is practicable only if the attorney is able to recover the fixed cost incurred for the first litigation. Therefore, if not all the victims take legal action, the intertemporal club will necessarily be of a smaller than optimal size, and the attorney will collect a fixed per capita fee that is necessarily lower. This will result in a lower incentive for the attorney.

Moreover, if the attorney does not have a legal monopoly on the follow-on legal actions, once the precedent has been produced it is foreseeable that free-riding colleagues will enter and crowd out the market, at a lower price that does not include the share of fixed costs. This is in essence the argument in favour of the natural monopoly, which in specific contexts is resolved precisely through the granting of legal monopolies; the law and economics literature has, for example, widely debated the case of knowledge and of the promulgation of specific intellectual property rights (Ramello, 2011).[27]

Naturally, an alternative to class action, as also more generally to regulation and tort law, is provided by an insurance system. Now, such a system is particularly effective when the assets of the injurer are not able to cover the damages, and thus produce the problem of the 'disappearing

---

[27] An eloquent example is Germany's 2005 enactment of the Capital Markets Model Case Act ('Kapitalanlegerthe Musterverfahrensgesetz' or 'KapMuG'), specifically designed to enhance investor protection through a system of test trials and linked actions. Interestingly, in order to solve the afore-stated free-riding problem through the free market, there is also a complex proviso measure expressly devoted to avoiding opportunistic behaviour by spreading the fixed cost of the test litigation among all the plaintiffs (Vorwerk and Wolf, 2007).

defendant', which in practice implies limited liability and hence a suboptimal level of precaution (Summers, 1983). In this case, insurance is a further means for transferring the risks and costs in exchange for a known benefit. This solution is sometimes the only accessible one (hence the financial insurance mandated by law, as in the US) for activities that may result in environmental damage, precisely to prevent certain subjects from being judgment proof (Boyd, 2002).

However insurance is at best a complement and not a substitute for the instruments and systems of tort law – including class action – for a number of reasons, the most obvious being that a frequent instances of collective actions have dealt precisely with insurance fraud (Issacharoff, 1997).

Hence the availability of a number of alternative protection instruments, among which is class action, is better able to cover all the areas at risk.

6. CONCLUSIONS

The different legal systems have gray areas, in which meritorious claims of victims may fail to be brought due to imperfections in the legal system, rather than due to lack of legitimacy. This is tantamount to a regulatory gap, which in practice leaves certain victims unprotected and certain wrongdoers unpunished. It therefore has a serious negative impact on the overall level of justice provided by a given system.

Yet, alongside the problem of justice, there emerges an equally serious problem connected with efficiency and individual behaviour: impunity creates an incentive to engage in harmful actions as source of profit, thanks to the possibility of transferring their cost to third parties. This has repercussions on the optimal number of accidents and on their social cost. As a result, the economic system becomes less efficient, and some investments are directed toward the production of accidents, i.e. the level of care moves away from its optimal point.

Class action is one of the possible remedies, which through an amendment of civil procedure makes it possible to reinstate the completeness of tort law in a large number of cases.

This chapter uses economic categories to show how the reorganisation of civil procedure is not merely aimed at providing a more efficient litigation technology, as hierarchies (and company law) might do for other productive activities, but that it also serves to create a idiosyncratic economic organization ultimately aimed at producing a set of goods, first and foremost among which are justice and efficiency.

It is thus possible to rediscover, through economic analysis, not only the productive function of this legal machinery, but also that partial compensation of victims and large profits for the class counsel, far from being a side-effect, are actually a necessary condition for reallocation of the costs and risks associated with the legal action.

Therefore, even though some commentators are uncomfortable with the idea of 'selfish' individual interests being used as an instrument for promoting collective welfare, class action has the potential to recreate, in the judicial domain, the same effects that individual interests and motivations, governed by the perfect competition paradigm, bring to the market.

Class action can thus re-establish the alignment between public and individual interests where there are no credible alternatives. This potential makes it – notwithstanding the implementation difficulties and possible distorting effects of its attendant economic opportunities – a desirable instrument for many insufficiently protected victims and, on the other hand, a fearsome adversary for the many injurers that continue to operate almost with impunity in many jurisdictions (and naturally fuel the opposition to the adoption of class action).

REFERENCES

Barzel, Y. (1997, 2nd edn), *Economics Analysis of Property Rights*, Cambridge, New York, Melbourne: Cambridge University Press.

Bernstein, R. (1977), 'Judicial Economy and Class Action', *Journal of Legal Studies*, **7**, 349–70.

Boyd, J. (2002), 'Financial Responsibility for Environmental Obligations: Are Bonding and Assurance Rules Fullfilling their Promises', *Research in Law and Economics*, **20**, 417–486.

Brown, John P. (1973), 'Toward an Economic Theory of Liability', *Journal of Legal Studies*, **2**, 323–50.

Calabresi, G. (1970), *The Cost of Accident*, New Haven: Yale University Press.

Cassone, A., and G. B. Ramello (2011). 'The Simple Economics of Class Action: Private Provision of Club and Public Goods', *European Journal of Law and Economics*, **32**, 205–224.

Cenini, M., B. Luppi and F. Parisi (2011), 'Incentive Effects of Class Actions and Punitive Damages Under Alternative Procedural Regimes', *European Journal of Law and Economics*, **32**, 229–240.

Chappe, N. (2011), 'Demand for Civil Trials and Court Congestion', *European Journal of Law and Economics*, **32**, 205–224.

Cornes, R. and T. Sandler (1996), *The Theory of Externalities, Public Goods, and Club Goods*, Cambridge, UK: Cambridge University Press.

Dam, K. W. (1975), 'Class Actions: Efficiency, Compensation, and Conflict of Interest', *Journal of Legal Studies*, **4**, 47–73.

Dana, J.D. and K.E. Spier (1993), 'Expertise and Contingent Fee: The Role of Asymmetric Information in Attorney Compensation', *Journal of Law, Economics and Organization*, **9**, 349–67.
Edwards, B. K., and R. M. Starr (1984), 'A Note on Indivisibilities, Specialization, and Economies of Scale', *American Economic Review*, **77**, 192–4.
Eisenberg, T. and G. P. Miller (2004), 'Attorney Fees in Class Action Settlements: An Empirical Study', *Journal of Empirical Legal Studies*, **1**, 27–78.
Eisenberg, T. and G. Miller (2010), 'The English vs. the American Rule on Attorneys Fees: An Empirical Study of Attorney Fee Clauses in Publicly-Held Companies' Contracts', New York University Center for Law and Economics, Working paper no. 52.
Epstein, R.A. (2003), *Class action: Aggregation, Amplification and Distortion*, University of Chicago Legal Forum, pp. 475–518.
Gallini, N. (2011), 'Private Agreements for Coordinating Patent Rights: The Case of Patent Pools', *Journal of Industrial and Business Economics,* **38**, 5–29.
Glaeser, E.L. and A. Shleifer (2003), 'The Rise of Regulatory State', *Journal of Economic Literature*, **41**, 401–425.
Heller, M. A. (2008), *The Gridlock Economy: How Too Much Ownership Wrecks Markets, Stops Innovation, and Costs Lives*, New York: Basic Books.
Hensler, D.R., B. Dombey-Moore, E. Giddens, J. Gross, E. Moller and M. Pace (eds, 2000), *Class Action Dilemmas. Pursuing Public Goals for Private Gain*, Santa Monica, CA and Arlington, VA: Rand Publishing.
Issacharoff, S. (1997), 'Class Action Conflicts', *University of California at Davis Law Review*, **30,** 805–833.
Klement, A. and Z. Neeman (2004), 'Incentive Structures for Class Action Lawyers', *The Journal of Law, Economics & Organization*, **20**, 102–124.
Koniak, S. P. and G. M. Cohen (1996), 'Under Cloak of Settlement', *Virginia Law Review*, **82,** 1051–1280.
Lee, E.G. and T.E. Willging (2007), *The Impact of the Class Action Fairness Act of 2005 on the Federal Courts*, Third & Forth Interim Report to the Judicial, Conference Advisory Committee on Civil Rules, Federal Judicial Center.
Mercuro, N. (ed., 1992), *Taking Property and Just Compensation: Law and Economics Perspective of the Takings*, Norwell, MA: Kluwer.
Nicita, A. and G.B. Ramello (2007), 'Property, Liability and Market Power: the Antitrust Side of Copyright', *Review of Law and Economics*, **3**, 767–791.
Peri, A. (2010), 'Obbligatorietà dell'azione penale e criteri di priorità. La modellistica delle fonti tra esperienze recenti e prospettive *de iure condendo*: un quadro ricognitivo', available at http://www.forumcostituzionale.it/site/images/stories/pdf/documenti_forum/paper/0225_peri.pdf
Porrini, D. and G.B. Ramello (2005), 'Class Action for Financial Losses: Deterrence Effects from Ex Post Regulation', Working paper, Università del Piemonte Orientale, Alessandria.
Porrini, D. and G.B. Ramello (2011), 'Class Action and Financial Markets: Insights from Law and Economics', *Journal of Financial Economic Policy*, **3**(2), 140–160.
Posner, R.A. (1994), 'What do Judges and Justices Maximize? The Same Thing Everybody Else Does', *Supreme Court Economic Review*, **3**, 1–41.
Ramello, G.B. (2011), 'Property rights and externalities: the uneasy case of knowledge', *European Journal of Law and Economics*, **31**, 123–41.
Rodhe, D.L. (2004), *Access to Justice*, Oxford and New York: Oxford University Press.

Silver, C. (1999), 'Class Actions – Representative Proceedings', in B. Bouckaert and G. De Geest (eds), *Encyclopedia of Law and Economics*, Cheltenham, UK: Edward Elgar, pp.194–240.

Summers, J. (1983), 'The Case of the Disappearing Defendant: An Economic Analysis', *University of Pennsylvania Law Review*, **132**, 145–85.

Vorwerk, V. and C. Wolf (2007), *KapMuG – Kapitalanleger-Musterverfahrensgesetz*, Munich: C. H. Beck.

Watson, A. (1974), *Legal Transplants: an Approach to Comparative Law*, Athens, GA: University of Georgia Press.

Yeazell, Stephen C. (1987), *From Medieval Group Litigation to Modern Class Action*, New Haven: Yale University.

8. Class action finance and legal expense insurance

Jürgen G. Backhaus

INTRODUCTION

In an interesting development, the *Wall Street Journal*[1] reported that Pfizer, in the name of Amy Schulman, its chief counsel, is sick and tired of having to pay billable hours for winning regulatory approvals. She wants to adopt a system of contingency fees to reward lawyers who win approvals for new drugs and applications. Those who fail to win approvals will not be compensated for their efforts.

Contingency fees are at the heart of class action finance. To this aspect we now turn in the eighth chapter.

1. THE ATTORNEY AS THE BANK AND PORTFOLIO CHOICE

Fee-for-service (in medicine or law) is a financial arrangement which unties the service and its respective outcome. Fee-for-service is the method of choice when irrespective of the outcome a well-prescribed standard and indisputable service needs to be rendered. For instance, for checking the well-functioning of a car, you want to opt for a fee-for-service arrangement in order to prevent the mechanic from making unnecessary repairs. Likewise, the services of a notary public need to be rendered according to prescribed rules and formalities. When the service is successful, we never hear about the case. But the fact that we never hear about a particular case does not mean that the service was successful. It may simply mean that a fault turned out to be inconsequential or just never surfaced. A totally different financial arrangement is called for when action is required that

[1] Koppel and Ashby (2009, p. 1).

cannot be suggested in advance, action which may require imagination and prudence, which may have to be daring, yet certainly not faulty. That is, the attorney in a class-action case may raze the borderline, but he is not allowed to cross it. For such arrangements, the principal is hard-pressed to monitor the agent, and here a contingency fee arrangement is called for. Pfizer may very well be right that winning federal approval for marketing a drug from the FDA requires imaginative action, which tests and to what extent is a matter of judgment and discretion, the attorney in charge of the case should have a strong say in these decisions.

2. SELECTIVE CHOICE OF ISSUES

A class action which has many plaintiffs unknown to one another involves already before the certification substantial investments with uncertain[2] outcomes. The outcomes are not risky, they are uncertain, and this is why there cannot be an insurance for them. Rather, it is the attorney himself, he who brings the action, who has to insure the risk of failure. He is the only one who can provide the insurance, as he is the only one who controls all the relevant information or at least can control it, if he is successful.

Since he has to provide insurance as self-insurance, he is limited to creating a pool of similar cases so as to spread the risk over a sufficiently large portfolio. This, however, has the implication that there may be fairly large partnerships of attorneys all specializing in similar cases, one bearing the risk of the other, while other dissimilar cases go completely unnoticed and are never brought. Due to the peculiarities of class action finance, class actions are therefore an incomplete remedy for market failure. Some types of market failure are remedied, and others are not. It cannot be said beforehand, which is which.

3. ANTITRUST IMPLICATIONS

The production function of a legal partnership specializing in class actions exposes substantial economies of scale and scope. The cost of bringing an action for a class of one thousand plaintiffs is not much different from the cost of bringing the same action for ten times as many. As is the case whenever we experience economies of scale, there is room for only one producer. Competition can only take place at the stage of selecting a case, but it is unlikely that many partnerships have specialized in any one

[2] Knight (1921).

particular case. Economies of scope imply that the issue space of potential legal cases is occupied not randomly, but strategically with each partnership specializing in a different legal issue, ideally positioned equidistantly. In this case, economies of scope would point to only one or at best two legal partnerships for any particular case in question. This lack of competition exacerbates those principal–agency problems discussed above (Chapter 6) under the term Rosenfield effect. In terms of antitrust policy, the bar has a specific role in monitoring its members. Self-regulation is preferable over outright state regulation, as a state regulatory agency would be hard pressed to generate the requisite information. (The internet affords a new solution. Angies list provides experience reports on roofers, dentists, and other professionals. Lawyers could readily be included.)

4. LEGAL EXPENSE INSURANCE

A selective set of cases lends itself to class actions, when antitrust implications play no role whatsoever. This can occur in cases which affect literally millions of people and can therefore serve interest group organizations as the organizing cement of their group. As Mancur Olson[3] had pointed out, the provision of public goods can come about through private initiative when interest groups throw in the public good as an added group benefit in order to bind members to the group. For instance, policemen may receive attractive rates for life insurance, fire brigades' men preferred rates for holiday trips, and the like. Likewise, the members of automotive associations have access to legal expense insurance, typically to deal with traffic related accidents. Legal expense insurance could, however, also kick in when for instance *Government Motors* (GM) lands a new model on the market with serious defects, inviting millions of complaints. In such a case, a Pinto type class action can readily be financed through legal expense insurance incurred by joining an automotive association.

5. ALTERNATIVE REMEDIES

Alternative remedies are far and in between. The most common is the consumer action, or more generally, the association action (Verbandsklage). This is a legal provision granting standing to self-appointed public interest groups. They can bring actions on behalf of identifiable, but unidentified affected consumers. This legal instrument is now widely used

[3] Olson (1965).

in Germany and seems to be the weapon of choice of Germany's current secretary of justice. Routinely, an association action clause is tagged onto regulatory legislation. The enforcement of the regulation is then left to private initiative. In the extreme, two underemployed attorneys-at-law together with families and friends form an association on behalf of some public concern, such as the well-being of crows. Under German law, seven members are required to form an association. Whenever some project, public or private, is deemed to interfere with the well-being of crows, this public spirited association will file a suit for a fee. The fee is paid by whoever has been named in the suit. If nothing comes of the suit, and the crows did not even notice it, at least the public spirited attorneys received a fee. It is obvious, that this can at best be a partial solution.

6. SUMMARY

In conclusion, class actions present principal–agency problems as a consequence of the need to finance them. These principal–agency problems can be so grave as to prevent class actions from being an always present remedy for market failure. Sometimes, they can be invoked, but sometimes they fail themselves.

REFERENCES

Knight, F. (1921), *Risk, Uncertainty and Profit*, Chicago: The Chicago Press.

Koppel, N. and J. Ashby (2009), '"Billable Hour" Under Attack', *The Wall Street Journal*, **254**(46), August 24.

Olson, M. (1965), *The Logic of Collective Action*, Cambridge and London: Harvard University Press.

9. Punitive damages and class actions

Francesco Parisi and Marta Silvia Cenini

1. INTRODUCTION

Punitive damages (or exemplary damages, as they are called in the United Kingdom) are damages that are awarded in excess of the plaintiff's actual harm when compensatory damages are insufficient to deter and redress wrongdoing. The law and economics literature (Polinsky and Shavell 1998; Shavell 2004) usually suggests that punitive damages[1] should be awarded when a tortfeasor has a significant chance of escaping liability for the harm caused. The economic function of punitive damages is that of deterring undetectable torts and tortfeasors that strategically rely on imperfect enforcement. These conditions are often found when litigation costs are very high or when it is difficult for victims to identify who injured them. Punitive damages should offset the deterrence-diluting effect of the chance of escape from liability. Given this function, punitive damages should be determined by multiplying the harm caused by the reciprocal of the probability of being found liable. Mathematically, let's consider the case of a unilateral accident and define the level of precaution undertaken by the prospective tortfeasor as x, which imposes a linear unitary cost w. As usual, p is the probability of creating an accident of gravity A. The probability of an accident is a function of x, with $p' < 0$ and $p' > 0$. The tortfeasor's liability when the accident actually occurs is L. Given any potential accident situation i, the social objective is to minimize the social cost function, given by the sum of precaution costs and expected accident costs:

$$\text{Min.}\,[w\,x_i + p_i(x_i)A] \tag{9.1}$$

[1] Generally, punitive damages can be awarded when the defendant's behavior is malicious, oppressive, gross, wilful and wanton, or fraudulent and are damages given to the plaintiff as a way of punishing the defendant.

The socially optimal level of care x_i^{**} will thus be characterized by first-order-conditions

$$w = -p_i'A \tag{9.1'}$$

That is where the social marginal cost of accident prevention equals its social marginal benefit.

The tortfeasor's objective is to choose a level of precaution that minimizes his private cost function, given by the sum of precaution costs and the expected cost of liability:

$$\text{Min.}\ [w\,x_i + p_i(x_i)L] \tag{9.2}$$

In the presence of enforcement errors, liability is not always successfully ascertained. Let's define e as the enforcement error and the probability that the tortfeasor will face liability for the compensatory damages in the event of an accident. The tortfeasor's expected liability will thus equal $L = Ae$. This implies that, in the presence of enforcement error, $e < 1$, the tortfeasor will face an expected liability that does not fully reflect the expected harm that he may cause to his victim. The injurer's private cost function (9.2) can thus be rewritten as:

$$\text{Min}\ [w\,x_i + p_i(x_i)Ae] \tag{9.3}$$

The privately optimal level of care x_i^* will thus be characterized by first-order-conditions

$$w = -p_i'Ae \tag{9.3'}$$

That is where the private marginal cost of accident prevention equals the private marginal benefit. By comparing the social optimality conditions in (9.1') with the private optimality conditions in (9.3'), it is easy to see that the social and private marginal benefit terms differ by the term e. This creates a divergence between private and social incentives. In economic terms, the enforcement error represents the externalization of social costs, leading tortfeasors to take too little precaution. In a regime where punitive damages can be awarded, this misalignment can be corrected by using a punitive damage multiplier m, bringing expected liability to $L = meA$. It follows that to make tortfeasors internalize the full social cost of their activity, L must be made equal to A. This can be done by multiplying compensatory damages by a value, m, which equal the inverse of the enforcement error (that is $m = 1/e$). This is the so-called 'punitive multiple'. In this way, the private objective function (9.2) will equal the social objective function (9.1), leading to a convergence of social incentives (9.1') and private incentives

(9.3'). From this, we conclude that in the presence of enforcement error, a punitive multiple equal to the inverse of the enforcement error restores efficient incentives. This derives from the basic tort law principle that, to achieve appropriate deterrence, tortfeasors ought to be threatened with an expected liability equal to the harm they caused. Courts should thus apply punitive damages and adopt a punitive multiplier to offset the diluting effects of enforcement errors. Only in this case will precaution be adequate, product price right, and risk-producing activities be at an optimal level.

Class actions have their own deterrent function. A class action is a procedural device used in litigation to consolidate actions for the protection of the rights of large numbers of parties whose cases involve a common question of law and/or fact. The law and economics literature identifies several economic functions of class actions, including economies of scale in adjudication through the consolidation of claims, access to justice and increased affordability of legal protection for plaintiffs whose claims involve amounts that are too small to be marketable to lawyers on a contingency basis. For the purpose of this chapter, we should stress that, by facilitating access to justice and allowing claims to be aggregated into a single proceeding, class actions make prospective defendants sensitive to the presence of small claims against – claims that would not constitute a credible threat if victims were forced to bring their claims through independent actions.

The effect of a class action remedy on tortfeasors' incentives can be described considering the case of a tortfeasor's action giving rise to n possible small harmful effects. The social objective is to minimize the social cost function, given by the sum of precaution costs and expected accident costs:

$$\text{Min}\left[wx_n + \sum_{i=1}^{n} p_i\left(x_n\right)A \right] \tag{9.4}$$

The socially optimal level of care $x_n{}^{**}$ will thus be characterized by first-order-conditions

$$w = -np_i'A \tag{9.4'}$$

That is where the social marginal cost of accident prevention equals its social marginal benefit.

The tortfeasor's objective is to minimize his private cost function, given by the sum of precaution costs and the expected cost of liability, which in this case takes the following functional form:

$$\text{Min}\left[wx_n + \alpha_o \sum_{i=1}^{n} p_i\left(x_n\right)L\right] \tag{9.5}$$

where α_o can take two alternative values: α_L representing the fraction of small claims that would be pursued in the absence of class actions; and α_C, representing the fraction of claims that would instead be pursued through legal action when class actions are made available. The availability of class actions increases the fraction of cases that will be pursued $\alpha_L < \alpha_C \leq 1$.

By deriving the optimal choice for a tortfeasor facing the risk of multiple small losses, x_n*, we can see that the privately optimal value will be characterized by first-order conditions

$$w = -\alpha n\, p_i{}' L \tag{9.5'}$$

Combining condition with the previously obtained result in (9.3'), it is easy to see that the tortfeasor's incentives will be consistent with the social objectives only for values of $e = \alpha = 1$. This again follows from the basic economic principle that, to achieve optimal deterrence, tortfeasors' expected liability should always equal the harm they cause.

By providing viable venue for small claimants, potential tortfeasors are faced with higher expected liability, which gives them stronger incentives to take optimal levels of precaution. In the law and economics literature, authors have suggested that class actions are appropriate when the litigation stakes are large in aggregate but small for any individual plaintiff.

Since the class action is a remedy created to provide justice to the highest number of victims, and since the remedy allows victims to aggregate claims, it should follow that a class action suit reduces the chance that the tortfeasor will escape liability. Similar to the effect of punitive damages, this brings the tortfeasor's expected liability closer to the actual harm that he caused. When this proposition is taken in conjunction with the previous economic reasoning, it would seem that punitive damages should not be awarded in the context of class actions, inasmuch as they would duplicate the effects already pursued though the latter remedies. However, recent cases have shown that the largest punitive damages were awarded in large-scale tort litigation: the verdicts against the tobacco industry are a historic example of the combined use of class action remedies and punitive damage awards.[2] Is the combined use of these remedies duplicative in its

[2] A famous class action verdict was rendered in Florida State Court against the tobacco industry: punitive damages were assessed at $144.87 billion, more than seventeen times the combined net worth of all major cigarette manufacturers. For further references, see Nagareda (2001a) and (2001b).

effects and possibly undesirable? Put differently, are those cases superimposing two remedies that perform similar functions?

In Part 2, we consider the interaction between these two remedial solutions. The previous analysis showed that the presence of enforcement errors, $e < 1$, and imperfect access to justice for small claim plaintiffs, $\alpha < 1$, have similar diluting effects on the tortfeasor's care incentives. Punitive damages and class actions can be viewed as performing a similar function in correcting the identified dilution effects of enforcement errors and imperfect access to justice. In the following, we suggest that, in spite of this common function, the two remedies operate using different mechanisms. These operational differences prevent them from being used interchangeably, and provide the basis for delimiting the respective domains of the two remedies under consideration. In exploring these differences we show under which conditions, when a choice is available, class actions should be preferred. The present analysis has been extended in Cenini et al. (2011) in order to examine the impact of procedural rules on the effectiveness of punitive damages and class actions. In Part 3 we provide examples in which imposing punitive damages, either alone or in combination with class actions, would instead lead to preferable outcomes. Part 4 concludes with some policy considerations.

2. DIFFERENCES BETWEEN CLASS ACTION AND PUNITIVE DAMAGES: COLLATERAL EFFECTS OF PUNITIVE DAMAGES

Punitive damages and class actions are instrumental to the creation of optimal deterrence. In both cases, deterrence is created by increasing the level of expected liability for the tortfeasor. This increase in expected liability is achieved through different means under the two remedies.

Punitive damages lead to an increase in expected liability by raising the amount of damages paid by tortfeasors. Class actions lead to an increase in expected liability by raising the numbers of claims that are likely to be brought against the defendant. The different margins on which punitive damages and class actions operate lead to a number of differences.

2.1 Moral Hazard

Punitive damages can be awarded in an individual action involving a limited number of plaintiffs. Punitive damages can also be applied to the widespread harm characterizing class action lawsuits. Either case presents the possibility of a moral hazard problem.

The term moral hazard refers to the tendency of a person who is imperfectly monitored to engage in behavior that is not in the interest of the principal, when their interests are not aligned (Rothschild and Stiglitz 1976). In the case of punitive damages, moral hazard refers to the possibility that the redistribution of risk changes victims' behavior, especially with regard to levels of precaution. Victims may have reduced incentives to take precautions, and an incentive to become an overcompensated victim. If punitive damages are assessed, the plaintiff potentially receives a windfall. Since punitive damages can result in her being better off than before the injury, she has an incentive to take inefficient levels of precaution and conceivably even contribute to the damage.

In a class action where punitive damages are not awarded, a problem of moral hazard almost never occurs. The plaintiff never receives compensatory damages greater than the actual damage. Incentives to take precaution could be even excessive relative to the efficient level. Class members often receive little benefit from class actions and sometimes are even harmed by taking legal action, as for example when the class counsels[3] are awarded large fees and class members are left with coupons or other awards of little or no value. The Class Action Fairness Act of 2005 has recently tried to get round this problem and has established that the court can approve a proposed settlement under which any class member is obligated to pay sums to class counsel that would result in a net loss to the class member *only if* she finds that nonmonetary benefits substantially outweigh the monetary loss (§1713). Under these circumstances, it is almost impossible that a class member could obtain damages exceeding the actual harm. Consequently, we can conclude that within a class action where punitive damages are not awarded a problem of moral hazard almost never occurs.

2.2 The Disappearing Defendant Problem

Assessing punitive damages in a class action suit also risks the disappearing defendant problem. When an individual action ends with a judgment in the millions, there is a high probability that the defendant will file bankruptcy. Consequently, the plaintiff who acted first will be compensated for his harm while the rest of the victims are left without protection. In other words, if the tortfeasor is insolvent, it has disappeared insofar as the victims are concerned and they will receive no compensation.

[3] The class counsels are the persons who serve as attorneys for the class members in a proposed class action.

With a class action, this problem would never (or at least rarely) occur. As a procedural device, class actions allow the aggregation of the highest number of legitimate claims against the same defendant that has allegedly caused harm. The settlement usually proposed at the end of the legal action, subjected to court approval, fixes the amount of money (or non-monetary benefits) that the defendant must pay to each class member. This settlement, if approved, binds all class members (or at least those members of the class who affirmatively agree to the settlement). Any discrimination between class members is not allowed and in particular, the Class Action Fairness Act of 2005 prohibits discrimination based on geographic location (§1714). The court approval is granted only if the settlement, voluntary dismissal, or compromise, is 'fair, reasonable and adequate', receiving greater scrutiny when the remedy is in the form of a coupon settlement (§1712 (e)). Courts must consider, among other aspects, 'the probable resources and ability of the parties to pay, collect, or enforce the settlement'.[4] Courts also must consider the effect of the settlement on other pending actions bearing a relationship to the instant action. It follows that within a class action a disappearing defendant problem would rarely occur or at least would be shared among all the injured parties.

2.3 Punishment

Punitive damages differ from class actions in their objective of imposing punishment on a tortfeasor whose behavior showed a conscious disregard for others.[5] As the Supreme Court has observed, 'Punitive damages are a civil penalty aimed at deterrence and retribution that further the state's interest in punishing unlawful conduct'.[6] Punitive damages should be awarded if and only if the tort was intentional.

While class action suits are not limited to this punitive function, one should query whether the state's interest in punishing unlawful conduct should be pursued within private law. A better alternative might be within the criminal system, where the benefits from sanctions are not to the

---

[4] Federal Judicial Center (2004, p. 242).

[5] California Civil Code §3294, entitled 'Exemplary Damages' (another name for punitive damages), reads: 'For Oppression, Fraud or Malice. In an action for the breach of an obligation not arising from contract, where the defendant has been guilty of oppression, fraud, or malice, the plaintiff, in addition to the actual damages, may recover damages for the sake of the example and by way of punishing the defendant'.

[6] *State Farm Mut. Auto. Ins. Co.* v. *Campbell*, Supreme Court of the United States, 538 U.S. 408 (2003).

advantage of only one person, and the punishment is proportional and strictly provided by the law.

More fundamental problems arise when courts impose damages in the millions of dollars on negligent tortfeasors, especially against manufacturers of defective products.[7] The three factors often seen as relevant to determining the appropriate size of a punitive damage award are the wealth of the defendant, the culpability of the defendant's conduct, the amount of compensatory damages awarded. Commentators (Wheeler 1983; Jeffries 1986; Bittle 1987) have noted a constitutional infirmity when massive punitive damages are awarded for a single course of conduct, given the Eighth Amendment's prohibition on excessive fines and the 'fundamental fairness' doctrine of due process of law. Both rules provide a constitutional limit on the size of punitive damage awards. Critics of large-sum punitive damages argue that the harshness of the penalty should be kept conceptually apart from the wrongfulness of the conduct and that the defendant's wealth should never affect the quantification of punitive damages (Bittle 1987).[8] Indeed, the Supreme Court, in *Honda Motor Co., Ltd.* v. *Karl L. Oberg*,[9] held that the Constitution imposes a substantive limit on the size of punitive damages awards and that there is a violation of due process clause where a party has been deprived of a well-established common-law protection against arbitrary and inaccurate adjudication, as may happen when punitive awards are awarded.[10] Accordingly, a growing number of states in

---

[7] In *Grimshaw* v. *Ford Motor Company*, Court of Appeal of California, Fourth Appellate District, Division Two, 174 Cal. Rptr. 348 (1981), analysed below, the jury assessed $ 125 million as punitive damages, reduced by judge to 'only' $3.5 million.

[8] In *Browning-Ferris Industries of Vermont, Inc., et al.* v. *Kelco Disposal, Inc., et al.*, Supreme Court of the United States, 492 U.S. 257 (1989), the Supreme Court rejected petitioner's claim that the punitive damage award violated the Excessive Fines Clause of the Eighth Amendment. The court held that the amendment's history and purpose evinced a legislative intent to apply it only to criminal prosecutions and punishments imposed by the government. The court also held that because petitioner failed to timely raise its due process challenge to the award, the claim would not be considered. Finally, the court held that neither federal common law nor the Excessive Fines Clause of the Eighth Amendment provided a basis for disturbing the jury's punitive damages award in the case. See also *Pacific Mutual Life Ins. Co.* v. *C. Haslip*, Supreme Court of the United States, 499 U.S. 1 (1991).

[9] *Honda Motor Co., Ltd.* v. *Karl L. Oberg*, Supreme Court of the United States, 512 U.S. 415 (1994).

[10] 'Punitive damages pose an acute danger of arbitrary deprivation of property, since jury instructions typically leave the jury with wide discretion in choosing amounts and since evidence of a defendant's net worth creates the potential that juries will use their verdicts to express biases against big businesses. Oregon has removed one of the few procedural safeguards which the common law provided

recent years have sought to change the way punitive damages are awarded, introducing absolute limits on punitive damages[11] or proportional caps based on compensatory damages.[12]

Finally, it is not useless to note that when the defendant is a firm – a common circumstance in cases involving extensive punitive damages – the retributive goal cannot be reached. Punishment can be addressed only against a culpable *individual* within the firm and not the firm as an abstract entity (Polinsky and Shavell 1998).

3. CASES IN WHICH PUNITIVE DAMAGES ARE EFFICIENT

3.1 Disgorgement Damage

The analysis in the previous paragraphs demonstrates the primary negative collateral effects of punitive damages. These cases suggest those instances where class action remedies should be preferred. We will now explore scenarios in which punitive damages are the more desirable remedy.

One instance in which punitive damages should be awarded is when the tortfeasor derives greater benefit from his illicit conduct than the amount of harm he causes. In this scenario, if the tortfeasor had to pay only compensatory damages, he would have a strong incentive to cause the harm, pay the damages and reap the benefit. As such, it becomes socially efficient to make the tortfeasor pay an amount that leaves him indifferent between the injury with damages (disgorgement) and or no injury. Damages paid to eliminate the tortfeasor's profit are referred to as 'disgorgement damages'. For example, when the editor of a newspaper publishes libelous statements, a court should take into account, among other things, the number of newspapers sold, which represents the defendant's profit derived from defaming the plaintiff. Even in the civil law tradition, where it is well known that punitive damages do not have a general application, libel defendants were

---

against that danger without providing any substitute procedure and without any indication that the danger has in any way subsided over time'.

[11] *See, e.g.,* GA. CODE ANN. § 51–12–5.1(g) (Supp. 1992) (limiting punitive damages for certain tort actions to $ 250,000); VA. CODE ANN. § 8.01–38.1 (Michie 1992) (limiting punitive damages on all claims to $ 350,000).

[12] *See, e.g.,* COLO. REV. STAT. ANN. § 13–21–102(1)(a) (West 1988) (limiting punitive damage awards in all civil actions to the amount of compensatory damages awarded); FLA. STAT. ch. 768.73(1)(a) (1991 & Supp. 1992) (limiting punitive damages in certain civil actions to three times the amount of compensatory damages awarded).

ordered to pay an amount of money higher than compensatory damages when found guilty.[13]

In these cases, it would still be better not to award the plaintiff the punitive damages, as we still have the problem of moral hazard. The sum could be given to a third party, an association, or the state. In recent years, some states have introduced the so-called 'split-recovery' provisions that allow the state to claim a portion of any punitive damages awarded.[14] This approach has been received favourably as it maintains adequate levels of deterrence and punishment for the defendant while reducing a plaintiff's windfall providing funds for the public's benefit.

---

[13] Regarding Italy, see Trib. Milano, Dir. Inf. 1992, 78 (1991), where the amount of damages was calculated with regard to how many copies of the newspaper had been sold; Trib. Roma, Dir. inf. e inf. 1993, 403 (1992). In a famous defamation case (*Gertz* v. *Robert Welch Inc.*, Supreme Court of the United States, 418 U.S. 323; 41 L. Ed. 2d 789 (1974), the Supreme Court refused to assess punitive damages because the States may not permit recovery of presumed or punitive damages when liability is not based on a showing of knowledge of falsity or reckless disregard for the truth. In an opinion by Powell J., expressing the view of five members of the court, it was held that:

> We also find no justification for allowing awards of punitive damages against publishers and broadcasters held liable under state-defined standards of liability for defamation. In most jurisdictions jury discretion over the amounts awarded is limited only by the gentle rule that they not be excessive. Consequently, juries assess punitive damages in wholly unpredictable amounts bearing no necessary relation to the actual harm caused. And they remain free to use their discretion selectively to punish expressions of unpopular views. Like the doctrine of presumed damages, jury discretion to award punitive damages unnecessarily exacerbates the danger of media self-censorship, but, unlike the former rule, punitive damages are wholly irrelevant to the state interest that justifies a negligence standard for private defamation actions. They are not compensation for injury. Instead, they are private fines levied by civil juries to punish reprehensible conduct and to deter its future occurrence. In short, the private defamation plaintiff who establishes liability under a less demanding standard than that stated by New York Times may recover only such damages as are sufficient to compensate him for actual injury. (418 U.S. 323, 351; 41 L. Ed. 2d 789, LEdHR18).

[14] The first states that introduced the 'split-recovery' provisions were Colorado, Georgia, Illinois, Iowa, Kansas, Montana, New York, Oregon, Utah. *See* COLO. REV. STAT. ANN. § 13–21–102(4) (West 1988); GA. CODE ANN. § 51–12–5.1(e)(2) (Supp. 1992); ILL. ANN. STAT. ch. 110, para. 2–1207 (Smith-Hurd Supp. 1992); IOWA CODE § 668A.1.2.b (1991); KAN. STAT. ANN. § 60–3402(e) (Supp. 1992); MO. REV. STAT. § 537.675.2 (Supp. 1992); N.Y. CIV. PRAC. L. & R. 8701(1) (McKinney Supp. 1993); OR. REV. STAT. § 18.540(1)(c) (1991); UTAH CODE ANN. § 78–18–1(3) (1992).

It is significant to note that, in this instance, the tortfeasor's utility, although illicit, will be used to increase the total social welfare. There are other cases, however, in which the illicit utility should not be allowed to increase social welfare. For example, consider a person who breaks the window of his neighbour's house because he enjoys the unhappiness his neighbour will experience (Shavell 2004, p. 245). In this case, society does not want to count the person's utility as an addition to social welfare. Instead, it wants to discourage the injurer's harmful act.

The same reasoning can be extended to other fields. For instance, when the factories pollute the environment, it is socially efficient to make the tortfeasor pay a sum equal to the injury with damages (disgorgement). This is equal to the profit derived from not using a less polluting system. It is worth noticing that Italy, a state where punitive damages are generally not awarded, introduced a type of penalty to be paid by tortfeasors for pollution-related infractions.[15] The law[16] considered, among other factors, the culpability of the defendant's conduct and the gain obtained by the tortfeasor (art. 18, §6). The law also provided that the sum would go toward an environmental protection fund (art. 18, §9 bis). Unfortunately, the new Environmental Code issued in 2006[17] eliminated these provisions.

We conclude that when the tortfeasor obtains greater benefit from his illicit conduct than the amount of harm he causes, he should be made to pay a sum greater than the actual harm. Under these conditions, punitive damages could be efficient. Note, however, that in all the instances analyzed above, the quantification of punitive damages does not depend on the enforcement error but on the profit gained by the tortfeasor. This suggests that when there is a high probability that the tortfeasor will escape liability because of transaction costs and when the aim is to bring the tortfeasor's expected liability closer to the actual harm he caused, the preferred remedy is the class action and not punitive damages. Note also that in these instances, the tortfeasor could be required to pay an amount equal to her profit in pursuance of the doctrine of unjust enrichment (Sacco 1959; Trimarchi 1962).

---

[15] The Constitutional Court of Italy (Corte Cost. n. 641, Foro it. 1988, I, c. 694 (1987)) stated that when an environmental damage occurs, tort law can assume a function of punishment.

[16] L. 349/86, so-called Legge Merli. Art. 18, §6 read: 'Il giudice, ove non sia possibile una precisa quantificazione del danno, ne determina l'ammontare in via equitativa, tenendo comunque conto della gravità della colpa individuale, del costo necessario per il ripristino e del profitto conseguito dal trasgressore in conseguenza del suo comportamento lesivo dei beni ambientali'.

[17] D.Lgs. 3 aprile 2006, n. 152.

Similar conclusions could be drawn when losses suffered by the victim are smaller than the total losses suffered by society, which always happens when the environment is damaged. Consider, for instance, the effects resulting from atomic bombs. Here even if all the people affected by this catastrophic event had taken legal action as a class, the entire damage suffered by society would not have been restored. In this case, the social cost is not entirely borne by the victim: punitive damages are efficient because they make the injurer internalize the total damage suffered by the whole of society. As with disgorgement damages, these punitive damages should be given to a third party and not to the victim to prevent a moral hazard problem.

3.2 Non-pecuniary Loss and Absolute Deterrence

Another instance in which punitive damages should be awarded is when health is at stake. Health, whether destroyed or damaged, is never fully replaceable (so-called irreplaceable commodities).[18] The losses are not pecuniary, which implies that it is very difficult for courts to estimate them. It follows that victims are usually not fully compensated for their losses arising from an accident that results in death or serious permanent injury. Research suggests that at present, damage awards for serious personal injury and death generally are not sufficiently large to induce potential injurers to take due care and engage in optimal activity levels (see Arlen 2000).[19] In 2001, the Supreme Court in *Cooper Industries, Inc.* v. *Leatherman Tool Group, Inc.* suggested that punitive damages historically compensated for noneconomic damages that were ignored by a less progressive legal system. The first time where punitive damages were awarded was in England in 1763. That case regarded a recovery for a non pecuniary loss, more precisely compensation for injured feelings.[20] In a case decided in Italy in 1994, the court awarded 2 million lire (equivalent to about 1 million euro) to people who had been exposed to toxic substances.[21] In this case, the calculation did turn on pecuniary considerations such as medical expenses, loss of working abilities, or the like. Instead, the aim was to restore a non-pecuniary loss. Note that when health is at stake it is almost

[18] A commodity is irreplaceable if its owner does not perceive any equivalent commodities available on the market.

[19] For the contrary view that victims of physical injuries may sometimes receive too much compensation, see again Arlen (2000), §11. See also Avraham (2003).

[20] See *Huckley* v. *Money*, 95 E. R. 768 (1763).

[21] App. Milano, GI 1994, I, 2, 961 (1994).

impossible that a problem of moral hazard will arise: few are willing to risk a long term health problem for pecuniary gain.

In these cases, a class action remedy could not substitute punitive damages, as the difficulty of estimating the exact amount of damages remains. In this case, punitive damages again do not depend on the 'punitive multiple'. Rather, the damages try to bring the tortfeasor's expected liability closer to the actual harm that he caused.

There is another reason that leads courts to assess punitive damages when health is at stake. Consider *Grimshaw* v. *Ford Motor Company*.[22] After a collision with another car, the vehicle manufactured by Ford burst into flames causing serious burns to the two people who were inside. The driver died a few days later of congestive heart failure as a result of the burns. The explosion was due to the placement of the fuel tank behind the rear axle, leaving a few inches of crush space. This was far less than in any other American automobile or Ford overseas subcompact. It was later discovered that this car had failed the manufacturer's fuel system integrity test. Ford nevertheless produced and sold the car to the public without doing anything to remedy the defects. Equipping the car to avoid the fuel tank explosion would have cost only $15.30 more per car.

The jury found Ford's behavior 'reckless' and blameworthy: to save only 15 dollars per car, the company had voluntarily chosen a solution imperiling the lives of the occupants in case of a collision. Discovery revealed this option was chosen because Ford calculated that it was more advantageous for the company to cause the harm and pay damages than to spend 15 dollars more per car, relying on the fact that very few people would actually sue. This suggests the benefit of aggregating plaintiffs through class actions.

It is important to note that even if the good isn't mass-produced, the tortfeasor should still pay punitive damages: in these cases society needs to create absolute deterrence. Since when health is at stake moral hazard will rarely occur, an assessment of punitive damages could be efficient.[23]

3.3 Introducing Frictions

Punitive damages could prove decisive when the harm caused by the tortfeasor is widespread but so small as to preclude a class action or an

---

[22] *Grimshaw* v. *Ford Motor Company*, Court of Appeal of California, Fourth Appellate District, Division Two, 174 Cal. Rptr. 348 (1981).

[23] We do not explicitly consider whether punitive damages could actually have a punitive purpose in the context of class actions. This does not contradict our results, however, as such cases are punishable by criminal law.

individual suit because of litigation costs and meagre compensatory damages. Punitive damages could represent the only factor able to induce the plaintiff, or a class of plaintiffs, to sue the tortfeasor and protect their legitimate claims when it would otherwise make little fiscal sense.

In this scenario, there could be a mixed equilibrium where the two remedies are combined and punitive damages are awarded within a class action. It is important to underline that punitive damages are necessary because they allow the class action to work. Put another way, punitive damages 'lubricate' the frictions that keep plaintiffs from bringing legitimate claims. To maintain equilibrium when combining these two actions, the relationship between punitive damages and the value of the action must be inversely proportional.

4. PROPOSAL AND POLICY CONSIDERATIONS

Many authors (Polinsky and Shavell 1998; Craswell 1996) argue that when victims are shareholders or customers of the firm, punitive damages are ineffective and should not be awarded. Since shareholders are the residual claimants of the firm's profits, they will be made worse off by awarding punitive damages. Customers, too, will suffer negative outcomes in the form of higher prices.

We are not entirely convinced. To begin with, the elasticity of demand implies that the firm cannot raise prices to the level it wants. Thus, it would not be possible to translate punitive damages into higher prices. Additionally, a higher price would lead the less efficient firm to exit the market, thereby strengthening its competitors.

When litigation costs are paid by the state, which sometimes happens when the class loses the action,[24] the plaintiff's aversion to risk becomes

---

[24] See for example Art. 15 of the Italian proposal presented by the Radical Party that says that if the class loses the action, the judge will liquidate the attorney's fee at expense of legal aid.

In the United States, class actions are always brought on a contingency fee basis. Class members do not ordinarily have to contribute to attorneys' fees or costs before settlement or judgment. In a class action for money damages lawyers who represent the class are generally paid out of the money that is recovered – called a 'common fund' – for the people they are representing. In class actions involving declaratory judgments or injunctive relief, lawyers may be paid by the people who hired them, or in some cases, by the people or companies they are suing. Attorney's fee awards are subject to court review and approval. Ordinarily, if an award is made in a common fund case, it will be awarded as a percentage of the total money available for the class. A benchmark award generally accepted by the courts is approximately 25 per irrelevant. The plaintiff will be indifferent between taking and not taking the action. With regard to the defendant, whether punitive damages represent a disruption cost is an empirical question that does not affect our conclusion.

REFERENCES

Arlen, J. (2000), 'Tort damages', in B. Bouckaert and G. De Geest, *Encyclopedia of Law and Economics*, Cheltenham: Edward Elgar, **2**, 682–734.

Avraham, R. (2003), 'Pain-and-Suffering Damages in Tort Law: Revisiting the Theoretical Framework and Empirical Data', Michigan Law and Economics Research Paper No. 03–001, *Northwestern Law & Econ Research Paper* 03–03, available at http://ssrn.com/abstract=382120.

Bittle, L.F. (1987), 'Punitive Damages and the Eighth Amendment: An Analytical Frame-work for Determining Excessiveness', *California Law Review*, **75**, 1433–50.

Bronsteen, J. and O.M. Fiss (2003), 'The Class Action Rule', *Notre Dame Law Review*, **78**(5), 1419–1454, available at http://ssrn.com/abstract=895093.

Cenini, M, B. Luppi and F. Parisi (2011), 'Incentive Effects of Class Actions and Punitive Damages Under Alternative Procedural Regimes', 32 *European Journal of Law and Economics*.

Craswell, R. (1996), 'Damage multipliers in market relationships', *Journal of Legal Studies*, **25**, 463–92.

Di Nola, S., D. Porcini and G. Ramello (2005), 'Class action, mercati finanziari e tutela dei risparmiatori', in *X Rapporto sul sistema finanziario italiano*, Fondazione Rosselli, 459–75.

Epstein, R. (2003), 'Class Actions: Aggregation, Amplification, and Distortion', *The University of Chicago Legal Forum*, 475–517.

Federal Judicial Center (2004), *Manual of Complex Litigation*, 4th edition, Eagan, MN: West Publishing.

Gallo, P. (1996), *Pene private e responsabilità civile*, Milano: Giuffrè.

Giuggioli, P.F. (2006), 'Class action e azioni di gruppo', Padova: Cedam.

Jeffries, J.C. Jr. (1986), 'A Comment on the Constitutionality of Punitive Damages', *Virginia Law Review*, **72**, 139–58.

Mesulam, S. (2004), 'Collective Rewards and Limited Punishment: Solving the Punitive Damages Dilemma with Class', *Columbia Law Review*, **104**(4), 1114–1149.

Miller, G. (1998), 'Class Action', in P. Newman (ed.), *The New Palgrave Dictionary of Economics and the Law*, vol. 1, New York: Stockton Press, 257–61.

Nagareda, R.A. (2001a), 'Engle v. R.J. Reynolds Tobacco Co.: Lessons In State Class Actions, Punitive Damages, And Jury Decision-Making', *Wake Forest Law Review*, **36**, 1129–55.

Nagareda, R.A. (2001b), 'Punitive Damages Class Actions and the Baseline of Tort', *Wake Forest Law Review*, **36**, 943–68.

---

cent of the total, although the award may be adjusted higher or lower, depending on the specific facts of a case.

Pardolesi, R. and B. Tassone (2003), *I giudici e l'analisi economica del diritto privato*, Bologna: Il Mulino.
Polinsky, A.M. and S. Shavell (1998), 'Punitive Damages: an Economic Analysis', *Harvard Law Review*, **111**, 869–962.
Rothschild, M. and J.E. Stiglitz (1976), 'Equilibrium in Competitive Insurance Markets: An Essay on the Economics of Imperfect Information', *The Quarterly Journal of Economics*, **90**(4), 630–49.
Sacco, R. (1959), *L'arricchimento ottenuto mediante fatto ingiusto*, Torino: UTET.
Shavell, S. (2004), *Foundations of Economics Analysis of Law*, Cambridge: Press of Harvard University.
Silver, C. (2000), 'Class Actions – Representative Proceeding', in P. Boukaert and G. De Geest, *Encyclopedia of Law and Economics*, Chetenham: Edward Elgar, **7**, 194–240.
Trimarchi, P. (1962), *L'arricchimento senza causa*, Milano: Giuffrè.
Wheeler, M.E. (1983), 'The Constitutional Case for Reforming Punitive Damages Procedures', *Virginia Law Review*, **69**, 269–356.

CASE REFERENCES

State Farm Mut. Auto. Ins. Co. v. *Campbell*, Supreme Court of the United States, 538 U.S. 408 (2003)
Honda Motor Co., Ltd. v. *Karl L. Oberg*, Supreme Court of the United States, 512 U.S. 415 (1994)
Pacific Mutual Life Ins. Co. v. *C. Haslip*, Supreme Court of the United States, 499 U.S. 1 (1991)
Browning-Ferris Industries of Vermont, Inc., et al. v. *Kelco Disposal, Inc., et al.*, Supreme Court of the United States, 492 U.S. 257 (1989)
Grimshaw v. *Ford Motor Company*, Court of Appeal of California, Fourth Appellate District, Division Two, 174 Cal. Rptr. 348 (1981)
Gertz v. *Robert Welch Inc.*, Supreme Court of the United States, 418 U.S. 323; 41 L. Ed. 2d 789 (1974)
Huckley v. *Money*, 95 E. R. 768 (1763)
App. Milano, GI 1994, I, 2, 961 (1994)
Trib. Roma, Dir. inf. e inf. 1993, 403 (1992)
Trib. Milano, Dir. Inf. 1992, 78 (1991)
Corte Cost. n. 641, Foro it. 1988, I, c. 694 (1987)

10. A case for information sharing in class action suits

Bruno Deffains and Eric Langlais

1. INTRODUCTION

There is a general agreement concerning two effects associated with the formation of a class action (CA thereafter). On the one hand, CAs entail aggregation and amplification effects, which are both individually and socially desirable. In practice, CAs are used to consolidate a large number of individual claims. Intuitively, individual rationality implies that the claims under a threshold depending on the litigation cost are deterred from filing a lawsuit. Thus, to the extent that CAs entail a decrease in the litigation cost, these smaller claims are allowed to enter into the litigation process. Moreover, once both the larger and the smaller claim file a suit against the same tortfeasor, he receives additional incentives to undertake a socially efficient level of care. This is because CAs lead to an increase in the probability of trial, given that when some victims are deterred from filing an individual suit, the defendant's probability of being sued is smaller than 1, and he does not have enough incentives to invest in the prevention activity. As a result, CAs also contribute to improving the preventive function of tort law.

On the other hand, CAs generate scale economies. Filing a suit against a large tortfeasor may be quite complex and expensive for an individual: it implies time and resources that may be expensive as compared to the capacity of the tortfeasor – such that a small plaintiff may be discouraged from filing against a large tortfeasor. In contrast, a CA allows a decrease in litigation cost per individual, or allows plaintiffs to invest in better experts than they did in the absence of a CA (since the cost is spread over all the members). Eventually, members of a CA may be specialized in some tasks depending on their skill. Adding to these internal or individual scale economies, there are also some external or aggregate scale economies. CAs entail a reduction in the number of individual court appearances, which is first beneficial for the members of the CA. But, it also induces an improvement in the organization of justice: once a CA is opened, the rate at which all claims are resolved is increased. In other words, CAs contribute to limiting the phenomenon of 'rationing by waiting' inherent in the organization of the judicial system.

Thus, the basic incentives to participate in a CA identified in the literature depends on the value of three key parameters:

(1) the number of individuals similarly situated with respect to a common defendant,
(2) the size of the loss borne by each party,
(3) the amount of administrative costs for an individual suit.

Nevertheless, some authors have suggested that members of a CA may develop strategic behaviours. Two contributors are worth noting. Che (1996) analyzes the role of asymmetries of information both between plaintiffs and the defendant and between the members of the CA. The author assumes that two kinds of plaintiffs (small claim, and large claim) sue against the same tortfeasor, and have the opportunity to join a CA or to file individually. He finds a multiplicity of equilibria: either no CA is formed, while there exists a potentially viable CA, or not all the plaintiffs are allowed to join the CA (and specifically, not all the smallest or weakest victims), but many opt out. Theoretically, the characteristics of each equilibrium, that is the composition of the CA, depends on the proportion of large stakes in the population of plaintiffs.

Marceau and Mongrain (2003) develop the idea that a CA has the characteristics of a public good. However, it is a public good which is privately produced because a CA is usually provided by only a subset of plaintiffs. Once the CA is created against a tortfeasor, all the victims have the opportunity to join it, and thus benefit from the provision of the good without having to incur the initial cost associated with the formation of the CA. For the representative member, this cost is a sunk cost, and it is borne only by the initiator of the CA. Hence, there is a problem of 'free-riding', which is formalized by Marceau and Mongrain as a war of attrition: on the one hand, each plaintiff has an incentive to wait for someone else to initiate the CA (because of the sunk cost) but on the other, he bears a penalty in waiting (time is also costly). The authors mainly demonstrate that the identity of the CA initiator depends on the rule of compensation awarded by courts to the CA members: small levels of damage averaging tend to give incentives to the holder of the smallest claim to be the initiator of the CA.

The existence of informational asymmetries and the characteristics of a public good explain that the exclusion of some plaintiffs may arise, and specifically the weakest victims. Nevertheless, it seems that another argument should counterbalance these effects that has not been yet formally investigated. When parties enter into the litigation process, they enter into a discovery process: before going to trial, parties collect evidences, testimonies, expertises and so on. Moreover, they share the information during the pretrial negotiation period.

But there are many reasons explaining that plaintiffs can also share the information they have collected when engaged in individual lawsuits. This is the case, for instance, when victims are injured by the same tortfeasor over a quite long period of time (e.g. asbestos or tobacco litigation, medical malpractice or product liability). In this context, plaintiffs do not simultaneously enter into the litigation process, but they enter sequentially (at different dates). Hence, we have to consider mainly the incomplete information for the first plaintiffs, since as time is passing, new evidences arrive and the 'state of the art' has changed.

As a result, some uncertainty is resolved from the time the first claims are settled to the period the later plaintiffs file. This implies positive informational externalities between plaintiffs because later filers benefit from the experience of the first plaintiffs. These externalities also allow later plaintiffs to update their beliefs on the likelihood to win at trial.

According to this view, a CA may be understood as a useful tool used by plaintiffs to internalize these informational externalities. Specifically, CAs allow the earlier victims to retain part of the benefits of these externalities, that otherwise they would never recover. The CA's attorney certainly plays an active role in the transmission of information between the members. When they become members of a CA, plaintiffs better perceive the existence of the correlation between the individual losses. Plaintiffs will become more confident about their chances of success at trial against the same defendant.

In our chapter, we focus on the impact of information sharing between plaintiffs and we compare the case where CAs are forbidden to the case where they are allowed. We consider that informational asymmetries exist mainly between parties and the judge. In many countries procedural rules hold such that parties have free access to the evidences and the various documents that the other party has gathered and will produce at trial. In contrast, some empirical works display that there exists a kind of heterogeneity in the decisions of courts, concerning similar cases. So once the parties have collected evidences, uncertainty remains as to the outcome at trial. A related problem is the emergence of new legal doctrines. For example in the United States, the problem with the asbestos litigation in the 1980s comes partly from the fact that the legal doctrine to apply was not yet developed. So in our work, the main source of uncertainty comes from the behaviour of the courts.

In the rest of the chapter, we exhibit the importance of three main features concerning the issue of CA formation: the characteristics of the discovery process (the technology of production of information: evidences, testimonies, expertises), the compensation rules set by courts (individual damage for individual suits or damage averaging for class action), and the size of scale economies on the litigation costs. Section 2 presents the model. In Section 3, we characterize a set of (subgame perfect) equilibria associated with the existence of the large class action. We show that when plaintiffs expect to never obtain 'bad news', a sufficient condition to file is that their priors are 'optimistic'. More specifically, we show that when plaintiffs expect to obtain at least one 'good news' in the future, such a CA is more likely to occur the smaller the proportion of plaintiffs having a small stake and the larger the scale economies on litigation costs. Section 4 considers the impact of alternative rules for damage applied by the courts (damage averaging vs individual damages), or lawyer's fees (contingent or proportional fees).

2. THE BASIC SET UP

2.1 Motivations

Consider a situation where the same individual, for example through the occurrence of several successive individual accidents, injures a group of victims. If CAs are forbidden, victims will enter sequentially into the litigation process, and will file individually against the tortfeasor. In this case, repeated trials entail positive informational externalities which are beneficial only to the later plaintiffs: the earlier plaintiffs who have worse or less fine information may undertake actions that otherwise they would not choose to follow had they obtained better information. In contrast, the plaintiffs who enter later on in the litigation process may benefit from the experience of the earlier ones and are allowed to make more accurate decisions regarding the various legal options that are available (file or exit; go to trial, settle or give up).

This is a passive transmission of information coming from the earlier plaintiffs, but a problem arises because the first plaintiffs have no means of benefiting from the information collected by their successors or to retain privately part of the benefits associated with the positive informational externality they create. From this perspective, the formation of a CA may be understood as a tool allowing the internalization of these externalities: the earlier plaintiffs could benefit from positive informational externalities. More generally, the formation of a CA makes the transmission of information between the plaintiffs easier. As a consequence, apart from economies of scale coming from the pooling of attorney's services, there exist strong incentives in favour of the formation of a CA which result from information sharing between plaintiffs: specifically, the pooling of individual information allows all of them to improve their individual assessment of the expected gain at trial.

We focus on these incentives to share information between plaintiffs suing the same tortfeasor and we investigate their consequences for the existence of a CA.

In our set up, the discovery process is such that:

1. Whatever the available information, plaintiffs are not confident with respect to their chances of success at trial, i.e. they cannot know whether the judge will be favourable to their case; on the one hand, it is relatively easy to assess the value of individual damages (which may be considered as a public information), but on the other hand, the cause of the victims' injury may be quite difficult or costly to establish; thus, the plaintiffs' individual assessment of the likelihood to win at trial are always smaller than 1.
2. Before entering into the litigation process, plaintiffs have common priors (same initial assessment of the likelihood that they will win at trial); but when they file a suit, and since they enter at different dates into the discovery process, they obtain different additional information: more specifically, the later the entry into the litigation process, the finer the information obtained; given that the new information allows each plaintiff to update his initial beliefs, this explains why the different types of plaintiffs have different posteriors beliefs.
3. The defendant has access to the same information as the plaintiff, for any date in the litigation process.
4. Each plaintiff evaluates (*ex-ante*) the opportunity to file a suit or to give up, knowing that he will benefit from a new information later on once he is engaged in the litigation process, and knows that this information will give a new assessment of his chances at trial, such that he will undertake *ex-post* the best decision (whether he exits, goes to trial or accepts the defendant's offer) conditionally on his information.

In this way, we can capture two salient points of the litigation process: i) Informational asymmetries exist mainly between the judge and the parties at trial. Thus, the main relevant source of uncertainty for parties is created by the behaviour of the court that is unknown *ex-ante*. ii) There are many reasons explaining why plaintiffs cannot be certain they will win at trial: scientific evidences are imperfect, some of them may be strongly controversial, there may exist a large disagreement between experts' opinions, judges may have bias of judgment, mistaken beliefs, and/or unfortunately reject some pieces of evidences.

As noted before, a related problem concerning collective accidents and mass tort CA is the emergence of new legal doctrines, which creates uncertainty for parties. Formally, we introduce this problem of information arrival and beliefs updating in a simple three-stage game, where two types of plaintiffs (large stake/low stake) file a lawsuit sequentially against a defendant. In a first stage, the first type decides either to sue individually or to initiate a CA; then, in the second stage, the second type decides either to file an individual suit or to join the CA when it has been previously formed; finally, in the third stage, the defendant makes one 'take-it-or-leave-it' offer either to an individual plaintiff or to the representative member of a CA.

In the next paragraph, we consider that two (types of) plaintiffs have been injured by the same individual either through two different individual accidental events occurring in a short period of time, thus implying repeated trials. They are supposed to be heterogenous in their claim of damage awards (or equivalently in the loss they have experienced): plaintiff denoted P_i has low stake θ_i, while plaintiff denoted P_j has a high stake $\theta_j > \theta_i$.

2.2 The Sequence of Individual Decisions

We consider a three-stage game, where plaintiffs enter sequentially in the litigation process against the defendant, such that P_i is the first filer. In stage 1, P_i may choose between two options: either he files or he exits. In this last case, everything is over for him, and then, P_j has only to decide for himself whether he enters and files individually, or if he exits. If P_i opts for filing, two options are available to him: either he can sue individually, or he can decide to initiate a CA, to which all individuals that have suffered a damage may join. In stage 2 beginning after P_i's move, P_j chooses either to sue individually or to register to become a member of the class action.

We assume that the membership is voluntary and open, such that the presence of a CA does not legally compel other plaintiffs to join it, and no individual plaintiff is denied membership against his wishes. In practice, Courts decide to maintain a CA or not, and prescribe deadlines for claimants' participation or opt out decisions. This framework reflects the equilibrium behaviours of plaintiffs, in such a way that after a limited period of time during which any individual has the opportunity to opt out of the CA, the membership becomes binding: no CA member can opt out, and no new plaintiff can opt in. Moreover, once a CA is formed, which requires that more than one plaintiff register, it sues on behalf of all its members. Here, no distinction is made between the case where the representative plaintiff who has initiated the CA litigates for all members, or the case where the active role is played by the CA's attorney. We assume that the delegation of the collective negotiation power to one of the members or to a third party leads to no agency problem and does not require an incentive scheme to monitor the efforts of the CA representative agent, who is supposed always to act in the best interest of all its members.

In stage 3, pretrial negotiations may also take place, leading to an amicable settlement of claims rather than their litigation at trial. That is, after a suit (individual or collective) is brought against the defendant, this one has the opportunity to make a take-it-or-leave-it offer to the other party (individual plaintiff or CA). Thus, either the defendant's offer is accepted (by a plaintiff or the CA), and thus the claim is settled, or it is rejected. In this event, we consider that either the claim goes to trial, or the plaintiff gives up.

As for the court's behaviour, it is assumed that the judge awards a compensatory damage equal to the claim of the defendant in the case of an individual suit, while he sets the damage obtained by each member of a CA equal to an index of the aggregate merit of the class, which is defined as $\Theta = \alpha\theta_i + (1 - \alpha)\,\theta_j$, with $\alpha \in]0,1[$ being either the proportion of plaintiffs i in the population of filers, or a parameter of the discretion power of judges. The role of this rule of damage averaging is part of the present chapter, and the distinction between those possible explanations will be discussed in the last part of the chapter.

The individual outcomes depend on the various litigation expenditures incurred by the plaintiff, since filing a suit is a costly activity. When filing an individual suit both plaintiffs bear the same litigation costs, which are of two kinds. The first one corresponds to the administrative registration of the claim, $C > 0$, which is supposed to be a sunk cost: whatever his decision, either he maintains his action until it is settled through a negotiation with the defendant or at trial, or he gives up after registration, the plaintiff never recovers this expenditure. The second one, $C_p > 0$, corresponds to litigation costs per se such as attorney fees, auditing or expertise costs and so on, that are borne only when the plaintiff files, to produce evidences in order to strengthen the court's beliefs that the defendant is liable. In contrast, joining a CA allows plaintiffs to litigate for smaller individual costs, $K_p > 0$. Moreover, members of the CA incur an additional sunk cost $K > 0$ (corresponding to registration costs and various administrative costs). We assume that:

$$\text{Assumption 1: } \theta_j > \theta_i > C_p \tag{10.1}$$

$$\text{Assumption 2: } 0 < K_p < C_p \text{ and } 0 < K < K_p \tag{10.2}$$

which means that if a plaintiff were aware of the defendant's liability, he would be prone to sue individually. Notice that the conditions in (10.2) put on the various transaction costs simply ensures that a CA entails scale economies on the various litigation costs: $C + C_p > K + K_p$. Scale economies achieved through the pooling of attorney's services and the decrease in the number of plaintiff's individual appearances in front of the court, are a classical motive that explains the great appeal of class actions.

The definition of the nature of both kinds of costs are introduced for ease of exposition. The clue of the story comes from the distinction between an entry cost which is paid in order that the plaintiff has an access to the litigation process, on the one hand, and a cost paid only when the plaintiff continues his suit until the end at trial, on the other hand. Notice that a more sensible interpretation would consider that C as K correspond both to administrative costs per se coming from the registration of the claim with the court plus the various sunk costs associated with the use of attorney's counsels (fixed costs such as filing costs, including expertise expenditures) during the pretrial period, whereas C_p as K_p would include more strictly only the expenditures incurred by the plaintiff when his case goes to trial, for instance those corresponding to the lawyer fees.

2.3 The Discovery Process and Individual Information

In our set up, as the plaintiffs enter sequentially in the litigation process, the timing of information arrival is stylized as follows:

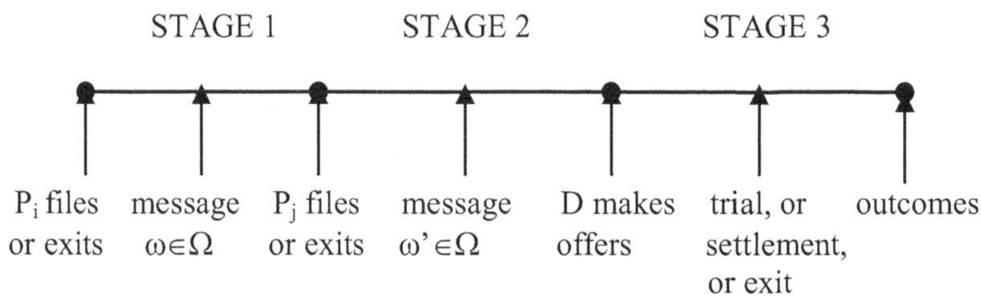

Figure 10.1 Stages in the litigation process

We consider circumstances where all the information which may be obtained (the set of all possible messages) by P_j is the same as what is available for the former P_i. Thus, everything goes as if the messages successively obtained by the litigants were initially drowned in the same set of messages.[1] But, basically, although both plaintiffs have access to the same technology of information, they do not have the ability to update their initial beliefs using the same information: plaintiff P_i enters first and only observes his own message, while plaintiff P_j observe a combination of two messages, consisting of his own message and plaintiff P_i's personal message.

Formally, let us denote Ω as the set of all available messages providing some piece of evidence with respect to the liability or guiltiness of the defendant. When P_i (respectively P_j) pays the litigation costs, he receives a message ω (respectively ω′) randomly picked in Ω, which will be used to improve his assessment of the likelihood that the defendant will be found liable/not liable at trial.

Since we consider the case of an aggregate technology of information, let us take as a primitive the joint probability distribution[2] $P : S \times \Omega \times \Omega \to [0,1]$, where $S = \{L, NL\}$ is the set of relevant states of the nature regarding the status of the defendant (Liable, Non liable) such that $p(L, \omega, \omega') \geq 0$ is the likelihood that the defendant is liable and the messages obtained respectively by plaintiffs i and j are (ω, ω'), while $p(NL, \omega, \omega') \geq 0$ is the likelihood that the defendant is non liable and the messages obtained respectively by P_i and P_j are (ω, ω').

2.4 Beliefs Updating Rules

We have to consider the various probabilities which are relevant in order to describe the informational status of plaintiffs, at each stage of the litigation process. Specifically, our general assumption implies that individuals have common priors, but that updating beliefs allow them to have different posteriors.

First, the primitives are connected to the plaintiffs' common priors on the defendant's liability in a simple way:

---

1 Thus, under some circumstances, plaintiff j may receive exactly the same message as plaintiff i: the weight of evidence or the significance of the message is increased in such a case.

2 See Hirschleifer and Riley (1997), Laffont (1988) for the basic case of an unidimensional technology of information. The specification in terms of joint probabilities is not the more natural or intuitive way to modelize the technology of information, but it is the more general! Anyway, any messages service reveals the existence of such a joint probability distribution. Here, we are more interested with the benefits associated with the process of beliefs updating allowed by this technology, than on the distortions coming from difference between pure individual subjective priors.

$$p_L = \sum_{(\omega, \omega') \in \Omega^2} p(L, \omega, \omega') \tag{10.3}$$

$$p_{NL} = \sum_{(\omega, \omega') \in \Omega^2} p(NL, \omega, \omega') \tag{10.4}$$

Using the available technology of information, the plaintiffs are also allowed to assess their chances of obtaining additional information. For example:

$$p^i(\omega) = \sum_{\omega' \in \Omega} p(L, \omega, \omega') + \sum_{\omega' \in \Omega} p(NL, \omega, \omega') \tag{10.5}$$

represents P_i's individual priors to obtain an individual message, when the message obtained by the other plaintiff is not observable. In our set up, where P_j files after P_i, we are interested in the case where P_j has the opportunity to observe also the message previously obtained by i; hence, the probability of such an event according to the technology of information at hand is:

$$p^j(\omega, \omega') = p(L, \omega, \omega') + p_{NL}(\omega, \omega') \tag{10.6}$$

As a consequence, P_j will update his beliefs according to the rule:

$$(R1): p^j(L|\omega,\omega') = \left[\frac{p(L,\omega,\omega')}{p(L,\omega,\omega') + p(NL,\omega,\omega')}\right] \tag{10.7}$$

when he observes both his own message and the message of the other plaintiff, but P_i can only condition his revision of beliefs as a unique message according to the rule:

$$(R2): p^i(L|\omega) = \left[\frac{£_{\omega' \in \Omega} p(L,\omega,\omega')}{£_{\omega' \in \Omega} p(L,\omega,\omega') + £_{\omega' \in \Omega} p(NL,\omega,\omega')}\right] \tag{10.8}$$

with:

$$p(L,\omega) = \sum_{\omega' \in \Omega} p(L,\omega,\omega') \tag{10.9}$$

In this context, the possible evidences that may be gathered during the discovery process does not change after that P_i eventually files and before P_j decides to enter. Nevertheless, P_j may benefit of the message obtained by P_i

(he benefits of the efforts undertaken by the former in the discovery process). Thus, he may update his likelihood of success according to both messages.[3]

3. EQUILIBRIUM ANALYSIS

We first introduce as a benchmark model the case of a system allowing only individual suits: thus two repeated trials occur. Then, we introduce the possibility of a class action, the plaintiff having the opportunity either to sue individually or to register a class action.

3.1 Precedents, Repeated Trials and Pure Individual Suits

When repeated trials occur (P_i's case is first settled), the last filer may benefit from the existence of jurisprudence or precedents as a result of a pure informational effect. We investigate how this involuntary sharing of information between plaintiffs affects the individual incentives to file.

Hence, assume that the CA is not allowed as a litigation option: the plaintiffs can file only an individual suit. Players' moves in stage 3 are the following: for the defendant, make an individual offer to each plaintiff; and each individual plaintiff may choose between: go to trial T; exit E; settle S. Let us denote $s(\theta_i,\omega)$ and $s(\theta_j, \omega, \omega')$ the settlement offer made by the defendant respectively to P_i and P_j, since it depends on the case and the information obtained.

When a case is litigated, any information which is revealed is always shared between the plaintiff and the defendant. In the present set up, the defendant always exercises his rights to the discovery process, since it allows him either to settle for an offer that is less than when the plaintiff is silent, and/or to litigate while saving the trial costs. The following lemma first solves the efficient decision of the defender and the response of the plaintiffs when the last stage of the game is seen as a 'one-shot' bargaining process, shown in Figure 10.2:

---

[3] In some circumstances, however, P_j may gather additional information, which is whether the evidence that should have been by the previous plaintiff (even when he only obtained partial information) is or is not always available or true. In other words, some events previously unbelievable are now available as pieces of evidence, and more specifically are seen as acceptable by the courts (unforeseen contingencies).

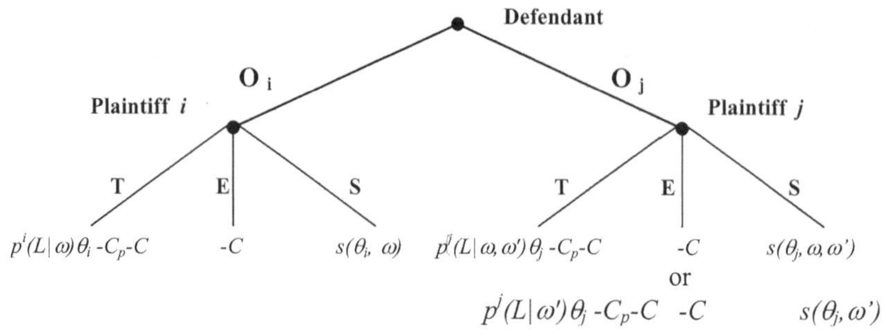

Figure 10.2 A 'one-shot' bargaining process

Lemma 1

Consider plaintiffs and the defendant's moves in stage 3:

i. For any message $\omega \in \Omega$, corresponding to the information obtained by P_i, the best 'one shot' individual offer made by the defendant to plaintiff P_i is: $s(\theta_i, \omega) = \max(0, p^i(L|\omega)\theta_i - C_p)$ P_i accepts this offer.[4]
ii. For any combination of messages $(\omega, \omega') \in \Omega \times \Omega$, corresponding to the information obtained by P_j, the best 'one shot' individual offer made by the defendant to the plaintiff P_j is $s(\theta_j, \omega, \omega') = \max(0, p^j(L|\omega, \omega')\theta_j - C_p)$. P_j accepts this offer.

The proof and those of all lemmas and propositions of the chapter are given in the Appendix.

Coming back to stage 2, P_j evaluates his own opportunity to file or not without the knowledge of the relevant message that will be available in the future, but only knowing the set of possible messages afforded by the available technology of information. Let us denote his expected utility level given the various possible messages that he may receive as follows:

$$Eu_j(\theta_j, p^j(L|.,.)) = \sum_{(\omega,\omega')\in\Omega^2} p^j(\omega,\omega')\max(0, p^j(L|\omega,\omega')\theta_j - C_p) - C \quad (10.10)$$

and given the priors, let us denote his expected utility level as:

[4] As far as Subgame Perfection is concerned, we should also consider the case where the plaintiff goes to trial, thus allowing for multiplicity of equilibria; however for concreteness, we adopt in the rest of the chapter the convention that the indifference between trial and settlement amounts to a strict preference for the settlement. See the discussion in Rasmusen (2001), Shavell (1989).

$$Eu_j(\theta_j, p_L) = p_L\theta_j C_p - C \tag{10.11}$$

The following lemma analyses when plaintiff P_j sues or gives up.

Lemma 2

i) Assume that only 'good news' is expected to arrive; then, information is not worth for P_j i.e.:

$$\text{if } \min\{p^j(L|\omega,\omega') \in \Omega\times\Omega \geq \frac{C_p}{\theta_j}, \text{then}:$$
$$Eu_j(\theta_j, p^j(L|.,.)) = p_L\theta_j - C_p - C \tag{10.12}$$

ii) Assume that there exists a unique combination of messages $(\hat{\omega}, \hat{\omega}') \in \Omega \times \Omega$ such that $p(L, \hat{\omega}, \hat{\omega}') \geq \frac{C_p}{\theta_j}$; then, information is worth for P_j, i.e.: $Eu_j(\theta_j, p^j(L|.,.)) - Eu_j(\theta_j, p_L) \geq 0$.

iii) Assume that there exists at least one combination of messages $(\hat{\omega}, \hat{\omega}')$ $\in \Omega \times \Omega$ such that $p(\mathrm{L}, \hat{\omega}, \hat{\omega}') \geq \frac{C_p + C}{\theta_j}$; then P_j always files individually, i.e. $Eu_j(\theta_j, p^j(L|.,.)) \geq 0$.

Part i) implies that if priors are 'optimistic' for P_j, then P_j always files, i.e. $p_L \geq \frac{C_p + C}{\theta_j} \Rightarrow Eu_j(\theta_j, p^j(L|.,.)) \geq 0$, but if $p_L < \frac{C_p + C}{\theta_j}$ then the plaintiff gives up $(Eu_j(\theta_j, p^j(L|.,.)) < 0)$.

Part ii) means that if priors are 'pessimistic' for P_j, then P_j may nevertheless file, i.e. we may have $Eu_j(\theta_j, p^j(L|.,.)) \geq 0$ although $p_L \leq \frac{C_p + C}{\theta_j}$.

Part iii) means that once very good news exists, the plaintiff always prefers to file an individual suit.

The same qualitative results also apply to P_i: in stage 1, he evaluates the opportunity to file or not without the knowledge of the relevant message that will be available in the future, but only knowing the set of possible messages afforded by the available technology of information. Let us define by:

$$Eu_i(\theta_i, p^i(L|.)) = \sum_{\omega\in\Omega} p^i(\omega) \max(0, p^i(L|\omega)\,\theta_I - C_p) - C \tag{10.13}$$

his expected utility level associated to the technology of information, and:

$$Eu_i(\theta_i, p_L) = p_L\theta_i - C_p - C \tag{10.14}$$

his satisfaction level associated to his priors, which are the same as the other plaintiff. Thus, we have:

Lemma 3

i) Assume that only 'good news' is expected to arrive; then, information is not worth for P_i, i.e.:

$$if\ min\{p^i(L|\omega), for\ all\ \omega \in \Omega\} \geq \frac{C_p}{\theta_i},\ then:$$
$$Eu_i(\theta_i, p^i(L|.)) = p_L\theta_i - C_p - C \qquad (10.15)$$

ii) Assume that there exists a unique message $\hat{\omega} \in \Omega$ such that $p(L, \hat{\omega}) \geq \frac{C_P}{\theta_i}$; then, information is worth for P_i, i.e.: $Eu_i(\theta_i, p^i(L|.)) - Eu_i(\theta_i, p_L) \geq 0$.

iii) Assume that there exists at least one message $\hat{\omega} \in \Omega$ such that $p(L, \hat{\omega}) \geq \frac{C_P + C}{\theta_i}$; then P_i always files individually, i.e. $Eu_i(\theta_i, p^i(L|.)) \geq 0$.

Said differently, lemma 2 and 3 display the conditions under which a plaintiff obtains an informational rent as a result of the discovery process. Information has a positive value in the present context only when the litigants know that bad news sometimes may be obtained. With additional information, a plaintiff updates his priors, and he is allowed to make the best possible decision in every circumstance, given that he can exercise an exit option if the information learned appears to be unfavourable for his case.

In this sense, the updating of beliefs may explain that holders of nuisance suits or pessimistic victims (conditionally on their priors: *i.e.* $p_L\theta - C_p - C < 0$) have an incentive to file, in the hope of learning good news in the future and pursue their action until trial. In this last case, it depends on stronger conditions on the technology of information.

This is highlighted in parts iii) of the lemmas. Each of parts iii gives a simple sufficient condition required whatever the priors (optimistic or pessimistic) in order to induce a plaintiff to file an individual lawsuit, saying that the plaintiff knows that there exists at least a very favourable message entailing a large probability that the defendant will be seen liable by the court. This last result may be understood as saying that it is of no use that a plaintiff expects to always receive a favorable message in the future, to induce him to file a suit: it is sufficient that there exists a single favourable message, given that in other circumstances, he will be induced to give up having only paid the administrative sunk costs.

In contrast, part i of both lemmas shows interestingly enough that when the available (technology of) information does not allow the possibility of bad events or news, such that the plaintiffs expect to obtain a positive payment from the defendant in any future event, then the discovery process provides no additional value in the sense that whether plaintiffs update their priors depending on the new message collected or use their priors, in both cases they undertake the same efficient decision.

Lemmas 1 to 3 lead to the following proposition.

Proposition 4

Assume that there exists at least one combination of messages $(\hat{\omega}, \hat{\omega}') \in \Omega \times \Omega$ such that $p(L, \hat{\omega}, \hat{\omega}') \geq \frac{C_p + C}{\theta_i}$; then there exists a Subgame Perfect Equilibrium where i) each plaintiff file individually, and ii) both cases are settled.

Remark that the requirement that there exists a $p(L, \hat{\omega}, \hat{\omega}') \geq \frac{C_p + C}{\theta_i}$ also implies that $p(L, \hat{\omega}, \hat{\omega}') \geq \frac{C_p + C}{\theta_i}$ meaning that any information delivered by the technology which appears as favourable for P_i is also good for P_j. As it is easily seen, this is a weak requirement in the sense that it is sufficient that plaintiffs are aware of the fact that there is one chance to obtain at least a good information, to induce them to file a suit. There is no need to be sure that good news always arrive in the future.

The next corollary is a straightforward consequence of the previous lemmas.

Corollary 5

If information has a positive value:

i. Any information favourable to the defendant (respectively, to the plaintiffs) reduces (increases) the settlement offer, as compared to the case where no additional information arrives.
ii. The probability of settlement is smaller than one.

Consider the case of the first plaintiff – the argument is the same in the other case. A favourable information for the defendant corresponds to a message such that $p_L > p^i(L|\omega)$ which implies $p_L\theta_i - C_p > p^i(L|\omega)\theta_i - C_p$. Now, in the case where information is worth, there is only a subset $\wedge_i \subset \Omega$ of possible messages for the first plaintiff such that $p^i(L|\omega)\theta_i - C_p > 0, \forall \omega \in \wedge_i$: then, the probability of settlement corresponds to the cumulative probability that the plaintiff obtains these favourable messages $\Sigma_{\omega \in \wedge i}\, p(\omega) < 1$.

3.2 Information Sharing and the Large CA

Consider now that class actions are available. Let us focus more specifically on the proper subgame beginning after P_j decides to adhere to the class actions. In stage 3, the defender makes an offer to the CA members, such that when the information pooled by the members of the class actions corresponds to the messages (ω, ω'), the settlement benefit of each member of the class actions is $s(\Theta, \omega, \omega')$.

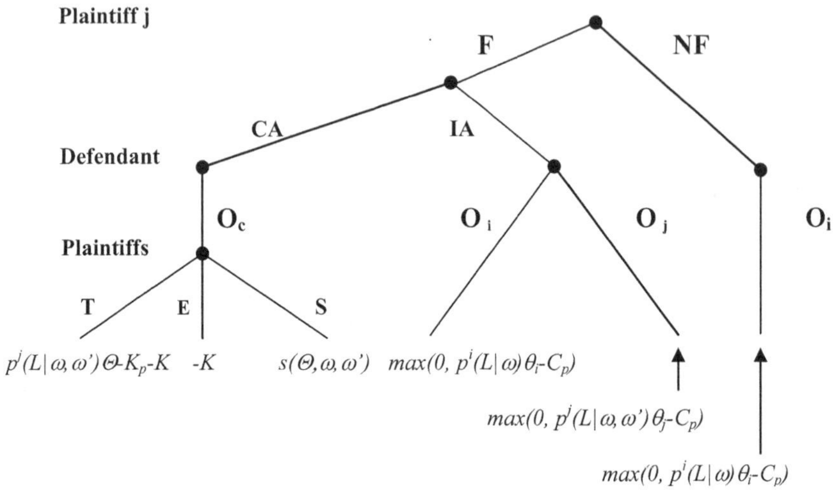

Figure 10.3 Subgames replaced by the defendant's best offer

Lemma 6

Consider the decision node in stage 3 where the defendant is facing a class action. For any combination of messages $(\omega, \omega') \in \Omega \times \Omega$, the best 'one shot' individual offer made by the defendant to the class action is: $s(\Theta, \omega, \omega') = \max(0, p^i(L|\omega, \omega')\Theta - K_p)$. The CA members accept this offer.

This implies that the defendant makes a positive offer to the class action soon as $p^j(L|\omega, \omega') > \frac{K_p}{\Theta}$. On the other hand, in any proper subgame in stage 3 beginning after that P_i gives up to initiate a class action, or after that P_i gives up to join it, the best individual offers of the defendant are those of lemma 1 (see also Figure 10.3 where these subgames have been replaced by the defendant's best offer).

We can now analyze the efficient decisions of P_j, considering separately the decision to join the class action or not (decision node following the entry of P_j), and finally the decision to file or not (decision node initiating the subgame of Figure 10.3). P_j's efficient decisions in stage 2 may be as follows.

Lemma 7

Assume that there exists a subset[5] of combinations of messages $\wedge_j \subset \Omega^2$ such that for any $(\omega, \omega') \in \wedge_j : p(L, \omega, \omega') \geq \frac{C_p + C}{\theta_j}$, and assume that $\alpha \leq \alpha^* \equiv \frac{C_p - K_p}{\pi^*(\theta_j - \theta_i)}$ where $\pi^* = \max \{p^j(L|\omega, \omega'), \text{ for all } (\omega, \omega') \in \wedge_j\}$. Then, i) P_j always files in the second stage, and ii) he prefers to join the class action when it has been initiated by P_i rather than to sue individually.

The following lemma focuses on the decision of the first plaintiff.

Lemma 8

Assume that there exists a subset of messages $\wedge_i \subset \Omega$, such that for any $\omega \in \wedge_i : p^i(L, \omega) \geq \frac{C_p + C}{\theta_i}$. Thus, P_i always files in the first stage, and he prefers to initiate the class action rather than to sue individually.

Using the material of lemmas 6 to 8, we have the following.

Proposition 9

Assume that: (C1) there exists a unique combination of messages (ω, ω') $\in \Omega^2$ such that $p(L, \hat{\omega}, \hat{\omega}') \geq \frac{C_p + C}{\theta_i}$, and (C2): $\alpha \leq \hat{\alpha} \equiv \frac{C_p - K_p}{p^j(L|\hat{\omega}, \hat{\omega}')(\theta_j - \theta_i)}$. Then, there exists a SPE where i) the class action is formed, and ii) the aggregate case is settled.

Proposition 9 displays a set of sufficient conditions in order that the large class action (encompassing both types of individuals) exists in equilibrium.

The result of proposition 9 is a direct consequence both of our specification of the technology of information, and of the assumption that the discovery process is perfect in the sense that there is a perfect mutualization of the information between plaintiffs and the defendant. In such a case, the two important issues are: 1) whether the first plaintiff prefers the structure of information defined by the set of his own personal messages, or the structure associated with the combination of two messages, his personal one and the information of the other plaintiff; 2) whether the second one obtains a higher payment when he becomes a member of the class action or not.

In our set up, P_j observes his own message and the first plaintiff's one whether or not he joins the class action; thus, he prefers to join the class action as long as the decrease in the litigation costs associated with the collective action ($K_p < C_p$) is not fully compensated by the decrease in the

---

[5] It is easy to see that this subset would be a singleton, *i.e.* the weakest sufficient condition required to have the same result as the lemma may be stated as follows: Assume that there exists at least one combination of messages $(\hat{\omega}, \hat{\omega}') \in \wedge_j : p(L, \hat{\omega}, \hat{\omega}') \geq \frac{C_p + C}{\theta_j}$, and assume that $\alpha \leq \frac{C_p - K_p}{p^j(L|\hat{\omega}, \hat{\omega}')(\theta_j - \theta_i)}$

expected payment awarded at trial given that the court uses an index of the aggregate claim in case of a class action ($\Theta < \theta_j$): (C2) corresponds to the requirement needed to insure the participation of P_j: it must be that the proportion of large stakes in population of plaintiff is high enough.

The result may be easily generalized, as in lemma 6, to introduce several messages being good news for plaintiffs in the sense of (C1). Nevertheless, consider the case where there is only a single combination ($\hat{\omega}$, $\hat{\omega}'$) satisfying (C1); then, the threshold $\hat{\alpha}$ may work as follows:

$$\text{Case 1: } p^j(L|\hat{\omega}, \hat{\omega}')\theta_i - \mathrm{K}_p > p^j(L|\hat{\omega}, \hat{\omega}')\theta_j - C_p \Rightarrow \hat{\alpha} > 1 \quad (10.16)$$

The inequality means that up to sunk costs, the expected outcome at trial of P_i when the class action is formed is larger than the expected outcome of P_j for an individual suit, given the nature of the information obtained by plaintiff (given $p^j(L|\hat{\omega}, \hat{\omega}')$). Then, any value of $\alpha > 0$ satisfies condition (C2), which is thus irrelevant in proposition 9. This is because in such a case, we also have:

$$p^j(L|\hat{\omega}, \hat{\omega}')\,\Theta - K_p > p^j(L|\hat{\omega}, \hat{\omega}')\theta_I - K_p > p^j(L|\hat{\omega}, \hat{\omega}')\theta_j - C_p \quad (10.17)$$

which insures that P_j always prefers to register the CA.

$$\text{Case 2: } p^j(L|\hat{\omega}, \hat{\omega}')\theta_i - K_p < p^j(L|\hat{\omega}, \hat{\omega}')\theta_j - C_p \Rightarrow \hat{\alpha} < 1 \quad (10.18)$$

As a result, the constraint on the proportion of small losses applies, with the threshold depending as follows on the parameters of the economy:

	$C_p - K_p$	$\theta_j - \theta_i$	$p^j(L\|\hat{\omega}, \hat{\omega}')$
$\hat{\alpha}$	+	–	–

On the other hand, the basic reason explaining why the first plaintiff initiates the class action, is that when the discovery process is perfect, the posteriors distribution $p^j(L|., .)$ is *more informative* in the sense of Blackwell (1953) than the posteriors distribution $p^j(L|.)$: for any message $\omega \in \Omega$, there always exists at least one message $\omega' \in \Omega$ such that: $p^j(L|\omega, \omega') > p^i(L|\omega)$ and one message $\omega' \in \Omega$ such that: $p^j(L|\omega, \omega') < p^i(L|\omega)$. Thus, the posterior beliefs $p^i(L|.)$ provides the plaintiff with some information which has been 'garbled' in the transmission as compared to the priors $p^j(L|., .)$. Anything goes as if the information associated to $p^j(L|., .)$ were sent, but it has been received by P_i with some additional noise, such that finally P_i recognized only the information attached to $p^i(L|.)$.

4. EXTENSIONS: DAMAGE AVERAGING, CONDITIONAL AND CONTINGENT FEES

It is straightforward to verify that when plaintiffs that have a large stake become the first filers, nothing more is added to the results, since the class action is formed under the same conditions as those in proposition 9. Thus, as far as the discovery process is perfect, the choice of the order of plaintiffs' entry introduce no strategic aspect. In contrast, alternative specifications of costs or compensation rules applied by the court may have more serious consequences.

In this section, we first consider the impact of alternative rules of damage awarded by courts, and specifically, the role of 'damage averaging'. Finally, we introduce alternative schemes for attorneys' fees and investigate their influence on the formation of a class action in the present set up.

4.1 Courts' Behaviour and the Damage Averaging Rule

The rule of damage award set by courts is of major importance if the entry of different plaintiffs entails a strategic aspect as is the case enhanced by Marceau and Mongrain (2003). It induces both the composition of the CA and the identity of the plaintiff who initiates the class action. Interestingly, this also occurs in our set up: we may suggest another interpretation of condition (C2) in proposition 8, which is a central condition for the occurrence of the CA to the extent that it monitors the behaviour of large stakes holders.

Assume that courts award a compensation to each member of a class action which is defined as the weighted sum of his personal claim and the aggregate value of the class action; formally: $d_s = \gamma\Theta + (1 - \gamma)\theta_s$, with $\gamma \in [0,1]$, for any P_s ($s = i, j$). In the following, γ will be termed the *degree of damage averaging*. When $\gamma = 1$, courts award the aggregate merits of the class action to each member, while when $\gamma = 0$, the courts award only individual damages. Straightforward manipulations show that:

$$d_i = (1 - \gamma(1 - \alpha))\theta_i + \gamma(1 - \alpha)\theta_j \tag{10.19}$$

$$d_j = \alpha\gamma\,\theta_i + (1 - \alpha\gamma)\theta_j \tag{10.20}$$

As a result, the following result applies.

Proposition 10
Assume (C1); then, there always exists a degree of damage averaging such that the large class action occurs in equilibrium, i.e. there exists a threshold

degree of damage averaging namely: $\gamma^* \equiv \frac{C_p - K_p}{p^j(L|\hat{\omega}, \hat{\omega}')(\theta_j - \theta_i)}$, such that for any $\gamma \leq \gamma^*$ the large CA is formed at equilibrium.

Once more, it is easy to see that if[6] $p^j(L|\hat{\omega}, \hat{\omega}')\theta_i - K_p > p^j(L|\hat{\omega}, \hat{\omega}')\theta_j - C_p$ holds, implying that $\frac{C_p - K_p}{p^j(L|\hat{\omega}, \hat{\omega}')(\theta_j - \theta_i)} > 1$, then all else equal the existence of a CA is compatible with any (positive) value of the level of damage averaging – or equivalently, the rule set by the court is of no matter. In the opposite case, however, the court has the opportunity to favour (or not) the formation of the CA, whatever the structure of the population of plaintiffs. Allowing a large degree of damage averaging, and plaintiffs having a large stake are deterred from participating in the CA when it has been initiated, since the decrease in litigation costs does not compensate the loss in terms of compensatory damage. Thus, it is a matter of precaution when courts set compensatory damages to members of a CA as close as possible to their individual claims.

4.2 Conditional and Contingent Fees

One way to understand the results of the previous section is the following: for plaintiffs, the opportunity to obtain additional information may work as a credible threat in order to obtain recovery from the defendant, although they may have pessimistic beliefs before trial. It is more usual in the literature to consider that litigation costs, specifically attorneys' fees, may be used strategically, playing the role of a device which commits plaintiffs who have pessimistic priors (holding nuisance suits) to file and sue until trial.[7]

In the case of CAs, specific attention has been paid to contingent fees (Klement and Neeman (2004), Lynk (1990, 1994), Miceli and Segerson (1991)) or to conditional fees (Emons (2004a,b), Emons and Garoupa (2004)). The rationale for the use of contingent or conditional fees to pay for attorney's services is twofold. The first advantage of contingent fees is that they induce the absence of risk in filing a lawsuit for the plaintiffs, since the risk is borne by the attorney: plaintiffs owe their attorney a fee only when there is recovery, *i.e.* when they win at trial. The other advantage is

---

6 This condition has a nice interpretation, saying that the expected payment obtained by a small loss holder when the court applies full individual damages to any member of a class action, is higher than the expected payment to a large stake holder suing individually.

7 See Rasmusen (2001) for an example; once a plaintiff sinks his litigation costs, he is commited to sue as far as he has any chance of success at all – in contrast, he gives up as soon as he is handled with a totally meritless suit.

that they enable plaintiffs to monitor the effort undertaken by the attorney in the time they spend on their clients' case, and gives them efficient incentives to maximize their client's recovery.

When *conditional fees* are introduced, a plaintiff pays the amount corresponding to his attorney's services only in the case where he wins at trial. Hence, the expected payment at trial is equal to the probability of winning (given the relevant information) times his damage award minus attorney's fees:

$$p^i\,(L|\omega)(\theta_i - C_p) : \textit{for } P_i \tag{10.21}$$

$$p^j\,(L|\omega,\,\omega')(\theta_j - C_p) : \textit{for } P_j \tag{10.22}$$

$$p^j\,(\mathrm{L}|\omega,\,\omega')(\Theta - K_p) : \textit{for a CA} \tag{10.23}$$

The following proposition[8] shows that in such a case, information has no role to play here, in the sense that the arrival of new information during the litigation process does not change the plaintiff's decision as compared to the decisions which would be made with no additional information over the information conveyed by the priors.

Proposition 11

Under both contingent and conditional fees:

i. Parties always settle.
ii. The value of information is null for both plaintiffs.
iii. The settlement offers are larger than under the fixed costs rule.

Proposition 11 shows that plaintiffs become neutral to the arrival of news when contingent fees are used, such that the decision to file depends only on their initial belief of the outcome at trial. This suggests that if contingent fees may solve agency problems between plaintiffs and their counsel, on the

---

[8] When *contingent fees* are used, a plaintiff pays an amount corresponding to a fixed percentage of the value of the claim only in a case of recovery, *i.e.* the costs corresponding to the payment of attorneys' services is proportional to the expected value of the claim; in such a case, the value of the expected outcome at trial is a given percentage of the claim:

$p^i\,(L|\omega)(1 - t)\theta_i : \textit{for } P_i$

$p^j\,(L|\omega,\,\omega')(1 - t)\theta_j : \textit{for } P_j$

$p^j\,(L|\omega,\,\omega')(1 - \tau)\Theta : \textit{for a CA}$

with t (respectively τ) $\in\,]0,1[$ being the percentage of the value of the claim in case of an individual action (collective action) charged by the attorney, and $t > \tau$.

other hand they may entail pervasive effects such as making victims not careful enough with the new information when it arrives.

The intuition is the following. Consider a plaintiff with an initial belief in his case, who wants to verify the quality of his claim at trial: he may use a simple 'test' corresponding to buying the services of a lawyer; this last one will inform the plaintiff whether he has a high probability to win at trial or a low one, and when alternative litigation strategies may be used at trial, contingent fees monitors attorney's efforts to choose the strategy leading to maximal recovery for the plaintiff. Proposition 11 tells us that this test is of no value for the plaintiff: his initial decision to enter or not depends only on his prior beliefs on his case, when contingent fees are used, since in case of an individual suit for example we have: $Eu_i(\theta_i, p^i(L|.)) = Eu_i(\theta_i, p_L)$ and $Eu_j(\theta_j, p^j(\mathrm{L}|., .)) = Eu_j(\theta_j, \mathrm{p}_L)$.

5. CONCLUSION

There is now an emerging literature on the economics of class actions and the incentives they generate for plaintiffs and defendants (e.g., Daughety and Reinganum,[9] 2009; Marceau and Mongrain, 2003; Klement and Neeman, 2004; Margherita and Saraceno, 2009; Sacconi, 2011; Teitelbaum, 2010). Most of these studies focus on negative externalities and the strategic use of class actions. The thrust of our chapter was to analyze how class actions can be considered as a discovery process enabling litigants to benefit from positive externalities of information. We showed in contrast that informational asymmetries between the parties and the judge play an important role in the organisation of class actions, and particularly explain the characteristics of the equilibrium concerning the plaintiffs' strategies.

REFERENCES

Blackwell, D. (1953), 'Equivalent Comparison of Experiments', *Annals of Mathematics and Statistics*, **24**, 265–272.

Che, Y-K (1996), 'Equilibrium Formation of Class Action Suits', *Journal of Public Economics*, **62**, 339–361.

[9] Related to our work, Daughety and Reinganum (2009) also use a dynamic model of the process by which multiple related lawsuits may be filed and combined. However, they do not pre-specify the order of moves (nor is any plaintiff's ability to file contingent on another filing); either plaintiff can file at any time. They examine several issues, including the actions a defendant may employ that may disrupt the formation of a joint suit.

Che Y-K and Yi J. (1993), 'The Role of Precedents in Repeated Litigation', *Journal of Law, Economics and Organization*, **9**, 399–424.
Daughety A. and Reinganum J. (2009), 'A Dynamic Model of Lawsuit Joinder and Settlement', *Working Paper*, Vanderbilt University.
Emons W. (2004a), 'Conditional Versus Contingent Fees', *mimeo*, University of Bern and CEPR.
Emons W. (2004b), 'Playing it Safe with Low Conditional Fees Versus Being Insured by High Contingent Fees', *mimeo*, University of Bern and CEPR.
Emons W. and Garoupa N. (2004), 'The Economics of US-style Contingent Fees and UK-style Conditional Fees', *mimeo*, CEPR.
Hirschleifer J. and Riley J. (1997), *The Analytics of Uncertainty and Information*, Cambridge University Press.
Klement A. and Neeman Z. (2004), 'Incentive Structures for Class Action Lawyers', *The Journal of Law, Economics & Organization*, **20**, 102–124.
Laffont J-J (1988), *The economics of uncertainty and information*, MIT Press.
Lynk W. (1990), 'The Courts and the Market: an Economic Analysis of Contingent Fees in Class-action Litigation', *The Journal of Legal Studies*, **19**, 247–60.
Lynk W. (1994), 'The Courts and the Plaintiffs' Bar: Awarding the Attorney's Fees in Class-action Litigation', *The Journal of Legal Studies*, **23**, 185–209.
Marceau N. and Mongrain S. (2003), 'Damage Averaging and the Formation of Class Action Suits', *International Review of Law and Economics*, **23**, 63–74.
Rasmusen E. (2001), *Games and information*, Blackwell Publishing.
Sacconi L. (2011), 'The Case Against Lawyer's Contingent Fees and the Misapplication of the Principal-agent Models, *European Journal of Law and Economics, forthcoming.*
Saraceno. M. (2008), 'Group Litigation, Access to Justice and Deterrence', *Working Paper No 2009*-04, Amsterdam Center for Law & Economics.
Shavell S. (1989), 'Sharing Information Prior to Settlement or Litigation', *RAND Journal of Economics*, **20**, 183–95.
Teitelbaum J. (2010), 'Allocation Rules and the Stability of Mass Tort Class Actions', *Working* Paper, Georgetown University Law Center.

APPENDIX

Proof of Lemma 1

Given that the administrative cost C is sunk, it is easy to see that when P_j obtains the message ω' after that P_i has received message ω, the defendant chooses a 'take-it-or-leave-it' offer in order to render the plaintiff indifferent between going to trial (suing) or accepting the offer: $s(\theta_j, \omega, \omega') = \max(0, p^j(L|\omega, \omega')\theta_j - C_p)$, where $p^j(L|\omega, \omega')$ follows R1. Symmetrically, when he faces the message ω with P_i, the defendant makes a 'take-it-or-leave-it' offer in order to render the plaintiff indifferent between going to trial (suing) or accepting the offer: hence $s(\theta_i, \omega) = \max(0, p^i(L|\omega)\theta_i - C_p)$, where $p^i(L|\omega)$ follows R2. Hence the result.

Proof of Lemma 2

i) Consider that $\min \{p^j (L|\omega, \omega'), \forall (\omega, \omega') \in \Omega\times\Omega\} \geq \frac{C_p}{\theta_j}$; thus, $\forall(\omega, \omega') \in \Omega\times\Omega$, it comes that $\max (0, p^j (L|\omega, \omega')\theta_j - C_p) = p^j (L|\omega, \omega')\theta_j - C_p$, such that:

$$\sum_{(\omega,\omega')\in\Omega^2} p^j (\omega, \omega') \max (0, p^j (L|\omega, \omega')\theta_j - C_p) - C$$
$$= \sum_{(\omega,\omega')\in\Omega^2} p^j (\omega, \omega') (p^j (L|\omega, \omega')\theta_j - C_p) - C \tag{A.1}$$
$$= p_L\theta_j - C_p - C$$

given that, by construction of the technology of information, we have both:

$$\sum_{(\omega,\omega')\in\Omega^2} p^j (\omega, \omega') = 1, \tag{A.2}$$

$$\sum_{(\omega,\omega')\in\Omega^2} p^j (\omega, \omega')\, p^j (L|\omega, \omega') = \sum_{(\omega,\omega')\in\Omega^2} p(L, \omega, \omega') = p_L \tag{A.3}$$

Hence the result.

ii) More generally, given that $\forall(\omega, \omega') \in \Omega\times\Omega : \max (0, p^j (L|\omega, \omega')\theta_j - C_p) \geq p^j(L|\omega, \omega')\theta_j - C_p$, we have after multiplying both terms of this inequality by $p^j(\omega, \omega')$ and then summing over all the possible messages:

$$\sum_{(\omega,\omega')\in\Omega^2} p^j (\omega, \omega') \max (0, p^j (L|\omega, \omega')\theta_j - C_p) - C$$
$$\geq \sum_{(\omega,\omega')\in\Omega^2} p^j (\omega, \omega') (p^j (L|\omega, \omega')\theta_j - C_p) - C \tag{A.4}$$
$$= p_L\theta_j - C_p - C$$

Hence $Eu_j (\theta_j, p^j (L|.,.)) \geq Eu_j (\theta_j, p_L)$, which is by definition the value of the information afforded by the available technology of messages. Thus, assuming a unique combination $(\omega, \omega') \in \Omega\times\Omega$: such that $\max (0, p^j (L|\omega, \omega')\theta_j - C_p) = p^j (L|\omega, \omega')\theta_j - C_p$, the result is direct.

iii) Let us assume that there exists at least one combination of messages $(\hat{\omega}, \hat{\omega}') \in \Omega \times \Omega$ such that $p(L, \hat{\omega}, \hat{\omega}') \geq \frac{C_p + C}{\theta_i}$; remark that this implies:

$$p^j (L|\hat{\omega}, \hat{\omega}') = \frac{p(L, \hat{\omega}, \hat{\omega}')}{p^j (\hat{\omega}, \hat{\omega}')} \geq \frac{C_p}{p^j (\hat{\omega}, \hat{\omega}')\theta_j} \geq \frac{C_p}{\theta_j} \tag{A.5}$$

As a result, it comes that:

$$\begin{aligned} Eu_j(\theta_j, p^j(L|.,.)) &= p^j(\hat{\omega}, \hat{\omega}')(p^j(L|\hat{\omega}, \hat{\omega}')\theta_j - C_p) \\ &+ \sum_{(\omega,\omega')\neq(\hat{\omega},\hat{\omega}')} p^j(\omega, \omega') \max(0, p^j(L|\omega, \omega')\theta_j - C_p) - C \\ &\geq p(L, \hat{\omega}, \hat{\omega}')\theta_j - p^j(\hat{\omega}, \hat{\omega}')C_p - C \\ &\geq p(L, \hat{\omega}, \hat{\omega}')\theta_j - C_p - C \end{aligned} \tag{A.6}$$

since by construction $\sum_{(\omega,\omega')\neq(\hat{\omega},\hat{\omega}')} p^j(\omega, \omega') \max(0, p^j(L|\omega, \omega')\theta_j - C_p) \geq 0$. Now, given that $p(L, \hat{\omega}, \hat{\omega}')\theta_j - C_p - C \geq 0$ by assumption, we obtain $Eu_j(\theta_j, p^j(L|.,.)) \geq 0$. Hence the result.

Proof of Lemma 3

Omitted (qualitatively the same as in lemma 2).

Proof of Proposition 4:

More specifically, we prove the following results.

Claim 12

Assume that there exists at least one combination of messages $(\hat{\omega}, \hat{\omega}') \in \Omega \times \Omega$ such that $p(L, \hat{\omega}, \hat{\omega}') \geq \frac{C_p + C}{\theta_i}$; then there is a Subgame Perfect Equilibrium which corresponds to the following set of actions:

(i) Each plaintiff files individually.
(ii) The defendant makes two individual offers:

$$s(\theta_i,\omega) = \max(0, p^i(L|\omega)\theta_i - C_p), \forall \omega \in \Omega \textit{ for } P_i, \textit{ and} \tag{A.7}$$

$$s(\theta_j,\omega, \omega') = \max(0, p^j(L|\omega, \omega')\theta_j - C_p), \forall (\omega, \omega') \in \Omega \times \Omega \textit{ for } P^j \tag{A.8}$$

(iii) Each plaintiff accepts[10] (at each decision node where he has to play) his specific individual offer proposed by the defendant, for every possible information he may receive.

---

[10] Remember that the present model allows for multiplicity of equilibria, since plaintiffs are indifferent in stage 3 between two actions T and S; but this introduces only technical difficulties, and we ignore other SPE.

Proof of claim 13

To prove (i) it is sufficient to remark that if there exists at least one combination of messages $(\hat{\omega}, \hat{\omega}') \in \Omega \times \Omega$ such that $p(L, \hat{\omega}, \hat{\omega}') \geq \frac{C_p + C}{\theta_i}$, then we also have:

$-p(L, \hat{\omega}, \hat{\omega}') \geq \frac{C_p + C}{\theta_i}$; thus, by part v) of lemma 2, P_j always files, given that he accepts any offer $s(\theta_j, \omega, \omega') = \max(0, p^j(L|\hat{\omega}, \hat{\omega}')\theta_j - C_p)$,

$-p^i(L, \hat{\omega}) \equiv \Sigma_{\omega' \in \Omega} p(L, \hat{\omega}, \omega') > p(L, \hat{\omega}, \hat{\omega}') \geq \frac{C_p + C}{\theta_i}$; thus, by part v) of lemma 3, P_i accepts the offer $s(\theta_i, \omega) = \max(0, p^i(L|\hat{\omega})\theta_i - C_p)$, and he always files. (ii) and (iii) are direct from lemma 1.

Proof of Lemma 6

As lemma 1, it is straightforward since K is sunk.

Proof of Lemma 7

Consider the subgame where the defendant offers $s(\theta_j, \omega, \omega')$ to P_j, which is accepted. Remark first that if the subset $\Lambda_j \subset \Omega^9$ exists, for any $(\omega, \omega') \in \Lambda_j$, P_j may obtain a positive payment equal to $\max(0, p^j(L|\omega, \omega')\theta_j - C_p) = p^j(L|\omega, \omega')\theta_j - C_p \geq 0$. Thus, following the proof of part v) in lemma 2, had he decided to sue individually, P_j's expected utility level would be positive since:

$$Eu_j(\theta_j, p^j(L|.,.)) \geq \sum_{(\omega,\omega')\in\Lambda j} p(L, \omega, \omega')\theta_j - C_p - C \geq 0 \tag{A.9}$$

given that by construction for any $(\omega, \omega') \in \Lambda_j : p(L, \omega, \omega')\theta_j \geq C_p + C$. Now for any message $(\omega, \omega') \in \Omega \times \Omega$, in order that P_j be better off when he joins the CA rather than to have sued individually, it must be that:

$$p^j(L|\omega, \omega')\Theta - K_p \geq p^j(L|\omega, \omega')\theta_j - C_p \tag{A.10}$$

which is true as far as $\alpha \leq \frac{C_p - K_p}{p^j(L|\hat{\omega}, \hat{\omega}')(\theta_j - \theta_i)}$. Hence assume that $\alpha \leq \alpha^* \equiv \frac{C_p - K_p}{\pi^*(\theta_j - \theta_i)}$ where $\pi^* = \max\{p^j(L|\omega, \omega'), \textit{for all } (\omega, \omega') \in \Lambda_j\}$; then for any $(\omega, \hat{\omega}') \in \Lambda_j$:

$$p^j(L|\omega, \omega')\Theta - K_p - K \geq p^j(L|\omega, \omega')\theta_j - C_p - K \geq p^j(L|\omega, \omega')\theta_j - C_p - C \tag{A.11}$$

Finally, after multiplying both the LHS and the RHS terms of this inequality by $p^j(\omega, \omega')$ and then summing over all the possible messages, we obtain:

$$Eu_j(\Theta, p^j(L|.,.)) \geq Eu_j(\theta_j, p^j(L|.,.)) \geq 0 \tag{A.12}$$

Hence the result.

Proof of Lemma 8

The crucial issue is whether the first plaintiff prefers the structure of information defined only by the set of his own personal messages, or the structure of information associated to the set of combinations of two messages, his personal ones and the messages of the other plaintiff. We shall show that the second one is *more informative* in the sense of Blackwell (1953) than the first one; as a result, P_i obtains a higher expected utility with the second one.

To understand this, remark that by (R2) for any message $\omega \in \Omega$ we have:

$$p^i(L|\omega) = \sum_{\omega' \in \Omega} \frac{p(L,\omega,\omega')}{\Sigma_{\omega' \in \Omega} p(L,\omega,\omega') + \Sigma_{\omega' \in \Omega} p(NL,\omega,\omega')}$$
$$= \sum_{\omega' \in \Omega} \left(\frac{p(L,\omega,\omega') + p(NL,\omega,\omega')}{\Sigma_{\omega' \in \Omega} p(L,\omega,\omega') + \Sigma_{\omega' \in \Omega} p(NL,\omega,\omega')} \right) \left(\frac{p(L,\omega,\omega')}{p(L,\omega,\omega') + p(NL,\omega,\omega')} \right) \tag{A.13}$$

which means that the following relationship linking P_i's the two types of posterior beliefs $p^i(L|.)$ and $p^j(L|.,.)$ always applies:

(1) $$\forall \omega \in \Omega : p^i(L|\omega) = \sum_{\omega' \in \Omega} \beta(\omega, \omega') \, p^j(L|\omega, \omega') \tag{A14}$$

with $\beta(\omega, \omega') = \frac{p^i(\omega, \omega')}{p^i(\omega)} < 1$ and $\Sigma_{\omega' \in \Omega} \beta(\omega, \omega') = 1$, meaning that the posteriors $p^j(L|.,.)$ are more spread than the posteriors $p^j(L|.)$, *i.e.* for any message $\omega \in \Omega$, there always exists at least one message $\omega' \in \Omega$ such that: $p^j(L|\omega, \omega') > p^i(L|\omega)$, and there always exists at least one message $\omega' \in \Omega$ such that: $p^j(L|\omega, \omega') < p^i(L|\omega)$. By definition, this amounts to say that the posteriors $p^j(L|.,.)$ are more informative than the posteriors $p^j(L|.)$. This is useful in the rest of the proof.

When P_i initiates a CA, and when P_j joins it, information sharing between plaintiffs leads to an expected utility level for the former which is by definition:

$$Eu_i\,(\Theta, p^j\,(L|.,.)) = \sum_{(\omega,\omega')\in\Omega} p^i\,(\omega,\,\omega')\max\,(0, p^j\,(L|\omega,\,\omega')\Theta - K_p) - K \tag{A.15}$$

with $p^i\,(L|\omega,\,\omega') = p^j(L|\omega,\,\omega')$, $\forall\,(\omega,\,\omega') \in \Omega^2$, whereas if P_i files an individual suit, he obtains:

$$Eu_i\,(\theta_i, p^i\,(L|.)) = \sum_{\omega\in\Omega} p^i(\omega)\max\,(0, p^i\,(L|\omega)\theta_i - C_p) - C \tag{A.16}$$

Hence, P_i initiates the CA more particularly soon as:

(2) $$Eu_i\,(\Theta, p^j\,(L|.,.)) \geq Eu_i\,(\theta_i, p^i\,(L|.)) \geq 0 \tag{A.17}$$

Let us exhibit simple conditions under which the RHS inequality in (2) is true. For that, assume that there exists a subset of message $\Lambda_i \subset \Omega$ such that any $\hat{\omega} \in \Lambda_i$ satisfies: $p^i\,(L,\,\hat{\omega}) \geq \frac{C_p + C}{\theta_i}$, which implies that $p^i\,(L|\hat{\omega}) \geq \frac{C_p}{\theta_i}$; as a consequence, it is easy to see that:

$$\begin{aligned} Eu_i\,(\theta_i, p^i\,(L|.)) &= \sum_{\hat{\omega}\in\Lambda_i} p^i(\hat{\omega})\,(\,p^i\,(L|\hat{\omega})\theta_i - C_p) - C \\ &\geq \sum_{\hat{\omega}\in\Lambda_i} p^i(L,\,\hat{\omega})\theta_i - C_p - C \\ &\geq 0 \end{aligned} \tag{A.18}$$

Remark now that by (1), we have $p^i\,(L|\hat{\omega})\theta_i - C_p = \Sigma_{\omega'\in\Omega}\,\beta(\hat{\omega},\omega')\,p^j\,(L|\,\hat{\omega},\omega')\theta_i - C_p$, for any any $\hat{\omega} \in \Lambda_i$, implying thus:

$$\begin{aligned} \sum_{\omega'\in\Omega} \beta(\hat{\omega},\omega')p^j(L|\hat{\omega},\omega')\theta_i - C_p &\leq \sum_{\omega'\in\Omega} \beta(\hat{\omega},\omega')(p^j(L|\hat{\omega},\omega')\theta_i - C_p \\ &\leq \sum_{\omega'\in\Omega} \beta,\hat{\omega},\omega')\max(0, p^j(L|\hat{\omega},\omega')\theta_i - C_p \end{aligned} \tag{A.19}$$

Pre-multiplying by $p^i\,(\hat{\omega})$, summing over all $\hat{\omega} \in \Lambda_i$, and finally rearranging, we obtain:

$$\begin{aligned} \sum_{\hat{\omega}\in\Lambda_i} p^i(\hat{\omega})(p^i(L|\hat{\omega})\theta_i - C_p) &\leq \sum_{\hat{\omega}\in\Lambda_i}\sum_{\omega'\in\Omega} p^i(\hat{\omega},\omega')\max(0, p^j(L|\hat{\omega},\omega')\theta_i - C_p \\ &= \sum_{\hat{\omega}\in\Lambda_i}\sum_{\omega'\in\Omega} p^i(\hat{\omega},\omega')\max(0, p^j(L|\hat{\omega},\omega')\theta_i - C_p \\ &\leq \sum_{(\omega,\omega')\in\Omega^2} p^i(\omega,\omega')\max(0, p^j(L|\omega,\omega')\theta_i - C_p \\ &= Eu_i(\theta_i, p^j(L|.,.)) \end{aligned} \tag{A.20}$$

Now, given that $\Theta > \theta_i$ and using assumption 2, it comes that: $Eu_i(\Theta, p^j(L|.,.)) \geq Eu_i(\theta_i, p^j(L|.,.))$. Hence (2) holds, and the lemma 8 is proven.

Proof of Proposition 9

Once more, we prove the following claim.

Claim 13

Assume that: (C1) there exists a unique combination of messages $(\omega, \omega') \in \Omega$ such that $p(L, \hat{\omega}, \hat{\omega}') \geq \frac{C_P + C}{\theta_i}$, and (C2): $\alpha \leq \hat{\alpha} \equiv \frac{C_P - K_P}{p^j(L|\hat{\omega}, \hat{\omega}')(\theta_j - \theta_i)}$. Then, there is a SPE associated to the following set of actions:

1 Each plaintiff files.
2 P_i initiates the CA, and P_j joins it.
3 The defendant makes three offers:

$$s(\theta_i, \omega) = \max(0, p^i(L|\omega)\theta_i - C_p), \forall \omega \in \Omega \textit{ for } P_i \tag{A.21}$$

$$s(\theta_j, \omega, \omega') = \max(0, p^j(L|\omega, \omega')\theta_j - C_p), \forall (\omega, \omega') \in \Omega \times \Omega \textit{ for } P_j \tag{A.22}$$

$$s(\Theta, \omega, \omega') = \max(0, p^j(L|\omega, \omega')\Theta - K_p), \forall (\omega, \omega') \in \Omega \times \Omega \textit{ for a CA} \tag{A.23}$$

4 At each decision node in stage 3 where he has to choose an action, each plaintiff accepts the offer (either individually or as a member of the CA) proposed by the defendant, for every possible information they may receive.

Proof of Claim 14

To prove 1/ and 2/ it is sufficient to remark that if there exists a unique combination of messages $(\hat{\omega}, \hat{\omega}') \in \Omega \times \Omega$ such that $p(L, \hat{\omega}, ! \hat{\omega}') \geq \frac{C_P + C}{\theta_i}$, then we also have:

$- p^j(L|\hat{\omega}, \hat{\omega}') \geq p(L, \hat{\omega}, \hat{\omega}') \geq \frac{C_P + C}{\theta_i}$; thus, if $\alpha \leq \frac{C_P - K_P}{p^j(L|\hat{\omega}, \hat{\omega}')(\theta_j - \theta_i)}$ by lemma 7, P_j always files and joins the CA initiated by the other plaintiff,

$- p^i(L|\hat{\omega}) \geq p^i(L, \hat{\omega}) \equiv p(L, \hat{\omega}, \hat{\omega}') + \Sigma_{\omega' \neq \hat{\omega}'} p(L, \hat{\omega}, \omega') > p(L, \hat{\omega}, \hat{\omega}') \geq \frac{C_P + C}{\theta_i}$; thus, by lemma 8, P_i always files and initiated the CA.

Finally, 3/ and 4/ are direct from lemma 5.

Proof of Proposition 10

It is sufficient to prove that, for any message pertaining to the subset $\Lambda_j \subset \Omega$ defined in lemma 6, and for any value of α, there always exists a $\gamma \in [0,1]$ such that:

$$p^j (L|\omega, \omega')\mathrm{d}_j - \mathrm{K}_p \geq p^j (L|\omega, \omega')\theta_j - C_p \tag{A.24}$$

with $\mathrm{d}_j = \alpha\gamma\theta_i + (1 - \alpha\gamma)\theta_j$, which is equivalent to:

$$\lambda \leq \frac{C_p - K_p}{p^j (L|\omega,\omega')\alpha (\theta_j - \theta_i} \tag{A.25}$$

Hence the result.

Proof of Proposition 11

Consider the case of the first type of plaintiffs. Equivalent arguments may be obtained in the case of the second plaintiff and in the case of a CA.

When conditional or contingent fees are introduced, the defendant's best offers to plaintiff i in stage 3 are the following, under assumption 2:

$$\begin{aligned} s(\theta_i, \omega) &= \max (0, p^i (L|\omega) (\theta_i - C_p)) \\ &= p^i (L|\omega) (\theta_i - C_p) : \textit{under conditional fees} \end{aligned} \tag{A.26}$$

$$\begin{aligned} s(\theta_i, \omega) &= \max (0, p^i (L|\omega) (1 - t)\theta_i) \\ &= p^i(L|\omega)(1 - t)\theta_i : \textit{under contingent fees} \end{aligned} \tag{A.27}$$

i) Thus, whatever the message, the plaintiff always obtains a positive payment – thus, he always accepts the defendant's offer.
ii) As a result, the plaintiff's individual expected utility level in case of individual suits is equal to:

$$Eu_i (\theta_i, p^i (L|.)) = p_L (\theta_i - C_p) - C = Eu_i (\theta_i, p_L) \tag{A.28}$$

Notice that by assumption 1: $Eu_j (\theta_j, p_L) > Eu_i (\theta_i, p_L)$. It is straightforward to see that individual suits are both beneficial for the plaintiffs soon as $Eu_i (\theta_i, p_L) \geq 0$, meaning that their common priors must satisfy: $p_L \geq \frac{C}{\theta_i - C_P}$.

(iii) Finally, both contingent and conditional fees (for a normalized cost : $t\theta_i = C_p$) allows for higher settlement offers, given that they induce a decrease in the expected payments from plaintiffs to their attorney:

$$p^i(L|\omega)\theta_i - C_p > p^i(L|\omega)(\theta_i - C_p) : \textit{under conditional fees} \tag{A.29}$$

$$p^i(L|\omega)\theta_i - C_p > p^i(L|\omega)(1 - t)\theta_i : \textit{under contingent fees} \tag{A.30}$$

as compared to the fixed costs system of the previous section.

11. Good law and economics needs better microeconomic models: the case against 'contingent fees' as application of agency models to the professions

Lorenzo Sacconi

1. INTRODUCTION

Economic analysis of the law aims at understanding whether legal rules are designed as adequate mechanisms of incentive strong enough to induce economic agents (for example firms, workers, tax payers or professionals) to contribute efficiently to the creation of wealth, production of a surplus, producing a public good or the reduction of a public bad or a risk.

One basic idea is that the law doesn't reach its goal directly but rather through affecting the economic agents' choices. They interact under the conditions put in place (in part) by a legal framework (and in part they react to these constraints) as far as economic agents are seen as (bounded) rational players participating in a game where the law sets the rules but doesn't uniquely determine outcomes. Outcomes are produced by how economic agents make their choices under the constraints set (or by taking advantage of the opportunities posted) by the rules – *inter alia*. Thus, legal rules may generate the effects a legislator desires – if it was a wise 'designer', but also unexpected outcomes in the case that actual incentives and opportunities of action were not appropriately considered. The result will be consequently a (Nash) equilibrium induced by the rules (since the law influences the 'rules of the game'), but not univocally determined because only the convergence of the players' learning and expectations toward a particular equilibrium point can explain why a given equilibrium has been reached, especially if multiple equilibria are possible.

Obviously, the purpose of such an analysis is not just predictive. It has instead a clear normative intent: the optimal design of the economic game – through incentives and constraints laid down by the law – by which a social welfare objective is indirectly reached. A *well* designed legal rule should define a game wherein an equilibrium is reached which corresponds to a social state such that some welfare properties desired by the legislator are satisfied. This endeavour takes for granted that only equilibria in the interactions among agents will constitute stable social states, but equilibria do not necessarily satisfy the welfare properties that a legislator may desire.

Nothing but an ideological prejudice (and a biased reading of the *Coase Theorem*) can lead to the conclusion that setting up a 'market' is the only welfare aim that a legal rule can pursue. Here assumed is that the established market will resemble a situation of 'perfect competition' closely enough, so that its equilibria will be socially efficient resource allocations. However, understanding legal rules as rules of a *game* (that is rules for strategic interaction) should suggest on the contrary that a perfect competitive market (or a close approximation to it) *could not exist* for every matter under consideration. The legislator's welfare objective may be for example the cooperative production of a *surplus* of social welfare through *idiosyncratic* relations and its *fair* distribution – objectives that aren't typically pursuable simply through a competitive market and are surely failed by an imperfectly competitive market. Rather they may be pursued through organized forms of cooperation and could be obtained through other institutions such as the firm, a public regulation, or self-regulated (through deontology codes) professions. Good Law & Economics demands adopting microeconomic models suitable for representing the salient features of a given field of interaction (transactions) among economic agents. They must be capable of realistically simulating the effects that superimposing a legal rule would produce through the interaction among the agents within the underlying economic reality. Otherwise, rules designed according to the mistaken hypothesis that a given field of interaction would satisfy the condition of an unsuited microeconomic model, could generate incentives that are completely perverse in that specific area.

Especially within the economics of professions an accurate accounting of the agents' information and knowledge (or what they are able to learn) should be executed. Given the proper modeling of the information available to the agents – what constraints it imposes on them, as well as the *transaction costs* these constraints imply – rational choices become predictable (at least in term of the *feasible equilibrium set* of the game). Otherwise, agents' decisions may contradict the designer's expectations.

Consider what could be the result of reforms of professional services like those introduced in many European countries where, with the intent to liberalize the market of professional services, together with the abolition of minimum tariffs also schemes of professionals' remuneration contingent on results have been legalized – i.e. 'lawyers' contingent fees'.[1] These are contracts allowing the professional's remuneration to be contingent upon the outcomes of the lawyer's activity, i.e. the judicial decision. This kind of remuneration has been in use for a long time in the US within the private law sector as well as, but more recently, in the United Kingdom (after the reform of legal services in the 1990s) and other European countries, even though they have been prohibited for a long time in continental Europe.[2] If the relationship between the professional and the client is seen according to the *principal–agent* model, contingency fees can be economically justified as an efficient incentive for the professional's effort.[3] The bulk of this approach is asymmetry of information between the professional (*agent*) – who is well informed about her own effort and characteristics, and the client (*principal*) – who is quite ignorant about the actual occurrence of such variables, but is nevertheless able to foresee the possible outcomes and define some sort of statistical correlation between the observable outcomes and the professional's efforts and characteristics.

The case is quite different, however, if the situation is seen as one of bounded rationality and incompleteness of contracts, so that some events are *ex ante* unforeseen and *ex post* asymmetrically gathered by the professional and the client. In such contexts (in part covered by what economists call *credence goods*) the client's *ex post* evaluation of results may require him to submit to an expert's judgment, typically a professional (Darby and Karni, 1973, Arrow 1963). Moreover, the professional–client relationship is

---

[1] This was one of the points of the heated debate that ensued the so-called Bersani Act, the Italian decree law on the liberalization of professions, when it was passed in the summer of 2006 (see *dl. 223, July 4th 2006*, and the *Law n.248, August 4th 2006*)

[2] Some authors stress a distinction between the US contingent fees system and what is called the UK-like *conditional fees system*. Under the second, a lawyer gets an upscale premium only if the case is won, but the upscale premium does not vary in function of the adjudicated amount (see Emons and Garoupa 2005). However, whether in the UK the premium is actually related to the amount adjudicated by the court is a matter of debate (Yarrow 2001).

[3] This is sometime argued not only *ex post* (after reform), but also 'ideologically' *ex ante*, as the economic policy justification of their introduction in the legal system. For instance, consider that the so called 2006 Bersani Act in Italy introduced the principle that 'professional's remuneration should be contingent on results' in general for all the professions, and it has been based on the widespread acceptance amongst the policy analysts (but not the professionals) that professions must be run according to economic models suitable for the firm's behavior, such as agency models.

a one of formal authority – the professional is in charge of making residual decisions over variables that cannot be included in the *ex ante* contract. Remunerations contingent on outcomes in these contexts can generate pathological incentives. For instance, the lawyer can discretionally decide to litigate only the more advantageous lawsuit and 'settle' all the less profitable cases within her 'clients portfolio', disregarding the 'access to justice' right of 'less-lucky clients'.[4]

Moreover, in the economic analysis of professions, the study of behavioral rules and motivations of the economic agent is particularly important. Behavioral microeconomics explains economic institutions and behaviors as a consequence of the complexity of individual agents' motivations and the composite nature of their utility function arguments. According to this point of view, an agent's utility function can't only represent her self-interested preferences, but also her endogenous motives for compliance with social norms, the importance of trust, the weight of social preferences and reciprocity (Gintis, Bowles, Boyd and Fehr, 2006). Utility functions should also represent preferences for reciprocal conformity to agreed-upon or shared basic principles of any social institution such as, for instance, the ethical code or ideals of a profession (Sacconi 1999, see also Grimalda and Sacconi 2002, 2005, Sacconi and Grimalda 2007). Accounting for these various prompts to act by means of a proper modeling of the economic agents' utility functions allows also for an approach to institution design which may take advantage of these more complex motivations, whereas these motivations would be crowded out by unsuitable incentive mechanisms (Frey 1997, see also Fehr, Klein and Schmidt 2001, Fehr and Gächter 2002).

This work proceeds as follows: Section 2 traces back lawyers' contingent fees to the principal–agent model and considers what we can learn from the economic literature that has pursued this line of modeling. Section 3 discusses whether a system of professionals remuneration conditioned upon outcomes is adequate for the professions in general. Section 4

[4] A related but different point is raised by Emons (2000) who sees the client–lawyer relationship as a context of *expertise* and *credence good.* The attorney may behave opportunistically in the assessment of the merit of cases (i.e. in telling whether the case requires standard effort or higher effort). Thus the lawyer decides to take too many undeveloped cases to the court, putting only standard effort in their preparation and neglecting the investment of additional effort necessary to develop completely the more difficult cases. On the contrary, this chapter characterizes the professional relationship as one where incompleteness of contracts is involved. The perverse effect is somewhat opposite than that enlightened by Emons: too many cases are dropped and hastily settled by the lawyer in order to concentrate his effort only on the mostly profitable cases.

introduces the idea that the professional relationship is not an *agency* relationship but rather an *authority relationship* based on *contractual incompleteness* (Williamson 1986, Grossman and Hart 1986, Hart and Moore 1990, Hansmann 1988, Hart 1995). This requires creating fiduciary relationships and the reliance on trustworthiness of the person holding a position of authority, as meant in organizational theory of formal authority (Simon 1951) and in philosophy of law (Raz 1985). Sections 5 through to 8 introduce a thought experiment aimed at checking the case for or against employing agency models for understanding the professional relationship and the pros and cons of contingent fees under different hypotheses about the underlying professional–client game, both informational and motivational. First, I consider the case when the principal–agent standard model could properly design the contractual relationship between the client and lawyer as long as it is understood according to the paradigm of complete even though information-asymmetric contracts (Section 6). Then (from Section 7 on), I show how a biased use of the standard agency model could instead create mistaken incentives in case the professional contract were incomplete and at the same time allowed for many relationships between a single professional and many clients. By two simple extensive form games it is shown that:

(*i*) in the case of a self-interested professional, notwithstanding that utilitarian overall efficiency is safeguarded, contingent fees lead to not respecting the fiduciary obligations with at least one client (to the detriment of Pareto optimality and equal, impartial, loyal respect for all the clients' rights and the obligation to promote all the clients' welfare) since only the *ex post* mostly remunerative cases are litigated (Section 7, the main negative result of the chapter).

(*ii*) In the case of a professional's willingness to comply with deontology standards – requiring impartial protection of all the clients' rights and claims, under a condition of minimal individual rationality – contingent fees lead nevertheless to neutralization of the deontological motivation and to a loss of efficiency in a utilitarian sense (Section 8, the 'impossibility of the charitable professional').

I admit here that deontological behavior is not completely altruistic and supererogatory – what would violate a condition of minimal individual rationality such that the agent cannot be paid less for higher effort than for lower effort. The professional's deontological behavior hence amounts to a condition of maximizing the professional's payoff under the constraint of *impartial*, *diligent* and *loyal* clients' treatment, which must be *fair* at least compared to the original contract that instituted the professional relationship. It follows that – even if the professional is committed by personal motivation to equal and fair treatment of all clients – unless her individual rent is very high, she is unable to escape from case (*i*) by redressing the unlucky client; (*ii*) by redress through a voluntary arrangement by which the professional personally pays for cross-subsidization between the cases of the two clients. The result is that deontology becomes indistinguishable from a suboptimal application of the contingent fees remuneration of lawyers, with inefficient (from a utilitarian point of view) total damage compensation for the clients, and perhaps with a violation of the luckiest client's claim to the best possible damage compensation for him. Thus, a typical *trade-off* ensues. Maximizing the professional self-interest under an incentive contract ('contingent fees') induces the maximization of aggregate utilitarian efficiency to the sacrifice of equality, impartiality and Pareto. On the other hand, constraining the professional's self-interest to be compatible with equality of clients' treatment, under the same contingent fees mechanism leads nevertheless to *due care* violations and a utilitarian efficiency loss.

A Pareto optimal, impartial, as well as efficient in a utilitarian sense, solution aimed at maximizing the total volume of damage compensation and at treating all clients impartially, loyally and diligently is considered in Section 9. There, contingent fees contract restrictions are put aside, and the lawyer's effective professional authority is acknowledged – so that she can renegotiate *ex post* the distribution of damage compensation among the three relevant players (herself and the two clients). She is allowed to resort to the global amount of damage compensation won from different cases litigated or conciliated on behalf of different, 'lucky' and 'unlucky' clients, in order to redress the unlucky from the decision of litigating only the most efficient and remunerative cases to the advantage of the luckiest. I make clear that this solution can be put in place only under behavioral assumptions such as the professional's *conformist preferences* (Grimalda and Sacconi 2005) or the workings of other mechanisms of endogenous norm *compliance*, like *reputation* (Sacconi 2000), which push the professional to comply with her fiduciary deontological obligations. Nevertheless, the main result of all these sections is that under a contingent fee contract, even if these motivations were available, the professional could not carry them out because of the logic of the contract which doesn't allow the pooling of different cases' damage compensations. I conclude that institutions like contingent fees do matter in pushing aside professional's fiduciary duties and also in making ineffective deontological motivations.

2. ECONOMIC ANALYSIS AND THE CASE FOR PRINCIPAL–AGENT MODELING OF THE PROFESSIONS

What is the economic *rationale* of the client–professional relationship? Is it a relationship between a principal and an agent where the principal hires the agent for a professional service with a clearly agreed-upon scope and predicted outcome, in which the agent's ability and effort are considered indispensable because of her superior knowledge? If this were the case, and if the principal succeeded in designing and enforcing a contract that provides incentives to obtain the desired service from the agent – at the cost of handing over some of his private rent – then we could say that the principal–agent model has captured the essence of the client–professional relationship. We will see, however, that things generally are not on these terms.

The most convincing way to argue in favor of a thesis is to consider the case that apparently demonstrates the opposite. The literature on lawyers' *contingent fees* (remunerations conditioned upon outcomes) actually supports the thesis that at least for damage litigations, it is possible to frame the provision of professional services in terms that are reminiscent of the incentive contract.

Contingent fees are extremely common in the USA for the remuneration of lawyers in damage compensation lawsuit, with the main exception being family litigations. Though the structure of contingent fees is not the same everywhere, it is in general based upon the lawyer's commitment when representing the client to accept bearing all or most of the legal action's burden without asking the client for a refund in a case of failure. At the same time, the client agrees to pay the lawyer a percentage of the compensation for damages if the case is successful. The professional's fee hence ranges from 33 per cent of the damage if the case is settled without trial, to 40 per cent if the plaintiff wins at trial or 50 per cent if a judgment for the plaintiff is settled on appeal. The principle is that the lawyer's complete remuneration varies according to the outcome, and that the lawyer bears the cost in a case of failure. In 1990 with the approval of the Courts and Legal Services Act reforming legal services in England and Wales, a weak form of *contingent fees* was introduced for the first time in a European country (see Benson 1979, Bowels 1994). The reform stemmed from a long and lively debate about the benefits and risks of introducing a contingent remuneration system for lawyers. The solution adopted was to introduce a hybrid remuneration scheme whereby the lawyer asks for a basic hourly fee that increases according to a pre-arranged upscale premium in case of a positive outcome of the litigation. This premium is not explicitly related as a percentage to the amount of the damage compensation (even though it is not completely clear whether it is conditionally adapted to its amount).

Economists rationalize *contingent fees* as an implication of the view that reduces the professional relationship in general to a *principal–agent* problem.[5] A principal and an agent agree on a contract according to which the principal will pay a remuneration f to the agent. The agent in turn will make an effort e to obtain an outcome (or result) x. The outcome is influenced by a random exogenous factor Θ and by e, so that $x(e, \Theta)$. In this way, the remuneration depends on three variables x, e, Θ, so $f = f(x,e,\Theta)$. The asymmetry in information is introduced by assuming that the agent has private information about e or Θ. In the first case, the agent even though uncertain about Θ – knows what her effort will be, so that *ex post* (after the contract signature) a *moral hazard* problem arises. In the second case, the agent has private information about the external factor that influences the quality or productivity of her services – for instance her own qualification, training, equipment etc – but the principal does know how to associate a quality/productivity parameter to the agent at the moment of signing the professional services contract. This yields *ex ante adverse selection.* In both cases, the principal does not know e or Θ, so the remuneration cannot be contingent on these variables.

Interpreting the lawyer–client relationship in these terms for cases of damage litigations – especially in terms of a *moral hazard* problem – was rather immediate (Rickman 1994). The outcome x is the amount of compensation for damages received in cases attended to by the lawyer. The lawyer's remuneration is f. The variable e is the effort made by the lawyer, while Θ could either represent his professional quality, training, equipment, updating, or exogenous variables that influence the lawsuit outcome, such as the court's behavior or the opposing lawyer's skills. In this context, the comparative efficiency of different contractual arrangements of the lawyer's fee is evaluated. A *remuneration scheme contingent on outcomes*, whereby the principal pays the lawyer $f(x)$ and takes $x\text{-}f(x)$ for himself, is contrasted with a remuneration *scheme based on effort*, such that given the hourly fee $f(e)$ and the hours spent, the lawyer's payment increases with effort ($d(f)/d(e)>0$).

If effort is an unobservable variable while outcomes *are* observable, but only statistically correlated to effort, then the optimal contingent contract

[5] Reference to moral hazard and principal agent modeling may be found in Schwartz and Mitchell 1970, Danzon 1983, Halpern and Turnbull 1983, Gravelle and Waterson 1993, Rickman 1994, Dana and Spier 1993. For a formulation of the theory in general see Salaniè (1997).

is one that provides an incentive to the lawyer, increasing the remuneration in states of the world (outcomes) where the amount of compensation for damages is statistically mostly correlated to high effort. On the contrary, a remuneration scheme directly based on (unobservable) effort allows the lawyer to act to his own advantage, which is to declare or spend more hours than necessary by the case. Hence a contingent fees scheme may be preferable for the client.[6]

If we interpret Θ as an exogenous random variable (for example the counterpart's ability or the court's behavior) the result is stochastic and it must include an evaluation of risk. A contingent remuneration of the lawyer shifts (partly or totally) the risk to the party most capable of handling it. The lawyer can actually differentiate and subdivide the risk between the many cases in his portfolio, while the client is idiosyncratically tied to the particular compensation for damages of his case. Admitting that the client is averse to risk, he will be indifferent in terms of expected utility between accepting a sure amount of money and the risky prospect of an expected compensation for damages from the case (i.e. litigate and win a higher compensation or lose the case). The expected monetary value of the risky prospect will therefore be higher than the monetary value of its certainty equivalent in utility. If, on the other hand, the lawyer is risk neutral, he is able to pay the certain monetary value (equal in terms of utility to the expected value of the client's case) insuring him against the case's uncertain outcome and getting as a payback the right of appropriating the uncertain damage compensation, that will represent a positive surplus to her. In fact, given linearity with the money of the lawyer's utility function, the expected monetary value for the compensation of damages will correspond for a lawyer to a utility value higher than the one paid to insure the client.

A remuneration scheme that insures the client against the costs of losing the case and guarantees him a sure value not dependent on the outcome,

[6] A recent vein of literature within the principal–agent framework compares the relative efficiency of two kinds of lawyers' remuneration schemes, both conditional on outcome – the US-style contingent fees and the UK-style conditional fees (see Emons 2007, Emons 2006, Emons and Garoupa 2005). In particular, Emons and Garoupa (2005) considers two contracts: the first (contingent fees) provides the attorney with a fixed baseline remuneration (possibly negative) if the case is lost, or the baseline plus a percentage of the damage compensation if the case is won. The second (conditional fees) provides the same baseline compensation if the case is lost, or the baseline plus a fixed premium if the case is won. According to Emons and Garoupa, contingent fees are relatively most efficient than other kinds of conditional remuneration, as far as they are analyzed within the standard principal–agent model.

and at the same time remunerates the lawyer in a way directly variable with the total amount of the lawsuit outcome is a kind of *contingent fee* that completely insures the client. Obviously, the most realistic hypothesis is that both are risk averse to some extent, and therefore the optimal design of the contract requires that the lawyer and client will share the risk. Usually lawyers' *contingent fees* set that both parties will partake of the risk, because the clients' and professionals' positive payoffs vary accordingly with the obtained compensation for damages, with the only exception of minimal entrance conditions. In the USA, the client is completely insured just about the risk of failure. In England, the client has to pay a base-line hourly fee, and therefore also the lawyer is partly insured against failure, while both share the risk associated with the extra expected compensation for damages.

On this base, it has been claimed that *contingent fees* increase the clients' access level to the judicial system for those clients that would not have been able to afford the case's cost or the risk of failure (which also includes payment of process costs) due to an insufficient income. The lawyer offers a remedy to financial markets' failures: on one side he anticipates the necessary capital for proceeding with the legal case that the client does not have, on the other side he allows the client to shift all or part of the risk of failure to the lawyer. This has efficiency effects because it gives the client the incentive to push his level of access to justice closer to the social optimum. It also has effects on fairness, because given a presumable higher risk-aversion level for poorer clients with respect to the richer professional, under a *contingent fees* scheme one can expect more egalitarian access to justice (Shwartz and Mitchell 1970, Danzon 1983, Swanson 1991, Rickman 1994).[7,8]

---

[7] However, dissenters' views underline that (a) *contingent fees* risk raising prices of legal performances due to the lawyers' possibility to renegotiate the percentage of compensation they obtained, after the client started a dependent relationship with them (lock-in effect) during the course of the case (Benson 1979, Swanson 1991); (b) conflict of interests between the lawyer and client could sharpen not about the effort in the single case, but about the lawyer's decision about which case to litigate and which to accommodate through a transaction with the counterpart: in particular, the lawyer will choose the case to litigate within his portfolio so as to maximize his total returns and not his single client's satisfaction (Benson 1979, Schwartz and Mitchell 1970, Danzon 1983, Gravelle and Waterson 1993, Rickman 1994); (c) the effect of the *contingent fees* on social efficiency is uncertain concerning the total level of the judicial system's tendency to litigation and on the extent of deterrence against hazardous behavior (that originate claims of damage compensations). In particular, proclivity of preventing such behaviors will be as greater as the lawyers' opportunistic inclination to accommodate lower-income cases with rebating

3. WHY PRINCIPAL–AGENT MODELS ARE UNSUITABLE FOR THE PROFESSIONS IN GENERAL

The above-mentioned assessments assume that the microeconomic representation of the client–professional relationship offered by the principal–agent model is appropriate. Furthermore, they appreciate the efficiency effects of the contractual arrangement under such hypotheses. These models emphasize the *ex ante* predictability of the set of all possible outcomes and the *ex post* ability to observe and verify the obtained outcome, which in this context is the amount of compensation for damages. This outcome must be recognizable *ex post* in its objective and independent existence, which means in terms of measurable characteristics that do not require for their description any observation of the lawyer's conduct during the case, and are clearly predictable before starting the case. This type of contract can be correctly implemented by a client just resting upon his knowledge of the compensation for damages obtained and enforced by the judge on the basis of the same information. In this section we do not concentrate on the particular application of *contingent fees* to lawyers,[9] but the possibility that such contractual mechanisms are paradigmatic of a more efficient regulation of liberal professionals in general.

First, if we could apply 'remunerations contingent upon outcomes' to professional activity in general, there would not actually be any trustor/

---

transactions. This depends on a parameter of identification between the lawyers' and clients' interests (Cooter and Rubinfeld 1989, Rickman 1994).

[8] Lester Brickman in the last few years has intensively campaigned against contingent fees (see Brickman 2003a, 2003b, 2005). In particular he raises a question about the competitiveness of the US market of legal services and contingent fees. What is interesting to the European reformers – who look for remuneration systems that may increase competitiveness of the professional services market – is that this point has been raised to give substance to the thesis that contingent fees enable lawyers specialized in personal injuries litigations to appropriate remunerations hundreds times higher than the corresponding hourly remunerations they would get if they charged exactly the hours put in cases. Attorneys – he says – apply a standard contingent fees (from 33 per cent to 50 per cent according to the State) to cases that are practically already won (even though the clients are uncertain about that) whereon they add practically no value in term of perspectives of substantial damage compensation for the plaintiff. Thus, they are able to appropriate remarkable rents that otherwise would go to their clients.

[9] If we hypothesize that the lawyers' contingent remuneration mechanism is introduced in a context of (not only asymmetric but also) incomplete information, then its application becomes problematic even to the typical case of compensation for damages. About this see sections 5 to 9 *infra*.

trustee relationship within the professional relationship. The client wouldn't 'put himself in the hands of' the professional, for an incentive contract actually remunerates the professional for what they give back for money, i.e. in a conditional way related to all possible, perfectly predetermined and *ex post* measurable outcomes. Thus there wouldn't be room for the typical fiduciary duties of loyalty and diligence (due care). What would count is the result. Actually, the typical principal–agent model of the agency contract is based not on trust but rather on *diffidence*: in a situation in which the agent can act with discretion – that is, when he could lie without being directly discovered – the principal predicts that the agent won't tell the truth and thus designs the contract in such a way that the agent becomes indifferent between telling the truth or not. It would make sense to speak of trustworthiness only if the principal could believe that when the agent has discretion he acts according to the principal's interests. But it is just because the principal cannot trust the agent that he designs an incentive contract that incorporates prizes and punishments to condition the agent to fulfill diverse output levels.[10] Fiduciary duties and economic principal–agent models do not go hand in hand as otherwise happens for the legal notion of agency relationship.[11]

---

[10] Economic models of reputation can be regarded differently (Fudenberg 1991). For a typical application to a case strictly analogous to that of the professions see Grief, Milgrom and Weingast (1994).

In reputation models, trust is represented by the probability that a player – the client – assigns to the types of the second player – the professional – i.e. his reputation to be an honest type or, to say it differently, by the probability that the professional identifies with a *type* that idiosyncratically follows a *commitment*. Under a reputation equilibrium (that is within an effective fiduciary relationship) the professional's rational choice consists in sustaining her reputation by means of a behavior coinciding with the client's expectations. We see then that trust does not necessarily imply that the professional acts altruistically – this does not occur in reputation models – but it implies that client believes that the professional will follow a principle (Kreps 1990) or is committed to a rule of conduct. The reconstructing of *reasons* for which this happens could be both self-interest in the long run or intrinsic preferences for reciprocal conformity. The two different (but not incompatible) hypotheses were considered by Sacconi (2000, 2006), Grimalda and Sacconi (2005) and Sacconi and Grimalda (2007).

[11] Brickman (2005) construes the origins of lawyers' fiduciary duties in the Common Law tradition, observing that they was further developed through agency law by the mid-nineteenth century (op. cit. p.1189). Thus it is the economic model of incentive contract, not the legal notion of agency, that conflicts with the idea of a fiduciary. This conclusion also accords with Brickman's discussion of how the US practice of contingent fees has progressively eroded the fiduciary obligations the lawyers owe to their clients, and in particular the decisions of the ABA Ethics 2000 Commission to reject amendments proposals concerning the reaffirmation of

In *second* place, the principal's and agent's cognitive and informative ability required by 'remunerations contingent upon outcomes' makes a general application of that model on the professional world difficult. These are (i) the *ex ante* predictability of the range of all possible outcomes and (ii) *ex post* observability and verifiability of actual outcomes.

Both these cognitive assumptions are unrealistic. The outcomes description is an inherent part of the description of each state of the world so that it cannot be separate by the description of the states space. The fact that a given outcome occurs in different states of the world may imply a quite different description of the outcome itself (for example, a 'high damage compensation' gained under favorable conditions is a different result than in unfavorable conditions – i.e. if the damage belongs to a socially and racially discriminated group; 'acquittal' of a guilty defendant is different than an innocent one; 'perfect recovery' from open-heart surgery is different from bronchitis). Even though we admit that the outcome to the client and the state of the world of which it is a part, are both perfectly observable *ex post,* nevertheless a certain outcome may *change its meaning* accordingly if it has been obtained in this or in that state of the world.[12] Let's now

---

fiduciary duties related to contingent fees. The amendments required the attorney to ask for a contingent remuneration only when the result of the lawsuit is genuinely uncertain, and substantial risk is involved in the determination of a case's outcome for each level of attorney's effort. Thus by accepting a fee contingent on outcomes the lawyer should face genuine risk (winning a percentage of the damage or losing the value of her investment). But notice that this is not the case of contingent fees, as far as their justification is given in the principal–agent model terms. Consider the case that, after signing the contract, the agent (attorney) but not the principal (plaintiff) learns accurately the state of the world (so that uncertainty vanishes for him), while effort remains his private information (a pure case of *hidden action*). Quite obviously a principal–agent model suggests giving the agent an incentive by paying him more for a higher outcome. But here the attorney does not face any risk *ex post*, when he learns the state of the world and decides the level of effort whereby a specific damage compensation is produced. A contingent fee under asymmetry of information is paid to the attorney for reasons of incentive, not because he faces genuine risk. Once the incentive mechanism justification for contingent fees is assumed, it seems natural that such amendments were rejected. Reasoning about agency in terms of the principal–agent incentive model is incompatible with the notions of the lawyer as a fiduciary.

[12] It follows that in order to overcome incompleteness of contracts, to take a full range of monetary payoffs (so to say from 1 $ to ten million) as it was a complete set of possible outcomes separable from our limited knowledge of the unforeseeable states of the world, is not an allowed move. When some unforeseen state is discovered the same amount of money will change its meaning as an outcome for the principal. Thus it is not admissible what Maskin and Tirole suggested in their *ad*

suppose that some state of the world has been discovered during the professional performance, and that it is completely new compared to the cognitive situation in which the client and professional had agreed on making remuneration depending on output levels. Since results to the client are understandable only when referring to the state of the world within which they occurred (significance is subjected to 'dependence on the context', or state-dependence), it is clear that a contractual obligation conditioned upon the occurrence of some consequence will be undetermined in a case in which that outcome occurred within a state of the world that was not among those states that the parties had foreseen. Simply the outcome cannot be recognized as the one whereon they had taken up contractual obligations. We notice here a particular *ex post* inability to 'observe'. Under unforeseen contingencies we can't observe or verify whether the contractual obligations has been complied with, simply because these contractual obligations conditioned on outcomes are *mute* in the face of unforeseen contingencies on which the outcome description depends.

For example, if we consider the medical profession, the outcome of medical services is not separate from the patient's treatment. A measurable physical result doesn't exist that is independent of the doctor's diagnosis and kind of treatment (actions and their quality). The consequences coincide with a subjective state of the patient, diagnosable only in the light of biomedical knowledge. To give a value to the services offered one has to be able to understand information about the treatment context and situations that come up in its process, and in order to judge the consequences one has to either be part of the profession or have the same skills as the doctor. The first is tacit information and the second is specialized information, which the patient usually is unable to use. In the last instance, medical services are part of *credence goods*. On the other side, during the cure the doctor can discover a state of health of the patient which was not noticed before. This may change the appropriateness of the treatment and the outcome depending on the state of the world. In this way, *ex ante* it is impossible to take specific obligations about the results obtainable in the presence of these unforeseen states of health.

The same occurs with the criminal lawyer. It is impossible to evaluate a court's decision independent from how truth has been reconstructed in the course of the trial due to the effect of the opposite actions of prosecutor, defend advocate, and how the judge oversees the case. To assess the court's

---

hoc reduction of incomplete contracts to a variant of the asymmetric information agency paradigm (Maskin and Tirole 1999, Tirole 1999).

ruling on a case you need an understanding of the case's context, and to make a judgment it is necessary to use 'tacit (or un-formal) information' obtained during the lawsuit. It is impossible to establish *ex ante* whether a sentence has been truly favorable or unfavorable just on the basis, for instance, of the entity of punishment inflicted and independent of the legal case's story. It wouldn't be meaningful to establish *ex ante* if a certain sentence is light or heavy independently of the evidence put forth as proof of the defendant's guilt or innocence during the trial. On the other hand, in order to evaluate on the basis of the legal trial story whether a certain sentence is either light or heavy, a client needs an expert's guidance. In particular, the verdict judgment is based on tacit knowledge of the legal trial and on a specialized knowledge of law that the client cannot acquire without legal assistance. Instead, the legal assistance for a guilty defendant would be an impossible mission and would be destined to forever being considered self-defeating to the professional. In addition, the truth reached during the trial is in part constructed and in part discovered in light of the evidence put forth which the professional cannot *ex ante* foresee. The significance of the outcome is 'dependent upon the state' which is revealed in the course of the trial. The set of all possible states (which cannot be identified with the number of conviction years ruled by a sentence) cannot be foreseen *ex ante* and listed so as to lead to a prior description of all possible outcomes. In this way, it is impossible to write a contract contingent on a trial's outcomes when they are connected to partially unforeseeable events.

4. PROFESSIONAL AUTHORITY UNDER INCOMPLETENESS OF CONTRACTS

A client–professional transaction should not be seen as a principal–agent relationship based on asymmetric information, but as an incomplete contract. By this I mean that professional services are not *ex ante* specified contingently on the occurrence of all possible states of the world. The contract is incomplete not only due to the costs of filling it, but also because, given their background information, parties *ex ante* do not even imagine all possible states of the world and therefore the appropriate services. The contract assigns a wide and vague mandate to the professional according to which she can decide discretionally, when states of the world are revealed, how the most appropriate service will be specified.

Moreover, often a professional service implies the client will conform to some requirement inherent to the same definition of the professional service. Examples are: doctors who treat patients and therefore establish, according to their diagnosis, the medical therapy the patient *should* follow; architects and engineers who set a project and then introduce specifications and readjustments along the working process that the building company *must* comply with; lawyers who study a case and readjust along the trial the strategy the client is requested to *follow*.

Professional's discretion ranges over *ex ante* non contractible decision variables, i.e. those decisions that *ex ante,* at the moment in which the client appoints the professional, cannot be subject to an explicit agreement. These decisions refer not only to acts made *ex post* by the professional, but also to the client's behavior.

Thus, a relationship of authority enters the picture according to Simon's definition (Simon 1951). A (the professional) has authority over B (the client) if B accepts (without keeping freedom of questioning them case by case) A's decisions within a given set of alternatives as the criterion of choice over actions that B himself will have to perform later (therapy observance, trial conduct etc.).

It is worth noticing that Simon introduces the authority relationship to make a distinction between the employment contract and the sale contract 'on spot'. In our case, however, the authority relationship develops in the opposite direction compared to the typical employment contract. It is the professional, the one who is 'hired', to exercise authority over the client, the 'one who hires' him. Using the current terminology of contract theory, it is the 'agent' who has authority over the 'principal'. Nevertheless, 'unforeseen events' play their typical role: if everything was predictable *ex ante* and the parties were equally informed, we could write a detailed contract in which for each state of the world the decisions of the professional and the subsequent conduct of the client would be set and signed by the parties. However, since states of the world are not *ex ante* entirely defined and listed, the professional is left with the authority to decide at the right time. This happens because the professional is the party who will be in the best informed position *ex post*.

According to a well-known definition by the philosopher of law Joseph Raz (1985), the authority's reasons to act – for those accepting a formal authority in relation to a given practice – are prima facie preemptive reasons: the client acts as requested simply because the person who is in the authority position 'says so' – any specific *assessment* of each recommendation per se is ruled out. If each recommendation were weighted and assessed by the client against every other reason to act, then we could not talk about professional formal authority. We would rather talk about logical and empirical abilities of persuasion towards the client (an advisory rather than authoritative function). An authority exists only if the authority's reasons to act preempt – i.e. 'take the place of' – the client's reasons for acting and overwhelm any other reason, just because they are those advanced by the authority itself. This definition describes appropriately the authority 'phenomenon' – the kind of reasons which matter in directing the client's action. But of course this phenomenon seems quite obscure and in need of further rational explanation. We go beyond the prima facie aspect of authority when we realize that preemptive reasons to act are reasons depending on (and explained by) preexistent and *independent* reasons that the client already had before the reasons with preemptive powers came into play (Raz 1985). Single actions within the range of accepted authority are executed due to the preemptive power that characterizes reasons put forward by an authority ('because it says so'), but the acceptance of this pre-emption power depends on the already existent client's reasons to act. Hence, for the professional to be put in a position of an authority means that the preemptive power exercised by the authoritative reasons to act are functional to pursuing reasons to act that the client already has independently of the claims put forward by the professional authority. This instrumentality of the authority relationship to pursuing in general goals or reasons that a client already had before the institution of the authority relationship, explains the preemptive-nature phenomenon of the authority's reasons to act: simply, without that feature it would not be able to carry out its function.

Concluding this section, we can say that the client–professional relationship is an authority relationship whereby the client *trusts* the professional, and legitimates her authority by accepting that her reasons to act exercise preemptive power over his own reasons to act, as far as this is an effective means to pursue in general the client's ultimate goals or interests. Such acceptance involves the trustor claim that authority given the trustee is functional to some preexistent goal, reason or interest the trustor himself already had before entering the authority relation (Davis 1987). This generates claims over the trustee which amount to her *fiduciary duties*. Actually, fiduciary duties are those that grant that the client's *independent reasons* to act are respected and that professional authority is based on *rational acceptation*. They give up completely the pretence to specify *ex ante* concrete actions or outcomes that the agent in the authority position should pursue or attain, and delimitate the trustor claim to vague and general principles and goals such as that he must pursue the trustor's best interest *loyally*, with *due care,* and in case the trustee has a number of simultaneous trustors, that he act *impartially* among them.[13]

[13] On fiduciary duties in their relation to authority see Flannigan (1989), Easterbrook and Fischel (1993).

5. HOW CONTRACTUAL INCOMPLETENESS IMPACTS ON LAWYERS' CONTINGENT FEES: A 'THOUGHT EXPERIMENT'

The result of the previous section is to characterize the professional relationship as an authority relationship. Therefore, we are moving in the area of contract incompleteness. The scope of this section is to introduce a 'thought experiment' aimed to test what may happen if an inadequate form of regulation were introduced in this area of transactions, with the typical structure of incentive agency contracts (as discussed in Section 2 devoted to lawyers' contingent fees). The experiment I suggest is therefore to simply apply this remuneration scheme in a context of incomplete contracting and then try to predict the consequences. The scope of a 'thought experiment' is not to ascertain the validity of a proposition in general, but just an attempt of falsification. To prove that undesirable effects are derived in a relevant case, which is constructed without restrictive ad hoc hypotheses and is representative of an entire class of relevant real-world situations, is enough to infer that an incentive mechanism may have negative policy consequences. Obviously, we are not confuting agency theory, for the simple reason that the unexpected effects come from a substantive economic reality which is different from the one on which the contingent remuneration scheme would have been correctly designed. From the theoretical point of view, the experiment is simply a 'mistaken' application. But, in order to assess policy implication, we cannot overlook errors that, by superimposing an unsuitable theoretical model to a reality that doesn't satisfy its initial conditions, result in effects that designers themselves did not desire and expect. In fact, the thought experiment deals with a normative mechanism that can be seen as a natural application of those reforming vision of the professions which are based on the dominant paradigm of agency theory applied into the particular legal environment of damages compensation cases.

The problem we are dealing with is well known in literature: after having insured the client against the failure of the case, the professional can have conflicting incentives when choosing which cases to litigate. He will only want to litigate the cases in his client's portfolio with greater expected utility, without bringing the level of respect for legality and client rights enforcement to the social optimum.

However, the aspect I want to focus on is of general interest. If the information in light of which the client and the professional sign *ex ante* the contract is incomplete, the contract wil not discipline all the possible states of the world that could come forth in the course of the case, nor all the possible damage that could be obtained by the lawyer. In this way, the lawyer has a margin of real discretion when he chooses the level of compensation to be claimed for under unforeseen contingents. In fact, in such a situation he can *ex post* decide on the amount when the relevant information has been revealed. This discretion increases the possibility for the lawyer to adjust the damage compensation claimed accordingly with the facts discovered as the case proceeds. The problem is whether this discretion can turn out to benefit the client.

Obviously, in a contractual scheme of pure insurance of the client (where the client definitely 'sells' the case to the lawyer at a certain price and gives up any conditional claim on the outcome), the discovery of unforeseen events, which lead to a higher damage compensation than those *ex ante* foreseeable, would only advantage the lawyer. In fact, he would appropriate the entire surplus deriving from lawyer and client joint action in the new contingencies. Not involving the client in the additional surplus sharing will implicate an additional risk of client's moral hazard (for example, during the trial). The prevalent scheme of contingent fees, it being based on a division of risk between the client and professional, does not run this risk. In fact, in this case the contract would impose that both the client and professional participate in the sharing of each possible *ex post* compensation, setting *ex ante* the percentage claimed by each part.

If the design of the percentage remuneration scheme was explicitly conditional on the concrete description of specific foreseen states of the world, the occurrence of unforeseen events could allow the lawyer to explicitly renegotiate the contract. However, accounting for this possibility would bring us out of the context of incentive contracts, seen as 'complete' contracts (even though with parties asymmetrically informed) set out *ex ante* conditionally upon every possible state of the world. That is, the principal–agent model would be directly put aside in order to permit the situation to be seen through the eyes of an incomplete contract renegotiation model. But my endeavor here is quite different: I want to explore what the effects could be of introducing incompleteness of knowledge in a context (maybe a mistaken contract arrangement) that does not allow in principle room for contract incompleteness.

Hence let us assume first that these contracts cannot be renegotiated, which means that the percentage obtained by the professional cannot deviate from a certain compensation portion whatever the outcome. In any case, the lawyer will only decide to litigate the cases that offer the highest expected utility *ex post*, in light of revealed information (and will litigate at all *ex post* losing cases), but those cases he decides to litigate will be compensated according to the provisos set out in the *ex ante* contract. My point is that such a rigidity in the incentive contract (which does not allow re-contracting *ex post* the client's compensation) is compatible with both the lawyer's self interest – who will decide to litigate only the most profitable cases, and the luckiest client's one – who fortunately *ex post* happens to be in the condition of profiting from *ex ante* unforeseen events. It will, however, result in a distributive inequity towards the unluckiest client, whose cases will be set aside and whose situation will worsen *ex post* due to the discovery of new opportunities. Specifically, in case the lawyer has bonded productive capacity, although he behaves efficiently so to maximize the total amount of damage compensation, this contractual scheme will prevent the lawyer from exercising his discretional power to serve all the clients. In this way, some clients, who had *ex ante* a positive expected compensation, will not be compensated at all for the damage.

6. A CLIENT–LAWYER GAME WHERE CONTINGENT FEES ARE SUCCESSFUL

We will first consider a typical agency problem within the context of complete but asymmetric information, characterized by the adoption of contingent fees. A plaintiff (the Principal) decides to consult the lawyer (Agent) to start off a case for damages against a defendant. In case the lawsuit is effectively brought to court, its result will be influenced by the occurrence of three possible states of the world – all of which the Principal and Agent foresee when signing the contract:

$$\Omega = \{\omega_1, \omega_2, \omega_3\} \tag{11.1}$$

If ω_1 occurs, the case is lost. If ω_2 or ω_3 happen, the case is won. The description of each ω_i includes elements like evidence (more or less certain) regarding the counterpart's responsibility; judge's attitude; defense lawyer's ability, etc. x is the compensation that the Agent is able to obtain, where x depends on the state of the world that will occur as well as on the effort e of the lawyer in litigating the case. Therefore, $x = g(\omega_i, e)$. For each state, the Agent can choose between two effort levels $e=\{e^\circ, e^*\}$, where the cost is $c(e^\circ) = 2.5$, $c(e^*) = 5$ (e^* is a given effort level that is necessary and sufficient for reaching the maximum possible level of compensation in each foreseen state, while e° is an insufficient effort level). So, we can define the possible outcomes

$$\text{If } \omega_1,\ x = 0,\ \forall e_i \in \{e^\circ, e^*\}, \tag{11.2}$$

$$\text{If } \omega_{2}, x = \begin{cases} 5 \text{ if } e^{\circ} \\ 10 \text{ if } e^{*} \end{cases} \tag{11.3}$$

$$\text{If } \omega_{3}, x = \begin{cases} 10 \text{ if } e^{\circ} \\ 20 \text{ if } e^{*} \end{cases} \tag{11.4}$$

Furthermore, there is an exit option for the Agent. Instead of litigating the case, she can settle it, accepting an offer $x_a = 2$ from the defendant. For her this option represents the minimum effort e_a, with a cost $c(e_a) = 1$. We can suppose that, by setting a professional relationship with the lawyer, the client makes a specific investment in collecting and communicating reserved information, without which in the relevant state of the world it would not be possible to obtain the above-mentioned compensation. This is a sunk cost. The Principal undergoes this sunk cost if he enters in the relationship, $k = 1.5$, or he does not undergo it if he does not enter in relationship, $k = 0$. This investment is non-monetary and cannot be insured by the Agent, who instead insures the Principal against the risk of having to pay for the monetary costs of losing the case.

Let us now consider payoff functions (linear in the money for simplicity) of the two players, Principal and Agent

$$U_P = x - f,\ U_A = f - c(e) \tag{11.5}$$

where f is the fee paid to the lawyer.

The hypothesis that the contractual regime is one of contingent fees is introduced in the model by setting $f = 0.5x$. The interaction between Principal and Agent is illustrated by the extensive form game represented in Figure 11.1. In the first move the Principal decides whether to enter (k) or not ($\neg k$) the relationship with the Agent. If he does not enter, the game ends with the payoff (0,0) respectively for the Principal and Agent. If he enters, the Agent decides on her first move between accepting the conciliation proposal (a), which produces a minimum compensation $x_a = 2$, with payoff (0.5,0) due to the Principal's sunk costs, and litigating the case (l). If he decides to litigate, then Nature will select one of three possible states of the world {ω1, ω2, ω3}.

Anyway, the agent must choose the effort level (e° or e^{*}) that she will devote to the case, before knowing in which sub-tree she will act because of the state of the world chosen by Nature (in the information context outlined).

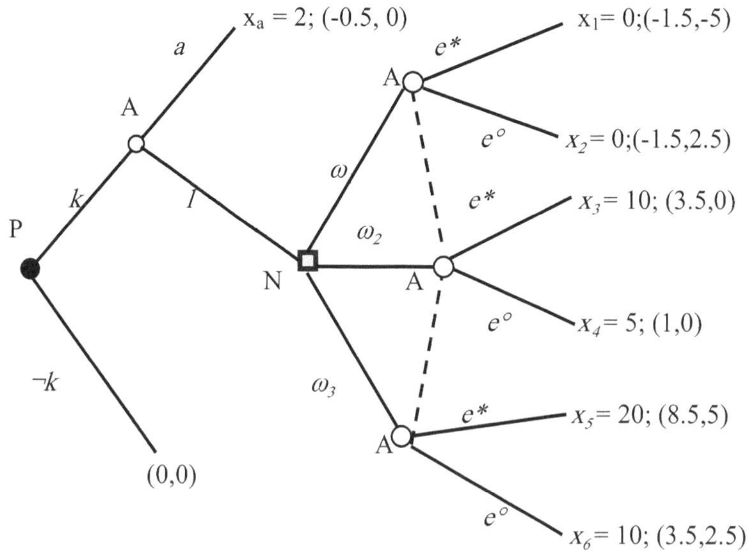

Figure 11.1 Ex ante game

At the end-edges of the game tree, we can see various possible compensations $\{x_1, x_2, x_3\ x_4, x_5, x_6\}$ and within bracket the associated payoffs respectively for the Principal and Agent, calculated under the hypothesis that the conditional contract – which fixes $f = 0.5x$ – is in force between the Principal and Agent, in accordance with the functional form of the payoffs defined above (from which for the Principal the cost of entrance k is subtracted). I assume that the probability distribution of the states of the world is $p = \{0.2, 0.4, 0.4\}$, and both players know it.

Clearly, in this game there is a moral hazard problem: the Agent has private information about her own action (the choice of effort in litigating the lawsuit), which she must nonetheless choose on the basis of her expected utility for each effort level, given the distribution of probability of states of the world (she is therefore uncertain about what state of the world will occur). Besides the state of the world occurrence, the Principal is unsure about the effort level chosen by the Agent. Under the hypothesis that the Agent decided to litigate the case, the Principal is not able to deterministically infer the Agent's effort level just by observing outcomes. In particular, neither from the compensation $x_1 = 0$ nor from the compensation $x_3 = x_5 = 10$ can he deduce if e° or e^*. Special attention should be given to the Agent's first move of whether to conciliate or not: in this case the client knows perfectly the professional's effort level. In any way, the payoff structure is not conditional upon effort and therefore the fact that the Agent's effort here is minimal does not implicate any sanction. Conciliating the cause is one of the lawyer's possible decisions within the legitimate discretion of the professional in the management of the case, admitted that expected utility from the lawsuit is less than the reciprocal advantage of a settlement (however, the Agent's payoff net of effort is zero). Imperfect information, introduced by the choice of nature (N) in the game, enables us to represent the asymmetric information between the Principal and the Agent.

Remember that payoffs in this game are assigned in accordance with the contingent remuneration scheme. In order that the contingent remuneration scheme constitutes an efficient incentive mechanism against the Agent's moral hazard (which means that this scheme is able to induce the Agent to choose a high effort level), the following Agent's incentives compatibility condition must be respected

$$f(x_5|\omega_3, e^*) - c(e^*) \geq f(x_3|\omega_2, e^*) - c(e^*) \tag{11.6}$$

otherwise, given the impossibility to distinguish between the results x_3 and x_6, in the state of the world ω_3, the Agent would have incentive to say that the state was ω_2 and apply the effort $e°$, obtaining the payoff

$$f(x_3|\omega_2, e^*) - c(e°) \tag{11.7}$$

by which she will get the rent $\Delta = c(e^*) - c(e°)$.

With a simple payoffs inspection it is possible to verify if such a condition is met. In order to calculate the equilibrium solution of this game under the incentive remuneration scheme, we should first consider Agent's expected payoffs resulting from her three possible strategies {(l, e*), (l, e°), (a, e_a)}, given the Principal's choice to enter k, under the probability distribution p on the possible states of the world $\omega_i \in \Omega = \{\omega_1, \omega_2, \omega_3\}$

$$EU_A(k; p; l, e^*) = \Sigma_i p_i U_A(k,l,e^*|\omega_i) = 1 \tag{11.8}$$

$$EU_A(k; p; l, e°) - \Sigma_i p_i U_A(k,l,e°|\omega_i) = 0.5 \tag{11.9}$$

$$EU_A(k; p; a, e_a) = \Sigma_i p_i U_A(k,a,e_a|\omega_i) = 0 \tag{11.10}$$

Second, consider the Principal's expected payoffs for the different possible strategy-combinations:

$$EU_P(k; p; l, e^*) = \Sigma_i p_i U_P(k,l,e^*|\omega_i) = 4.5 \tag{11.11}$$

$$EU_P\,(k;\,p;\,l,\,e^{\circ}) = \Sigma_i\, p_i U_P\,(k,l,e^{\circ}|\omega_i) = 1.5 \tag{11.12}$$

$$EU_P\,(k;\,p;\,a,\,e_a) = \Sigma_i\, p_i U_P(k,a,e_a|\omega_i) = -\,0.5 \tag{11.13}$$

$$EU_P\,(\neg k;\,p;\,a,\,e_a) = \Sigma_i\, p_i U_P(\neg k,a,e_a|\,\omega_i) = 0 \tag{11.14}$$

$$EU_P\,(\neg k;\,p;\,l,\,e^{\circ}) = 0 \tag{11.15}$$

$$EU_P\,(\neg k;\,p;\,l,\,e^*) = 0 \tag{11.16}$$

The solution is a Nash equilibrium in dominant strategies ($k;\,p;\,l,\,e^*$) such that the Principal enters and the Agent responds by choosing to litigate the case and to pursue it with high effort. Hence, in this simplified case the contingent fees scheme – which is provided through the payoff functions – gives the Agent proper incentive to act in equilibrium according to the Principal's interests: the damage compensation is at a social optimum, even though the Agent gets some rent.

7. IMPOSSIBILITY OF THE FIDUCIARY RELATIONSHIP UNDER A PRINCIPAL–AGENT MODEL OF THE PROFESSIONAL'S REMUNERATION

Let us now introduce the typical hypotheses of the critical thought experiment.

7.1 Not Just Asymmetric but also Incomplete Information

The game must now be seen under a situation of *incomplete information*: states of the world *ex ante* foreseen by the players do not exhaust all the possible situations that effectively may occur once the relationship is established through the Principal's entrance (k). After the Principal's entrance, the Agent understands that there is a further possible state of the world. In fact, she receives information about the fact that an alternative state of the world ω_4 involves a result different from those she had generally considered until that moment. Other than incomplete, the information is asymmetric in the sense that only the Agent learns of this opportunity, whereas the Principal continues to perceive the situation as it was *ex ante*. In substance, the incomplete and asymmetric nature of information can be expressed by this statement: *ex ante* (before the Principal entered) both see the game as represented in Figure 11.1; but, *ex post*, after the Principal has entered, the Agent and not the Principal sees the game as represented in

Figure 11.2. The peculiarity of the state of the world ω_4 is that it reveals the possibility of a compensation $x_{10} = 42$ as a consequence of an exceptional effort e^{**} made by the Agent with a cost $c(e^{**}) = 8$. *Ex ante* this effort level was not accounted for as it was not seen as necessary to obtain any available damage compensations under the possible states of the world. This can be considered, for example, the result of a preliminary investigation started off by the Agent, who discovers relevant facts about the counterpart (for example, evidence that was not known by the client at first on the hazardous conduct of the counterpart who caused the damage, or the judge's particular orientation in previous similar cases). The set of the *ex post* possible states for A is now expressed by:

$$\Omega_{A\ ex\ post} = \{\omega_1, \omega_2, \omega_3, \omega_4\} \tag{11.17}$$

With a probability distribution $p_{A\ ex\ post} = \{0.1, 0.2, 0.2, 0.5\}$

The principal is not able to learn about the existence of such a possibility unless it is not signaled by the Agent through the related behavior which results in the outcome x_{10}.

Only in this case the Principal realizes (as the Agent does) that at the end-edges of the game tree there is the extended set of the possible compensations $\{x_1, x_2, x_3, x_4, x_5, x_6, x_7, x_8, x_9, x_{10}, x_{11}, x_{12}\}$, and within bracket the associated additional payoffs respectively for the Principal and Agent, calculated under the previous hypothesis about the contingent fee contract (see Figure 11.2).

7.2 Trade-off Among Simultaneous Legal Cases

The Agent is involved in two simultaneous contractual relationships with two different Principals, P1 and P2. She therefore has two analogous cases C1 and C2 in her portfolio. In both cases, the information for the two parties is perceived as incomplete, but *ex post* only in C1 does the Agent learn that there is the possibility of an additional *ex ante* unknown state of the world ω_4, which implies the possibility of a compensation exceptionally high conditioned upon an exceptionally high effort e^{**}. Therefore, in the Agent's eye the two cases are different *ex post*: C1 appears as the game in Figure 11.2, while C2 remains in the configuration in Figure 11.1. The two principals P1 and P2 still continue to see the cases as represented in Figure 11.1, unless the Agent signals the existence of an additional state of the world by reaching compensation $x_{10} = 42$.

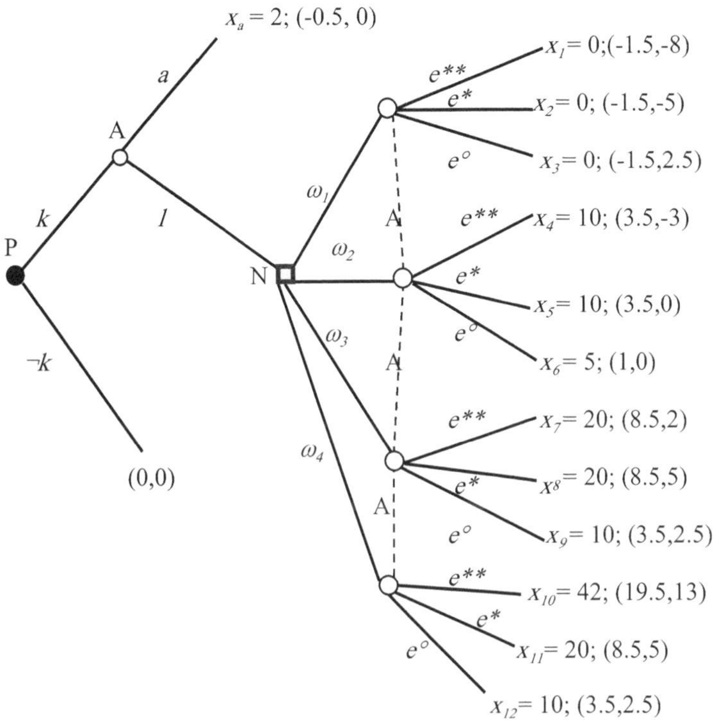

Figure 11.2 Ex post game

7.3 Bounded Effort Capability

A further relevant assumption is that the Agent's effort and productive capability is bounded from above by the maximal effort that she may put in litigating the two cases altogether. For instance

$$c_{max}(e) = 10 \tag{11.18}$$

Consequently, if she decides to litigate both cases, then she is not able to employ the required effort e^{**}, which costs $c(e^{**}) = 8$. She could litigate a case with the highest required effort only if she decided to accept to conciliate one of the two cases. In fact, $c(e^{**}) + c(e_a) = 9 < c_{max}(e)$. But on the contrary $c(e^{**}) + c(e^{*}) = 13 > c_{max}(e)$, $c(e^{**}) + c(e^{\circ}) = 10.5 > c_{max}(e)$. So, while the occurrence of an unforeseen state improves P1's prospects, at the same time P2's prospects are not unchanged, but rather they worsen because it is not given that the Agent can litigate both cases if she takes advantage of the occasion in C1.

The fact that the contract is incomplete means that the Agent is not bound by any clause to litigate each case at any level of predefined effort. She could also not litigate either and settle both. The contingent fee contract does not state *what* conduct the Agent should comply with – not even in terms of a general criteria – but rather just a payoff structure, such to indirectly induce the Agent's conduct. Since it is the lawyer who signals what events become possible as an effect of the learning process within the game, the client learns the unforeseen states of the world only due to the lawyer's behavior. Therefore, the client is not able to discern between *ex ante* unforeseen states of the world if not in the *ex post* perspective, i.e. after the Agent's choice. Whether the incentive structure of contingent fees is able to induce efficient behavior and to align the Agent's behavior with the two principals' objectives must be ascertained.

Hence it is necessary to calculate what the lawyer's best response would be in the two situations C1 and C2. To this end, I will first calculate her expected *payoff* in each case, for each strategy, and then the combined *payoff* of the two cases. I will identify the Agent's payoff function in the *ex post* perspective with $U^t_A(\cdot)$.

In case C1 the Agent's expected *payoff* for the four *ex post* possible strategies, given the new probability distribution $p_{A\ ex\ post}$ on the states of the world $\Omega_{A\ ex\ post} = \{\omega_1, \omega_2, \omega_3, \omega_4\}$, are

$$EU^t_A\,(k;\, p_{A\ ex\ post};\, l,\, e^{**}) = \Sigma_i\, p_i U^t_A(k.l, e^{**}|\omega_i) = 5.5 \quad (11.19)$$

$$EU^t_A(k;\, p_{A\ ex\ post};\, l,\, e^{*}) = \Sigma_i\, p_i U^t_A(k.l, e^{*}|\omega_i) = 3 \quad (11.20)$$

$$EU^t_A(k;\, p_{A\ ex\ post};\, l,\, e^{\circ}) = \Sigma_i\, p_i U^t_A(k.l, e^{\circ}|\omega_i) = 1.25 \quad (11.21)$$

$$EU^t_A(k;\, p_{A\ ex\ post};\, a,\, e_a) = \Sigma_i\, p_i U^t_A(k.;a, e_a|\omega_i) = 0 \quad (11.22)$$

In case C2 the expected *ex post payoff* remain unchanged given the distribution p on the set of possible *ex ante* states $\Omega = \{\omega_1, \omega_2, \omega_3\}$, thus $EU^t_A = EU_A$ (see sec.6).

The overall A's expected payoff of choosing the strategy l in the case C1 with the level of effort e^{**}, and at the same time choosing the strategy a in the case C2 is

$$EU^t_A\,[(k;\, p_{A\ ex\ post};\, l,\, e^{**}|C1);\, (k;\, p\,;\, a,\, e_a\,|C2)] = 5.5 \quad (11.23)$$

while A's expected payoff of litigating both cases with a level of effort e^* is

$$EU^{t}_{A}\,[(k;\, p_{A\ ex\ post};\, l,\, e^{*}|C1);\, (k;\, p;\, a,\, e^{*}|C2)] = 4 \qquad (11.24)$$

As a result, *once the two clients P1 and P2 have entered into a professional relationship paying the cost k, the Agent's best response in the two linked games is to litigate (strategy l, e**) the case C1 and conciliate (strategy a,* e_a*) the case C2.*

To the end of calculating the equilibrium strategies of the game, what counts is the state of information that the principals P1 and P2 have at the moment that they must choose their strategy. Before the Agent's move they see the game as in Figure 11.1. In particular with reference to P2, before the specific investment *k* has been undertaken, he predicts having an expected *payoff* of 4.5 which is enough to convince him to invest in the case. Given the representation of the problem *ex ante*, they are led to select *k* in both of the cases. Compounding players' P1, P2 and the Agent's best responses, the ensuing equilibrium under imperfect and asymmetric information is:

(a) *ex ante P1 and P2 invest k and enter both cases C1 and C2;*
(b) *in the ex post perspective, Agent chooses (l, e**) in case C1 and (a) in case C2.*

Nevertheless, in the counterfactual reconstruction that the clients P1 and P2 may carry out in light of the information revealed by the Agent's conduct, this combination of strategies doesn't coincide with what would have been chosen by players if the information at their disposition had immediately been what they learned at the end of the game.

In fact, let us consider the *ex post* expected utility of the damage compensation level for the two principals. By '*ex post*' it is intended the principal P1's expected payoff after she is informed by the Agent about the existence of possibility ω_4. While the principal P2, who faces the same game *ex ante* as well as *ex post*, has the same range of expected payoffs as in the previous example – not including ω_4, the P1's expected payoffs are *ex post* affected by the possibility of the new state. Conditional on the Agent's various strategies, they are represented as follow:

$$EU^{t}_{P1}(k;\, p_{A\ ex\ post};\, l,\, e^{**}) = \Sigma_i p_i U_{P1}(k,l,e^{*}|\omega_i) = 10.55 \qquad (11.25)$$

$$EU^{t}_{P1}(k;\, p_{A\ ex\ post};\, l,\, e^{*}) = \Sigma_i p_i U_{P1}(k,l,e^{*}|\omega_i) = 6.5 \qquad (11.26)$$

$$EU^{t}_{P1}(k;\, p_{A\ ex\ post};\, l,\, e^{\circ}) = \Sigma_i p_i U_{P1}(k,l,e^{\circ}|\omega_i) = 2.3 \qquad (11.27)$$

$$EU^{t}_{P1}(k;\, p_{A\ ex\ post};\, a,\, e_a) = \Sigma_i p_i U_{P1}(k,a,e_a|\omega_i) = -0.5 \qquad (11.28)$$

P2's *ex post* expected payoffs conditional on the Agent's various possible strategies are the same as the case analyzed in the previous section (see Figure 11.1).

If principal P2 reconstructs his expected payoff under the hypothesis of the Agent's rational strategy choice, then he would realize that *ex post* he can only gain an expected *payoff* of –0.5. Consequently, his perspective is radically changed when compared to the moment in which he entered, only due to the muted situation of case C1 although the structure of the game that represents the case he is interested in remained unchanged from the passage of the *ex ante* to *ex post* perspective. Before the specific investment *k*, after analyzing the expected result of both the games, he predicted having an expected *payoff* of 4.5 which was enough to make him invest in the case. Nevertheless, after the communication of the new possible states of the world transmitted by the Agent's choice, he realizes – once he is locked-in – that he cannot get back his initial sunk investment. Thus, if he had been able to anticipate this change deriving from the linkage of the two cases C1 and C2, the principal P2 wouldn't have entered into a professional relationship with the Agent. I summarize this point by saying that principal P2 *regrets* his *ex ante* decision.

How serious is this fact according to a social welfare point of view? Let us now calculate the total expected payoff jointly gained by the two clients under any possible strategy chosen by the Agent. Under the Agent's strategy $(l, e^{**}|C1;\ a|C2)$ the clients' joint expected compensation for damages is:

$$EU^{t}_{P1}(k;\ p_{A\ ex\ post};\ l,\ e^{**}) + EU_{P2}(k;\ p;\ a,\ e_{a}) = 10.55 - 0.5 = 10.05 \qquad (11.29)$$

whereas, under the strategy $(l,\ e^{*}\ |C1, C2)$ it is instead:

$$EU^{t}_{P1}(k;\ p_{A\ ex\ post};\ l,\ e^{*}) + EU_{P2}(k;\ p;\ l,\ e^{*}) = 6.5 + 4.5 = 11 \qquad (11.30)$$

Therefore, the two principals' joint utility for their expected total compensation is greater if the Agent chooses (l, e^{*}) in both cases than if she chooses (l, e^{**}) in C1 and (a) in C2, as will happen nevertheless under the predicted equilibrium point.

Let us observe that this assessment of the joint prospect of the two clients implies that some observers (or clients themselves) are able to compare their utility numbers and summate them, i.e. this reflects a utilitarian view on social welfare based on the clients' interpersonally comparable utilities. This preludes to asking the question: what are the *ex post* global efficiency properties resulting from the Agent's best response? In other words, does the Agent act so as to maximize the social welfare *ex post*? If the relevant standpoint for evaluating social welfare were the clients' aggregate utility, the answer would be clearly *not*. From the *ex post* perspective the equilibrium solution not only implies that P2 regrets his decision, but also that the equilibrium doesn't maximize the clients' joint payoff. This is also the answer to the question 'is the professional complying with her fiduciary obligation to maximize the wellbeing of her clients (in utilitarian sense)'?

However, there is a different standpoint wherefrom social welfare may be assessed, which includes also the professional – and of course goes beyond the idea of a utilitarian fiduciary obligation to maximize the joint wellbeing of the clients. It is simply maximizing the aggregate welfare of all the parties involved in a decision, disregarding their social or personal position (i.e. their identity as professionals or clients). In order to calculate this, we simply have to consider the sum of the two principals', P1 and P2, expected utilities and that of the Agent. Under the Agent's best strategy, social welfare is:

$$\begin{aligned} W^* = {} & EU^t_A[(k; p_{A\ ex\ post}; l, e^{**}|C1); (k; p; a, e_a|C2)] \\ & + EU^t_{P1}(k; p_{A\ ex\ post}; l, e^{**}) \\ & + EU^t_{P2}(k; p; a, e_a) = 15.55 \end{aligned} \tag{11.31}$$

Otherwise, under the linked Agent's strategies (l, e^*), social welfare is:

$$\begin{aligned} W^{**} = {} & EU^t_A[(k; p_{A\ ex\ post}; l, e^*|C1); (k; p; a, e^*|C2)] \\ & + EU^t_{P1}(k; p_{A\ ex\ post}; l, e^*) \\ & + EU^t_{P2}(k; p; l, e^*) = 15 \end{aligned} \tag{11.32}$$

Thus, the Agent's equilibrium choice is – in utilitarian sense – efficient *ex post*.

Summing up, two hard *social justice and welfare* problems arise:

(a) there is a distributive iniquity concerning the treatment of the two principals P1 and P2, such that P2 *ex post* can only regret having entered into a relationship with the Agent – i.e. P2 complains about *unfairness* of his treatment because of the preference accorded to client P1's interests. He also complains about *disloyalty* in the Agent's conduct, and as far as it amounts to subtracting expected effort from litigating a case, he also complains about a lack of *due care*.

(b) In case the professional is seen as constrained by a utilitarian obligation to maximize her clients' joint wellbeing, her equilibrium behaviour violates this fiduciary obligation. To say this differently, if social

> welfare is attached just to the effects of the lawyer's action on the enforcement level of the clients' legal rights, then the Agent's equilibrium behaviour in the context of incomplete information makes the level of rights enforcement *suboptimal in a utilitarian sense.* It also leaves a Principal completely unsatisfied – i.e. passing to this solution would not be a *Pareto* improvement, because the solution is not unanimous among the rights holders. This is not to say that the alternative solution would be Paretian per se (in fact principal P1 does prefer the Agent's equilibrium choice). But considering that to the second solution (see 11.30) is attached a higher utilitarian social welfare value, one would say that there is room for an accommodation (in terms of Kaldor–Hicks efficiency) able also to gain P1's acceptance of the second solution, which is not available to the first (see 11.29) (as far as only the two principals payoffs are concerned).

Nevertheless, the Agent's individually rational conduct *ex post*, leading to a game equilibrium given the rational *ex ante* actions of principals P1 and P2, is efficient in a more general utilitarian sense, for it maximizes the sum of all the players' utilities. We see this social efficiency in a utilitarian sense (using the hypothesis of interpersonal utility comparability) from the fact that the Agent and principal P1 in the new context obtain jointly an additional rent such to earn more than what principal P2 loses.

The conclusion concerning contingent fees is mixed: it fails the basic requirements of clients' Pareto optimal treatment, equality of treatment and the obligation to the clients' wellbeing. But giving up equality and unanimity, it exploits the opportunity of litigating a case with the best effort e^{**} that allows reaching maximum utilitarian efficiency, a goal that any wise design of an institutional rule should also account for. A typical trade-off between fairness (deontology) and social efficiency (welfarism) seems to ensue.

8. IMPOSSIBILITY OF THE 'CHARITABLE PROFESSIONAL'

It is quite immediate to recognize the solution the lawyer could devise to the forgoing dilemma in order to regain fairness, Pareto dominance and the commitment to clients' overall wellbeing, and at the same time preserving efficiency and rationality in her behavior. She could redress client P2 with a side utility payment to be added to client P2's expected *payoff* coming from the Agent's choice a of not litigating the case C2. Such integration would make the client P2 indifferent between the prospect that the Agent puts *effort* e^* into her lawsuit case and the prospect that she conciliates the same case. To this end, the lawyer could rely on her own *payoff* gained from the choice to litigate the case C1 with effort e^{**} if it is great enough. Hence, I call this conduct the *charitable professional solution.*

Because in order to make simpler utility comparisons I here assume that the lawyer and the clients are both neutral to risk, a side payment equal to 5 would leave client P2 in a state of indifference compared to what he had figured out in the moment in which he decided to enter into a relationship with the lawyer. The necessary condition is, however, one of the Agent's *individually rational participation:*

$$EU^t_A\,[(k;\, p_{A\ ex\ post};\, l,\, e^{**}|C1);\, (k;\, p\,;\, a,\, e_a|C2)] - T \\ \geq \\ EU^t_A\,[(k;\, p_{A\ ex\ post};\, l,\, e^*|C1);\, (k;\, p;\, l,\, e^*|C2)] \qquad (11.33)$$

where T is the utility side payment that is transferred from the Agent to the principal P2 and makes the latter indifferent. In fact, the Agent's utility level when she litigates both the trial with effort e^* is the one under which the Agent cannot go without losing incentive to choose the strategy $[(l, e^{**}|C1), (a|C2)]$. Hence, it is necessary that the additional rent the Agent earns conciliating C2 and litigating C1 with maximal effort is not less than what makes P2 indifferent

$$\Delta_{P2} \leq \Delta_A \qquad (11.34)$$

where

$$\Delta_{P2} = [EU_{P2}(k;\, p;\, l,\, e^*) - EU^t_{P2}\,(k;\, p;\, a,\, e_a)] \qquad (11.35)$$

and

$$\Delta_A = \{EU^t_A\,[(k;\, p_{A\ ex\ post};\, l,\, e^{**}|C1);\, (k;\, p\,;\, a, e_a|C2)] \\ - EU^t_A\,[(k;\, p_{A\ ex\ post};\, l,\, e^*|C1);\, (k;\, p;\, l,\, e^*|C2)]\} \qquad (11.36)$$

A simple payoffs review demonstrates that the condition is not satisfied in our context. In fact the Agent, under her best response strategy, obtains expected payoff 5.5. Instead, by adopting the alternative strategy $(l, e^*|C1, C2)$, the Agent could secure himself an expected payoff of 4, which means that the Agent has no more than 1.5 *utils* at her disposal to redress client P2. But the side utility payment that would leave P2 indifferent on the contrary is 5, which would reduce the Agent to an expected payoff of 0.5, and violates her participation condition.

As a consequence, the structure of the contingent contract doesn't allow the Agent the personal arrangement that I called the 'charitable solution', consisting of a side payment taken from her own fee to redress the client P2 from the Agent's choice to coalesce with principal P1 at the expense of P2. The structure of the lawyer's contingent remuneration therefore makes the lawyer's deontological conduct incompatible with her basic incentives, even when the latter had the willingness to constrain the maximization of her own expected utility by the commitment of not damaging client P2 with respect to his initial expectations, treating both clients fairly and maximizing their joint payoff.

If, therefore, the lawyer felt *obliged* for deontological reasons to pursue the interests of both clients equally, then she could only choose the inefficient strategy $(l, e^*|C1, C2)$, that doesn't allow her to take advantage of the disclosed opportunity thanks to learning *ex post* about the possible new state of the world. Let us call this Agent's conduct the *inefficient–egalitarian professional solution*.

Hence, when the Agent's deontological constraint is strong enough, we have an egalitarian but inefficient implementation of the contingent fees mechanism, because the individual rationality participation condition isn't consistent with the efficient allocation of the Agent's effort. But not litigating with effort e^{**} case C1, as far as it treats equally the two clients, may also be seen as a violation of the duty of *due care* toward client P1, who legitimately *ex post* claims to be redressed by a damage compensation proportional to the prospects of his individual case. In other words. the Agent does not serve the best interest of principal P1.

Thus contingent fees, *(i) under the constraint of equality of clients' treatment, implies an infringement of a deontological obligation toward principal P1, (ii) whereas, under the assumption of self-interested personal utility maximisation, it leads to an infringement toward the principal P2* (a harder violation indeed, as it was associated with a betrayal of the initial expectation the principal had when he entered the contract and the generation of a sharp distributive inequality), *which amounted to acting both unfairly and in conflict of interests*.

Efficiency and impartial respect of legal rights in this context come into conflict due to the contractual incentive structure wherein the Agent operates. As a consequence, to treat the client–professional relationship as an agency problem through an incentive contract leads to a professional's disloyalty (which is the legal equivalent to 'moral hazard') toward at least one of her clients, and/or to the violation of social efficiency (in utilitarian sense). A result that may be included in the growing literature on the perverse effects of incentive contracts (see for example Frey 1997, Fehr, Klein and Schmidt 2001, Fehr and Gächter 2002).

To be sure, deontological behavior in our context doesn't amount to pure altruism.

Deontology is seen as the result of a fair (even though hypothetical) agreement amongst the clients and the lawyer, whereby the lawyer commits herself to treat them equally, without discrimination, and fairly with respect to their initial understanding of the scope of professional services, but on the other hand the lawyer grants herself a claim to earn a higher income for higher effort.[14]

9. POOLING DAMAGE COMPENSATIONS IN ORDER TO MAXIMIZE OVERALL WELL-BEING AND GUARANTEEING FAIR TREATMENT TO ALL THE CLIENTS

Does an alternative contractual arrangement exist where, if the Agent's behavior were driven by fiduciary obligations to her clients, this behavioral drive could manifest its positive effects? In other terms, does an institutional arrangement of the lawyer–client relationship exist such as to allow using incomplete contract flexibility in order to exploit the opportunity represented by the state ω_4 in the mutual advantage of the Agent and the two principals P1 and P2?

Consider that if the Agent operated for a single Principal in two linked cases like C1 and C2, then the latter could be redressed for the lawsuit conciliated by the additional rent accruing to her from the possibility of winning case C1 in the unforeseen state. Assume that in order to redress the gain lost in the second case C2 the damage compensation from case C1 can be involved. Then the conditions for the Principal's acceptance of conciliating the case C2 are guaranteed by the fact that, under the obvious hypothesis of intrapersonal comparable utilities, the client gets more from case C1 than he loses in C2. Under the more demanding hypothesis of interpersonal utility comparability, we can try to transfer this reasoning to the side payment between Principals P1 and P2. In this case, the Agent can use the total damage compensation obtained from all the litigated and not litigated cases to generate all the clients' payoffs. This means that she can use the compensations obtained in case C1, litigated on behalf of client P1, to redress client P2 for the lack of compensation in case C2. Resorting to total

[14] For a wider discussion of professional ethics and also the lawyers deontological codes see Bayles (1981), Dietrich and Roberts (1997), Dzienkowski (1996), Koehn (1994).

compensation allows then a side payment which makes P2 indifferent between litigating or not case C2 – taking as reference point what principal P2 would have expected from litigating his case with *effort* e^* –, and at the same time to satisfy the Agent's participation condition. This amounts to requiring:

$$\Delta_{P2} \leq \Delta_{A+P1} \tag{11.37}$$

where

$$\Delta_{P2} = [EU_{P2}(k; p; l, e^*) - EU^{t}_{P2}(k; p; a, e_a)] \tag{11.38}$$

and

$$\begin{aligned}\Delta_{A+P1} = \{&EU^{t}_{A}[(k; p_{A\ ex\ post}; l, e^{**}|C1);(k; p; a, e_a|C2)] \\ &+ EU^{t}_{P1}(k; p_{A\ ex\ post}; l, e^{**})\} \\ - \{&EU^{t}_{A}[(k; p_{A\ ex\ post}; l, e^*|C1); (k; p; l, e^*|C2)] \\ &+ EU^{t}_{P1}(k; p_{A\ ex\ post}; l, e^*)\}\end{aligned} \tag{11.39}$$

which is obviously satisfied. Let's call this conduct the *ethically responsible professional* solution.

This solution is made difficult, however, by the fact that the lawyer should be able to decide how to distribute *ex post* the compensation among himself, the client P1 and the client P2 as well. But *this is not allowed by the contingent contract structure*, according to which the more 'lucky' client has a right to a prefixed percentage of the damage compensation obtained in his case independently of the outcome. If, on the contrary, the lawyer had formal authority in the *ex post* decision about the division of total damage compensation between clients, she could make some redress across them. This implies that the lawyer manages the damages compensation for different lawsuits like a trustee of a mutual fund, to which the clients confer the cases. She exercises all the decisional rights concerned with her position of authority, but she acts in favor of the clients as beneficiaries, to whom in a successful case she pays no less compensation than the expectations they had before entering into the fiduciary relationship, plus a rent depending on the profitability of their case.

In a nutshell, exercising deontology requires more discretion than the contingent contract allows, because the latter does not allow *cross-subsidization* between clients and cases. Still, the professional's higher discretion requires *ex post accountability* in terms of the professional's compliance with deontology obligations to act loyally and impartially towards both clients. The scheme of the proposed solution in fact is the following:

a. A fiduciary relationship with an obligation owed to each client of pursuing her best interest is set, which is constrained by symmetric obligations owed to third parties, other clients included, requiring the Agent to grant fair and impartial treatment of all clients;
b. the lawyer is allowed to settle *ex post* the amount of damage compensation due to clients and her *own fee*, under the constraint that these decisions have to satisfy loyalty and fairness obligations owed to all clients;
c. the lawyer conciliates the less advantageous case and obtains the maximum compensation from C1;
d. the lawyer redresses client P2 by a side payment taken away from the compensation of case C1, in such a way to grant him a payoff equal to $EU_{P2}(k; p; l, e^*)$. On the remaining compensation a proportional fee will be applied according to the existing arrangement among the parties.

That is equivalent for the lawyer to have the authority to bargain *ex post* the fee with the 'lucky' client in such a way to have at her disposal enough resources to redress the 'unlucky' client. Given that the lawyer acts with respect for the deontological obligations, this would allow her to respect fairly the claims of the 'lucky' client as well. A logical reference point for fairly adjudicating these diverse claims is the *ex ante* hypothetical contract in which the professional would have committed herself to all clients with the obligation of pursuing their interests according to the reasonable expectations that have led them to enter into the relationship with the professional. If *ex post* unforeseen events show up causing a potential welfare surplus, such opportunities can be utilized only under the condition that their exploitation could have been agreed upon also in the *ex ante* perspective. This means that these opportunities do not cause detriment to any of the parties. It is reasonable that in the *ex ante* perspective, in case it were predicted that there was such a large profit in C1 to suggest conciliating the case C2, the client P2 would have consented to this course of action. In fact, it was mutually advantageous for all the clients, himself included. A redress such that the client P2 becomes indifferent between litigating or conciliating his own case, defines the condition for him to accept such an eventuality.

According to this model, remunerations of the professional and the clients are understood as the result of a three players cooperative game for their mutual advantage. It is quite obvious that the Agent carrying out effort e^{**} must be paid a payoff that is not less than when she carries out effort e^*. At the same time it must be recognized that the client P1's case C1 is what allows maximizing the aggregate compensation, which amounts to saying that player P1 contributes the opportunity ω_4 to the cooperative surplus. Hence, quite naturally player P1 claims most of the surplus associated with the possible state ω_4 with respect to the baseline compensation obtainable in the alternative less profitable states. But player P2 seems to have a veto right. The *ex ante* contract obliged the lawyer to litigate both cases in order to grant each client *i* at least the expected payoff $EU_{Pi}(k; p; l, e^*)$. Thus he must permit the lawyer to put aside case C2 in order to be able to litigate case C1 with the highest effort, and he will afford such a permission only when this will grant him at least the *a priori* expected payoff.

10. CONCLUSION

Let us conclude with some remarks on what has been shown so far. As far as the arrangement of the professional's remuneration (put forward in the last section) is concerned, everything depends on whether the conduct complying with fiduciary obligations is performed in equilibrium. It is obvious that whenever this condition is not met and if we do not have any explanation for the rationality of respecting an obligation such as 'maximize impartially all the clients' interests under the constraint of respecting the professional's participation condition', then the contractual arrangement with higher professional's discretion would involve a greater space for the Agent's abuse of her authority. The professional could try to completely appropriate the surplus associated with the new opportunity revealed by the state of the world ω_4, leaving the client P1 barely with what she expected at the moment she entered into the professional relationship and at the same time without *ex post* redressing the client P2. In fact, the client P1 would receive a damage compensation identical to what he would receive if his case had the structure of a game like that shown in Figure 11.1, so that his payoff wouldn't reveal to himself and the client P2 the existence of an opportunity like ω_4.

Therefore, in order to sustain a professional authority relationship, the hypotheses about conformist preferences for deontology are crucial. A fully fledged modeling of conformist preferences of the professional community, as well as the single professional, is beyond the scope of this chapter.[15] However it would show the following. Granted indifference with the material payoff, that the Agent gets by carrying out effort e^*; she has a

[15] Nevertheless see Grimalda and Sacconi 2005, Sacconi and Grimalda 2007 for the analogy with the non-profit organization and Sacconi (2006) for the analogy with CSR self-regulation.

positive psychological incentive to implement cross-redressing between the clients. Moreover, the professional would also be ready to give up part of her material surplus in order to make room for a fair redress of the 'unlucky' client. The necessary condition for the existence of such a *psychological Nash equilibrium* (for general reference see Genakopulos et al. 1989, Rabin 1993) would be that the renouncement in terms of material payoff is not too high with respect to the gain in term of psychological utility, which ensues from the conformity to a deontological code as far as it is believed to be complied with by the whole profession.

It should be admitted that considering professional ethics just as ineffective 'cheap talk' and mere 'window dressing', without any relation to the reasons for clients to accept the profession's authority, is quite an unrealistic explanation of a phenomenon lasting from the very beginning of the professions as social institutions. A more realistic approach is to maintain that professionals' conduct adheres to the general hypothesis of motivational complexity. According to this hypothesis, to some extent self-interest is paired off with a disposition to conform deontological obligations owed to clients, as far as these are agreed upon and accepted by the professional community and there are shared expectations of their observance on the part of the other members of the profession.

Institutions and contractual arrangements, however, matter in fostering or depressing these alterative motivations. The main conclusion I have reached in this chapter in fact is that as long as the ongoing contractual structure asks for professionals' remuneration contingent upon outcomes, professional deontology cannot show any effectiveness in directing the professionals' conduct.

In the first case (Section 7), given the agent's participation condition and self-interested maximization of the Agent's payoff, we are led to violate fairness of treatment, loyalty toward client P2 and the fiduciary commitment to improve both clients' wellbeing. In the second case (Section 8), admitting just a minimal condition of individual rationality as a participation condition, not only utilitarian efficiency is violated but also the right of the client P1 to a diligent treatment of his case.

In the third case (Section 9), an institutional and contractual mechanism, allowing for more discretion but also for compliance with all fiduciary duties, is presented. It is consistent with the hypothesis that the professional is motivated by conformist preferences for reciprocal compliance with fiduciary obligations. But the arrangement under which (admitted conformist preferences) all the deontological tenets are satisfied – i.e. *equality* and *impartiality* of treatment for all the clients, *loyalty* and *due care* in discharging professional obligations owed to each client – reaches this goal simply by violating the requests inherent in the contingent fees mechanism.

In fact, this mechanism does not permit pooling *ex post* the damage compensations gained by litigating distinct cases belonging to different clients, and distributing them according to a fairness criterion.

Hence contingent fees make its behavioral hypotheses about the prevailing selfishness of professionals a self-fulfilling prophecy. Starting from this assumption, and by institutionalizing contingent fees as a remuneration scheme for professional services, what is obtained is necessarily the same as the premise. In equilibrium any conduct conforming effectively to a professional obligation of impartial and loyal pursuing of the best interests of all her clients cannot be observed.

REFERENCES

Arrow, K. (1963), 'Uncertainty and the Economics of Medical Care', *American Economic Review,* **53**, 941–73.

Bayles, M. (1981), *Professional Ethics*, Belmont, California: Wadsworth.

Benson, Sir H. (1979), *Final Report of the Royal Commission on Legal Services* (I & II), Cmnd 7648, London: HMSO.

Bowels, R. (1994), 'The Structure of the Legal Profession in England and Wales', *Oxford Review of Economic Policy*, **10**(1), 18–33.

Brickman, L. (2003a), 'The Market for Contingent Fee-Financed Tort Litigation: Is It Price Competitive?', *Cardozo Law Review*, **25**(1), 102–165.

Brickman, L. (2003b), 'Effective Hourly rates of Contingency Fees Lawyers: Competing Data and Non-Competitiveness', *Washington University Law Quarterly*, **81**(3), 653–736.

Brickman, L. (2005), 'The Continuing Assault on the Citadel of Fiduciary Protection: Ethics 2000's Revision of Model Rule 1.5', *University of Illinois Law Review,* 1181–1216.

Camerer, C., G. Lowenstein, and M. Rabin (eds) (2004), *Advanced in Behavioral Economics,* Princeton: Russell Sage Foundation.

Cooter, R.D. and D.L. Rubinfeld (1989), 'Economic Analysis of Legal Disputes and Their Resolution', *Journal of Economic Literature*, **27**, 1067–97.

Curran, C. (1998), 'Regulation of the Professions', *The New Palgrave Dictionary of Economics and the Law*, vol. 3, (P.Newman ed.), London: MacMillan, pp.247–54.

Dana, J. and K. Spier (1993), 'Expertise and Contingent Fees: the Role of Asymmetric Information in Attorney Compensation', *Journal of Law, Economics, and Organization*, **9**(2), 349–67.

Danzon, P.M. (1983), 'Contingent Fees for Personal Injury Litigation', *Bell Journal of Economics*, **14**(1), 213–24.

Darby, M. R., and E. Karni (1973), 'Free Competition and the Optimal Amount of Fraud', *Journal of Law and Economics*, **16**(1), 67–86.

Davis, M. (1987) 'The Moral Authority of a Professional Code', in *Authority Revised*, NOMOS XXIX, J. Roland Pennok and John W. Chapman (eds), New York: New York University Press.

Dietrich, M., and J. Roberts, (1997) 'Beyond the Economics of Professionalism' in J. Broadbent, M. Dietrich and J. Roberts (eds), *The End of the Professions?*, London: Routledge.

Dzienkowski, J.S. (ed.) (1996), *Professional Responsibility Standard, Rules, Statutes,* (1996–97 Edition), St. Paul, Minn.: West Publishing Co.

Easterbrook, F.H. and D.R. Fischel (1993), 'Contract and Fiduciary Duty', *Journal of Law and Economics*, **36**(2), 425–51.

Emons, W. (2000), 'Expertise, Contingent Fees, and Insufficient Attorney Effort', *International Review of Law and Economics*, **20**(1), 21–33.

Emons, W. (2004), *Playing It Safe with Low Conditional Fees versus Being Insured by High Contingent Fees*, Discussion Paper 04.19, University of Bern, www-vwi.unibe.ch/theory/papers/emons/lcf.pdf.

Emons, W. (2007), *Conditional Versus Contingent Fees*, *American Law and Economics Review*, **8**(1), 20–23.

Emons, W. and N. Garoupa (2005), 'US-style Contingent Fees and UK-style Conditional Fees: Agency Problems and the Supply of Legal Services', *Managerial and Decision Economics,* **27**(5), 379–385.

Fehr, E., A. Klein and K.M. Schmidt (2001), *Fairness, incentives and contractual incompleteness,* CESIFO Working paper, no.445, Munich. Germany.

Fehr, E. and K.M. Schmidt (2000), 'Fairness Incentives and Contractual Choices', *European Economic Review*, **44**(4–6), 1057–1068.

Fehr, E. and S. Gächter (2002), *Do Incentive Contracts Undermine Voluntary Cooperation*?, Institute of empirical research in economics, Working paper no.34, Univ. of Zurich.

Flannigan, R. (1989), 'The Fiduciary Obligation'*, Oxford Journal of Legal Studies*, **9**(3), 285–94.

Frankel, T. (1998), 'Fiduciary Duties', *The New Palgrave Dictionary of Economics and the Law,* vol. II, (P.Newman ed.), London: Macmillan, pp.127–132.

Frey, B. (1997), *Not just for the money*, Brookfield: Edward Elgar.

Fudenberg, D. (1991), 'Explaining Cooperation and Commitment in Repeated Games', in J.J. Laffont (ed.) *Advances in Economic Theory, 6th World Congress*, Cambridge, UK: Cambridge University Press.

Geanakoplos, J., D. Pearce and E. Stacchetti (1989), 'Psychological Games and Sequential Rationality', *Games and Economic Behavior*, **1**(1), 60–79.

Gintis, H., S. Bowles, R. Boyd and E. Fehr (eds), (2006), *Moral Sentiments and Material Interests*, Cambridge, Mass: MIT Press.

Gravelle, H.S.E. and M. Waterson (1993), 'No Win, No Fee: Some Economics of Contingent Legal Fees', *The Economic Journal*. **103**(420), 1205–1220.

Grief, A., P. Milgrom and B.R.Weingast (1994), 'Coordination, Commitment and Enforcement: The Case of Merchant Guild', *Journal of Political Economy*, **102** (41), 745–75.

Grimalda G. and L. Sacconi (2005), 'The Constitution of the Not-For-Profit Organisation: Reciprocal Conformity to Morality', *Constitutional Political Economy,* **16**(3), 249–76.

Grossman, S. and O. Hart (1986), 'The Costs and Benefit of Ownership: A Theory of Vertical and Lateral Integration', *Journal of Political Economy*, **94**(4), 691–719.

Halpern, P. J. and S. M. Turnbull, (1983), 'Legal Fees Contracts and Alternative Cost Rules: An Economic Analysis', *International Review of Law and Economics*, **3**(13), 3–26.

Hansmann, H. (1988), 'Ownership of the Firm', *Journal of Law, Economics and Organisation,* **4**(2), 267–304.
Hart, O. (1995), *Firm, Contracts and Financial Structure*, Oxford: Clarendon Press.
Hart, O. and J. Moore (1990), 'Property Rights and the Nature of the Firm', *Journal of Political Economy*, **98**(6), 1119–1158.
Koehn, D. (1994), *The Ground of Professional Ethics*, London: Routledge.
Kreps, D. (1990), 'Corporate Culture and Economic Theory' J.Alt and K.Shepsle (eds), *Perspectives on Positive Political Economy*, Cambridge: Cambridge University Press.
Maskin, E. and J. Tirole (1999), 'Unforeseen Contingencies and Incomplete Contracts', *The Review of Economic Studies,* **66**(1), 83–114.
Mattews, R.C.O. (1991), 'The Economics of Professional Ethics: Should the Professions be More Like Business?' *The Economic Journal,* **101**(407), 737–50.
Pratt, J.W. and R.J. Zeckhauser (1985), *Principals and Agents: The Structure of Business,* Boston, Mass.: Harvard Business School Press.
Rabin, M. (1993), 'Incorporating Fairness into Game Theory and Economics'. *The American Economic Review* **83**(5), 1281–1302.
Raz, J. (1985), 'Authority and Justification' *Philosophy and Public Affairs*, **14**(1), 3–29.
Rickman, N. (1994), 'The Economics of Contingent Fees in Personal Injury Litigation' *Oxford Review of Economic Policy*, **10**(1), 34–50.
Sacconi, L. (1999), 'Fondamento ed efficacia delle deontologie professionali', S. Zamagni (a cura di) *Le professioni intellettuali tra liberalizzazione e nuova regolazione*, Milano: EGEA, 21–96.
Sacconi, L. (2000), *The Social Contract of the Firm,* Berlin: Springer.
Sacconi, L. (2006), 'CSR as a Model of Extended Corporate Governance, an Explanation Based on the Economic Theories of Social Contract, Reputation and Reciprocal Conformism', in F. Cafaggi (ed.), *Reframing Self-regulation in European Private Law*, The Netherlands: Kluwer Law International, pp.289–341.
Sacconi, L. (2007), 'Incomplete Contracts and Corporate Ethics: A Game Theoretic Model under Fuzzy Information', in F. Cafaggi, A. Nicita and U. Pagano (eds), *Legal Orderings and Economic Institutions*, London: Routledge, pp.310–351.
Sacconi, L. and G. Grimalda (2007), 'Ideals, Conformism and Reciprocity: A Model of Individual Choice with Conformist Motivations, and an Application to the Not-for-Profit Case'. in: P.L. Porta and L.Bruni (eds), *Handbook of Happiness in Economics*, London: Edward Elgar, pp.532–570.
Salaniè, B. (1997), *The Economics of Contracts, A Primer*. Cambridge Mass.: The MIT Press.
Schwartz, M.L. and D.J.B. Mitchell (1970) 'An Economic Analysis of the Contingent Fees and Personal Injury Litigation' , *Stanford Law Review*, **22**, 1125–62.
Simon, H. (1951), 'A Formal Theory of Employment Relationship', *Econometrica*, **19**(3), 293–305.
Swanson, T.M. (1991), 'The Importance of Contingent Fee Arrangements', *Oxford Journal of Legal Studies*, **11**(2), 193–226.
Tirole, J. (1999), 'Incomplete Contracts: Where Do We Stand?', *Econometrica*, **67**, 4, 741–81.
Williamson, O. (1986), *The Economic Institutions of Capitalism*, New York: The Free Press.
Yarrow, S. (2001), 'Conditional Fees', *Hume Papers on Public Policy* , **8**, 1–10.

12. Collective litigation versus legislation: a rent-seeking approach to class actions

Sophie Harnay and Alain Marciano

A traditional conception of courts considers them as meeting the individual demands of litigants to fill the gaps in legislation. The argument can easily be extended to collective litigation in which a collective demand to courts can be interpreted as the consequence of inadequate public regulation. However, although class actions were at first adorned with any virtue, the abuses and excesses observed since the 1990s in the USA and the emphasis put on the costs that they may bring on firms and collectivity have modified this overall positive perception. This chapter argues that despite their well-known drawbacks, class actions nevertheless entail some advantages that should not be underestimated. More precisely, we argue that class actions and political lobbying in the political market may provide groups with two alternative rent-seeking technologies, allowing groups to obtain their desired legal outcome that may therefore take the form either of a favourable legislation or a favourable judicial ruling. However, although much of the economic literature has been devoted to studying the choice between litigation and settlement, the choice between litigation and legislation has been quite overlooked. Furthermore, the rare papers that consider the choice between litigation and legislation do not consider the collective dimension of litigation through class action but only individual suits. This chapter is an attempt to suggest some elements to fill this gap. More precisely, among other determinants, we suggest that the choice of a group between the two technologies of influence – that is, the choice between 'legislative activism' and 'judicial activism' – may be determined by their relative capacity to allow group members to overcome the collective action problem that plagues both the legislative and the judicial channel. The first section analyses why collective litigation and legislative influence may actually provide interest groups with two ways to demand for favourable decisions. The second section examines the collective action problem in both cases and the instruments – especially the legal ones – that may be used to solve it. The third section analyzes a possible forum shopping by interest groups that may be driven by the availability of both litigation and legislation as rent-seeking devices. The fourth section summarizes the argument and provides some elements of conclusion.

1. (COLLECTIVE) LITIGATION VERSUS LEGISLATION: ALTERNATIVE WAYS TO SEEK RENTS?

1.1 Public Choice versus Law and Economics

Law can take different forms, such as statute law, case law, administrative regulation, and self-regulation. Correspondingly, various kinds of lawmakers are involved in the process of law-making: legislators, courts, agencies, bureaucracies, and even private agents issue legal contents implying the creation of economic incentives towards agents. Now, all legal forms cannot be considered as substitutes or interchangeable and bearing analogous meanings at both the formal and informal levels. Neither are they intended to perform similar roles in the economic and social fields. On the contrary, some legal forms are intended to perform better in different fields and, therefore, expected to prevail in certain frameworks. For instance, in the USA, legislation is expected to prevail in certain legal frameworks and situations, such as public law, while private law is rather expected as the favourite playground for litigation. Therefore, despite several major exceptions and overlapping, legislation and case law may be seen schematically as concerned with specific legal fields respectively.

On this account, legislation and litigation are traditionally treated separately in the economic analysis. On the one hand, legislative activity, processes and outcomes mostly fall within the scope of public choice analyses. Within that framework, legislations are analyzed as a market process exchange in the political market and mostly thought about in terms of the interest groups theory of government. Along this line, organized pressure groups interested in specific legislations compete for political favours in the political market. For their purpose, they engage in rent-seeking expenditures, defined as 'expenditures of real resources undertaken by individuals or groups of individuals in order to either obtain an increase in their wealth by securing government franchises, or to avoid a cost or reversal of an exclusive right' (McNutt 2002, p. 166). Symmetrically, lobbying expenditures can take the form of rent-defending expenditures as well, intended to protect a favourable situation, whatever its origin. Different channels of political influence are considered within this framework. For instance, a straightforward way to influence legislation is to invest in financial or time contributions on campaigns. On the supply side of the political market, politicians, bureaucrats, and other political actors as well are considered as rent setters obtaining compensation of various types against the provision of favourable legislations. The equilibrium is obtained in the market by pairing demanders and suppliers of legislation. For that equilibrium, groups maximize their gains and exert their optimal amount of political pressure, given the productivity of their expenditures and the other groups' expenditures. Finally, legislation is seen as the outcome of the relative efforts of interest groups. Further, due to the well-known collective action issue, small well-organized groups are expected to benefit mostly from legislations, at the expense of most diffuse interests less able to resist legislative pressure (Tollison 1982 for a survey; Becker 1983). Since small groups are more efficient in controlling and deterring free-riding by their members, they are more likely to obtain favourable legislation in the political market, mostly at the expense of larger groups.

On the other hand, litigation is mainly treated by the law and economics literature. As for the public choice analysis of legislation, literature is extensive. It is, however, possible to distinguish two main trends in the law and economic analyses of litigation. A first set of works puts forward the motives and preferences of litigants as the driving force for legal evolution (Rubin 1977; Priest 1977; Goodman 1978). In that view, parties act as gatekeepers in the legal change process, since a court can produce a precedent only if a plaintiff has brought a case before the court. From that standpoint, thus, judicial rules differ from legislative processes through which legislators are always entitled to issue political decisions in any field they wish without any restriction and seizure consideration. By contrast with this first representation of judges 'passively' responding to litigants decisions, a second set of works focuses on the role of courts in legal changes. Assuming a judicial preference for efficiency, it accounts for a general trend of common law towards efficiency (See for instance Posner 1986). Now, it is important to note that, within these analyses, litigants may not really have a demand for the production of favourable precedents but simply for a favourable solution to the current case. For instance, when they do not value the production of a precedent but are interested only in the resolution of the current conflict because they do not anticipate the repetition of the game and their involvement in a similar conflict in the future (Bailey and Rubin 1994). Another explanation for litigants not issuing a demand for precedents as durable decisions but mainly for their bringing a solution to a specific conflict is that no property rights or compensation is associated with precedents. Precedents and legal rules, in that view, have the features of a public good. This allows future users to free ride on the legal expenditures efforts of former litigants without contributing themselves to the development of case law. This in turn might lead to insufficient production of precedents in the litigation market. However, it is noteworthy that even in this case, litigants play a major role in triggering legal production, since the supply of precedents by courts is a by-product of the demand for conflict resolution. In that view, thus, some amount of precedents might be produced nevertheless, despite the collective good nature of case-law, as long as litigants have a sufficient incentive to issue a private demand for conflict resolution.

With few exceptions, thus, there are few bridges between public choice and law and economics analyses of legislation and litigation. When the link between legislation and litigation is considered, litigation is usually seen as a remedy against legislative incompleteness and expected to fill the gaps in legislation, when the latter does not exist or is unsuitable. In this view, laws are incomplete because they do not specify what is to be done in every situation, and courts create law when an unspecified contingency occurs and the dispute between parties is brought before the court. This conception of litigation puts courts and judges in a situation of 'interstitial legislators', as Oliver Wendell Holmes once claimed. Therefore, we argue in the following section that the differences between legislation and litigation may have been exaggerated in some aspects.

1.2 Litigation – Another Rent-seeking Device?

Although most of the application of rent seeking theory has focused on politicians and public officials, legal expenditures by parties are very much similar to a specific type of rent-seeking contest legal expenditures at trial and, to a large extent, can be seen as lobbying expenditures of a specific type. Now, few works develop the parallel so far. For instance, Landes and Posner (1979) remark that their analysis of common law and litigation is also relevant for the study of statute law and legislation but do not develop their point. Following up this line, Rubin (1982) draws a parallel between forces that shape statute law and common law, noting that litigation and legislation do not differ intrinsically but that parties use whichever method of legal change is most efficacious to reach their goal. In the same vein, Katz (1988) builds a model very close in mind to those developed by rent-seeking analyses. In his model, parties in a dispute choose to invest in litigation expenditures so as to produce legal arguments and to influence the judicial decision. The probability to win is then defined as a positive function of the expenditure on legal resources of the party and a negative function of the other party's expenditure. Within this framework, 'the judge chooses the winner partly on the basis of the argument made by the parties, partly upon the exogenous merits of the case, the relevant burdens of persuasion, and partly on random factors, including political considerations and any judicial biases' (Katz 1988, p. 129). Tellingly, Katz explicitly recognizes that his results 'may have application to the general phenomenon of rent-seeking under uncertainty' and that 'litigation behaviour can be seen as a special case of [political lobbying]' (Katz 1988, p. 139). However, litigants are not assumed to have an interest in the production of a durable precedent, but only to be interested in a favourable solution to their dispute – which prevents the analysis to take law-making into consideration explicitly. By contrast, Bailey and Rubin (1994) are the first to develop an overall analysis of the forces that change statute law, including interest groups having a specific interest in having law modified. The change can be obtained consciously – following a litigation strategy – or unconsciously – following an evolutionary process. They find that cases will be litigated rather than settled if one party has a greater interest in the case as precedent than does the other. In that view, thus, the judicial decision has an explicit precedential value in the eyes of litigants. Therefore, as cases are litigated, the law will come to change for the benefit of the party with the biggest interest in case law. In their own words, they 'find a strong parallel in common law to the forces that change statute law, including rent seeking by special interest groups' (Bailey and Rubin 1994, p. 467), writing that 'rules that survive are the "fittest" in the sense that they survive, reflecting a temporary balance in the rent-seeking pressures of the day, but [that] little else can be said about them' (*Ibid.*, p. 469) and concluding, very in a rent-seeking vein, that 'law will tend to evolve in a direction favouring that type of litigant that is less numerous (or that can organize into a class of less numerous groups) with respect to a particular type of case' (*Ibid.*, p. 473). Farmer and Pecorino (1999) develop the analogy between legal expenditures and lobbying expenditures a step further. They also consider legal expenditures as a specific channel for rent seeking and adapt a traditional rent-seeking model so as to take the specificities of the litigation process into account. For instance, they introduce the objective merits of a case[1] and various fee arrangements systems within a rent-seeking framework. More precisely, they study the impact of different fee arrangements designs on the choice of a litigant to bring a suit before a court. They compare the effect of the American rule, under which both parties have to bear their own legal cost under the American rule with the effect of the English rule, under

---

[1] Katz (1988) also introduces considerations on case quality in his model.

which the losing party at trial not only bears its own cost but also those of the winner. Perhaps the most accomplished work following up the line of the analogy between political rent-seeking and litigation, Rubin, Curran and Curran (2001) model the legislative and judicial games and their expected returns, and they predict which option, either litigation or legislation, will be selected by the group. In their model, contending interest groups compete either to defend or change the existing law, according to their position of plaintiff (the so-called 'challenger') and defendant (the so-called 'incumbent'). They define the probability that the legislature changes the law as a function of both the simultaneous relative efforts of the two groups respectively and of a given parameter of the legislature's receptiveness for a new law. In the same manner, the probability that the judiciary changes the law is also a function of the relative efforts of the groups and of the effectiveness of their efforts in triggering a change in precedents. Parties compare the expected payoffs from the two rent-seeking methods. The solution of the game is a Nash equilibrium that is determined by three factors that interest groups consider when making their decision to sue in a court or to lobby the legislators. These three factors are the ratio of the interest-group cost to the cost of legislative effort, the ratio of the other group's costs of legislative effort to its judicial cost effort, and the ratio of the defendant's technological advantage in the courts to its advantage in the legislature, determined by the receptiveness of both producers to change the law respectively.

1.3 Collective Litigation and Rent-seeking

Now, the aforementioned analyses never consider the case for *collective* litigation, especially through class actions. At the very best, collective litigation is mentioned only in passing. Then, analyses simply assume that a similar analysis holds for individual litigants and groups as well, that is, individual lawsuits and class actions, without consideration for specific problems that may arise from the collective nature of collective litigation. For instance, Bailey and Rubin (1994, p. 469) merely define parties as 'a member of the class of actual or potential injurers' or 'an actual or potential victim, or an organization of such individuals', without distinction between individual and collective litigation. However, this restrictive conception of litigation – reduced to its individual dimension – dismisses class action as a collective influence mechanism. Indeed, since a class–action lawsuit can be brought by a *group* of individuals against persons or firms having violated the law and inflicted injury, the parallel with collective action by groups appears straightforward. As a *collective* device available to a group of people sharing common interests, collective litigation provides groups with another instrument of collective action, besides traditional channels of political influence through lobbying in the political market.

Here, the analogy between a class in class actions procedures and a group is obvious. Thus, although public choice analyses do not usually discuss the definition and characteristics of a group in great detail – most of the time, they consider it sufficient that a common objective is shared by group members to assume the existence of a group as well – it can easily be claimed that a class – such as it is defined in class action procedures – satisfies the definition of an interest group. For instance, Mueller (2003, p. 473) writes that 'in every case the force behind the formation of an interest group is the belief that its members have *common* interests and goals', which clearly holds true for a class. Indeed, the usual conception considers a class as an aggregation of individual members.[2] In that view, the commonality of goals and interests plays a major role in class formation and definition and this echoes Mueller's definition of an interest group. This is clear for instance from Rule 23 of the Federal Rules of Civil Procedure (FRCP) in the US class-actions system, that specifies that '[o]ne or more members of a class may sue or be sued as representative parties on behalf of all only if (1) the class is so numerous that joinder of all members is impracticable, (2) there are questions of law or fact common to the class, (3) the claims or defenses of the representative parties are typical of the claims or defense of the class, and (4) the representative parties will fairly and adequately protect the interests of the class'. Like a group, thus, a class shares at least common interests and goals. However, this does not mean that class actions do not come up against a free-riding and collective action problem, like it is the case in the political market as well.

2 COLLECTIVE ACTION IN POLITICAL RENT-SEEKING AND CLASS ACTION

2.1 The Collective Action Issue in Class Actions

We have shown that political lobbying and class actions provide groups with two channels of collective action. Also, in the first section, we have already mentioned that rent-seeking activities are affected by possible free-riding behaviour by group members in the political market. Usually,

---

[2] A second conception conceives the class as an entity distinct from its components. A consequence of this conception is that it rules out any problem of contribution of individual members to the collective effort. See Coffee (2000, pp. 380ff.).

class actions are considered more immune to free-riding and collective action issues than political action in the legislative market. Indeed, a traditional argument supporting class actions against individual claims in addressing cases that involve common questions is that the former entail economies of scale and avoid the duplication of legal costs associated with individual litigation. Since they allow for economies of scale, class action open the door to litigation that individuals could not afford otherwise individually.

However, for the economies of scale argument to be relevant, class members are expected not to free-ride on the litigation effort of the others – since the outcome of collective litigation is clearly a club good. Within that framework, class members find themselves in a group-like situation in which they have an incentive to free-ride, since the outcome of collective litigation is appropriated collectively whereas the cost of contributing is borne at the individual level. Therefore, under this well-known situation of collective action, no class member has an incentive to act for the group, despite their commonality of interests. Further, the representative claimant may also lack the incentive to incur the costs of the class action and contribute to production of a collective good, when he or she knows that the benefit of his or her private action will lead benefits to all class members. In other words, a representative claimant, as an individual litigant, may not accept to contribute to the litigation process and to play the role of a first-mover when he or she expects the others to free-ride on his or her individual effort. This parallels the well-known situation of an individual litigant facing the 'dilemma' of contributing to the precedential system – since a precedent, as a rule, is a collective good and can be used by any agent without charge, a litigant has no individual incentive to contribute to the stock of precedent, once his or her own case has been solved and when he or she does not reckon on being involved in a similar conflict in the future again.

Further, behind the weak incentive of class members to contribute to the production of a club good, the collective action problem within a class may still be reinforced by dissension between class members. Indeed, various types of internal and external conflicts may divide the class (Coffee 2000). For instance, conflicts may arise when members have heterogeneous preferences over some points, such as the repartition of punitive damages or of the settlement when their case is settled. This may also be the case when present and future claimants diverge on the level of current and future damages – for example, the former may favour high damages compensating them for their actual loss, whereas the latter may prefer lower damages to be paid on the current period and preserving the solvency capacity of the injuror until futile claims mature. Another reason for class members not to go along with each other may also derive from their various degrees of risk tolerance. An additional source of divergence may also derive from the interests of the representative and the rest of class members being misaligned, leading to a delegation situation such as it is depicted within agency models.

Now, despite the conditions for free-riding by individual litigants, class actions do not appear to collapse under the effect of class members' free-riding behaviours systematically. Even, by contrast with what can be observed in the legislative market, large groups, obviously, do resort to class actions to defend their interests – see mass tort litigation for instance. This paradoxical situation could be explained as the consequence of some external provisions that may help to guarantee that class actions do not come up against collective action problems systematically. Indeed, in class actions, lawyers are allowed to vindicate the rights of a large group of people where no individual party has sufficient economic incentive to bring suit on his own. Several facilitative devices can be mentioned here supporting the argument. For instance, that lawyers are allowed to sue on behalf of an entire class of plaintiffs without obtaining their consent tends to lower the cost of forming a group (Haymond and West 2003, p. 92). The fee arrangements towards lawyers also provide a decisive instrument to facilitate the emergence of class actions (Rubenfeld 2006). Here, the fact that in a US class action plaintiffs' attorneys advance the litigation's expenses against a contingent fee calculated as a fraction of the class recovery provides a remedy against the incentive problem of an individual litigant unwilling to bear the cost of initiating the action without certainty about the outcome and the behaviour of other potential plaintiffs – in other words, such a fee arrangement can be seen as a way for lawyers to subsidize class actions. Another facilitative practice in class actions that allows to overcome free-riding and to reduce the cost associated with launching an action is that some attorneys keep a 'team' of 'professional plaintiffs' ready to act as representative plaintiffs in class actions, in exchange for a compensation from the lawyer which contributes to lower the cost of starting a class action for the representative (Perino 2006, p. 4).

Some judicial practices and procedural requirements may also be construed as facilitating class actions. Thus, interestingly, Rule 23 provides a precise definition of a class that has no counterpart for a group in the political literature. It puts forward not only the commonality of interests and goals but also the homogeneity in preferences that seems to be a decisive feature of a class as well. More precisely, the homogeneity of preferences is guaranteed by the right to opt out for any member requesting exclusion from the class action (under Rule 23(c) of the US FRCP). In this respect, the obligation to give notice to the members of the class once the class is certified and their right to exclude themselves from the proceeding – that is, in other words, the necessity that a member consents to his or her participation in the class action – differentiates a class from a 'mere' group where no explicit consent is required. Alternatively, the fact that only the class members who have chosen to opt out explicitly are not bound by the judgment is another difference with the political lobbying process that does not allow for possible exclusion, once a statute is passed. Furthermore, Rule 23(c) specifies that 'the judgment in an action maintained as a class action under subdivision (b)(1) or (b)(2), whether or not favorable to the class, shall include and describe those whom the court finds to be members of the class [and] the judgment in an action maintained as a class action under subdivision (b)(3), whether or not favorable to the class, shall include and specify or describe those to whom the notice provided in subdivision (c)(2) was directed, and who have not requested exclusion, and whom the court finds to be members of the class'. Finally, the definition of a class seems both more precise and explicit than the definition of a group within the political market. The clarity of the definition may also serve to overcoming free-riding in class actions and perform as a guarantee that class actions not come up against collective action problems. In other terms, the fact that legal provisions help to check the commonality of interests and goals and the homogeneity of preferences among class members may provide class actions with an external device to solve a possible collective action problem. This echoes the 'separate and "selective" incentive(s)' that Olson (1965, p. 51, quoted by Mueller 2003, p. 473) calls on, on the account that they constitute an inducement to act collectively so as to allow for the production of collective goods. Finally, thus, the rules of procedure governing class actions, as they are written down in the US FRCP, may perform as those 'separate and "selective" incentive(s)'.

2.2 Lawyers' Opportunistic Behaviour in Class Actions

In addition, class actions are also plagued by another type of free-riding in relation to the principal–agent relationship between plaintiffs and attorneys. Indeed, like it is the case in most agency relations, the agent, *i.e.* the lawyer, is more informed or has more expertise than the principal, i.e. class members. As a consequence, he or she is able to exploit this informational asymmetry for his or her own benefit, which leads to opportunistic behaviours at the expense of the principal best interest. The problem of monitoring that derives from this situation opens the door to a free-riding behaviour by class members, since ways to hold attorneys accountable to the class members are usually costly and may therefore be affected by a collective action problem – a class member individually has no incentive to invest resources in controlling the attorney as the monitoring outcome is a club good whose benefit will accrue to all class members, including those who have not participated in the production of control. As a consequence, self-interested attorneys are able to adopt opportunistic behaviours. For instance, they will seek only for their own profit and engage in undue class actions bordering on 'legal extortion' on defendants (Haymond and West 2003), at the expense of class members, or they will maximize their fees and choose a wrong timing in settlement. Furthermore, the compensation of 'professional plaintiffs' by lawyers for their participation in action is another brake on effective control, since they will have only few incentives to control the lawyers effectively.

Now, paralleling those legal devices intended to facilitate class formation and class action, additional legal instruments are also oriented towards the resolution of the agency problem between lawyers and class members. Obviously, the problem of aligning the lawyers' interests with the interests of their clients is not specific to class actions but concern all kinds of litigation (Dewatripont and Tirole 1999). But the extent of lawyers' abuses in class actions has led to a strong criticism of class actions themselves and, therefore, to the search for remedies against those abuses. In the USA, thus, legislative and regulatory provisions have been introduced to make attorneys' monitoring more accurate and reliable. For instance, in the field of securities class actions, the US Private Securities Litigation Reform Act (PSLRA) of 1995 introduced the lead plaintiff provision intended to improve the monitoring of lawyers by class members. In a situation where 'plaintiffs' lawyers typically control securities class actions because they are insufficiently monitored by the relatively unsophisticated individual investors that often serve as representative plaintiffs' (Perino 2006, p. 4), the 'hope' behind the PSLRA is that 'because institutions have the largest claims in class actions, [...] they may be able to capture enough of the gains from active monitoring to at least partially overcome the collective action problem' (*Ibid.*, p. 7). To put it in other words, because of their large financial interest in the case, because they are alleged to possess a higher legal expertise than individual plaintiffs, and also because they can legitimately be expected to be repeated players in the game, the PSLRA expects and encourages institutional investors to assume primary control over lawyers. Thus, the PSLRA provides that 'once appointed by the court, the lead plaintiff selects a lead counsel for the class, subject to court approval, [...] and monitors it' (Perino 2006, p. 8; Weiss and Beckerman 1995). Among other legal provisions, the US Class Action Fairness Act of 2005 also strengthens the control of attorneys' fees when they are seen as excessive relative to the benefits accrued to class members.

Therefore, absent those devices intended to overcome the free-riding problem in class actions, one could expect some classes to remain latent, which would prevent some legal arrangements (either judicial rulings or settlements), as club goods, from emerging. Clearly, such devices intended to facilitate the emergence of a class and to have the class actions proceedings perform well have no counterpart within the political market. For instance, no instrument is available in the political market to allow for the 'crystallisation' of latent interests as organized groups and the effective formation of a group mainly remains contingent on its size, without consideration for possible devices that may help a group to overcome its collective action problem. In the same manner, although interest groups may be confronted with similar control problems towards professional lobbyists to those faced by class members towards attorneys, no specific attention is drawn on that specific agency problem within the political market and the large bulk of literature on the issue of delegation in class actions has no parallel in the public choice literature. From that standpoint, interest group analyses focus on the outcome of lobbying activities of interest groups that have already formed and are active in the political arena, but do not consider explicitly the channels through which they have been able to emerge. Now, the fact that some judicial procedures may mitigate the cost of collective action – for instance, through the aforementioned class action facilitation – whereas no similar device exists in the political market may induce some groups to resort preferably to collective litigation rather than to invest in lobbying expenditures in the political market. The next section examines their choice between collective litigation and legislation.

3. FORUM SHOPPING BETWEEN LEGISLATION AND CLASS ACTION

3.1 Interest Groups' Choice between Political Lobbying and Class Action

As a consequence of the lack of devices aimed to overcome the collective action problem in the political market, larger groups may be penalized for the benefit of smaller groups that do not need specific incentives to form. Therefore, some statutes, public interest legislation, and pro-consumers legislation, may not be produced although they would benefit mostly to large groups unable to overcome the collective action problem. In that view, class actions may provide a valuable remedy against the consecutive over-representation of smaller groups over larger ones and a way to overcome the opposition of powerful and well-organized interest groups that may thwart the enactment of socially beneficial regulation. In other words, large groups may also be willing to invest in class actions in order to obtain favourable case-law when their high costs of organization prevents them from an easy access to efficient pressure in the political market and when they are provided with legal means to overcome the collective action problem through class actions. As a way of voice for groups with large diffuse interests and high costs of organization, thus, class actions may perform valuable social functions in a public interest view. One could expect, thus, that small and well-organized groups mostly intervene in the political market while large groups that would remain latent in the absence of external help to overcome their collective action problem preferably resort to class actions. Such a 'positive' conception of collective litigation that attributes virtues to class actions lawsuits, by contrast with a political market mainly viewed as 'monopolized' by small groups defending well-organized interests, justifies the current movement promoting the introduction of class actions in French law and accounts for the strong support of consumers' associations and minority shareholders – that is, large groups characterized by high costs of organization – to the project (Magnier 2005).

Now, the collective action argument does not imply that only large groups will carry out class actions. Indeed, smaller groups may also have a vested interest in class actions, as long as class actions diversify their channels of influence. Therefore, groups may adopt a forum shopping behaviour between legislation and litigation. Since a group wishing to change the law may have the choice between bringing cases before a court or lobbying legislators, the problem becomes to determine which method of influencing legal decision-making is the most efficacious to achieve its intended goals. The problem may thus be twofold. On the one hand, it is to determine whether to resort either to litigation or to political lobbying if litigation and legislation are substitutes. On the other hand, it is to determine the optimal combination of litigation and legislative investment if litigation and legislation are complements. In that case, they may be used jointly or successively by groups so as to reach their intended purpose. For intance, groups may use litigation as a regulatory strategy to force companies to accept regulatory policies and litigation may in some cases lead to major regulatory changes (Viscusi 2002).

Therefore, the choice of a rent-seeking method by interest groups may be driven by several determinants. First, it may be a function of their own size and of the corresponding cost of organization. In that view, the success of class actions lawsuits in rent-seeking technologies may be largely determined by their capacity to overcome the collective action problem. Whenever class actions are efficient in overcoming the problem of collective action, or when external incentives decrease the organization cost of a group, an actual trade-off between political lobbying and collective litigation as competing technologies of rent-seeking can occur. When legal provisions do not supply the conditions of efficient rent-seeking through collective litigation, groups will preferably resort to political lobbying – at least, as long as the group is effective in the political market. A telling illustration of this idea is given by the French '*actions en representation conjointe*' such as designed in Article L. 452–2, al. 1, *Code monétaire et financier* (*Loi du 8 août* 1994). Albeit quite close to US class actions in goal and intent, they remain rather unusual, mostly due to strong conditions discouraging a wider use. For instance, while representation is understood in a quite comprehensive manner in US class actions, the French understanding of the representative mechanism is much more limitative – restricted to a narrowly defined list of authorized associations – and, therefore, prevents potential litigants to resort to class actions massively (See Magnier 2005, for an application to corporate governance matters in France). From this situation, it is obvious that, in France, collective litigation cannot seriously compete with legislators as a rent-seeking technology so far. As a matter of fact, part of the current debate about the development of a 'real' class action procedure relies on this premise. In other words, without effective tools and legal conditions intended to overcome collective action in the judicial area, collective litigation may be doomed to remain an empty shell. Second, the choice between legislation and litigation may also be influenced by the exogenous availability of legal devices helping – or not helping – to overcome free-riding. For instance, the availability of some legal instruments in a given legal system is obviously a constraint on the groups' choice between litigation and legislation. This partially accounts for the supporters of class actions in France arguing that their introduction would provide the French domestic legal system with enhanced advantages in the current context of increased legal competition with foreign systems (Magnier 2005). Third, groups can also be expected to make their choice rationally according to the relative productivity of both types of expenses, to the sensitivity of courts and legislators to their argument, to the cost of political and judicial representation and procedures relatively. Fourth, the choice may also depend on the rent-extraction behaviours of third parties and groups may thus be expected to favour a channel of influence that minimizes the transfers associated with rent extraction (McChesney 1997; Haymond and West 2003).

3.2 A Cooperative View of Legislation and Litigation?

A related question deals with the interest of legislators to facilitate class actions. In a classical rent-seeking framework, rule makers (politicians, regulators, agencies, courts...) can be seen as rent setters. Their power to organize transfers from one group to another group puts them in the position to extract a part of the rent they transfer (Appelbaum and Katz 1987; McChesney 1987, 1991). Therefore, the interest of legislators to organize and facilitate class actions may be limited, since they may have an incentive to put barriers on the entry of contending suppliers – i.e. courts – in the legal market, so as to preserve their own rent and their rent-extraction capacity as well. In other words, they could be expected rather to limit competition in rent extortion than to increase it. Now, paradoxically from that standpoint, most devices facilitating class actions appear to be of legislative origin. How then to explain legislative contribution to class actions rationally? A first explanation refers to a traditional motive of legislative delegation to courts. The costs of direct legislative decision-making, including not only the direct financial costs of decision but also the transaction costs associated with negotiating to reach a majority in the Congress, provide courts with an incentive to delegate their decisional capacity to the judiciary. Second, legislative incompleteness, combined with the expectation that courts may be more responsive than legislators to changing circumstances, may also account for delegation. Third, legislators may attempt to shift political responsibility towards courts as politically sensitive issues are concerned (Salzberger 1993; Salzberger and Voigt 2002). Along that line, they may try to claim political responsibility for decisions positively received by voters while disclaiming any responsibility for unpopular policies. Further, legislators may choose to delegate decision-making to courts mostly in those fields that are less profitable – that is, in which interest groups are less willing to invest or to a lesser extent because the rent at stake is lesser than in alternative fields. Fourth, legislators may agree to delegate their decision-making power to courts knowing that judicial rulings defer to legislation; in that sense, the delegation cost to legislators may be low – or, in a way, 'reversible' – as long as they keep the possibility to overturn judicial decisions. A fifth explanation, also consistent with an interest group analysis, is that class actions may be supported by some powerful pressure groups. For instance, lawyers as a professional group may be very supportive of class actions in the USA, due to their high financial interests in the matter. Their support may thus even account for the evolution and successive reforms in the field of class actions, leading to substituting political channels of rent extraction with legal ones (Haymond and West 2003). In a similar manner, the movement promoting the introduction of 'real' class actions in the French legal system may be interpreted as driven by self-interested lawyers seeking for additional sources of revenue and opportunities. Within that framework, the promotion of class action lawsuits may even be seen as a rent-defending strategy carried out by the French profession of lawyers in a context of increased legal competition to remedy their alleged comparative disadvantage in comparison with foreign counterparts benefiting from the class action technology – in other words, for fear that legal competition might induce French plaintiffs to file class actions lawsuits abroad because that legal technology is not supplied by domestic courts, legislators may meet the domestic demand for class actions. The demand for a class action procedure in the corporate governance field provides a good example of such a situation (Magnier 2005, p. 53).

4. CONCLUSION

Legislation and litigation may thus provide interest groups with two strategies to obtain legal changes, either through the political market or courts. Now, both political and judicial markets are affected by a collective action problem, which may not be solved in a similar way in both cases. More precisely, small groups are able to solve their collective action problem in the political market due to their limited size, whereas large groups mostly remain deprived from influencing legislation. Therefore, the latter may be most likely to resort to collective litigation, since class actions do actually provide interest groups with some external devices – of legal nature – to deter free-riding by class members. In other words, the choice of a preferred channel of influence is dependent on several determinants that are contingent not only on the size of the group, but also on the legal system in which they operate. Yet, our analysis still requires considering several important elements. One important element is that collective litigation and legislative pressure do not necessarily yield similar legal outcome as far as their nature is concerned. For instance, in a huge proportion of cases, collective litigation brings about to a settlement that does not allow for the production of a legal rule or precedent. Such 'settlement class actions' therefore require to be considered more carefully in our analysis, since they may obviously impact the litigation *v.* legislation strategy of groups. In other settings, litigation may also represent a support and basis for future regulation (Viscusi 2002), which may also modify the influence strategy of a group.

Other differences between litigation and legislation may limit the relevance of the analogy as well, although they may not directly affect the choice made by groups between both channels of influence but mostly have consequences at the social level. For instance, class actions do not allow for citizens' interests to be explicitly represented and, unlike the case of the regulatory changes, do not entail any mechanism to ensure that their outcomes are in society's best interests. Major procedural differences exist as well. For instance, judges can only decide on those cases that come before them and, alternatively, are obliged to decide on cases once they are seized – which is typically not the situation for politicians. Furthermore, the design of recruitment and compensation structures for judges and politicians is far from being similar. In addition, there is a requirement for judges to motivate their decision, whereas politicians are not bound by such an obligation theoretically. The adversorial *v.* inquisitorial nature of the judicial system may also play a role in the choice of the group between litigation and legislation. More precisely, within an inquisitorial system, the fact that a judge does not only 'buy' the arguments of parties or is influenced by their argumentation as a function of the level of their expenses may decrease the groups' incentive to invest in litigation expenditures, since they may reveal less profitable in some cases. In addition, another point should be considered according to the type of litigation considered. Following Abraham (2002), one can distinguish two types of class actions, respectively 'backward-looking litigation', in many aspects similar to conventional tort litigation and mostly oriented towards insurance and compensation of injured parties, and 'forward-looking litigation', intended to modify law and to influence agents' incentives for the future. Our analysis holds mainly in the latter case but appears far less relevant in the former case.

REFERENCES

Abraham, K. (2002), 'The Insurance Effects of Regulation by Litigation', in W.K. Viscusi (ed.), *Regulation through Litigation*, Washington, DC: AEI Brookings Joint Center for Regulatory Studies, pp.212–232.

Appelbaum, E. and E. Katz (1987), 'Seeking Rents by Setting Rents: The Political Economy of Rent Seeking', *The Economic Journal*, **97**(387), 685–99.

Bailey, M. J. and P.H. Rubin, (1994), 'A Positive Theory of Legal Change', *International Journal of Law and Economics*, **14**, 467–77.

Becker, G.S. (1983), 'A Theory of Competition among Pressure Groups for Political Influence', *Quarterly Journal of Economics*, **98**(3), 371–400.

Coffee, J.C. (2000), 'Class Action Accountability: Reconciling Exit, Voice, and Loyalty in Representative Litigation', *Columbia Law Review*, **100**(2), 370–439.

Dewatripont, M. and J. Tirole (1999), 'Advocates', *Journal of Political Economy*, **107**(1), 1–39.

Farmer, A. and P. Pecorino (1999), 'Legal Expenditure as a Rent-Seeking Game', *Public Choice*, **100**, 271–80.

Goodman, J.C. (1978), 'An Economic Theory of the Evolution of Common Law', *Journal of Legal Studies*, **7**, 393–406.

Haymond, J. and J. West (2003), 'Class Action Extraction', *Public Choice*, **116**, 91–108.

Katz, A. (1988), 'Judicial Decisionmaking and Litigation Expenditure', *International Review of Law and Economics*, **8**, 127–43.

Landes, W.M. and R.A. Posner (1979), 'Adjudication as a Private Good', *Journal of Legal Studies*, **8**(2), 235–84.
Magnier, V. (2005), 'La class action, un remède efficace?', *Cahiers de droit de l'entreprise*, **4**, 53–5.
McChesney, F. (1987), 'Rent Extraction and Rent Creation in the Economic Theory of Regulation', *Journal of Legal Studies*, **16**(1), 101–118.
McChesney, F. (1991), 'Rent Extraction and Interest-Group Organization in a Coasean Model of Regulation', *Journal of Legal Studies*, **20**(1), 73–90.
McChesney, F. (1997), *Money for Nothing: Politicians, Rent Extraction, and Political Extortion*, Cambridge, MA: Harvard University Press.
McNutt, P. (2002), *The Economics of Public Choice*, (2nd edn.). Cheltenham, UK: Edward Elgar.
Mueller, D.C. (2003), *Public Choice III*, Cambridge: Cambridge University Press.
Olson, M. (1965), *The Logic of Collective Action*. Cambridge, MA: Harvard University Press.
Perino, M.A. (2006), 'Institutional Activism through Litigation: An Empirical Analysis of Public Pension Fund Participation in Securities Class Actions', *Legal Studies Research paper*, **55**, St. John's University School of Law, available at http:///ssrn.com/abstract=938722.
Posner, R.A. (1986), *Economic Analysis of Law*, (3d edn.), Boston: Little Brown.
Priest, G. (1977), 'The Common Law Process and the Selection of Efficient Rules', *Journal of Legal Studies*, **6**(1), 65–82.
Rubenfeld, W. B. (2006), 'Why Enable Litigation? A Positive Externalities Theory of the Small Claims Class Action', *Public Law and Legal Theory Research Paper Series, UCLA School of Law*, **10**, available at http://ssrn.com/abstract=890303.
Rubin, P.H. (1977), 'Why Is the Common Law Efficient?', *Journal of Legal Studies*, **6**, 51–63.
Rubin, P.H. (1982), 'Common Law and Statute Law', *Journal of Legal Studies*, **11**, 205–223.
Rubin, P.H, C. Curran and J.F. Curran (2001), 'Litigation versus Litigation: Forum Shopping by Rent Seekers', *Public Choice*, **107**(3–4), 295–310.
Salzberger, E.M. (1993), 'A Positive Analysis of the Doctrine of Separation of Powers, or: Why Do We have an Independent Judiciary?', *The International Review of Law and Economics*, **13**(4), 349–79.
Salzberger, E.M. and S. Voigt (2002), 'Choosing Not to Choose: When Politicians Choose to Delegate Powers', *Kyklos*, **55**, 281–310.
Tollison, R. (1982), 'Rent Seeking, a Survey', *Kyklos*, **35**(4), 575–602.
Viscusi, W.K. (ed.) (2002), *Regulation through Litigation*, Washington, DC: AEI Brookings Joint Center for Regulatory Studies.
Weiss, E.J. and J.S. Beckerman (1995), 'Let the Money Do the Monitoring: How Institutional Investors Can Reduce Agency Costs in Securities Class Actions', *Yale Law Journal*, **104**(8), 2053–2127.

PART 3

Comparative legal views: issues, national experiences and a proposal

13. Class actions in private enforcement of EC antitrust law: the Commission Green Paper*

Francesco Denozza and Luca Toffoletti

1. THE GREEN PAPER AND THE PRODUCTION OF DETERRENCE

The Green Paper of the European Commission, on *Damages actions for breach of the EC antitrust rules*[1] promotes the development of private enforcement of antitrust rules in the European Union. In doing so, the Commission addresses a number of reasons why private suits, and damages actions in particular, are important and need to be incentivised in EC antitrust. Both the functions of compensation and deterrence of damages actions are taken into consideration. As to compensation, the Green Paper contains such a strong statement as the following: 'it is desirable that victims of competition law violations are able to recover damages for loss suffered, if competition law is to better reach consumers and undertakings and enhance their access to forms of legal action to protect their rights'.[2] Deterrence is surely at issue as well: the Commission clearly states that 'Enhanced private enforcement will (...) increase the incentives of companies to comply with the law, thus helping ensure that markets remain open

* An earlier version of this work was presented at the conference 'Introducing Class Actions in Europe – A Comparative Law and Economics Perspective', Alessandria, January 26–27, 2007 (Università del Piemonte Orientale, Department of Public Policy and Public Choice- POLIS)

1 December 19, 2005, COM (2005) 672, hereinafter the 'Green Paper', with the annexed *Commission Staff Working Paper Annex to the Green Paper*, hereinafter the 'Staff Working Paper' (when not specified, general reference is to the set of two documents as a whole).

2 Staff Working Paper, para. 4.

and competitive'.[3] Neither one or the other of the two functions, though, is apparently given preference as a policy goal, or is said to be in fact predominant over the other.[4]

Still, the Commission, in line with its whole reform policy it has been bringing about for almost a decade now, very clearly indicates that it wants antitrust enforcement to be decentralised. Spreading the burden of enforcement over private citizens in the EU, other than over National Competition Authorities (after the 'Modernisation Reform' with Regulation 1/2003, NCAs have the powers and the duty to apply the whole range of the EC Treaty antitrust rules, with sole exceptions of merger control that remains governed by a mutually exclusive relationship between EC and Member States' jurisdictions) is in fact a powerful means to achieve the goal of liberating the scarce resources of the Commission itself. Those resources would be finally allocated to certain limited in number, but highly ranked in priority, tasks of enforcement in the Commission's agenda and overall antitrust policy.

Behind this idea one can unmistakably recognize the assumption that private enforcement, once fully or satisfactorily developed,[5] shall be able to *substitute* public enforcement. In certain areas at least, public enforcement would take a step back relying on the current, or upcoming, initiatives of private parties to realise the same ends.

---

[3] Staff Working Paper, para. 5.

[4] Indeed, irrespective of the weight of compensation, even if one thinks compensation to be the only aim of private actions, every damages claim does add to the existing level of deterrence. One cannot obtain compensation of victims without interfering with deterrence. The Green Paper reference to *Courage* (European Court of Justice, case C-453/99, *Courage v Crehan*, [2001] ECR I-6297), which states that the right of 'any individual to claim damages for loss caused to him by a contract or by conduct liable to restrict or distort competition (…) discourages agreements or practices, which are frequently covert, which are liable to restrict or distort competition' (para. 26–27), seems to confirm this underlying ambiguity. On the relationship between deterrence and compensation see Section 4 below.

[5] The Green Paper goes through all the perceived obstacles to such development, envisaging intervention on all or most of the factors that currently prevent it. Whilst in this chapter we deal solely with the introduction of class actions – or similar devices (see below on the definition) – the drastic increase in the level of private enforcement activity would in all likelihood only be achieved by means of a full-scale reform. The analysis we make here is not dependent, in our view, on the very many interactions of those various areas of the envisaged intervention. As we will make clear in Section 3 below we look at class actions' introduction both (a) for their effect of boosting private damages suits and (b) for some specific directions they may induce in such a boost.

Since the sole end of public enforcement, within the EC antitrust framework, is deterrence,[6] private enforcement is then attributed, in this respect, to the function of producing deterrence. More precisely it is attributed to the task and capability of producing *equivalent* amounts of deterrence to those produced by public enforcement.

Whilst this is not fully spelled out in the Green Paper, we argue that nevertheless the conception of private enforcement as a substitute supplier of deterrence is an important idea underlying the envisaged reform and is indeed implied by the way it is proposed.

2. CLASS ACTIONS AND THE PRODUCTION OF DETERRENCE

In all likelihood, the envisaged reform will not be able to do away with class actions. Not only are they considered in the Green Paper amongst the devices to introduce so as to achieve a satisfactory level of private enforcement activity, but they also represent the cure to one of the most formidable obstacles to damage suits: the sub-optimal incentive to sue, and incur the costs of litigations, for victims of so many antitrust violations that produce very small individual injuries to a very large number of persons.

In this respect if one intends private suits to substitute the efficacy of Public enforcement in yielding deterrence, that obstacle must be removed. In a sense, one can say that to introduce class actions is tantamount to introducing private enforcement *tout court*. The drastic underdevelopment of damage suits in the EC and throughout all Member States has been recently evidenced in detail in the survey made for the Commission in a 2004 Report.[7] As noticed, the Green Paper makes a whole scan, on the basis of what emerged from that survey, of all the different factors standing against the spread of damage suits in Europe: there is no doubt that introducing class actions alone would not be enough to reverse the current status of 'total underdevelopment'. Nor is there any doubt, though, that

---

6 As opposed to the US system whereby public agencies bring private suits before the courts (other than prosecuting offenders under criminal law when applicable: a task we do not consider here being not applicable to EC antitrust), in EC as is known the Commission (as well as all NCAs) combines investigating *and adjudicating* powers: when a violation is ascertained, they may issue administrative fines against the infringers. Public enforcement never gets in touch with civil liability issues: national courts have wide discretion and autonomy in adjudicating rights in this respect.

7 Waelbroeck, Slater and Even-Shoshan (2004).

without class actions, even the adoption of all other considered measures would not be enough.

'Class actions' is used here in a very broad sense. A significant amount of uncertainty seems to affect the discussions on enforcement reform as to the precise scope of a reference to 'class actions', due in part to the existence, in certain EU jurisdictions, of statutes or draft statutes allowing a form of collective suit which differs, sometime to a significant extent, from US-like class actions.[8] Though significant differences certainly occur between different devices of collective representation (one of the most important being that amongst so-called 'opt-in' and 'opt-out' systems), in this chapter we will not discuss the specificities of such differences: reference is made, with 'class actions', to all forms of collective or group representation that allow a potentially large number of individuals, having in common the way they have been exposed to the negative effects of a conduct representing an infringement of the antitrust laws, to suit the alleged injurer under a single judicial initiative, with the effect of being all awarded damages within that very same single suit.

We use such a broad notion of class actions because we want to discuss the effects that their introduction could cause within the perspective of the production of deterrence. Relevant effects on deterrence should be yielded by any of the proposed kind of collective representation suits.[9] Indeed, it follows from their definition as proposed here above that they will produce the increase in deterrence that represents the topic addressed in this chapter. It is the change from a private enforcement framework without class actions to one in which they will be available, we assume, that would determine the emergence of private enforcement as a significant deterrence factor.

3. PRIVATE AND PUBLIC ENFORCEMENT CONCURRING IN THE PRODUCTION OF DETERRENCE

If EC antitrust is going to have class actions for damages suit, both private and public enforcement will play a concurrent role in producing deterrence, as is envisaged in the Green Paper: they will ultimately stand on a level

[8] An illustration of the current situation throughout Member States in this respect is in the Green Paper, para. 195–197 of the Staff Working Paper.

[9] At least in the sense that the differences amongst them should not determine any significant difference as to the amount of deterrence increase that their introduction should produce.

basis, in that deterrence to would-be infringers may stem from either the possibility of an investigation leading to administrative fines, or the possibility of private suits leading to payment of damage awards (or, of course, a combination of the two: but what counts is that one or the other perspective *alone* may significantly deter the potential wrongdoer).

As noticed, this outcome is not at all discussed in the Green Paper as being problematic.[10] On the contrary, it seems that the underlying assumption is that the relationship between the two enforcement activities is linear: so that for every additional unit of private activity that is injected into the system, a unit of public activity may be withdrawn, yet leaving an unchanged aggregate level of deterrence.[11]

We argue that this assumption is not correct. Damages actions have intrinsic limitations as devices for the production of deterrence. Moreover, the way they interact with public enforcement depends on a number of variables: they may or may not be able to supplement appropriate amounts of deterrence when public enforcement no longer intervenes.

The introduction of class actions cannot be discussed without taking into consideration that a boost in damages actions could produce significant distortions on deterrence.[12]

---

[10] There apparently is only one point of concern for the Commission at the moment, which regards the interaction with leniency programmes. We will briefly illustrate this issue in Section10, below.

[11] Let us assume we currently have a level of deterrence, made up by public enforcement alone, a level that we measure 100. Once class actions are introduced, expected damages awards emerge as a relevant cost in the cost/benefit analysis of wrongdoers: let us assume we can measure this effect in 50. Aggregate deterrence would be then 150. If 100 had been already the optimal level (it should, assuming public enforcement activities are aligned to the appropriate standard), enforcement from public agencies' activity may, and should, be reduced to 50.

[12] Much of the discussions seems to concentrate on the good and bad of class actions, the opportunity of importing them into different frameworks, as the European Jurisdictions are indeed, in respect to their original context, the US legal system (in general, and specifically as to antitrust enforcement devices and institutional organisation). Here we argue that before discussing which is the most appropriate way to boost damages actions, we need to have a more clear picture of the consequences that such a boost may determine in our antitrust enforcement system as is today at EU level and as well in most Member States' jurisdictions.

4. SOME PREMISES ON THE (SUPPOSED) CONFLICT BETWEEN DETERRENCE AND COMPENSATION

A narrowing of the focus on the way private damages actions interfere with deterrence, which is what we deal with in this chapter, calls for an explanation of how we think these problems, and their possible solutions, relate with another function served by damages actions: compensation.

On this some preliminary remarks are needed, given the huge number of studies dealing in general with the function of tort liability, and in some cases with the alleged conflict amongst a deterrence function and a compensation function of damages actions.

4.1 Three Groups of Choices Lying on Autonomous Grounds

In essence, and with the sole purpose of putting forward some premises in the aim of trying to avoid that what follows is misunderstood, we think that every policy of repression of socially undesirable activities implies for the regulator to make choices which can be classified in at least three different groups.

The first group includes those choices related to the definition of illegal conducts. Within this category falls as well the definition of the necessary degree of fault for illegality to arise (and sanctions be triggered), since on these choices depend degree and modality (more or less prevention devices) with which certain activities are to be made.

A second group relates to the management of risks: risks that the undesired activities be nonetheless made. Here at issue is the decision on the level of possible ex-ante interventions (e.g. permits to condition certain activities to the adoption of safety measures), on monitoring, on appropriate deterrence levels, on how to ensure that wrongdoers be caught, and so on.

Within the third group are choices relating to the management of consequences: consequences of those illegal activities which are undertaken notwithstanding the rules on their illegality (and the adopted deterrence measures). Here fall the choices on compensation due to victims, on the effectiveness of sanctions as punishment, and so on.

Needless to say that the choices made at each of the three levels do have implications on the choices that can be made at the other two. For example, it is out of the question that the choice made at the first level between having an unconditional ban of certain acts, or banning them only when they are inefficient, implies that management of risks and of consequences see to it that choices made at these latter two levels do not contradict the first choice. Notwithstanding these interrelations among the choices made at the different levels, we argue that the three groups are eminently and conceptually independent, one from the others.

4.2 Compensation and Deterrence as Interfering Instruments, and Not as Alternative Values

The distinction amongst the three levels helps, then, to understand a phenomenon that does not seem to receive enough attention in the many discussions on the matter in which such distinction is ignored. We allude to the fact that it is well possible to conceive a set of rules, with perfect internal consistency, in which the first level choice is inspired by *equity/fairness* considerations, or rights-based conceptions (e.g. the right to be not murdered is protected regardless of any cost-benefit calculus), the second level choice is instead inspired by *efficiency* considerations (it is decided that it is not convenient to use all the resources that would ensure that any risk of violation is removed – refraining, e.g., to employ two policemen in the endless patrol of every individual potentially being a murderer – thereby establishing a certain level of acceptance of risk), whereby the third level choice is inspired by reasons of retributive *justice* (a sanction – thirty years imprisonment – is imposed because it is deemed proportional to the seriousness of the committed crime, not for its ability to deter or to compensate the victim).

If one considers the distinctions amongst the three levels hereby underlined, many discussions on the function of tort liability may appear useless, or in any case ill conceived. This is the case, in particular, of the discussion (which, given the scope of this chapter, is of most direct interest here), on the relation between deterrence function and compensation function of damage actions. In the framework that we propose, the two matters lie on different grounds: the first (deterrence) relating to management of risks and the second (compensation) to management of consequences of a committed tort.

This does not mean that all problems disappear: it means though that the relationship between the two functions must not be seen in terms of a radical alternative of values, but rather in terms of the interferences which, as we already noted in general, are always possible, also between choices which lie on different levels. To make an example, a legislator deciding to manage the risks using deterrence (other than, e.g., prevention) and choosing to allocate this task to damages actions, may design the latter so as to have criteria to define the recoverable damages aimed at obtaining optimal deterrence. When managing the consequences of the tort, the legislator may still decide that making the victims whole is the first priority. In this case he or she could revise the criteria of damages recovery (those set forth at and within the second level) that should result unfit to achieve this second purpose. Interferences, and the need to go about with balancing evaluations, would then arise. Still, the lawmaker has also the choice to leave the criteria unaltered and intervene with insurance or public subsidy systems for the victims incurring insufficient damages recovery. In this way the independence between the two tiers of choices would be reintroduced.

These remarks may also apply to the issue of deterrence in antitrust law. Once established that we are at level two (thus we assume a given definition of what is illegal), the issue is then: what is the relationship with level three, that of the management of consequences? Here as well, similarly to what we have just observed in general, nothing would prevent the lawmaker from designing damages actions so as to enhance its efficacy as to deterrence. He or she could then freely decide whether the victims of anticompetitive conducts should be left to their fate (i.e., able to recover only that amount – be it much or little – which could be granted to them as a consequence of damages action not designed in view of their compensation), or they should in any case reach full recovery of their suffered prejudice (possibly by means of the activation of supplemental devices, which may range from subsidies for the least compensated to high taxation of punitive damages in excess of actually suffered prejudices).

4.3 Can Damages Actions Adequately Perform a Deterrence Function?

Upon this premise, and in this context, we can finally state precisely the purposes of this chapter. We want to draw the attention to a number of difficulties that in many situations prevent private damages actions, as they are currently conceived (i.e. with all their limitations as to causation, burden of proof, quantification criteria, and so on, which are more or less present in all European jurisdictions) to adequately perform a deterrence function. From the observation of such failures one can then infer consequences both with regard to coordination amongst private and public enforcement, and with regard to the possible amendments to current rules on private damages actions.

We want to remark that this leaves unaffected the question about the opportunity to compensate victims, a question that arises at a different level and that urges its own solutions. The answer can be either negative or positive, the latter case implying the need to set up further devices, apt to correct the negative effects that may flow from the intervention made on the damages action rules with a view to increasing its deterrence potential.

4.4 Three Goals for a Deterrence Policy and the Appropriate Measure of the Sanction in Relation to Each of Them

A deterrence policy may pursue different goals. The possibility of achieving them, and the very same possibility of defining and articulating them, clearly, varies in relation to the situations and the kind of conducts that comes into play. In this chapter we will consider three possible (in our view, reasonable) goals, with reference to a context of wilful conducts (we will not consider, therefore, problems relating to prevention activities, a matter which is likely to be quite marginal in antitrust law – with the exception, as we shall see, of the prevention activities consisting in abstaining from behaviours which are nonetheless lawful, in order to avoid the risk that errors in the evaluation of the boundaries of the notion of illegality may lead to being sanctioned also for conducts the legality of which may be argued).

The three goals we shall take into consideration are the following:

1. The first is to disincentivise certain conducts on absolute terms, regardless, that is, of a cost-benefit analysis made on a case by case basis.
2. The second goal is to discourage only those conducts from which the wrongdoer obtains benefits that do not outweigh the costs imposed on third parties.
3. The third goal is to prevent certain conducts which are valued negatively, avoiding however to discourage certain others, albeit similar, still deemed neutral or even beneficial.

These goals may be pursued by means of adopting different measures.

Some of them may relate to the setting up of the necessary devices so as to avoid that the prohibited conducts remain hidden. These are the devices that in the classical proposition of the question, which compares the net benefits of the wrongdoer to his or her costs, represented by the amount of the sanction discounted by the probability for the wrongdoer of being caught, impact on this latter element. In this chapter we will not deal with this issue. We will discuss as if we acted in a context (if obviously implausible for antitrust application, however useful for a theoretical exploration) in which the value of p is always equal to 1.

We will thus consider exclusively the problems relating to the measure of the sanction.

In this perspective, and coming back to the possible goals of a deterrence policy, we then have that:

- To reach the first goal we only need to have that the sanction be higher then the expected gain of the wrongdoer; when this condition is met, unless the wrongdoer himself makes calculation mistakes, the conduct is discouraged for all rational profit-maximizers.
- To achieve the second goal we rather need that the sanction be exactly equal to the aggregate net costs borne by third parties; once this equality holds the rational agent will decide to realise the forbidden conduct only when his or her net benefits are higher than the aggregate net costs imposed on third parties. Thus yielding an increase in social welfare.
- The third goal requires more complex interventions, and particularly a graduation of the sanction in relation to the seriousness of the offence.

5. DAMAGES ACTIONS AND OPTIMAL DETERRENCE MODELS: THREE DISPARITIES

In three different contexts, those in which each one of the above defined goals are pursued, disparities emerge between the prescriptions of optimal deterrence models and the sanctions brought about by damages awarded to victims of antitrust violations. We analyse such disparities making two assumptions.

The first assumption is that no public enforcement concurs in creating the total amount of sanctions, i.e. as if there would be no other consequence for the violator than the payment of damages to victims, nor any cause of detection of infringements other than the initiative of private plaintiffs. This assumption would help to show, we argue, how private enforcement yields deterrence on its own. We will then add into the picture the concurring role of public enforcement again, to reconsider the production of an optimal aggregate level of deterrence from a perspective that looks at private enforcement as decentralised activities that cannot be influenced by public policy.[13] In this perspective the effects of private enforcement may, and have to, be measured in themselves, with a view to design a policy of public enforcement to be consistent with such effects.

[13] This is indeed the very essence of private enforcement brought about by class actions. When civil suits are brought by public prosecutors or governmental agencies, as is the case in the Federal US jurisdiction, a policy decision lies behind such enforcement activities. Here we concentrate on the suits brought by the victims, which are by definition decentralised devices for the production of deterrence.

The second assumption regards the conception of damages. We do take into consideration the fact that damages actually obtainable by victims, as awarded by Courts, differ, and may do so to a significant extent, from the notion of private losses or private costs that are used in economics. Since our purpose is to discuss the implications on deterrence of the private enforcement's boost to be caused by the introduction of class actions, we refer to realistically recoverable damages, which in turn represent the amounts that potential wrongdoers include in their cost-benefit calculus. As is known, the difference at issue stems prominently from the notion of legal causation: not every single costly consequence of a conduct may be considered as having been 'caused', within the meaning accepted and used in court adjudications, by such conduct. The well- known and long-debated juridical question on the boundaries of causation is certainly of relevance when addressing policy options for private enforcement; still, it seems to have been, surprisingly, overlooked almost entirely in the Green Paper. For the purposes of the following analysis it is enough to bear in mind that damages as awarded by courts – the definition of damages we use here – do not correspond to the notion of private cost which is used in optimal deterrence analysis. Other than causation, further difficulties implied by the features of the judicial adjudication, such as difficulties of proof, or precise quantification of the suffered prejudice (even if of the kind included within the boundaries designed by the notion of legal causation), may concur in widening the gap.

Finally, we do not consider the competitors' actions for damages. First of all, class actions are eminently a device that serves the needs of the customers of the infringers (injured competitors normally have sufficient incentives to bring individual suits; the introduction of class actions should not interfere with the level of competitors' lawsuits). Second, it is customers' harms that bear the closest correlation with the profitability of the infringers and hence it is in customers' claims that damages may be most significantly looked at to see how they come close to a notion of optimal sanction for deterrence purposes. The loose (if at all existent) connection between the grant to competitors of a right to recover their harm and deterrence purposes is well known.[14]

In the following paragraphs we suggest that Damages as above defined diverge from these three quantities that play a fundamental role in the

---

[14] See, e.g., Hovenkamp (1999, pp. 645, 650) (optimal deterrence model's application to exclusionary practices a 'radical departure' from existing law of damages, but competitors' suit, as they are, nevertheless, serving certain socially desirable functions, like early detection of injuries to consumers).

literature on the design of the optimal deterrence: (a) the gain of the violator; (b) the social loss; (c) the seriousness of the offence.

6. DAMAGES AND WRONGDOER'S GAIN

The first, basic prescription implied by a deterrence purpose is that sanctions must prevent the illegal conduct, and hence that the expected loss for the potential wrongdoer has to be higher than the expected gain if we want her or him to abstain from a certain conduct that is qualified as illegal.

The simple formula is then that damages must be higher than the expected gain, times the percentage of detection ('p'):[15]

$$Damage > Gain\ (*1/p) \tag{13.1}$$

The level of deterrence created by judicial award of damages does not necessarily keep up with this basic prescription even in the simplest of cases. Violations like hard-core cartels, those in respect of which class actions are deemed to be fairly appropriate remedies,[16] show different level of consistency with the rule.

In price fixing cartels, we do have that damages equal the violators' gain: the latter being the so-called monopoly overcharge, or the difference between the cartel price and the competitive price (or the level of price in the same market before the cartel formation, or in neighbouring markets), times the sold quantities; the former being the same price differential (times the purchased quantities, which in aggregate, assuming all victims bring an action – or that a class action is brought – equal the cartel members' aggregate gain).

In market allocation cartels the above does not seem to hold anymore. Here the cartel members profit out of a number of cost reductions, other

[15] As already noted, we exclude from the analysis the percentage of detection, assuming that it equals 1. Changes in this variable should not affect the implications we derive in this chapter from the disparities of damages and the other considered quantities. Once established that damage is an amount that varies to a significant extent depending on the nature of the case and violation at issue, as we argue, the chances to have optimal deterrence level by means of private enforcement decrease regardless of the amount of p. The simple propositions we recall from optimal sanction analysis also assume that all parties are risk neutral and enforcement costs are zero. Another general assumption is embedded in the static nature of the models employed in the analysis (incentives in a dynamic framework, which would alter the determination of the optimal amount of sanction, are not considered).

[16] The consumer harm flowing from price fixing cartels is normally widespread, fragmented, and of relative ease of measurement in court.

than the overcharge. Relying on a set of clients (or territories) securely allocated to them and isolated from competitive pressure, they will be able to avoid costs for promotion, innovation, and the like.

Hence, whilst in price fixing we have that

$$\textit{Damage} = \textit{The overprice} = \textit{The overcharge} = \textit{Gain} \tag{13.2}$$

in market allocation we have

$$\textit{Damage} = \textit{The overprice} < (\textit{The overcharge} + \textit{Avoided Costs} =)\ \textit{Gain} \tag{13.3}$$

Moreover, the avoided costs part of the gain may hardly be measured, let alone be incorporated in recoverable damages.[17]

The level of deterrence produced by private enforcement, even by the most efficient one (with p equal to one and all victims bringing actions or being entitled to their share of the award), then: (a) is different depending on the nature of the infringement, and (b) may be sub-optimal, leading to underdeterrence.

7. DAMAGES AND SOCIAL LOSS

We now consider a second, more complex prescription, according to which sanctions must be designed so as to not only prevent illegal conducts, but also avoid preventing illegal conducts that nevertheless are occasionally efficient.

This is a very well known proposition in deterrence analysis; its underlying purpose is to adjust the level of deterrence to factor in a standard of social desirability, based on the efficiency norm.[18]

It is important to remember, in considering this norm of optimal sanction design in an antitrust framework, that the conducts at issue in this context are treated with strict illegality as those in the previous one: we are not referring to conducts whose legality in the first place is to be determined

---

[17] As opposed to the efficiencies produced by practices considered in Context 2 (Section 7 below) this kind of advantages, those of the 'quiet life' enjoyed by the monopolist or, here, the cartel members, are not incorporated in static models on which deterrence analysis is based.

[18] See, e.g., Posner (2001, p. 267): 'To impose a violator a cost (...) equal to the cost that his violation imposed on society (...) is a criterion of efficiency and hence an especially appropriate one to use in designing remedies for antitrust violations'. A detailed illustration in Landes (1983).

on the basis of a balance between the anticompetitive effects and the efficiencies they bring about (as, e.g., under the 'exemption' test provided for in para. 3 of art. 101 of TFEU).[19] In fact, even hard core cartels (as all other behaviours treated by antitrust law with a rule of strict illegality) may produce, on occasions, efficiencies.[20]

In this second context the prescription is to design the level of sanction so that the infringer, in case the efficiencies are significant, shall in any case do the illegal conduct, even after having paid the sanction.

The rule is then that damage must equal to (but not higher than) the total social loss, where the total social loss is formed by the monopoly overcharge, the deadweight loss (DWL),[21] and all other losses (all third parties' net costs):[22]

$$Damage = (Overcharge + DWL[\ +other\ losses^{23}]=)$$
$$Total\ Social\ Loss\ (*1/p) \qquad (13.4)$$

When the cost savings produced by the efficiencies are higher than the DWL, after paying damages the infringer shall still remain with a net gain: even after the overvcharge has been entirely offset, the gain will lie in the

---

[19] The exemption test under art. 101.3 of the TFEU may be equated, for the limited purposes of the distinction illustrated in the text, to rule of reason analysis as opposed to per se illegality in US antitrust law.

[20] On efficient cartels and appropriate remedies see e.g. Posner (2001, p. 267).

[21] The deadweight loss is the most typical factor of divergence between damages as awarded upon litigation and a measure of optimal sanction as per deterrence analysis. Nonetheless, it is argued that the harms suffered by excluded consumers (those third parties who are damaged because, having a lower reservation price, they substitute away towards an inferior product once the price is increased by the violators) should and could, effectively, be made recoverable: see Leslie (2006), suggesting that parens patriae suits brought by state attorneys generally may be the most suitable instrument for such a purpose.

[22] The proposition is expressed by Landes (1983, at 656) as follows: 'The rule for determining the optimal fine or damage award is simple to state: the fine should equal the net harm to persons other than the offender'.

[23] Other losses, as e.g. the costs of litigation and other enforcement costs, are in effect a deadweight loss and can be included in this latter notion (their existence shall make the DWL larger than if only determined by inefficient substitution). Other losses of a different kind to be included in deterrence analysis are those arising from competitors' investments, when they are wrongfully excluded: Hovenkamp (1999, p. 651), and see Hovenkamp (1989, pp. 1–17), where the author remarks that this latter kind of costs, of particular relevance, cause a systematic underestimation of the social costs of infringements, thereby yielding to underdeterrence. The notion of total social loss intends to include the harms of all parties other than the violators.

positive difference between the produced efficiencies less DWL. And if efficiencies more than compensate social losses, society has a net benefit.

Should damages be only equal to the overcharge, the infringement would take place (the infringer gains from the efficiencies) when society still suffers a loss (arising out of the inefficient substitutions).[24] On the contrary, when damages are higher than total social loss, in case of efficiencies a socially desirable conduct (in this perspective) is nevertheless prevented.

Let us consider two examples: agreements to block innovation, and to price discriminate.

When the infringers collude to jointly delay the introduction of innovative processes or products on the market (in order, for example, to fully exploit existing and already stocked, but inferior, product lines)[25] a number of private costs arise, a kind of costs which are very difficult to measure; but they are certain, widespread and of a significant extent: those are the lost benefits in term of enhanced quality, or safeness, or environmental protection, and so on. This means that damages are lesser than total social loss: a situation leading to underdeterrence.

If instead the purpose or effect of collusion is to price discriminate between purchasers, the recoverable damages shall be equal to the increase in price suffered by some of the customers and the total social loss would be equal to the imposed aggregate increase in price (plus the inefficient substitutions as in the first example) *minus* the aggregate decreases in price resulting from the discrimination (the price paid by those who pay less than before). The damages are then higher than the total social loss, resulting in overdeterrence.

---

[24] This is, indeed, the reason why the sanction should not be *less* than the sum of the overcharge and the deadweight loss: when efficiencies may flow from a cartel or other illegal conduct, they can make the violation profitable even if outweighed by social losses (i.e., if they are, no matter how small but, lower than the DWL they would always accrue to the violator after having paid a damage that offset the entire overcharge). Hovenkamp (1999, p. 30) notes that the inclusion of the costs from inefficient substitution in the recoverable damages incurs a serious obstacle in the fact that those are costs borne by individuals who are not the direct purchasers of the monopolised goods (i.e. those consumers who no longer buy the goods after the increase in price, and who opting for a substitute product, by definition an inferior one, suffer a reduction in their surplus), thus likely not having standing (to US Courts standards) to bring an antitrust damages action. But see Leslie (2006, p. 559).

[25] On the antitrust treatment of conducts blocking innovation see Symposium, 'Antitrust and the Suppression of Technology in the United States and Europe: Is there a remedy?', (1998) 66 Antitrust LJ 415 and see particularly Flynn (1998, p. 487). See also Maugeri (2007).

The situation depicted in the last example could be of general relevance in light of the wide position taken by the European Court of Justice on standing in antitrust actions (see *Courage* and *Manfredi*, where 'anyone' is the word used to define those who have standing).[26] When standing is conceived in very broad terms, many situations, other than price discrimination (with its intrinsic duality of better off/worse off parties) may be figured. If, for example, employees are to have standing, those who lost their jobs as a consequence of illegal predation, resulting in their employer (the ousted undertaking) being liquidated, may sue the predator for damages, claiming their lost wages; but those losses (and possibly all social losses) could be more than offset by the avoided damages to the predator's employees: those who would have been fired absent the predation, due to the competitive pressure their employer would have suffered from its excluded rivals, were they still in the market.

8. DAMAGES AND SERIOUSNESS OF THE OFFENCE

Lastly, in a third context optimal deterrence analysis provides the indication that sanctions have to be designed so as not to discourage the undertaking of legal efficient actions that occur around the ones that are considered illegal.

Here the task is completely different from the previous ones, in that the illegal conduct cannot be defined precisely: the opposite of hard core cartels (whether or not cartels from time to time produce offsetting efficiencies, there is reasonable certainty that they normally do not and therefore a regime of per se illegality is chosen). When one cannot rely on precise definitions, as is the case for very many antitrust violations, the prescription is to consider marginal deterrence.

Marginal deterrence analysis advocates finely adjustable sanctions. In this perspective the norm that comes from deterrence analysis is then to graduate sanctions, according to the degree of seriousness of the offence, so that efficient conducts that cannot be distinguished precisely from the ones to be proscribed at the moment when their legality or illegality is decided may not be discouraged.

Coming to the disparity with damages, private enforcement cannot keep up with this norm since the sanction is of the on/off type: once illegality is

[26] Case C-453/99, *Courage v. Crehan*, [2001] ECR I-6297 and joined cases C-295/04-C-298/04, *Vincenzo Manfredi et al. v. Lloyd Adriatico Assicurazioni*, [2006] ECR I-6619.

ascertained (and therefore the liability of the infringer is derived), all suffered damages have to be restored.[27]

A significant example for this scenario is the antitrust treatment of rebates. Rebates are the typical conduct that lies very close to a number of legal, efficient ones. Even in the strictest conceptions, let alone the many perspectives from which a more lenient treatment is called for,[28] there is significant room for rebates that deserve to be encouraged, being recognised as efficient. A recent US antitrust class action shows how the perspective of paying damages may yield a very high, possibly disproportionate, level of deterrence. The action was brought by retail pharmacies (tens of thousands in the class) alleging that drug manufacturers colluded in denying them discounts they granted to hospitals and other large health care organisations.[29]

The recoverable damages were the denied discounts times the purchased quantities: possibly a very high amount with significant deterrent potential. Though we may figure that due to the nature of the infringement there might have been room for a successful defence,[30] magnitude of risk created by the largeness of the class was apparently enough of an incentive for the defendants to settle. A settlement was agreed for $408 million: an amount that in itself stands out in comparison to the administrative fines issued for

---

[27] Damages may be a superior device to a *fixed* fine: as Hovenkamp (1999, p. 644) notes, in a price fixing cartel (and in the presence of the trebling rule) the violators are discouraged in setting a higher increase in price thereby making the collusion more detectable, as opposed to setting a lower overcharge, thus reducing the probability of being discovered and sanctioned. Should they risk being charged with a fixed fine, they should rather set the higher increase in price (only increasing one risk – of being caught – and not two – being caught *and* pay higher damages). Here, though, we are referring to the (highly) variable fines which can be (and are) set by the Authorities in the EU framework.

[28] The institutional position most inclined to apply economic analysis to the treatment of rebates granted by dominant undertakings, whilst still allowing room for illegality, within EU is probably the DG Competition discussion paper on the application of Article 82 of the Treaty to exclusionary abuses, 2005, para. 7.

[29] In *re Brand Name Prescription Drugs Antitrust Litigation* (N.D. III. June 21, 1996, 7 Trade Reg. Rep. (CCH) P71, 449) a class action was brought by retail pharmacies alleging drug manufacturers and wholesalers conspired to deny them discounts granted to other parties. An illustration of the case and of the settlement's terms in Calkins (1997).

[30] Although the case was tried under a per se illegality rule, being characterised as a case of collusion among the pharmaceutical manufacturers, we here want to underline that rebates, and price reductions, normally deserve in-depth analysis so as to avoid that normal, pro-competitive behaviour may fall under the antitrust prohibitions. The issue is of particular significance within EU, where as is known rebates granted by dominant undertakings fall under a very strict regime.

this kind of infringements in the EU, where the enforcer is able to use its discretionary power in graduating the amount of the fine in accordance with the seriousness of the violation.[31]

9. PRIVATE AND PUBLIC ENFORCEMENT: THE QUESTION OF THE COEXISTENCE AND COORDINATION OF CLASS ACTIONS WITH A SYSTEM OF ADMINISTRATIVE FINES

A first conclusion to be drawn from the above is that private enforcement cannot be considered something that, when boosted (or at all started as we imply it will with class actions introduction in EC Antitrust), simply adds some further deterrence on top of the previously existing level. Nor is it correct to think that it may substitute public enforcement in certain areas, as the Commission apparently suggests in the Green Paper.[32]

Our view is that, also in the perspective of deterrence alone,[33] private and public enforcement should be conceived as complements, in the specific sense that they produce *different qualities* of deterrence.

---

[31] See the Commission's Guidelines on the method of setting fines imposed pursuant to Article 23(2)(a) of Regulation No 1/2003 (2006/C 210/02).

[32] In particular, in the Green Paper the Commission seems to adopt the view that in certain areas of enforcement the administrative activity may be abandoned, relying on the surging private actions (which are implied to be certain, due to proper incentives to be introduced along with them: we argue that even if class actions would be undertaken under these assumptions – proper incentives, therefore certainty of insurgence and related certainty of the production of a deterrence effect – one cannot rely on the *proper* level of deterrence to be created, or recreated when public enforcement is to accordingly withdraw).

[33] As already noted we do not consider in this chapter the effects of the introduction of class actions on compensation. There certainly is a complementary relationship between damages actions and the administrative fines system in that the former allows victims to be compensated, whilst the latter does not. Here we focus our attention on the complementary relationship between the different kinds (other than levels) of deterrence produced by the two systems. The policy choice consisting in the introduction of class actions in EC antitrust undoubtedly has to take into consideration the need to enhance the compensation of victims. Certain implications in this respect arise, nonetheless, out of deterrence analysis: the need for compensation decreases as long as the level of deterrence comes closer to the optimum; where all would-be infringers are deterred, no violation and hence no victim occur; when would-be infringers are deterred from inefficient violations alone – see above, Section 6 – the need for compensation is anyway reduced to a significant extent. See Posner (2001, p. 266) (objective of compensation subsidiary to deterrence). Still, compensation may well be a value in itself, whose pursuit may

Their interaction is not linear: relying on a finally mature private enforcement to provide additional level of deterrence then balanced with a general reduction of enforcement activities by the Public Authorities may not be a sound policy.

A more specific and in-depth analysis should be put in place to evaluate whether one can reasonably foresee that the concurring existence of public and private enforcement on a level basis – and within the existing framework and tradition of Antitrust Law in EU – would yield to overdeterrence or underdeterrence.

We argue, though, that it is at least possible to anticipate both effects, depending on the kind of practices at issue.

10. SOME EXISTING PROPOSALS FOR COORDINATION

The problem of coordinating public enforcement with collective private damage suits has stimulated indeed some interesting analysis and proposals.

One suggests putting class actions on auction so as to adjudicate the right to enforce amongst public enforcers and private parties, to the best offer price.[34]

Another one recommends concentrating a phase of damage suits, the assessment of damages in aggregate, to a public consultant (which could be the National Competition Authority, it is suggested) making thus available to all potential private claimants an overall estimate, to be apportioned in single claims by the courts.[35]

A third one is in the Green Paper. It is indeed the only reference to the problem one can find in it, and it addresses the need to protect the effectiveness of so called leniency programmes, exempting the informer (who is stimulated to report the existence of the cartel in exchange for

---

be driven by considerations that have nothing to do with efficiency alone. For reference in the Green Paper to such a conception see e.g. para. 7 of Staff Working Paper, which refers to the aim of 'bringing competition law closer to the citizen' by means of enhancing their 'opportunities to enforce directly effective rights in the field of competition', such that 'greater awareness of and engagement in competition law on the part of European citizens' will be encouraged.

[34] Rosenberg and Sullivan (2005). A similar idea (in a different context and expressed in much broader terms) is in Posner (2001, p. 276), who suggests a right of first refusal to be conferred to enforcement agencies to bring damages suit.

[35] Rüggeberg and Schinkel (2006).

immunity from fines) from all or part of his tortious liability in subsequent private damage suits.[36]

11. A SELECTIVE USE OF CLASS ACTIONS AND A SUPPLEMENTAL ROLE FOR PUBLIC ENFORCEMENT: SOME INDICATIONS FOR FURTHER ANALYSIS

We are not sure of the practical feasibility of the first two proposals, and we find that the third one is a very limited one. Based on the remarks we made so far, we now may try to put forward some final possible indications for further analysis. The question in our view should be whether it is appropriate to introduce class actions *as a general instrument*, available for all violations.

Before we come to that, let us first consider that class actions may not even be such an effective means of deterrence, compared to other available solutions to promote damage claims.

An interesting device is certainly the so called Small Claims Procedure, that the Commission envisages in a proposal published in 2005.[37] Instead of gathering private suits with collective representations, the underlying idea of the proposal is to simplify small individual claims, up to 2,000 Euro, making them available at barely no cost for the plaintiff (no mandatory lawyer representation, claims may be filed with a simple fill-in form, the court is granted wide discretion on evidence and assessment of damages, thereby lowering the claimants' burdens).

Clearly this would be attractive in many antitrust cases, especially in so-called follow-on actions, whereby public authorities already ascertained violations and, as may be the case with price fixing, assessed the amount of the overcharge. The impact on deterrence would be much higher than with class actions since settlement becomes impossible (this would also impact in some respect on the widespread concerns that class actions generate a number of unmeritorious claims). Interestingly, the Green Paper considers them as a possible device to serve the needs of consumer redress, in addition to class actions.[38]

---

[36] Staff Working Paper, para. 224, with reference to the Commission Notice on Immunity from fines and reduction of fines in cartel cases, (2006/C 298/11).

[37] Commission's Proposal on an European Small Claims Procedure, COM(2005)87.

[38] Staff Working Paper, para. 192. No consideration of the consequent overall amount of deterrence then produced seems to be given in the occasion by the Green Paper.

One tends to be fairly convinced then, also in light of this very last section of the Green Paper, where such a powerful deterrence supplier, as the Small Claim Procedure indeed appear to be, is thought to work alongside class actions, that the Commission is not concerned at all about the possible overdeterrence consequences (nor does a different impression come from the noted concern for the efficacy of leniency programmes: here as well, deterrence needs only to be preserved, in the eyes of the Commission).

As argued in the preceding paragraphs, the results that come from looking at the prescriptions of optimal deterrence, should instead urge more reflection on the various ways that class actions may be able to interact with current deterrence levels, in the specific institutional framework – EU Antitrust – in which they are bound to function.

In this respect we think that a selective approach should be adopted, one that would pick the most appropriate areas for the new device: the areas where class actions, in themselves, are apt to yield the most satisfactory level of deterrence.

In doing so, since the continuing parallel enforcement activity of the public agencies is, of course, out of question, one should also keep in mind that when class actions should result in underdeterrence, public enforcement is always able to supplement with its activity, whilst, on the contrary, when the yielded sub-optimality is overdeterrence, no correction may be made.

Recalling our previous analysis, we have that underdeterrence is most likely to occur in context 1 (Section 6) and context 2 (Section 7), whilst overdeterrence is expected in context 3 (Section 8) – and is also arising, to a lesser extent, in context 2.

In context 1, which refers to the most traditional focus of public enforcement, the fight against cartels, there will always be some public enforcement activity to be added. So would be in context 2. Here, though, we would have another problem specifically arising out of class actions, at least in the way they are conceived in the US: the commonality requirement does not fit with the task of setting damages coming from inefficient substitution (the DWL); this being a further obstacle for mass damage claims, private enforcement would be even more unable to lead to sufficient levels of deterrence. Here as well public enforcement may always supplement with additional activity.

If overdeterrence is the problem where conducts are precisely defined as illegal (context 2) the extent of it should be, in any case, low and so the costs of introducing class actions. To the contrary, in context 3 the superiority of a public enforcement, as is in the EU, that is empowered to issue graduate fines, is clear in comparison to private enforcement. Here we have already an intrinsic potential for overdeterrence that should not be increased with class actions.

Our conclusions are then the following two.

First, we should consider the opportunity, and the costs, to introduce class actions only for cartels (or to prevent the use of them for certain practices: exclusionary practices and those subject to rule of reason analysis/exemption test under art. 101.3 TFEU).

Second, we need to adopt a different perspective in which it is private enforcement that plays a leading role. It serves compensation goals, and in doing so it yields a certain level of deterrence. Public enforcement as we have it, is in the position to complement private activities using its role of central institution and its gradable fining powers.

REFERENCES

Calkins, S. (1997), 'An Enforcement Official's Reflections on Antitrust Class Actions', *Arizona Law Review*, **39**, 413–440.

Flynn, J.J. (1998), 'Antitrust Policy, Innovation Efficiencies, and the Suppression of Technology', *Antitrust Law Journal*, **66**(2), 487–525.

Hovenkamp, H. (1989), 'Antitrust Protected Classes', *Michigan Law Review*, **88**, 1–48.

Hovenkamp, H. (1999), *Federal Antitrust Policy – The Law of Competition and its Practice*, (2nd edn), St. Paul, Minn: West Publishing Company.

Landes, M. (1983) 'Optimal Sanctions for Antitrust Violations', *University of Chicago Law Review*, **50**, 652.

Leslie, C.R. (2006), 'Antitrust Damages and the Deadweight Loss', *The Antitrust Bullettin*, **51**(3), 521–67.

Maugeri, M. (2007), 'Private Enforcement e diritto antitrust: le prospettive comunitarie', *working paper*, available at http://www.fscpo.unict.it/Eventi/Maugeri_Private_enforcement_e_diritto_antitrust.pdf (17 May).

Posner, R.A. (2001), *Antitrust Law*, (2nd edn.), Chicago: University of Chicago Press.

Rosenberg, D. and J.P. Sullivan (2005), 'Coordinating Private Class Action and Public Agency Enforcement of Antitrust Law', *Harvard Discussion Paper*, **523**, available at http://ssrn.com/ abstract=795524 (August).

Rüggeberg, J. and M. Schinkel (2006), 'Consolidating Antitrust Damages in Europe: A Proposal for Standing in line with Efficient Private Enforcement', *Amsterdam Center for Law & Economics Working Paper*, **4**, available at http://ssrn.com/paper=903282.

Symposium (1998), 'Antitrust and the Suppression of Technology in the United States and Europe: Is there a remedy?' , *Antitrust Law Journal*, **66**.

Waelbroeck, D., D. Slater and G. Even-Shoshan (2004), *Study on the conditions of claims for damages in case of infringement of EC competition rules*, available at http://ec.europa.eu/comm/competition/antitrust/others/actions_for_damages/comparative_report_clean_en.pdf (31 August).

14. The enforcement of management passivity duty in take-over law: class action or government action?*

Fernando Gomez and María Isabel Saez

1. INTRODUCTION

The behaviour of managers (in a broad sense, encompassing also the Directors) towards a tender offer for the acquisition of a company is crucial for the likelihood of success of the offer, and thus for shareholders' welfare. The European Directive on Takeover Bids contains, following English Law on this matter, a passivity rule – or duty of abstention – forcing managers to abstain from actions that may influence the outcome of the tender offer, exempting only those that can lead to higher-price offers. The rule, however, does not appear to be straightforwardly desirable for many commentators, and for many legal systems as well. For instance, US Law does not contain such a rule, and among the European countries implementing the Directive, several have made use of the opting-out provisions allowed in the Directive.

We think, however, that there are good reasons, both at the theoretical and at the empirical level, supporting the efficiency of the passivity rule. In fact, Section II of this chapter, besides characterizing the duty, provides several economic rationales for the optimality of the passivity rule in Takeover Law, particularly in the European context of mandatory and competitive bids.

Our main focus, nevertheless, does not lie in the substantive efficiency properties of the issue of enforcement. We think that a central point missing in the debate on the passivity rule is precisely a crucial one: how the rule is enforced. Without appropriate enforcement, the rule would be

* We are grateful to Jesús Alfaro, Jose Bonilla, Javier Garcia de Enterria, Cándido Paz-Ares, and participants at the Conference on Class Actions in Alessandria (Italy), for helpful comments and suggestions. All remaining errors are, of course, our own.

almost worthless, given the powerful incentives of the agents – the managers – to violate the duty. Moreover, inadequate enforcement levels may be self-reinforcing, due to the power of lax social norms in this area in most European markets.

The class action suit is the general way of protecting and compensating shareholders for directors' duty violations, but we claim that it does not serve as a powerful deterrent of potential infringements of the passivity duty. In Section 3 of the chapter we argue, with the help of a very simple game-theoretical model, that class action suits by disappointed shareholders in the aftermath of the failure of the tender offer, are structurally unable, specially in Europe, to provide adequate levels of enforcement against reluctant directors. In Section 4 we consider how Government action, through monetary fines, incapacitation, and in the extreme, criminal sanctions, although not without problems of its own, can be seen as the only promising source of more effective enforcement of the passivity rule, not the least through its influence on virtuous social norms that can reduce the cost and expand the effect of governmental enforcement activities.

2. REGULATION DOES MATTER IN TAKEOVER LAW: THE MERITS OF THE PASSIVITY RULE

2.1 Public Bids for Acquiring Control of a Listed Company

The success of public bids for acquiring control of a listed company depends, at least in theoretical terms, on the decision of its owners, the shareholders, who can decide whether or not to sell to the bidder. Nevertheless, there are other players with ample possibilities of influencing the result. Antitrust and public regulation often give the Government the power to alter the course of the bid with their veto or their conditions and requirements. But, as acknowledged by many commentators, it is management of the target company who frequently holds the key to control of the company even though managers and Directors are not, *de iure*, their owners.[1] For this reason, some legal systems impose a duty of passivity or abstention in the presence of a public tender offer for control.

[1] This is the most important issue regarding takeovers: who are better decision-makers, the managers or the shareholders? Normally, the managers make better decisions in the business field, because they are specialized, and they have the position to do so: they have the internal information of the company and the bargaining power. So, in theory, they are in the best position to sell the company to the best bidder and in the best conditions for the shareholders. [See Bainbridge

The passivity duty assumes the obligation of not interfering in the natural course of a bid to acquire company securities off shareholders. In particular, it attempts to prevent managers from deploying any device aimed at causing the bid to fail.[2] The argument we shall now endeavour to put forward is that the passivity duty, or duty of abstention, generally *works towards efficiency*. As part of the legal system, it helps to create value for companies and for society as a whole.

2.1.1 Passivity duty ensures managers do not obstruct third-party bids

The passivity duty ensures that managers are not going to obstruct a bid for acquisition made by a third party to the shareholders. A duty of abstention is the traditional legal solution on how to manage conflicts of interest, when the self-interest of an agent directly endangers the capacity to act in the interest of the principal. Managers occupy a fiduciary position in relation to their principals, the shareholders, who seek to obtain the maximum return on their investment, including accepting an advantageous bid. However, managers of the target company have powerful incentives to block a bid, as they know that if it is successful, they will in all likelihood lose their jobs, with the ensuing loss of rents. The conflict of interest involved can be so intense as to lead to the impression that it disables them from independently acting in the interest of the shareholders. Not in vain, as acknowledged by the relevant literature, do anti-takeover bid strategies constitute one of the most aggressive demonstrations of agency costs – of the gap between shareholder interests and the personal interests of the managers.[3] Consequently, the initial reaction would suggest that the most reasonable way to proceed is to force them to remain on the sideline of the securities acquisition process promoted by the acquiring and perhaps even

---

(2005)]. But the problem here is that the risk of disloyalty is very high (Walking and Long (1984)). All these reasons, with the efficiency of the market for corporate control, favour the shareholders as decision-makers: See, Cramton and Schwartz (1991, pp. 27ff.)

[2] The basis for the passivity duty, according to legal commentators in jurisdictions imposing such a duty, is that managers

> … as agents for the shareholders, administrators must always act in the interest of the major shareholders, without hindering the course of the bid as, once a hostile takeover bid has been formulated, it is the shareholders' duty to decide for themselves, without interference from the administrators, whether to accept or reject it, as shareholders are the best judge of their own interests: Fernández de la Gándara and Sánchez-Álvarez (2002, p. 232).

[3] See, on this point the classical financial literature, Asquith (1983, pp. 51ss.); Bradley, Desai and Kim (1983, pp. 183ss.); Easterbrook and Jarrell (1984, pp. 227ss.).

rival firm. This obligation, furthermore, does not interfere in the mechanics of the bid, made directly to the shareholders, leaving each to decide individually whether it is in his or her interest to sell.

2.1.2 Anti-takeover measures

Anti-takeover measures constitute a barrier to the development of a market for corporate control. Prohibiting them increases the chances of a successful outcome for takeover bids, and this, in turn, encourages new bids and, with them, a more active and healthy market for corporate control. A buoyant market for corporate control promotes, in principle, corporate value. The reason for this lies in the fact that it is one of the most effective mechanisms available for disciplining administrators and for succeeding in improving management and productivity of firms. And, as is well known, management costs, like any other business costs we could mention such as those related to technology or human capital, raise the cost of production. It is therefore advisable to reduce them, if feasible. Regardless of other enforcement schemes based on the use of sticks, and carrots such as compensation schemes, it is truc that takcover bids have a decisive impact on the prospective welfare of managers, and consequently, possess great disciplining potential. As the probability of a takeover bid is contingent on performance, it can become the incentive many administrators need to undertake to improve management.[4] Empirical studies show that companies recording a higher incidence of receipt of bids belong to low productivity industrial sectors.[5] If companies create value, society as a whole benefits from it. It should come as no surprise that among the control mechanisms on managers, takeovers are the one that raise the greatest resistance amongst those who find themselves subjected to their rigour.

2.2 Passivity Duty: Managers' Duties of Loyalty towards Shareholders

The *passivity duty belongs, in the legal understanding of most countries imposing it, to the duties of loyalty on the part of managers towards shareholders*. These duties are essentially geared to prohibiting managers from taking advantage of their privileged position – as being in charge of the corporate machinery – in detriment to shareholders in situations of conflict of interest. What is the function of these duties of loyalty? The general duty of loyalty serves as a gap-filling tool, enabling ongoing completion of the corporate contract, by definition incomplete. It works like a compass,

---

[4] This idea is highly credited in the financial literature; see for all, Jensen (1988).

[5] Morck, Shleifer and Vishny (1990).

allowing us in a particular situation to distinguish between loyal and disloyal behaviour and to update the number of issues of fresh opportunistic behaviour that might have been detected.

Given their fiduciary position, managers are, at least legally, bound to take business decisions with the sole purpose of maximising the shareholders' interest. This type of fiduciary relationship forces them to defer their private interests to shareholders' interest. Quite another matter is whether the shareholders, the principal in whose interest the duty of loyalty is imposed, decide to authorize the manager a given behaviour falling within the duty. This may confirm the idea that general prohibitions entail costs, because they are not desirable in each single contingency, even if, in general, they are.

Concerning our passivity duty, an important issue would be whether the rule should be thought of as mandatory, or merely a default rule, which shareholders may dispense with. The matter is not just one of each firm's agency costs, but also, and above all, of achieving a more efficient corporate sector. The reason in favour of making the passivity rule mandatory in nature lies in the negative externalities giving rise to anti-takeover bid strategies vis-à-vis the potential market agents. The efficiency of the market for corporate control transcends internal conflicts of interest in a firm, and from this perspective shareholder interests are not always in line with market efficiency. Naturally, shareholders have a greater interest in facilitating the corporate control market than managers, but less than the social optimum would like. There may be a problem of free-riding affecting the individual shareholder so that her private interest can lead to a thwarting of the bid and, along with this, a narrowing of the market.[6] The reasonable solution indicates that we should balance this sub-optimality of the private decision, with the costs of making the rule mandatory, which are substantial. The legal system enforcing a passivity rule for a longer time, and thus with the longest standing experience in these matters, English law, has traditionally opted to treat passivity duty the same way as all the other duties of loyalty and to leave the prohibition in the hands of the shareholders in each specific set of circumstances. The idea is that if shareholders understand that the inclusion rather than the exclusion of anti-takeover bid measures acts in their favour, they have every right to pursue their interests in whatever manner they deem fit, without having the legal system meddling with the decision in the name of overall efficiency.

It is, in fact, generally sensible for prohibitions specifying the duties of loyalty to be reversible, for an exception to be possible, specifically when

---

6 Grossman and Hart (1980, pp. 42–43).

efficiency would dictate this move.[7] But this should not, however, lead us to think that given that the rule is a default rule, then the content is largely irrelevant. That making it permissive or prohibitive is unimportant, given that shareholders are always free to alter it in the specific situation. The default rule matters, and is likely not to be changed as easily as one could abstractly think.[8]

And in this respect, the passivity duty is an extreme one. The risk of opportunism on the part of the manager, in a conflict of interest situation is generally high, but there is often room for mutual benefit of derogating the duty in particular circumstances (efficient self-dealing, for instance). In the case of a hostile takeover bid, however, the situation confronting managers is a particularly dramatic one. As a result, the generally applicable default rule should be the one with the largest scope of application, a better fit for the largest number of circumstances – in this case, the prohibitive rule given the scale of the conflict in this context – although there may be some instances in which the prohibition is not efficient. Now, the default character of the rule guarantees that in these – rarer – cases, reversibility is possible.

In addition, in Corporate Law generally, the reversibility of a rule does not work equally well from the two sides involved. Anti-managerial rules are easier to amend than pro-managerial rules, which sacrifice shareholder interests.[9] This point of view, moreover, is the one that adapts best to the hypothetical choice of shareholders, had they anticipated the rule applicable prior to the company's becoming listed on the stock exchange. This is the reason why the decision by European Member States to opt in or opt out of the passivity duty provided in Article 9 of the Takeover Directive is not an impartial decision. Leaving other considerations aside, that we shall be commenting on later, it is clear that greater overall shareholder protection is achieved if Member States adopt the prohibitive rule rather than the permissive one, and without precluding the fact that, in both cases, shareholders should have ultimate power in any given situation.

---

[7] Bainbridge (2002, p. 308).

[8] This is what is known in theory in contracts as the stickiness of default rules – departing from the additional legal rule is a costly process, not only because of the costs and disadvantages involved in drawing up the alternative clause, but also because our cognitive bias in favour of the status quo makes this an attractive solution on more occasions than strict rationality would indicate, see Kahneman, Knetsch, and Thaler (1990, p. 1325). This bias has been tested in legal contracting: Korobkin (1998, p. 608). On the general consequences of stickiness, see, Ben-Shahar and Pottow (2006, p. 651).

[9] See, Bebchuk and Hamdani (2002).

2.3 Passivity Rule as an Element in the Design of an Efficient Takeover Regime

Takeover Law has a determinant effect on the physiognomy of the market for corporate control. In this context, the law does matter. However, there are reasonable indications to think that the passivity rule is an important element in the design of an efficient takeover regime.

Both theoretical and empirical analyses seem to be on the side of the passivity rule. In theory, the appeal of a resistance policy by managers against a bid may be backed by their position in the company: there is little doubt that they have the best information on the target company's real state, and they can be actively involved in a negotiation process with the bidder. These features make them potentially useful for defending shareholders' interests when the occasion arises. What happens is that, as explained, we need to include another factor in the analysis, namely the serious conflict of interest in which managers are immersed – let us not forget that their job is at stake if the bid succeeds. This strong source of incentive distortion should make us fear that the scales are tipped on the side of a passivity duty, at least as a default solution.[10] This theoretical result seems to have been well confirmed by the empirical studies on the subject.[11] Studies showing the effects that anti-takeover measures have on the value of the company seem to be conclusive of the sign of those effects. Tobin Q's indicate behaviour in accordance with the passivity duty appears to create value. And the opposite effects, that anti-takeover strategies reduce company value,[12] are also well-established.

---

[10] Passivity may appear to be a highly drastic solution, but the truth of the matter is that we do not possess any other means of correcting this distortion. For example, we know that so-called 'golden parachutes', or the fact that managers may also be relatively large shareholders of the company, can moderate the intensity of the conflict of interest, but cannot, by themselves, eradicate it.

[11] There are several empirical studies showing that hostile takeover bids create value for shareholders, to cite some classic examples, see Jensen and Ruback (1983, p. 10); Jarrell and Poulson (1989, pp. 12, 16). In the European context, see Goergen and Renneboog (2004, pp. 9ss.). It is a different matter from this to assert that all hostile take-over bids are *ex-post* efficient, or even that, as whole, and statistically, take-over bids increase the *ex-post* value of the target company, and thus, social welfare. The bidder's reasons for launching a takeover bid are diverse, and often they may be not socially desirable (empire building). But the evidence seems to show that, for the shareholders of the target company, takeovers create value.

[12] This is the evidence provided by Gompers, Ishii and Metrick (2003, p. 107). Furthermore, the empirical studies assert that defences like poison pills or greenmailing lower the price of securities, see for all, Jarrell, Brickley and Netter (1989); Malatesta (1992). There is one study that points at the finding that managerial

At this juncture, a curious dissociation occurs between the academic theories and regulation on the two sides of the Atlantic, with the noteworthy exception of the United Kingdom. In the US, the literature is, in the majority, persuaded of the efficiency of the passivity rule, but the legal regime, in the hands of the individual States, is aligned with managerial preferences (to the delight of corporate lawyers!).[13] To such an extent is this true, that studies attempting to explain why legislators or shareholders prefer the inefficient rule to the efficient one[14] are mushrooming. Many of these considerations are behind the now traditional debate over the effects of interstate competition concerning the evolution of Corporate Law.[15] History is recorded in a very different way in continental Europe. Here, following the authority of the English model on the subject, the passivity rule was taken on by several legal systems, and initially failed to give rise to

---

resistance does not seem to harm target shareholders: target management is associated with an increased likelihood of competing bids, and with larger shareholder value between the initial tender offer and the outcome of the bid: Jennings and Mazzeo (1993, p. 883). The notion of managerial resistance in this study, however, is much broader than the restricted actions by the passivity rule, because any indication of displeasure with the offer – even purely verbal – qualifies as resistance. The passivity rule does not preclude in any way the managers from expressing opinions critical of the bid, and even less from finding competing bidders. In fact, the Takeover Directive mandates that managers have to express an opinion on any public bid (art. 9.5):

> The board of the offeree company shall draw up and make public a document setting out its opinion of the bid and the reasons on which it is based, including its views on the effects of implementation of the bid on all the company's interests and specifically employment, and on the offeror's strategic plans for the offeree company and their likely repercussions on employment and the locations of the company's places of business....

[13] The classical literature remains valid, see Easterbrook and Easterbrook (1981, pp. 1161ff.); Gilson (1981, pp. 819ss.). The topicality of this literature can easily be tracked in recent contributions, see, for instance, Gilson (2001, pp. 491ff.); Bebchuk (2002a, pp. 973ff.).

[14] The most recent theories question the quality of corporate governance in the field of company by-laws. It is common to find provisions facilitating the protection of managers from takeover risks, Bebchuk, Cohen and Farell (2004).

[15] In the United States, Takeover Law is state law, not federal law. That is why the discussion is about the merits or de-merits of competition among States (Romano (1993, pp. 843ff.); Kahan and Kamar (2002, pp. 679ff.). The most successful explanation says that the law is pro-manager because managers have legally the key to re-incorporation v. Bebchuk, Cohen and Farrell (2002); Bar-Gill, Barzuza and Bebchuk, (2006) (see also the comments of Gómez and Sáez, (2006, pp. 161ss)).

much debate because the rule had practically no effect on the market.[16] Until, that is, the actual appearance of the first wave of hostile takeover bids by foreign companies. The majority of legal commentators then started to discredit the rule. And we would predict that most European countries will end up supporting the defensive conduct of administrators as there are good – self-interested – reasons for them to do so.

The state of mind of European legal commentators on this issue illustrates the deep-seated distrust of the appeal of the market for corporate control. The suspicions are numerous and varied. *The first line of resistance is ideological in nature.* A very widespread view held on takeovers sees them as purely redistributive transactions, spurning their aptitude for being productive and welfare-enhancing. The problem with this is that it enshrouds the belief that a change of hands of the control takes place at the cost of stakeholder interests, especially employees' interests. In the extreme, managers who defend themselves from a takeover are thought to be protecting jobs. This is likely to produce an alliance of interests between managers and employees, to the detriment of shareholders' interests.[17] Governments can join in if the political contingency takes them in this direction (European Governments are more inclined to take up the side of the employees than the investors' side). The answer is simple – employment protection belongs to a different – and more compelling for politicians – political dimension, than efficient regulation of takeovers.

The second line of resistance is structural in nature. The high concentration of capital in European companies constitutes a structural barrier to takeovers. Offers will only be successful if they can count on insider consent, dramatically reducing the number of companies susceptible to being a target to a takeover bid.[18] Pro-takeover legislation is therefore thought to lead inevitably to few companies wishing to be listed on the stock exchange. This analysis does not reflect reality, though. The truth is that takeover regulation has little impact for capital concentration and, if it has some, it is in the direction of promoting dispersion. Concentration cannot be explained as a result of opposition to takeover bids, but rather as a result of the private benefits of control, which is what motivates the

---

[16] For an illustration of the Spanish case, see Garrido (2002, pp. 2719ff.).

[17] Bertrand and Mullinathan (1999), report on the relationship between anti-takeover defences and corporate costs.

[18] Berglöf and Burkart (2003, p. 179), establish the fact that over 50% of listed companies in Austria, Belgium, Germany and Italy have a controlling partner holding the majority of the voting rights. Concentration rates in the rest of Europe remain high with 43.5% in the Netherlands, 20% in France, 34.5% in Spain and 34.9% in Sweden.

refusal by company controllers to disperse ownership.[19] From this perspective, concentration continues to exist because the control block market is more lucrative for the controlling agent than the securities market is. It is true, however, that there is an interest in Europe in revitalising capital markets for the purpose of reducing the cost of the capital and increasing the investment opportunities of firms. This objective of making stock markets more attractive entails improving the way we regulate the securities market, but also Corporate Law too. And precisely in this context, takeover regulation fulfils a pro-dispersion function. The development of capital markets will necessarily lead to a higher rate of capital dispersion and, with it, agency costs will rise. The experience in Continental Europe of checking agency costs through legal measures is small, as we did not have to deal with the problem: controlling shareholders have been responsible for keeping agency costs within tolerable margins. In the absence of other mechanisms for keeping managers in check, mechanisms requiring time and cost, the market for corporate control can act as a substitute.

The third line of resistance is technical, and includes the legal arguments raised against the passivity duty. The starting point is the fact that Takeover Law gives rise to inefficient deals. This view is inadequate. Any system of regulating takeovers faces a fundamental trade-off between efficiency and value-reduction.[20] And for this reason, legislation does matter. The optimal regulation would be capable of always promoting productive deals and always curbing unproductive ones. In other words, from the viewpoint of managerial incentives, promoting takeovers when the managerial performance and company returns are poor, and discouraging them when they are good. Critics of takeovers defenders of this premise assume that, as takeovers are by nature expropriatory, managers serve better shareholders' interests under the right of resistance than under a passivity rule. This idea is structured along two lines of argument.

The first stresses the differences existing between States concerning the quality of Corporate Law and the productivity of their firms. As a consequence, they consider that levelling the playing field is the priority. The danger they fear is that, subject to market forces, value-destroying deals takes place, because the target company falls into the hands of an expropriating raider. If a raider, subject to few legal controls in its national

[19] See, Bebchuk (1999). The association of the private benefits of the control and the concentration of capital is contrasted, see La Porta, López de Silanes, Shleifer and Vishny (2000, p. 3).

[20] This basic analysis is the one used in the financial literature, to approximate to the takeover theory, see for all, Tirole (2006, pp. 425–30).

legislation, acquires a foreign company, there is a risk that the expropriator's objective will be channelled a larger or smaller fraction of existing value into his own pockets.

The second line of argument gathers around the preconception that markets are imperfect and incapable of properly pricing companies.[21] Transpiring from this analysis is the existence of a high number of undervalued companies. Now, the managers' duty of resistance against the takeover bidder serves, in the first case, to curb an unproductive acquisition and, in the second, to raise the price of an unacceptably low bid. In short, it boils down to saying that the passivity duty produces inefficiencies, whereas the duty of resistance protects both shareholder interest and the general interest.

On the face of it, these arguments may sound persuasive, but they are not, on more detailed reflection. It is true that the market for corporate control has two weak points – the risk of expropriation, and the risk of undervaluation. What happens is that, in Europe, these systemic costs are offset to a reasonable extent. The expropriation risk is hampered by the compulsory takeover, and the undervaluation risk is weakened thanks to competing takeover bids. Both instruments undoubtedly entail their own costs too, as we shall clarify below. But both are prevalent in Europe, and it is this environment of compulsory takeovers and competing takeover bids which should serve as our benchmark.

2.3.1 Compulsory takeover regime

The equal opportunity rule underlying the compulsory takeover regime is a very effective weapon for curbing expropriatory sales. A compulsory takeover raises the costs of launching a takeover bid because the offer made for the control block needs to be extended to the rest of the stakeholders. This discourages unproductive deals, as it is highly unlikely that an expropriator will acquire a company in order to draw private benefits from the control if the cost of doing so cancels out the expected profit. The drawbacks of the rule deserve to be given some remarks, though. A compulsory takeover is potentially a costly rule because it inhibits market development,[22] and curbs not only inefficient deals, but also other efficient ones too (it can lock the controller inside even though the bidder were to enhance company value).[23] This suggests that the rule is ideal for protecting shareholders in

---

21 Black and Kraakman (2002, p. 521).

22 Berglöf and Burkart (2003, pp. 196–18).

23 Bebchuk (1994).

contexts involving high private benefits of control – the case in several European jurisdictions.

2.3.2 Competitive bidding auction system

The risk of undervaluation, if it exists, is counteracted by the auction promoted by competing takeover bids. In addition, the passivity duty does not forbid the search for better bidders. Managers can always do this without violating their fiduciary duties (art. 9.2 Takeover Directive). If the original bid is not very high, what can be expected to happen –particularly with a little help from the managers of the target company – is that competing bids are made that improve the price. Consequently, if the quotation price does not reflect the value of the target company and the initial bid is timid, this produces an invitation-to-call effect between competing bidders who will then bid upwards.[24] In fact, perhaps the most serious drawback of a competitive bidding auction system affects the acquirer instead of the target. We are referring to the risk of undervaluation produced by the so-called winner's curse.[25] There is certainly no doubt that the competing takeover bid system has another side to it.[26] Like the equal opportunity rule, it may inhibit, to some extent, the market for corporate control. Subsequent bids can seriously punish the initial offeror, who has incurred the costs of preparing and submitting the bid, that are frequently high, discouraging thus, the presentation of initial bids. And if there is no initial tender offer, there will be no competing tenders either. What is not doubtful, though, is that, either through formal auction, or through informal soliciting of new bids by the managers of the target, competition among bidders increases bid value.[27]

---

[24] Fishman (1988); Jennings and Mazzeo, (1993, p. 883) find empirical evidence of this effect.

[25] The winner's curse arises in common value auctions, not in private value auctions. In common value auctions, property valuation is the same – but uncertain – to all bidders, whereas in private value auctions, the bidders' private – and different – preferences are taken into account. Cramton and Schwartz (1991) understand that in the takeover context, the common value auction model is generally a better approximation to reality. The risk of falling into the winner's curse, and ending up paying too much is deemed to be particularly dangerous in market for corporate control: See Naraiya (1998); Black (1989, pp. 623–8).

[26] See Sáez (2003).

[27] Cramton and Schwartz (1991).

3. THE PROBLEMS WITH PRIVATE ENFORCEMENT OF THE PASSIVITY RULE

3.1 What if Enforcement is What Really Matters?

In the preceding section we have tried to give reasons supporting the idea that the passivity rule is, on the whole, an efficient ingredient of Takeover Law. In fact, the Takeover Directive, and the Law in several European jurisdictions, adopt it as the default regime.

But this is not enough. We all know that 'Law in books' does not necessarily mean 'Law in action'. This is especially true in a rule such as this that arouses powerful – and concentrated – resistance against its application. The key to the rule being effective – and not a trivial adornment of the legal regime – lies in the enforcement strategy adopted by the legal system. There is a twofold argument behind this idea. On the one hand, if the rule is to be regularly observed, it needs to catch on in the corporate culture and be considered by market operators as a valuable rule of fair play. It is very difficult – and in any event enormously costly – to enforce a rule that is in no way internalised by the community at which it is aimed. If opposition to it is very strong, the rule will end up succumbing, save in exceptional cases.

On the other hand, the success or failure largely depends on timing. Managers as a group can be expected not to twiddle their thumbs and do nothing. They have powerful incentives to try to make the rule fail, and they can rely on the contacts and influence to succeed in tipping the scales in their favour. As a result, in this game of opposing forces, the winning conduct (whether of resistance or passivity) is very likely to be the one succeeding in being the first to become established as a corporate social norm. For this reason, the longer the rule takes to become rooted as a social norm, the higher will be the risk of managers' political pressures succeeding. When that time comes, the corporate social norm will prevail however inefficient it may be.

The theory we intend to present below is that private disciplining mechanisms of the passivity duty are defective. Implementation of the rule in the market, in our view, calls for a well-designed and publicly-perceived sanctioning system. Otherwise, the passivity duty will cease to be seen as such, and the rule will gradually lose its legitimacy.

The first step in our task attempts to show that private enforcement – essentially articulated through class actions brought against managers violating the passivity duty – does not meet the expectations. The traditional enforcement system for duties of loyalty is liability through shareholders' class actions. The parties harmed by the disloyal actions of managers are the ones suing for damages. To our knowledge, no actual cases have been brought for infringement of the passivity duty. This is a bad sign about the effectiveness of an enforcement mechanism. Moreover, there are other reasons for being suspicious of the strength of shareholders' class actions as enforcers of the passivity rule: on the one hand, there are structural impediments affecting those suits which prevent that the harm suffered by shareholders when defensive tactics are used by managers to be translated into a damage payment at the expense of the latter; on the other hand, there are functional impediments that determine – even if the structural obstacles were removed – that shareholders' suits, if not combined with other enforcement mechanisms, would make an inefficient system of sanctions with poor deterrent capacity. The second step would take up public enforcement as the mechanism holding more promise for an effective application of the passivity rule.

3.2 A Game-theoretical Model of Class Actions vs. Public Sanctions in the Enforcement of the Passivity Rule

With the help of a simple game-theoretic model it is possible to illustrate the conceptual inadequacy of shareholders' class action suits to enforce the passivity rule of managers facing a hostile take-over. In the next sub-section we will present and discuss some additional complicating factors that will make the shortcomings of securities class actions even more apparent in the enforcement of the passivity rule.

In the first game, players act under a passivity rule enforced by shareholders' class actions against managers.

Let's assume that in the presence of a hostile take-over bid,[28] the managers of the target company can choose between two actions: passive or active (in the sense of resisting or opposing the bid). If managers remain passive, there is an exogenous probability, p, that the bid will be accepted by shareholders, and thus, succeed in allowing control of the target by the bidder. In this case, the bid is successful, and shareholders obtain a premium of t (over their existing baseline value, which we normalize to 0). Managers, on their part, are simply sacked by the successful bidder, and obtain their outside – of the target company – best alternative revenue, which we also normalize to 0. If the bid fails (for reasons beyond the scope of our simple model: shareholders reject it because they expect a more profitable offer in the future, or believe the bid does not reflect the true

[28] Given that we focus on the enforcement of the passivity rule, we disregard the strategic nature of the bidding behaviour by the would-be controller.

value of the company; or there are antitrust concerns that make the Government block the take-over, for instance) shareholders continue enjoying their baseline value (normalized to 0) and managers continue enjoying their rents r over their next best alternative.

If, on the contrary, managers actively oppose the bid, we assume that the probability of success of the bid falls to $q<p$. We also assume that the behaviour of managers obstructing the bid has a cost, z, which is borne by the target company: the cost of the litigation challenging the bid, or the cost of the other defensive tactics deployed by management.

If, given the active opposition by management, the bid succeeds (remember, with the reduced probability q), the payoffs to managers and shareholders are the same as in the previous sub-game, that is, (0, t).

One may be – correctly – tempted to question the assumption that in case the bid succeeds, shareholders will not have to face the costs of the defensive tactics, because the premium they will cash over their baseline value will remain unchanged – from the passive managers sub-game level – at t. In reality, who bears in the end those costs does not affect our reasoning, as long as managers can escape facing, through legal liabilities or other means, the cost of their defensive actions. If the tender offer cannot be changed after being public – a rule prevailing in many European legal systems[29] – it is the bidder who, at least initially, bears the cost of defensive tactics, because he acquires a company with a diminished value, namely in the amount of z. Why is it plausible to assume that the bidder will not be able to recover such costs from the exiting managers? The reason is twofold. First, it is doubtful whether the use of defensive tactics in violation of the passivity rule can justify the imposition of liability vis-à-vis the bidder, even if successful. The passivity rule, at least in Continental Europe, is a consequence of the general duty of loyalty in favour of existing shareholders, not in favour of external parties, regardless of whether they are potential hostile bidders, or future shareholders. There would be no breach of duty towards the bidder on which to base managers' liability. Second, even if breach of duty towards the prospective acquirer could be found in theory, the *ex-post* nature of the liability finding make it much more probable that the defensive tactics deployed by managers will not be deemed by Courts to be in violation of the passivity rule. The reason lies that, by definition, we would be discussing liability once the take-over bid

---

[29] The common rule is that an offer can be revised only to the extent necessary to implement an increased or improved offer, and the right of withdrawal (Rule 32.4 and Rule 34 of the English Takeover Code; and art. 13 of the European Directive 2004/25/CE).

has been successful, and given the course of events it seems harder for a Court to consider that the failed tactics were in fact prohibited defensive ones.

When, in the presence of active opposition by managers, the bid fails, shareholders have to decide whether to sue the managers for violation of the passivity rule. If they opt for not suing the managers, payoffs for managers and shareholders will respectively equal (r, -z). If shareholders disappointed with the failure of the tender offer file a class action suit, they will be able to recover from the managers the loss of a chance of obtaining the premium t over the baseline value of the company. We build the best scenario here for the shareholders' class action: we assume away legal costs of bringing the class action; we assume that the class will be adequately represented by legal counsel faithfully pursuing the interests of the class; we assume that there is no legal error in the determination of liability; and we assume that by the Court's decision – or in settlement – the shareholders' class will receive in damages the amount lost as a consequence of the managerial breach of the passivity rule, less the fee obtained by the class action lawyers: t (p-q) (1-δ).[30] We also assume – essentially, because the amount should legally go to the company, and not to a group of disappointed shareholders, and because it will be difficult (and require different types of evidence than that showing the amount of t (p-q)) – to determine – that the shareholders will not recover the cost of the defensive measures themselves, z, which will not be included in the damage award.

Managers, in turn, have to pay damages – covering both shareholders' and class action lawyers' shares – and their own legal defence costs, f. We further assume – something that is not automatic, particularly if the case is settled before trial – that the losing managers will also lose their jobs and their accompanying rents.

In Figure 14.1 we represent in extended form the game described in the preceding paragraphs. It is clear that without specific values for the parameters r, t, z, p, and q, we cannot generally characterize the equilibria of this game. But it is also the case that for a substantial range of values of r and q, it is likely that managers will not be induced to refrain from defensive tactics post-tender offer, given that managers do not always face the consequences – any consequence, in fact – of the violation of the passivity rule. There is an ostensible underenforcement problem. The larger is z, the

[30] We assume the fee paid by the group of shareholders as a contingent fee, even if this arrangement is still formally not acceptable in several Continental European jurisdictions, but the assumption, we think, better reflects the existing experience in other places on securities class actions. It does not affect the qualitative nature of the implications of this simple model.

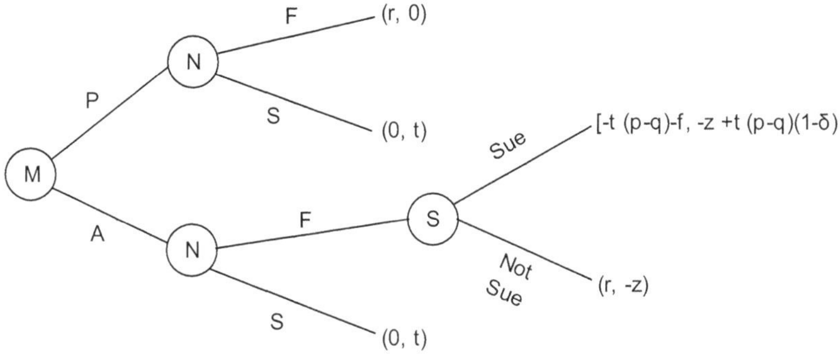

Note: (-, -) = payoffs to (manager, shareholders).

Figure 14.1 Game in which players act under a passivity rule enforced by shareholders' class actions against managers

larger is the social loss resulting from this inadequate level of enforcement of the passivity rule. An important qualification here is that the enforcement shortcomings of the shareholders' class action mechanism are hard to tackle through specific legal policy measures in this field. All the relevant parameters r, t, z, p, and q, are either entirely out of reach of legal measures, or are the result of general and complex elements of a legal system.

In the second game we represent the interaction, governed also by a passivity rule, albeit under a different enforcement regime. Now, the violation of such a rule is subject to penalties imposed by the Government, more specifically by the public agency regulating the securities market. The players are thus now three, managers, shareholders, and the Government.

As before, managers of a target company after a take-over bid are confronted with the choice of two strategies. On the one side, a hands-off strategy, that implies no interference with the bid. In this case, as in the previous game, there is an exogenous probability, p, of the bid being successful, and shareholders obtaining a premium of t (over their existing baseline value, which we again normalize to 0). Managers, on their part, will be fired by the successful bidder, and will be left with their normalized best alternative employment revenue of 0.

If the bid fails, for exogenous reasons, shareholders continue enjoying their baseline company value (normalized to 0) and managers continue enjoying their rents r over their next best employment alternative. Both in the case of success and of failure of the bid, the Government is not affected by the outcome, given that we assume that it is neutral towards the fate of the tender offer as such.

On the other side, managers may opt for using defensive tactics to knock down the bid. If this occurs, the Government may react by sanctioning the managers. If the Government does not impose sanctions, the bid will continue its due course, and will succeed (with the decreased probability q) or fail in the end. Payoffs for managers and shareholders will be identical to the ones in the previous game, for both the success and the failure of the bid. The Government, in turn, if it allows the violation of the passivity rule to go unsanctioned, will suffer some disrepute,[31] and thus incur a cost of –d, regardless of the fate of the bid.

The Government can impose a penalty on the managers, something that entails some sanctioning costs, c, but will also bring the amount of the penalty, s. We assume that the penalty is monetary, although in later sections we will discuss other alternative penalties as well. If the Government effectively sanctions the violating managers, the bid will also continue its course, and we assume – modestly, in terms of the effectiveness of public enforcement – that the probability of success will be unaffected by the sanction, and thus will remain at the low level of q. Moreover, whatever the fate of the bid, the managers sanctioned by the Government will be fired. The resulting net payoffs are thus (-s, -z, s-c) in case the bid fails, and (-s, t, s-c) if it succeeds.

Two additional factors are relevant at this point. First, that the lack of sanctioning response from the Government, does not mainly obey to insufficient detection of the illegal behaviour, nor, at least to a large extent, to the desire to avoid the risk of legal error. Given the open and public nature of a take-over process, and the heavy involvement of regulatory agencies in many of their landmarks, and given the fact that many defensive tactics, by their very nature (litigation, release of poison pills) have to take place in the open, the likelihood that a violation of the passivity rule will remain undetected by the Government is definitely low. Factual uncertainty being very exceptional, the risk of error in the imposition of the sanctions will also be correspondingly so, although it will not be zero. Even if the actions take place in the open, and are of a voluntary nature – there is little or no chance that they occur by negligence or inadvertently – there may be some legal uncertainty regarding the proper qualification of the relevant actions. We think, however, implausible, that the failure of the regulatory agency to take action in a given case is due to the problems of detection or legal error. It seems more likely that they are due to lack of resources to act,

[31] It is immaterial whether the source of this cost for the regulatory agency is the unsatisfied desire that justice be done, and social welfare promoted, or more pragmatically, the loss of prestige and authority in future regulating and sanctioning activities.

or to collusion with the managers (a factor we do not explicitly include into our model, although c could be interpreted as including the foregone advantages of colluding with the managers who violated the passivity rule).

The second factor refers to the role of shareholders' class actions in the presence of Government sanctions. Typically, the latter will not rule out or pre-empt the former. On the contrary, once the Government has imposed a sanction on managers for breach of the passivity duty, if the bid turns out to be, in the end, unsuccessful, the chances that a class action will be filed, and the likelihood of success of such an action, will be significantly enhanced. This means that the payoffs of the players in part of the Government sanction sub-game that follows it are, with high likelihood: $(-s - t(p-q) - f, -z + t(p-q)(1-\delta), s-c)$ in case the bid fails, and $(-s, t, s-c)$[32] if it succeeds.

In Figure 14.2 we represent in extended form the game described in the preceding paragraphs – without the latter qualification on the parasitic class action suits following the Government sanction.

It is clear that without specific values for the parameters r, t, z, s, c, d, p, and q, we cannot generally characterize the equilibrium strategies of this game. It is clear that if the amount of the sanction, s, is low, and/or the cost of governmental sanctioning, c, is high, it is likely that we will encounter an underenforcement problem with respect to the passivity rule. But if the value of s is sufficiently high, and of c sufficiently low, we could encounter adequate levels of enforcement, that would induce the passivity actions by managers that we argued were desirable in the first section of the chapter. Moreover, the enforcement deficits that may erode Government action are not out of the reach of improvements in legal policy. Though not entirely unconstrained, s is largely under the control of the legal policy-maker, and the same is true of c (even if collusion will probably be harder to tackle).

This gives public enforcement through sanctions an inherent advantage over shareholders' class actions as an effective instrument to enforce the passivity rule.

This prominent role of public enforcement is reinforced in the presence of the already mentioned parasitic shareholders' suits which would supplement some of the flanks left by public enforcement, and would allow the latter to economize on some of the relevant dimensions (for instance, private damages following the public sanction make it possible to keep the level of deterrence of wrongdoing with lower levels of sanction, something

[32] It may even be the case that the payoffs for the players are $(-s-z, t, s-c)$ if the Government sanction provides the successful bidder with sufficient cause of action against the managers in order to recover the direct costs of the defensive tactics.

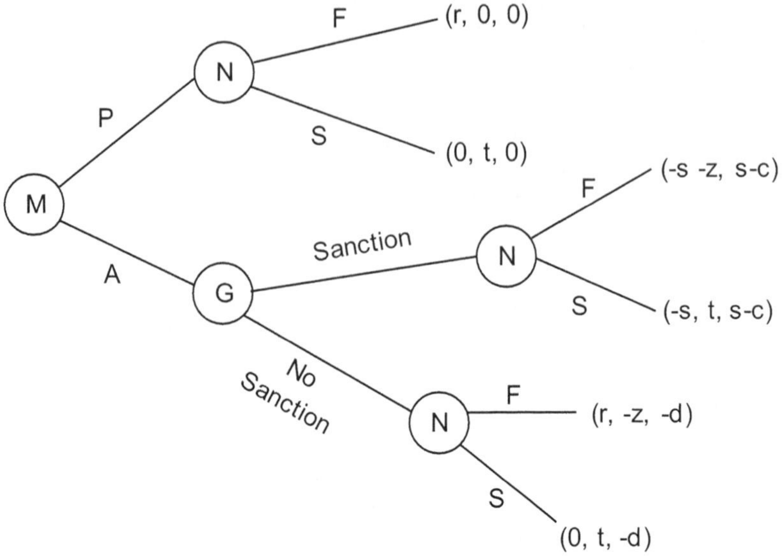

Note: (-, -, -) = payoffs to (manager, shareholders, government).

Figure 14.2 Game in which players act under a passivity rule, the violation of which is subject to penalties imposed by the Government

that may be socially beneficial if the sanction is in itself costly, like a non-monetary sanction).

The interaction with parasitic shareholders' class action suits would look as depicted in Figure 14.3.

It is again obvious that class actions following the track of previous sanctioning action by the securities regulator would increase deterrence of violations of the passivity rule, as the damage payment may add up to the fine already imposed upon the manager. This does not imply that those parasitic suits are worth their cost in social terms. In fact, in our simple model we have not explicitly considered the social costs of the class action mechanism, neither here nor when considering the private enforcement instrument alone.[33] But it is clear that in association with public enforcement, class actions cannot be more socially costly than when functioning essentially in association as an enforcement mechanism. In fact, quite the contrary is to be expected. When the violation has already been established

[33] We have not considered explicitly a social welfare function either, although we believe it is unnecessary for the purposes of showing the disadvantage of private enforcement in our context.

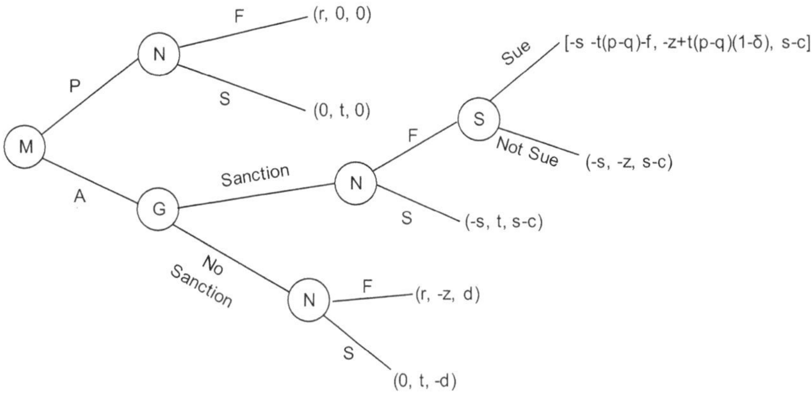

Note: (-, -, -) = payoffs to (manager, shareholders, government).

Figure 14.3 Interaction with parasitic shareholders' class action suits

and sanctioned by the regulator, it is highly likely that the costs of the class action will be lower. The issue of liability will be straightforward, and the litigating efforts of both the class action counsel,[34] and defence lawyers, will concentrate on the amount of damages to be paid. So public enforcement seems not only a promising enforcement mechanism in itself, but also enhances the deterrent potential of private enforcement (at least, reducing its costs, though more realistically, also increasing the probability of success of the class action and the amounts of compensation recovered). La Porta, Lopez-de-Silanes, and Shleifer,[35] argue that in the field of securities law, public enforcement by the regulator (through investigative powers, for instance, that can obtain documents, or testimonies from parties involved) produces information that has public good character: criminal and civil litigation can be built upon it.

[34] The increased simplicity of the case would not only reduce litigation effort and cost, it would also decrease the agency costs in the relationship between the class and the class attorney, given that the selection and monitoring of the latter would be simplified. For instance, in cases in which only the damage amount is at stake (liability is already a given) it is easier to use an auction to select the law firm that would represent the class. This was the method used in the class action against the auction houses Christies and Sotheby's: *In Re Auction Houses Antitrust Litigation*, 197 F. R. D. at 71, 85 (S. D. N. Y. 2000). The use of auctions to select counsel, however, has fierce critics: Bebchuk (2002b); Fisch (2002). Some economic literature is more positive of auctions as incentive mechanism for class action lawyers: Klement and Neeman (2004).

[35] La Porta, Lopez-de-Silanes and Shleifer (2006, p. 12).

In fact, there seems to be empirical evidence confirming the existence of this positive effect of public enforcement on private enforcement. Cox and Thomas[36] have found that the dollar amount of the settlement obtained in a private action is positively and significantly correlated with a number of factors (provable losses, total assets) among which the presence of an SEC enforcement action is relevant.

In the following section we discuss in more depth some additional factors that make more transparent the inadequacy of class actions suits to enforce the passivity rule.

3.3 Why Shareholders' Class Actions Make a Bad Disciplining Mechanism for the Passivity Duty

From the preceding sub-section we can derive the implication that in the context of the passivity rule, shareholders' class actions are, theoretically, ill suited to be, on their own, an effective enforcement tool. The essential problem of class actions – or other private actions, for that matter – as an enforcement mechanism here, is that it has poor deterrence power because the anticipated sanction by the infringer is essentially ineffective, both in legal [see 3.3.1 below] and reputation terms [see 3.3.2 below]. This latter aspect warns us that private litigation is not a suitable system for efficiently implementing the corporate rule of manager passivity in the face of a takeover bid [see 3.3.3 below].

3.3.1 Threat of private lawsuits does not deter the violation of the passivity rule

The threat of private lawsuits does not deter the violation of the passivity rule because the level of exposure of managers who infringe their duty to the effective imposition of liability is low, and the panoply of sanctions ineffectually weak.[37] This leads to an expected liability which is very likely to be notably lower than the benefits from infringing the duty. In fact, if we judge it from an *ex ante* perspective, in a cost-benefit analysis prior to a decision as to whether or not to carry out sanctionable conduct in relation to the passivity rule, managers would not find it too hard to be inclined towards active opposition to a hostile takeover bid.

---

[36] Cox and Thomas (2004).

[37] Eisenberg (1999, p. 1276), soundly admits that if the only reason for violating the duty of loyalty is exposure to a legal sanction, agents will regularly violate the duty.

(i) For a start, the likelihood of offenders being effectively declared liable is low. As was apparent in the game-theoretical model, not all infringements result in suit, only if the bid fails in the end is a private lawsuit imaginable. Moreover, it should be even more difficult for the matter to be actually brought to Court if we take into account the low litigiousness actually involved.[38]

On top of this, there are noteworthy technical difficulties based on liability law for the shareholders' suit to prosper: shareholders would need to show, besides the violation of a duty – and let's assume this is an easy condition to establish – the amount of harm suffered – and what if market value of the company did not go down significantly after the bid failed, but shareholders believe the long-term value with current management would be lower than the bid? – the causal link between the breach of duty and the losses incurred by shareholders, as well as proximate causation issues.

Furthermore, added to the foregoing must be the small amount of experience acquired by European Courts in deciding upon these matters, which makes them more prone to failing to detect breach of duty. The traditional lack of training of the judges in financial matters, and the formalistic attitude, the belief that Courts function as executors of what the Law pre-ordains, typical of Continental European judicial juridical ethos, makes Courts, overall, more inclined to 'legalise' conduct that is dishonest, but formally in compliance with the rule.

(ii) Liability, when imposed, would not likely be too costly, because the sums involved are inefficiently low. This malfunction is, in fact, common to the infringement of other duties of loyalty on the part of the managers.[39] Civil liability is a remedy – at least in Europe – with a scope inherently limited to compensating the damage caused. Damage payment is not allowed to go any farther, reaching the plane of pure and simple sanction – such as with US punitive damages. Thus, if managers are found liable, in the worst – for them – scenario they only face compensation of proven harm or, alternatively, when harm is too hard to quantify, (as may frequently happen in this context), to

[38] The low level of confidence in the effective functioning of Courts in relation to illicit action linked to the securities market is an empirically proven fact in the US, a system with, at least allegedly, higher levels of litigation and Court involvement in corporate wrongdoing: See Cox and Thomas (2002); Pritchard (2002).

[39] See Cooter and Freedman (1991). This question has been studied in a Civil Law setting by Paz-Ares (2003).

disgorge the benefit obtained through the violation of the duty (an amount not too easy to quantify either in this setting).

(iii) Moreover, if found liable, managers would not personally incur any great loss: their liability as managers is ordinarily insured, and with insurance premiums paid by the company itself.[40] To a large extent the victim of the breach of duty – the stockholders – shoulder their own harm *ex-ante*, albeit leaving behind serious transaction costs. If, exceptionally, insurance coverage were to be excluded, the risk, for reasons mentioned in (ii) will typically not be extremely high.

(iv) In the worst case scenario for the managers, namely a high damage judgment in favour of the adversely affected shareholders that is not covered by D&O insurance, typically the manager will not face full liability, as he will likely be judgment-proof. Liability, particularly if the company is a large one and the class of harmed shareholders is large, will exceed his assets. Insolvency and personal bankruptcy discharge will protect the infringer from having to face all of the consequences of his or her action.[41]

This cost-benefit calculus becomes more tainted towards infringement, the greater the incentives managers face to breach the duty, or the greater the benefits arising from breach. Such is the case of the passivity duty: the benefits are most tempting (strong incentives exist for administrators to defend themselves), and the costs become externalised (few restrictions exist for not doing so). As we have shown, the inability of shareholders' class action suits seen, to deter managers from infringing the passivity rule does not only lie in the low expected sanction (probability of imposition multiplied by the magnitude), but also in the fact that the infringer's conduct entails some costs that will affect the pockets of the innocent parties, and not the guilty.

And we need to remember that in a takeover the stakes are high for the manager: job retention, and the ensuing private benefits (and they may be presumably high, if we take into account the fact that the bidder is prepared

---

[40] The empirical evidence available to us seems to confirm this idea. Rarely does liability personally affect the manager. The cases in which personal wealth is touched, besides cases of criminal liability, tend to be those in which the company itself is insolvent, or has had financial problems in finding insurance coverage. See Coffee (2006).

[41] Insolvency is one of the main drawbacks to the use of *ex post* monetary sanctioning instruments to regulate conduct. It is a well-known result in the Law & Economics literature that insolvency produces under-deterrence, and may even determine a shift in the design of optimal liability standards: See Ganuza and Gómez (2008).

to increase the value of the firm by reducing the agency costs). If defensive tactics allow managers to thwart the tender offer, and keep job and benefits, the cost of expected liability is very likely to be worth it. If they win, they achieve their goal, and do not pick up the price tab, but instead the parties presumably harmed by their conduct do – the shareholders. If they lose, the negative consequences for the firm of the defensive measures adopted will substantially be a problem for the new management.

Observe that this is not only a question of redistribution of company resources, but also of social costs. Since a negative externality exists that liability is unable to internalize, an excess amount of defensive measures against a takeover would be adopted, with respect to the social optimum. And, moreover, such measures will have a negative effect on social welfare: launching a bid for control will be more costly, so the likelihood of their occurrence will be reduced, and as a result the market for corporate control narrows.[42] This is why private enforcement does not meet the expectations, and we can only hope that, given the negative implications for social welfare, public enforcement will be able deterrence deficit in this field.

3.3.2 Shareholders' class actions do not appear to entail significant reputational penalties for managers

We should not forget that social reproach is a very effective non-legal enforcement mechanism. Managers, as most other people in different walks of life, are not only concerned about their monetary income, but also about their reputation in their social sphere. For instance, a well-designed compensation system is a good way to provide managerial incentives and lower agency costs.[43] This is not the case with exposure to liability for breach of a duty of loyalty.[44] From a purely monetary point of view, we have argued that liability towards shareholders brings little dissuasion. This is why the reputational element must also be taken into account, so that the legal

---

42 Indeed, from an economic perspective, in essence the argument put forward is that, for deterrence purposes, the expected sanction, if we ignore enforcement costs, ought to equal social harm. This is the classic stance of Becker (1968, pp. 169–70). The problematic question would naturally be how to measure social harm. Be that as it may, what unquestionably transpires from the foregoing is that private enforcement is very far from being capable of succeeding in bringing the expected sanction close to the magnitude of the social loss from the infringing conduct.

43 Jensen and Murphy (1990). Remuneration has its limits. Instead of reducing them, it may cause higher agency fees if not offset by efficient mechanisms of good governance, see Bebchuk and Fried (2004).

44 Some theoretical findings suggest that reputational penalties, and not pecuniary sanctions are the main threat to which managers sued for disloyalty are subjected, see Black, Cheffins and Klausner (2006).

sanction can also take its toll in terms of prestige and reputation.[45] If, for instance, as the result of a shareholders' suit, managers would lose the chance to sit in other governing boards (because they would be deemed untrustworthy for such positions), they would have serious reason for abstaining from defensive tactics in a given situation.

Apparently, shareholders' suits do not involve social stigma for managers, at least in the country that has studied this matter more attentively.[46] It may be able to do so in a legal environment where loyalty is well established as a corporate social norm, and where a striking case of fraud takes place. In general terms, however, it seems to perform poorly also with respect to the deterrence power of social stigma. This is especially true for conduct related to the securities market. Empirical studies indicate reputation only appears to be sensitive to private enforcement when this is accompanied by public enforcement.[47] On the other hand, other types of sanction have greater reputational consequences, clearly criminal sanctions or those levied by public institutions. The reason is twofold. First, civil lawsuits frequently can often be purely strategic and spurious, and the market – correctly discounts the noise in the information to this effect.[48] And given

---

[45] Initially, the role of the market's strict reputational penalties was overrated, see Klein and Leffler (1981); Fama and Jensen (1983). Today we know that it should go along with a legal sanction, in order to achieve adequate levels of deterrence.

[46] Empirical data bear this out. Litigiousness vis-à-vis managers is highly discounted, and does not appear to correspond to reputational penalties, quite the opposite rather. Only sanctions imposed by the SEC give a signal of managerial disrepute to the market, see Helland (2006). It could be thought that the US case, where shareholders' suits are not infrequent, may not be a good benchmark for the European case, where they are rare events, and specifically so in relation to listed companies. The rarer the suits, the argument would go, the greater the stigmatising potential of the effective findings of liability. Although we do not have empirical evidence on this issue, our guess would be exactly the opposite: in the place in which liability works more effectively, there is little trace of reputational penalties being added to it, there where it hardly works managerial reputations go along an entirely different path. Indeed, if the argument we reject were right, any increase in the number of suits, which would increase the level of the legal sanction, would also raise the number of spurious claims and nuisance suits, and this would, in turn, reduce the informational value and the reputational penalties associated with the suits.

[47] Furthermore, studies indicate that the likelihood of civil suits being successful goes up considerably when accompanied by a sanction by the regulator, Cox and Thomas (2003).

[48] It is not surprising that the studies run on the American market demonstrate that the majority of the lawsuits for fraud are brought against large companies (the so-called 'deep pockets'), concentrate on certain specific industries, and affect

that a large fraction of the lawsuits for fraud in the securities market are frivolous, news of their bringing does not throw any – reliable – negative light on the managers. This is even more obvious in the takeover field. The battle for control can lead all the parties involved to use the Courts as part of offensive or defensive strategies. The fact that the parties mutually accuse each other, rightly or wrongly, of almost anything in a Civil Court, comes within the regular scene of things. Criminal and regulatory charges, although they can also be frivolous, can be reasonably expected to be so with a much lower rate of occurrence.

The second reason lies in the fact that most – even the founded ones – shareholders' suits are settled before trial, and without a Court or a jury having the chance of passing a judgment of liability. The possible reputational signal thus, gets substantially, if not entirely, muted.

3.3.3 Private shareholders' suits

The additional problem of private shareholders' suits in enforcing a passivity duty is that they *do not constitute an efficient mechanism for implementing an ethos of honesty and fair play in takeovers*. If the legally prohibited conduct is socially perceived as disloyal and reprehensible, enforcement and compliance become easier. The process is clear. Managers – as the rest of us – care about esteem and reputation. If the system of community values rewards the honesty of an agent, what normally happens is that this way of thinking is internalised by the agents, and ends up impregnating institutions, and company law itself. Social extra-legal enforcement works at two levels. Instrumentally, the legal sanction joins the social sanction in terms of reputation – the infringing manager has a tainted record and companies will punish him by not hiring. But, as we know, the deterrent effect of reputational penalties in this respect is linked to the level of detection of norm violation. Nevertheless, the second level of enforcement, the internalisation of the duty as a personal rule of conduct, is more effective, because it operates even when infringement is hard to detect. That being so, the problem in many European countries is that the passivity rule is a legal, albeit not a social norm (see (i) below), and this confronts us with the challenge of implementing the social norm (see (ii) below), and with the risks we can encounter (see (iii) below).

(i) It is certainly true that we do not have here a rule with strong social support. The reason is not difficult to discern: The passivity rule is in

---

companies with volatile securities. A high level of frivolous and strategic suits can be expected: See Alexander (1991); Bohn and Choi (1996); Choi (2004).

Continental Europe essentially a product of a foreign – English – influence in Securities Law. This, rationally, should not lessen the value of the norm. It embodies a solution that is overall efficient and, as a social norm, it is a public good of some value (in the absence of a social norm, the costs generated by enforcement of the legal norm are very high[49]). But, to a certain extent, it is artificial. Takeover Law is adopted cold by the most Continental European legislators, taking advantage of the proven experience of the London Panel. There, the City financiers are the ones to decide, privately and voluntarily, whether or not to subject themselves to a compulsory code of conduct.[50]

Looked at closely, the provenance of the norm is not so important, in other words, the party producing the rule – be it public authorities or market self-regulation (at the end of day, the Continental legislators take up the norm generated by the operators of a relatively efficient market, instead of concocting one).[51] The decisive factor is something else: *the interest groups operating in a market.*[52] If the interests of the most powerful group essentially concur with the dictates of efficiency, the market will provide itself with rules protecting investors, and with mechanisms guaranteeing their enforcement and compliance. On the other hand, if the most powerful groups are those with a personal interest in private benefits, market regulation

---

49 In the area of duties of loyalty in fiduciary relationships, social norms play an irreplaceable role. Were this not so, in order to balance the equation, the internal 'monitoring' system would need to be strengthened, and punitive damages applied [amongst Continental commentators, this controversial measure is defended by Paz-Ares (2003, pp. 27–8)]. Even so, it is undeniable that both options are extremely costly.

50 The traditional social norm is opposed to hostile takeover bids. These were deemed in the past to be bad for industry, and a dishonest means of acquiring the control of a company. This attitude is gradually changing. The point of inflection in Great Britain was marked by the battle for *British Aluminium*. Sponsored by the Bank of England, the market players furnished themselves with some rules of conduct, all of which were determined by the interests of investors and the market. On this issue, see Armour and Skeel (2006).

51 The specialised literature has devoted a great deal of attention to this circumstance. The options under debate are self-regulation, following the English model, competition between States in the matter of regulating the securities market, or the creation of a powerful and efficient regulator [as shown by Choi (2000); Romano (1998); Prentice (2006)]. Experience asserts that different systems work in certain contexts and not in others. The fundamental factor is to know whether the incentives for individuals or the institutions issuing the rules are in line with the development of social welfare, or whether they serve other self-centred interests.

52 This is the thesis (sound in our view) expressed by Armour and Skeel (2006).

will be structured according to those interests, regardless of efficiency.[53] Thus, in the English case, the market for corporate control substantially lies in the hands of institutional investors. In continental Europe, it lies fundamentally in the hands of the control blocks. And their respective interests, in the scenario of public tender offers, are divergent. Insiders, whether managers in the case of dispersed ownership, or controlling shareholders in the case of concentrated ownership, do not approve of the fact that the market can wrench control away from them. Control gives them the – legitimate – power to take corporate decisions without minority shareholders, and the – illegitimate – power to obtain private benefits. If the market is dominated by insiders, it is to be expected that they will agree on rules of play that fit in better with their interest in maintaining control. Quite a different situation arises when the market is controlled by investors. Then they will support the takeover bid system, and particularly the passivity rule, because it is a mechanism that serves their interests and gives them the final say on how to maximise the value of their investments.

(ii) The previous reflections lead us to the conclusion that the passivity rule should be introduced, at least to a certain extent, as a social norm for it to be efficient. What happens is that it is no easy task to implement the passivity duty as a social norm. Precisely for this reason, enforcement becomes imperative. Then, sure enough, in order for passivity to form part of the rules of the game shared by the players, they need to feel committed to the non-use of such arts. As a result, the participants in the market for corporate control will be obliged to respect the letter and the spirit of the norm. Now, the idea we think unavoidable to stress is that, in order to succeed in implementing and enforcing this commitment, the major role in disciplining and sanctioning should fall to the market regulator, and not to shareholders' class action suits.

And this is so for two reasons. The first warns us that *public enforcement holds a disciplining power for the passivity duty that is more effective than private enforcement*. This is unquestionable when it comes to the general regulation of a market. We have already pointed out the factors making it difficult for shareholders' private suits to send an effective deterrent message, in view of the probable paltry nature of expected liability. In addition, the authority of the regulating body means that the legal sanction now sends out a clearer

[53] Pirrong (2002).

message that defensive measures are reprehensible, and this corresponds to a higher likelihood of loss of reputation on the part of infringers. We shall return to these questions later.

The second idea refers to the *unsoundness of leaving the leading role to the Courts, as happens with private suits*. Regardless of the technical dysfunctions arising from substantive law, Courts are inherently improperly placed to impose the passivity duty. Three reasons back this statement: the high risk of strategic litigation; the risk that judges will be subject to a pro-managerial bias when it comes to applying the passivity rule, thereby rendering it less effective; and the risk of under-investment on the plaintiff's side.

The *risk of strategic litigation* may consist, when the bidding contest is still open, in using the Courts as a ploy to delay the entire takeover process. The usual pattern would be for the managers of the company subjected to a hostile takeover bid to go to Court in order to gain time.[54] But there is no doubt that leaving the task of deciding on breach of the passivity duty exclusively or almost entirely up to the Courts, does very little in favour of the efficiency of the system. Firstly, because the passage of time runs against the bidder, and Courts operate slowly. Secondly, because to initiate legal proceedings against management is to give cause for the defendant to use all the legal tricks within their reach to prolong and hamper the proceedings, and with it, maybe, the takeover process. Uncertainty represents a very high cost to the bidders.

The *risk of undesirable bias* refers to the fact that if the Courts are in charge of defining and supervising enforcement of the passivity rule, it is predictable that they will be inclined towards favouring management to a greater extent than is desirable.[55] This is easily

---

[54] Litigation as a defensive tactic against a takeover bid is well referred in several studies, see, Jarrell (1985).

[55] This is undoubtedly a relevant factor for understanding the bias towards favouring defensive tactics shown by the Supreme Court of the State of Delaware in the US. In a regulatory framework of managerial primacy based on the business judgment rule, and with powerful detractors of the passivity rule, but also with powerful foundations for the duty of loyalty, the Court adopts an intermediate position and sets up the test of proportionality in the *Unocal* decision: in order to assess the legitimacy of a defensive measure, it must be checked to see whether it is proportionate to the threat (see Gilson and Kraakman (1989)). The result would have been very similar in Great Britain had the Courts been left to pass judgment on the passivity duty, as demonstrated by the few decisions existing in the late 1960s/early 1970s. In substance, they do not stray very far from the *Unocal* doctrine: See Armour and Skeel (2006, pp. 69–70).

explained. It is intuitive for almost everyone – including judges – to admit that fraud or deceit represent undesirable and reprehensible conduct. This is not the case with the use of defensive measures. At the limit – or so it will be claimed – all that managers do is defend the company from a threat. And managers will systematically allege that the tender offer, whatever its nature, is below the value of the firm, a statement, whatever true or false, difficult to refute in Court. This corresponds with widespread cognitive dispositions of lay people in financial matters, and Courts are lay people in such matters. This should make us fear that they will apply the passivity rule with legal rigour, but without the conviction generated by internalization of the underlying norm. This basic stance can show up when judgment is passed on a specific case. If the particular circumstances involved lead judges to believe that the tender offer is inadequate, they may be tempted to do justice in the specific case, and be soft in enforcing the prohibition.[56] This dysfunction can be exploited by 'active' managers and their team of lawyers, who will attempt to discredit the tender offer. The retrospective bias (if a better offer appears, then the first was too low, and thus opposition to the bid was justified) that has already been well identified by the behavioural law and economics literature, can be a temptation difficult to resist.[57]

The *risk of underinvestment in litigation on the side of the plaintiff is an additional important factor.* The incentives to invest in litigation are asymmetrically distributed in such cases. Defendants – the managers whose behaviour is taken to Court under the passivity rule – will have their legal expenses subsidized by the Company, albeit they reap full benefits of the legal proceedings: The benefits of winning the case are only enjoyed by managers, but not the costs, which are borne by the target company itself. This is very likely to incline managers to defend themselves with teeth and nails if taken to Court, and also to be generous – with other people's money – when it comes to reaching an agreement with the plaintiff on redressing the damage caused.[58] Moreover, litigation to enforce the rule will typically be carried out *ex*

---

[56] Clearly, the risk of this happening is greater in Common Law settings, but we cannot rule out its having a certain influence in Civil Law settings. It would seem clear that judges would be more reluctant to impose a high damage award when they believe that the conduct is not morally reproachable, see Coffee (1984, p. 1150).

[57] See, Sunstein (2000).

[58] In the jurisdictions with most experience in securities market fraud litigation, it has been proven that the parties are prone to reaching financial agreements within the confines of the coverage guaranteed by the insurance policy covering on the civil

post by disappointed shareholders – and we have already recounted the difficulties existing for *ex post* litigation of the rule. But there is also the chance that the offeror decides to challenge in Court the defensive tactics by the managers on the basis of a passivity rule infringement. This additional enforcement effort, however, is threatened by the fact that the incentives for the bidder to request the Court to enjoin the defensive strategy of the target are weakened due to the even more skewed distribution of costs and benefits of trial: if the claim by the offeror wins, the plaintiff reaps the benefits, but so do the plaintiff's potential competitors (once the target has been stripped down, another bidder could appear on the scene and take advantage of the situation to make a better offer). In this respect, the gains are in large part a public good (non-rival for all potential bidders). The costs, however, fall individually on the party bringing legal action. Just the opposite of what happens with the managers–defendants.

(iii) In this context, we cannot refrain from highlighting a serious danger affecting enforcement strategies for passivity duty, which is the rule of reciprocity. This rule is contained in Art. 12, in connection with Art. 9, both of the Takeover Directive. In essence, it provides that Member States can subject the passivity duty to a reciprocity precondition. That is, they can allow in their National laws, any company to opt out of the legal passivity duty when the foreign bidding firm is not subject to this duty in its national legislation. This is not the appropriate place for a thorough treatment of the rule, something others have already started doing.[59] But there is certainly room for highlighting an idea we indicated earlier, which is that *the reciprocity option reflects a lack of convinced opinion on the merits and superiority of the passivity duty*. The States with most experience in this field, such as Great Britain, have not joined the reciprocity bandwagon. This is reasonable for them as, if the legislation adopting the rule is pro-investor and pro-market – as we take it to be – it will continue to be so regardless of

accountability of the administrators. This means that it rarely happens that managers contribute personally to the agreement. The numerous empirical studies carried out over the past 15 years testify to this. For a general overview, see for all, Coffee (2006).

[59] See, Brecht (2004), who is critical of the measure, based on the understanding (in our belief soundly so) that it hampers the control market; Gatti (2005) who is optimistic about the effectiveness of the reciprocity rule.

whether the players are native or foreign. The opposite case is indicative of the fact that the values behind the legal regulations are, in reality, different. Instrumentalising the passivity duty ends up taking its toll.[60]

It is our impression that reciprocity will in the end leave its mark on the passivity duty. It would help to shatter its extra-legal (moral if you prefer) support, that is essential for securing it as a social norm. If reciprocity governs, the regulating body will lose the moral authority to sanction. It will not be possible for the regulating body to take up a harsh stance against the parties violating the passivity duty without resulting – or appearing to be – arbitrary (all depending on whether the foreign bidder is English or German, for instance) and excessive. Deep down, it will seem as if native bidders are given a stricter deal than foreign bidders. This will end up lowering the disciplining tone, and the final blow may not take long, if we bear in mind the power wielded by the interest groups opposed to the rule in Continental Europe.

4. THE ROLE OF PUBLIC ENFORCEMENT

4.1 The Conditions Making Public Enforcement Attractive

The preceding section has presented a bunch of reasons leading us to think that the enforcement of the passivity duty is not satisfactorily solved through private lawsuits, essentially *ex post* shareholders' class actions.[61] We have been able to show that private enforcement, even though it is the

---

[60] It is misleading, and naïve, to think that reciprocity serves the interests of the investing public and the efficiency of the market. This evokes an old doctrinal dispute over loyalty duties and their effectiveness. A polemical piece by Macey and Miller (1990), argued that breach of the duty of loyalty should be subject to an efficiency scrutiny in order to decide whether or not it should be subject to sanctions. This idea arose numerous opposing arguments. But for our purposes, the fundamental one is that it misses the expressive force of the Law. The message it sends out is that telling the truth or lying is merely instrumental. This is an undesirable message, because the corporate obligation to be loyal and tell the truth would lose validity and the market would not know who, where, and when to trust (see Ayres (1991)).

[61] In fact, the existence, or lack thereof, of the class action as a scheme to aggregate small lawsuits by individual shareholders or investors, appears to be statistically insignificant for explaining the size and development of the securities market: La Porta, Lopez-de-Silanes and Shleifer (2006, p. 11). It is true that this empirical study claims to show that the quality and extent of disclosure and liability

traditional instrument to deter breach of duties of loyalty, is not overly effective, and less so in respect of the passivity duty.

In order to verify the possible existence of greater effectiveness of public enforcement, we would need to confirm three conditions. The first is legitimacy: it is a matter of corroborating that regulatory intensity is associated with public benefit. The second is aptitude: we should confirm whether it is an effective mechanism for enforcing the non-intervention of administrators during the takeover bid process. The third is cost-benefit analysis: any statement on effectiveness requires that the benefits that are undoubtedly produced by public enforcement can be financed at a bearable cost, otherwise it would not be viable.

The fundamental reason for sustaining legitimacy and aptitude of public enforcement is its capacity to reduce social costs. If managers know they have an unsanctioned margin of manoeuvre at their disposal for defending themselves against the threat of a hostile takeover bid, they will make use of it. The consequences would be twofold. On the one hand, on top of the fact that they produce a loss to the company, they block productive deals. On the other hand, dynamically, they discourage the appearance of other bids, if would-be bidders anticipate that the likelihood of their tender offers being successful is considerably reduced by opposing managers. The market for corporate control would be not insignificantly narrowed.

Public institutions, particularly securities market regulators, are well placed to reduce those costs. They can compensate for the lack of significant enforcement on the part of private shareholders' actions. Secondly, because for the passivity rule to be effective it needs to be internalised by those who have a duty to observe it. And this can be attained, at least to a certain extent, by a committed sanctioning strategy making enforcement credible. Moreover, the credibility and prestige of the regulators would impose an additional loss of reputation to the infringer who is sanctioned, and that would not otherwise exist.

In passing, let's make a point on legislative policy regarding this issue. The Takeover Directive is naïve in considering that the shareholders' interest is duly protected by giving them the option of making the statutory choice of applying passivity duty, even when the national legislation has opted out of this, that is, does not impose it as mandatory in nature.[62] The

standards is a more important factor for the development of capital markets than public enforcement. We will take up this claim later in the text.

[62] For the contrary view, see Gatti (2005, pp. 75–6). It is true that this is a default rule, but it is not easy to reverse a pro-administrator rule to a pro-shareholder rule, for reasons well-known in the literature: Bebchuk and Hamdani (2002).

reason is simple: if national legislation does not include passivity duty, it will be difficult for the relevant State to invest in resources to install an efficient system of public enforcement. And as we have seen, since private enforcement proves to be inadequate, it is reasonable to predict that the shareholders' interest will be left unprotected from both sides of the enforcement toolkit.

The third condition is the one requiring deeper investigation on our part.

4.2 The Relative Pros and Cons of Public Enforcement of the Passivity Rule

4.2.1 The pros

The advantages of public enforcement of the passivity rule do not imply that we should do away with shareholders' suits without further ado. Quite the opposite in fact, what it means is that the public enforcement should carry the weight, and Court enforcement through private lawsuits would be a complementary function – and more effective than in isolation, as we have already shown, when private actions follow the tracks of public enforcement.

The theoretical advantages of public enforcement of the rule lie in the following factors.

First, it is an *ex ante* mechanism, and more flexible than private enforcement in the available remedies. Courts generally decide *ex post*, and in a framework delimited by the specific case in question. They are responsive and reactive to harm caused. On the other hand, public enforcement emphasizes *ex ante* dissuasory mechanisms or controls.[63] What is involved here is a question of intensifying the functions of supervising and reacting quickly and vigorously in the event of breach. Public enforcement can react swiftly, and before the consequences of harm from the infringing conduct appear, or at least before they are irreversible. On occasions, it is even possible to predict a conduct beforehand, and enjoin its occurrence. On the contrary, the takeover bid period can be extended to no useful purpose if we give ample room to the Courts, the takeover process will be significantly delayed and encumbered, and with it the market for corporate control.

---

[63] See, Shavell (2004, pp. 572ff.) for a summary of the canonical economic theory of the relative advantages and disadvantages of *ex post*, privately initiated remedies based on monetary sanctions – such as liability – and of *ex ante*, publicly administered control mechanisms. It is not surprising that some factors, like the information available for the public authorities in contrast of the information available for private people, the size and effective application – judgment-proof problems as paramount factors –, and the cost of imposing the sanctions, are the most relevant factors in the comparative analysis.

Public monitoring tasks are, in principle, costly disciplining mechanisms. Even so, in the event of defensive tactics in hostile takeover bids, allocating funds to monitoring seems to be indicated. It so happens that conduct in breach of the passivity duty is clearly visible, in addition to the fact that there is a limited number of takeover bids that can be placed during the same period, thereby allowing public regulators to concentrate their attention, and the enforcement funds available, on the tender offer under way – Courts have a much more diverse caseload at any given time. A high level of detection of infringement can be attained at a relatively low cost. On the other hand, as it involves prohibited behaviour of a voluntary nature for the potential infringer, there is no excessive risk of over-compliance. A manager can perfectly achieve compliance with the rule – and at a very small cost, at least direct cost – by refraining from carrying out the prohibited behaviour.

Typically, the securities regulator is the maximum authority in the securities market. Its decisions are complied with in the market, and its authority holds sway amongst operators. It has broad sanctioning powers on all matters affecting the securities market, powers well-established and subject to administrative procedure. Decisions and sanctions by the regulator have a major impact on the market and on the relevant public: they are a highly visible instrument and the message they send out in relation to its disciplining efforts quickly spreads.[64] From this point of view, as resources are limited, a large part of the secret to success consists in a wise choice of the sanctionable targets, in order to be able to succeed in indicating the rigour of the discipline and in discouraging undesirable behaviour.

Of course, adequate performance by the regulator should not be taken for granted. The two conditions on which the prestige of the regulating institution in fulfilling its duties depends, are professionalism and impartiality.

(i) The note of *professionalism* claims that its officers have credible expertise in regulating financial activities. This expertise makes them ideal for detecting sophisticated behaviour that would otherwise pass unnoticed by a non-specialist. It also holds an additional advantage. As the regulating body focuses its disciplining efforts on the passivity duty, it records and updates the list of infringing conducts. This is a more dynamic system for identifying disloyal strategies than the judicial precedent. It also has greater direct repercussions: the enforcement strategy of the regulating body affects the entire market,

64 Cox and Thomas (2003).

that of the Courts affects the parties in dispute, although it has public echo as well, and some value as judicial precedent. A financial slant in the detection of infringing conduct may well displace a more legalistic stance. This marks a substantial difference in relation to the catalogue of conduct that is de facto subject to sanction, which is likely to be extended.[65] Litigants seek redress, and legal action takes places only in cases in which direct harm to private parties has materialized. On the other hand, the regulating body may act against any infringing conduct. A broader range of cases and companies, thus, are susceptible of being potential targets of its penalising arm. Looked at carefully, the big losers in this system are the lawyers – lawsuit attorneys at least – and perhaps this is justified.[66] Comparative experience shows that in litigation concerning the securities market there is a lack of alignment between the interests of the litigating lawyers and social welfare.[67]

(ii) The *impartiality* note reminds us that the regulating body should serve market efficiency, and not the private interests of some of its participants. It pursues the prohibited conduct without preferential treatment pro or contra. This is the key element for the credibility and prestige of the institution. And one of the weakest points of a regulatory agency body, because in reality there is a high risk of connivance with the political or economic powers. We shall return to this point later.

Third, an efficient system of sanctions should count on a catalogue of possibilities adapted to the entity of the breach. The mere possibility of starting proceedings against managers is reason enough for them to mind

---

65 The empirical studies attempting to measure the effectiveness of private and public enforcement on the subject of the securities market highlight the fact that the targets pursued by the two disciplining mechanisms do not coincide. It is common knowledge that litigants are governed by expected value criteria, seeking 'deep pockets' and significant losses, whereas the regulating body may centre its efforts on smaller firms and pursues indicators of financial predicament, which point to companies with higher risk of committing fraud and that will lead to irreversible losses: See Cox and Thomas (2003).

66 Not only from the point of view of costs. In principle, damage payments do not constitute social costs, they are merely redistributive transfers. But it is undeniable that litigation costs should be taken into account at the time of assessing the private enforcement system. Litigation is an expensive way of solving disputes. And the most significant net cost is that of legal services, see Jackson (2005).

67 The problem of badly adjusted incentives in litigation making it impossible to attain the optimal amount of private suits against illegal actions in the marketplace is well known in the literature: See, Coffee (1986); Macey and Miller (1991).

their conduct, if we bear in mind the adverse publicity to which they will be exposed. The traditional sanctions imposed by regulatory bodies come in the form of fines or pecuniary sanctions. Two questions need to be borne in mind in relation to fines. The first is that for them to be properly calibrated, their amount, in expected terms, should fit the sum of social costs. The second tells us that for fines to be more dissuasive, they should directly affect managerial assets and not the company's equity capital or that of the insurer. In short, in these conditions, if the level of detection is high, as would seem to be a clear possibility with public enforcement, the sanctions will not need to be very high in order to ensure reasonable deterrence. Even so, if the regulating body does not dispose of sufficient means to carry out satisfactory monitoring, high fines will induce would-be infringers to comply – although the higher they are, the more difficult it will be for managers to possess the assets to pay them. Moreover, note that even though these payments are perceived as costs by the managers, strictly speaking, they are not.[68] They are resources transferred from one party to another and can be reassigned to other purposes.

In addition, these corrective measures should be reinforced by others whose effectiveness makes them inalienable. Clearly, injunctions, and incapacitating sanctions come in this category. Faced with obstructionist behaviour by administrators, what is most urgent is to stop it. This is the best way of protecting investors' interests – forcing the administrators to cease their defensive conduct, or to correct the course of events before it leads to worse harm. For their part, incapacitating sanctions for acting as manager of a public company, or suspending the right to operate in the securities market, may give a powerful blow to the reputation of administrators, and thus be very effective in triggering social sanctions. For all that, this type of sanction needs to be meted out cautiously as it entails significant costs. For a start, compliance costs (making sure the guilty administrator does not directly or indirectly violate the incapacitation order). But it also entails a social cost because it has the adverse effect of dissipating human resources and their productive capacity.

4.2.2 The cons

Monitoring conduct of managers in the event of a hostile takeover bid is a costly effort. Thus, the effectiveness of the regulatory agency in achieving proper deterrence of undesirable behaviour is subject to serious budget constraints, and also political restrictions.

---

[68] See Jackson (2005).

Personal and material resources devoted to compliance with the rule should be translated into detection levels. Investment effort should take into account the country's population and wealth. Studies indicate that Common Law countries devote a larger budget – not only in absolute terms, but also in relative terms too, whichever way you look at it, to the agencies regulating the securities market.[69] This may suggest that development of a capital market not only depends on the pro-investor regulatory effort but, and very especially, on *enforcement*. The market for corporate control will not achieve efficiency de facto, despite its doing so de iure, if the market lacks a tough regulating body.

In a recent paper,[70] La Porta, Lopez-de-Silanes, and Shleifer, present evidence challenging the importance of public enforcement for the development of securities markets. They claim, with the help of data assembled from a questionnaire of lawyers in almost 50 countries on laws and regulations affecting the securities markets. And their findings result in rules on disclosure requirements and specific liability of market participants (issuers of securities, underwriters, auditors) being the most important predictors, among legal variables, of market development. Public enforcement (which covers the independence, regulatory, investigative, and sanctioning powers of the regulatory agency, and also criminal law rules) are less important, with the exception of the regulatory powers of the securities agency. Thus, private enforcement[71] seems to carry the weight, over public enforcement, in developing healthy securities markets.

Two objections should be raised here, however. First, on a general basis, the legal variables they employ do not adequately measure enforcement, particularly private enforcement. They merely assume that private enforcement exists and is active, just because disclosure rules and liability standards for market participants exist, and are clear and exacting. But they do not attempt to measure it. Actual agency activity –not even budget – is not part of the study. It seems as if it is 'Law in the books' and not 'Law in action' that has been considered. Moreover, several of the elements classified under private enforcement – essentially, those concerning disclosure – seem to influence not just private enforcement, but public enforcement as well.

---

69 Ibidem. For instance, if one compares some European countries with the US, we see that Germany comes off very badly from the comparison. The data available shows that the US invests $ 83 943 per billion dollars of stock-exchange capitalisation, whereas France produces figures of $ 19 041, and Germany $8896.

70 La Porta, Lopez-de-Silanes and Shleifer (2006).

71 With the exception of class actions, which do not seem to play an important role: Ibidem.

Second, and more to the point for the purposes of our chapter, is that their study refers only to the IPO market, that is, to initial public offerings of securities. That is, the underlying problem addressed by the legal variables underlying their study is that of an asymmetric information interaction between a company (and its advisors, or gate-keepers) and investors, the future shareholders. In the passivity rule setting, we are confronted by an agency problem between managers and current shareholders as principals. The same is true with other instances of breach of fiduciary duties by managers. And although some of the problems faced by private shareholders' suits may be common to both settings, they are more acute in the agency problem, and some of them are not at all present in the IPO scenario (much lower probability of occurrence, more difficult proof of liability, more difficult proof of causal link, low probability of the case being brought).

On a different line, there is also politics affecting the sanctioning action of the regulatory agency. The question here concerns the independence of the regulating body vis-à-vis the powers capable of undermining it. Most commentators now accept that the Government should not interfere in the workings of the regulating body, putting pressure on the agency as a function of political contingences. Notwithstanding, it is true that Government intervention in the decisions taken by economic regulatory agencies may be lower than in others with a higher political profile. And if on the odd occasion the Government falls into the temptation to interfere, the reaction on the part of the financial press and market operators may be crushing. The same thing happens in relation to the European institutions that in the economic sphere of activity operate clearer rules of the game than in other spheres. To sum up, without being too optimistic, one can think that the trend with this type of interference is, overall, on the decline in Europe, insofar as markets gradually acquire size and weight, and Governments cement democratic tradition (which usually, in pure empirical terms, converges with liberal postures where financial markets, not necessarily other economic matters, are concerned).

Interference is not only to be feared from politicians, however. Regulatory agencies should not be influenced by pressure groups from the market itself. This threat is even more worrying, if that were possible, than the previous one and more difficult to control because intervention from these types of group tends to be more subtle than political pressure. Major listed companies have great force and influence as they comprise the market's most important customers. And more so in relatively narrow markets, like many in Continental Europe still are. The regulating agency (its personnel, naturally) moves in a close environment involving constant contact with market participants, and this can end up leading to a certain abeyance to private interests in detriment to general interests. The case for corruption is acute but, can be checked, at least to a large extent, through by an efficient remuneration system, and adequate sanctions. In our view, the most serious risk is that of the old boy network, to a very tight network of reciprocal arrangements in social and corporate relationships. This network may well find its way into the relationships with regulatory agencies, and interfere with the healthy exercise of public enforcement efforts, particularly in a delicate – and controversial – setting such as that of the passivity rule.

5. CONCLUSIONS

Public enforcement (not just in this area, but generally) is no magic solution. It entails serious direct and indirect costs, and will probably leave important deterrence gaps. We think, however, that in the field of the passivity rule, private enforcement, focused on shareholders' class actions, is doomed to fail as an effective deterrent tool. The obstacles to the deterrent effect of private enforcement in this area are numerous, and difficult to overcome. They are either inherent to liability as a remedy in the legal toolkit, or are deeply rooted in the legal tradition of Continental European systems, such as the horror at punitive damages.

Of course, one could legitimately ask oneself, why bother so much about the passivity duty? Why should we engage the costly machinery of private and public enforcement on this matter? We have tried to present reasons why one should consider such a duty as an efficient ingredient of Takeover Law. Maybe it is not a central feature of Corporate Governance, and maybe its contribution to the reduction of agency costs is only modest. But wherever it is in place, it is a piece of the delicate institutional setting on which the market for corporate control may grow and develop. And it is a piece hard to replace, if it fails.

REFERENCES

Alexander, J. (1991), 'Do the Merits Matter? A Study of Settlement in Securities Class Actions', *Stanford Law Review*, **43**, 497–598.

Armour, J. and D.A. Skeel (2006), 'Who Writes the Rules for Hostile Takeovers and Why? The Peculiar Divergence of US and UK Takeover Regulation', *Georgetown Law Journal*, **95**, 1727–2007, available at www.ssrn.com.

Asquith, P. (1983), 'Merger Bids, Uncertainty, and Stock Returns', *Journal of Financial Economics*, **11**, 51–83.

Ayres, I. (1991), 'Back to Basics: Regulating How Corporations Speak to the Markets', *Virginia Law Review*, **77**, 945–97.

Bainbridge, S.M. (2002), *Corporation Law and Economics*, New York: Foundation Press.

Bainbridge, S.M. (2005), 'Unocal at 20: Director in Corporate Takeovers', *Law-Econ Research Paper*, **19**, available at http:/www.ssrn.com., (September 7).

Bar-Gill, O., M. Barzuza and L. Bebchuk (2006), 'The Market for Corporate Law', *Journal of Institutional and Theoretical Economics*, **162**, 134–71.

Bebchuk, L. (1994), 'Efficient and Inefficient Sales of Corporate Control', *Quarterly Journal of Economics*, **109**(4), 957–93.

Bebchuk, L. (1999), 'A Rent Protection Theory of Corporate Ownership and Control', *National Bureau of Economic Research*, *NBER Working Papers*, **7203**, available at http:/www.ssrn.com.

Bebchuk, L. (2002a), 'The Case Against Board Veto in Corporate Takeovers', *University Chicago Law Review*, **69**, 973–1035.

Bebchuk, L. (2002b), 'The Questionable Case for Using Auctions to Select Lead Counsel', *Washington University Law Quarterly*, **80**, 889–99.

Bebchuk, L., A. Cohen and A. Farrell (2002), 'Does the Evidence Favor State Competition in Corporate Law?', *California Law Review*, **90**, 1775–90.

Bebchuk, L., A. Cohen and A. Farrell (2004), 'What Matters in Corporate Governance?', *Discussion Paper, Harvard John M. Olin for Law, Economics and Business*, **491**, available at http:/www.ssrn.com.

Bebchuk, L. and A. Hamdani (2002), 'Optimal Defaults for Corporate Law Evolution', *Northwestern University Law Review*, **96**(2), 489–520.

Bebchuk, L. and J. Fried (2004), *Pay Without Performance: The Unfulfilled Promise of Executive Compensation*, Cambridge, MA and London: Harvard University Press.

Becker, G. (1968), 'Crime and Punishment: An Economic Approach', *Journal of Political Economy*, **76**, 169–217.

Ben-Shahar, O. and J. Pottow (2006), 'On the Stickiness of Default Rules', *Florida State University Law Review*, **33**(3), 651–82.

Berglöf, E. and M. Burkart (2003), 'European Takeover Regulation', *Economic Policy*, **36**, 172–213.

Bertrand, M. and S. Mullinathan (1999), 'Executive Compensation and Incentives: the Impact of Takeover Legislation', NBER Working Paper, 6830, available at http:/www.ssrn.com.

Black, B. (1989), 'Bidder Overpayment in Takeovers', *Stanford Law Review*, **41**, 597–653.

Black, B. and R. Kraakman (2002), 'Delaware's Takeover Law: the Uncertain Search for Hidden Value', *Northwestern University Law Review*, **96**, 521–66.

Black, B., B.R. Cheffins and M. Klausner (2006), 'Outside Directors Liability', *Stanford Law Review*, **58**, 1055–1159.

Bohn, J. and S. Choi (1996), 'Fraud in the New Issue Market: Empirical Evidence on Securities Class Actions', *University of Pennsylvania Law Review*, **144,** 903–982.

Bradley, M., A. Desai and E.H. Kim (1983), 'The Rationale Behind Interfirm Tender Offers: Information or Synergy?', *Journal of Financial Economics,* **11**, 183–206.

Brecht, M. (2004), 'Reciprocity in Takeovers', in G. Ferrari, K.J. Hopt, J. Winter and E. Wymeersch (eds.), *Reforming Company Law and Takeover in Europe*, Oxford: Oxford University Press.

Choi, S. (2000), 'Regulating Investors not Issuers: A Market-Based Proposal', *California Law Review*, **88**, 279–334.
Choi, S. (2004), 'The Evidence of Securities Class Actions', *Vanderbilt Law Review*, **57**(5), 1465–1528.
Coffee, J.C. (1984), 'Regulating the Market for Corporate Control: A Critical Assessment of the Takeover's Role in Corporate Governance', *Columbia Law Review*, **84**, 1145–1296.
Coffee, J.C. (1986), 'Understanding the Plaintiff's Attorney: the Implications of Economic Theory for Private Enforcement Through Class and Derivative Actions', *Columbia Law Review*, **86**, 669–727.
Coffee, J.C. (2006), 'Reforming the Securities Class Action: An Essay on Deterrence and its Implementation', *Columbia Law Review*, **106**, available at www.ssrn.com.
Cooter, R. and B.J. Freedman (1991), 'The Fiduciary Relationship: its Economic Character and Legal Consequences', *New York University Law Review*, **66**, 1045–75.
Cox, J.D. and R.S. Thomas (2002), 'Leaving Money on the Table: Do Institutional Investors Fail to File Claims in Securities Class Actions', *Washington University Law Quarterly*, **80**, 855–81.
Cox, J.D. and R.S. Thomas (2003), 'SEC Enforcement Heuristics: an Empirical Enquiry', *Duke Law Journal*, **53**, 737–80.
Cox, J.D. and R.S. Thomas (2004), 'Public and Private Enforcement of the Securities Laws: Have Things Changed since Enron?', *Notre Dame Law Review*, **80**, 893–907.
Cramton, P. and A. Schwartz (1991), 'Using Auction Theory to Inform Takeover Regulation', *Journal* of *Law, Economics, & Organization*, **7**(27), 33–45.
Easterbrook, F.H. and D.R. Easterbrook (1981), 'The Proper Role of a Target Manager in Responding to a Tender Offer', *Harvard Law Review*, **94**(6), 1161–1204.
Easterbrook, F.H. and G.A. Jarrell (1984), 'Do Targets Gain from Defeating Tender Offers?', *New York University Law Review*, **59**, 277–99.
Eisenberg, M.A. (1999), 'Corporate Law and Social Norms', *Columbia Law Review*, **99**, 1253–92.
Fama, F. and M.C. Jensen (1983), 'Separation of Ownership and Control', *Journal of Law and Economics*, **26**, 301–325.
Fernández de la Gándara, L. and M. Sánchez-Álvarez (2002), 'Limitación de la Actuación del Órgano de Administración de sociedad Afectada por el Lanzamiento de una Oferta Pública de Adquisición', *Revista del derecho de sociedades*, **18**, 231–38.
Fisch, J.E. (2002), 'Lawyers on the Auction Block: Evaluating the Selection of Class Counsel by Auction', *Columbia Law Re*view, **102**, 650–728.
Fishman, V.M. (1988), 'A Theory of Pre-emptive Shareholder Takeover Bidding', *RAND Journal of Economics*, **19**, 88–101.
Ganuza, J. and F. Gómez (2008), 'Realistic Standards: Optimal Negligence under Limited Liability', *Journal of Legal Studies*, **37**(2), 577–94.
Garrido, J.M. (2002), 'La Actuación de los Administradores de una Sociedad Frente a una Opa Hostil', in AA. VV., *Derecho de Sociedades. Libro Homenaje a Fernándo Sánchez Calero*, Madrid: Estudios de sociedades.
Gatti, M. (2005), 'Optionality Arrangements and Reciprocity in the European Takeover Directive', *EBOR*, **6**, 553–79.

Gilson, R.J. (1981), 'A Structural Approach to Corporations: the Case Against Defensive Tactics in Tender Offers', *Stanford Law Review*, **33**, 819–891.

Gilson, R.J. (2001), 'Unocal Fifteen Years Later (and what we can do about it)', *Delaware Journal of Corporate Law*, **26**, 491–513.

Gilson, R.J. and R. Kraakman (1989), 'Delaware's Intermediate Standard for Defensive Tactics: Is there Substance to Proportionality Review', *Business Law*, **44**, 247–67.

Goergen, M. and L. Renneboog (2004), 'Shareholders' Wealth Effects of European Domestic and Cross-border Takeover Bids', *European Financial Management*, **10**(1), 9–45.

Gómez, F. and I. Sáez (2006), 'Competition, Inefficiencies, and Dominance in Corporate Law. Comment', *Journal of Institutional and Theoretical Economics*, **162**, 161–7.

Gompers, P., J. Ishii and A. Metrick (2003), 'Corporate Governance and Equity Price', *Quarterly Journal of Economics*, **118**, 107–155.

Grossman, S.J. and O. Hart (1980), 'Takeover Bids, the Free-rider Problem and the Theory of the Corporation', *Bell J. Econ*, **11**, 42–3.

Helland, E. (2006), 'Reputational Penalties and the Merits of Class-Action Securities Litigation', *Journal of Law and Economics*, **49**(2), 365–395.

Jackson, G.E. (2005), 'Variation in the Intensity of Financial Regulation: Preliminary Evidence and Potential Implications', *Yale Journal on Regulation*, **24**(2), 101–139, available at www.ssrn.com.

Jarrell, G.A. (1985), 'The Wealth Effects of Litigation by Targets: do Interests Diverge in a Merger?', *Journal of Law and Economics*, **28**, 151–77.

Jarrell, G.A. and A. Poulson (1989), 'The Return to Acquiring Firms in Tenders: Evidence from Three Decades', *Financial Management*, **18**(3), 12–19.

Jarrell, G.A., J. Brickley and J. Netter (1989), 'The Market for Corporate Control: the Empirical Evidence Since 1980', *Journal of Economic Perspectives*, **2**(1), 49–68.

Jennings, R.H. and M.A. Mazzeo (1993), 'Competing Bids, Management Resistance, and the Structure of Takeover Bids', *Review of Financial Studies*, **6**(4), 883–909.

Jensen, M.C. (1988), 'Takeovers: their Causes and Consequences', *Journal of Economic Perspectives*, **2**, 21–48.

Jensen, M.C. and K.J. Murphy (1990), 'CEO Incentives – It's not How Much you Pay, but How', *Harvard Business Review*, **68**(3), 138–53.

Jensen, M.C. and R. Ruback (1983), 'The Market for Corporate Control: the Scientific Evidence', *Journal of Financial Economics*, **11**, 5–50.

Kahan, M. and E. Kamar (2002), 'The Myth of State Competition in Corporate Law', *Stanford* Law *Review*, **55**, 679–749.

Kahneman, D., J. Knetsch, and R. Thaler (1990), 'Experimental Tests of the Endowment Effect and the Coase Theorem', *Journal of Political Economy*, **98**(6), 1325–48.

Klein, B. and K.B. Leffler (1981), 'The Role of Market Forces in Assuring Contractual Performance', *Journal of Political Economy*, **89**(4), 615–641.

Klement, A. and Z. Neeman (2004), 'Incentive Structures for Class Action Lawyers', *The Journal of Law, Economics, and Organization*, **20**(1), 102–124.

Korobkin, R. (1998), 'The Status Quo Bias and Contract Default Terms', *Cornell Law Review*, **83**, 608–687.

La Porta, R., F. López de Silanes, A. Shleifer and R.W. Vishny (1997), 'Legal Determinants of External Finance', *Journal of Finance*, **53**, 1131–50.
La Porta, R., F. López de Silanes, A. Shleifer and R.W. Vishny (2000), 'Investors' Protection and Corporate Governance', *Journal of Finance*, **58**, 3–27.
La Porta, R., F. Lopez-de-Silanes and A. Shleifer (2006), 'What Works in Securities Laws?', *Journal of Finance*, **61**, 1–32.
Macey, J.R. and G.P. Miller (1990), 'Good Finance, Bad Economics: An Analysis of the Fraud-on-the- Market Theory', *Stanford Law Review*, **42**, 1059–1092.
Macey, J.R. and G.P. Miller (1991), 'The Plaintiffs' Attorney's Role in Class Actions and Derivative Litigation: Economic Analysis and Recommendations for Reform', *University of Chicago Law Review*, **58**, 1–118.
Malatesta, P. (1992), 'Takeover Defences', in P. Newman (ed.), *The New Palgrave Dictionary of Money and Finance*, vol. 3, London: Macmillan, pp. 363–636.
Morck, V.R., A. Shleifer and R. Vishny (1990), 'Do Managerial Objectives Drive Bad Acquisitions?', *Journal of Finance*, **4**, 31–48.
Naraiya, N. (1998), 'The Winner's Curse Hypothesis and Corporate Takeovers', *Managerial and Decision Economics*, **9**(3), 209–219.
Paz-Ares, J.C. (2003), 'La Responsabilidad de los Administradores Como Instrumento de Gobierno Corporativo', *InDret*, **4**, 1–61.
Pirrong, C.S. (2002), 'A Theory of Financial Exchange Organization', *Journal of Law and Economics*, **43**(2), 437–72.
Prentice, R.A. (2006), 'The Inevitability of a Strong SEC', *Cornell Law Review*, **91**, 775–99.
Pritchard, A.C. (2002), 'Who Cares?', *Washington University Law Quarterly*, **80**, 882–88.
Romano, R. (1993), 'Competition for Corporate Charters and the Lessons of Takeover Statutes', *Fordham Law Review*, **61**, 843–84.
Romano, R. (1998), 'Empowering Investors: A Market Approach to Securities Regulation', *Yale Law Journal*, **107**. 2359–430.
Sáez, M.I. (2003), 'Una Aproximación al Derecho de las Opas Competidoras (a propósito de una reforma reciente)', *RDBB*, **92**, 747.
Shavell, S. (2004), *Foundations of Economic Analysis of Law*, Belknap Press of Harvard University Press.
Sunstein, C.R. (2000), *Behavioural Law and Economics*, New York: Cambridge University Press.
Tirole, J. (2006), *The Theory of Corporate Finance*, Princeton and Oxford: Princeton University Press.
Walking, R.A. and M.S. Long (1984), 'Agency Theory, Managerial Welfare, and Takeover Bid Resistance', *Rand. Journal of Economics*, **15**(1), 54–68.

15. The constitutional impact of class actions in European legal systems

Jörg Luther

The transplant of class action into European Legal Systems has to face several questions arising from the European Constitutionalism. Legal comparison helps to understand that the European future of class action depends first of all on how we understand the European origins (Section 1) and the diversity of European legal cultures and societies (Section 2). The political choice of the European lawmakers can be conditioned by specific reasons of economical rationality and cultural reasonability. They are obliged to hold in balance different national and supranational constitutional rules and principles. An assessment of the constitutional impact could be helpful if we take into consideration aspects such as the law making competences (Section 3), the fundamental social and economical rights (Section 4) and the rights of action and defence (Section 5). The following remarks, however, try just to start a comparative debate from an Italian point of view (Section 6).

1. THE EUROPEAN ROOTS OF THE 'CLASS ACTION'

Comparative lawyers look to the 'class action' as an institution of the federal and state law of the United States grounded on the English *'representative action'*.[1] This history should need further research from a larger comparative perspective, looking also at the roman law rules of *'pro alio agere'* through special forms of '*procurator ad litem*', such as the '*duoviri*' in the cases of *municipia,* the '*quivis ex populo*' beneficiary of a *poena* in the

[1] For a critical reconstruction see Yeazell (1987, pp. 38ff), preceeded by Marcin (1974), and followed by Giussani (1996, pp. 4ff). For the European mentality of the medieval experience see Grossi (1995, pp. 87ff).

case of 'public' or 'popular' actions and the '*defensor absentis*' admitted by the praetor if presenting a '*cautio iudicatum*'.[2]

Anglo-American historians consider *class action* often modern because *representative action* was already a pre-modern practice in a pluralistic context of local communities and representation through elders and clan-leaders. Lord Nottingham's Manual of Chancery Practice (1674) described the following rule for the later so called 'bills of peace':

> A bill to settle the customs of a manor wherein a multitude of tenants are concerned may be exhibited by any three in name of the rest, so as they produce before the Register a sufficient authority to enable them to sue in the name of the rest, and so as they be responsible for the costs.[3]

In *Brown* v. *Vermudden,* the Chancery decided therefore that the 'defendants and all the Miners' should pay customary rights of a tithe, while the defendants had been chosen by the miners at the request of the acting parish.[4] Later the representative action was applied to groups of shareholders and unincorporated associations (friendly societies), even in case the identification of all of them had become impracticable.[5] When the English courts of law and equity merged in 1873, even damage actions were allowed provided that 'more than one person has the same interest in a claim'. On the one hand, the representative has neither to be appointed nor to give information to represented persons, on the other hand the court's decision is binding them, but 'may only be enforced by or against a person who is not a party to the claim with the permission of the court'. In this context, restrictive interpretations prevailed for long time, excluding claims originated by separated contracts or aimed to different relief and defences.[6]

The representative action has been restricted even in the United States under federal *diversity jurisdiction*, with Equity Rule 48 of 1843 denying explicitly binding effect for 'absent parties'.[7] The turn from *representative*

---

[2] See Kaser and Hackl (1996, pp. 209ff.). The historical dimension is still lacking in the pioneeristic work of Cappelletti (1983).

[3] Quoted by Yeazell (1987, p. 132).

[4] 22 Eng. Rep. 796, Ch. 1676.

[5] *Chancey* v. *May*, 24 Eng. Rep. 265 (Ch. 1722), *Adair* v. *New River Company* 32 Eng Rep. 1153 (Ch. 1805).

[6] *Markt Co Ltd.* v. *Knight Steamship Co. Ltd*, 2 KB 1021 (1910). See Mulheron (2004, pp. 77ff.); Andrews (2007), 291ff.

[7] 'Where the parties on either side are very numerous, and cannot, without manifest inconvenience and oppressive delays in the suit, be all brought before it, the court in its discretion may dispense with making all of them parties, and may proceed in the suit, having sufficient parties before it to represent all the adverse intents of the plaintiffs and the defendants in the suit properly before it. But in such

litigation towards *class action* was prospected only in the second half of nineteenth century, when binding effects were prospected[8] and rule 48 was used for taxpayer suits and actions against picketing.[9] In 1912 the new Rule 38 relied on questions 'of common or general interest to many persons constituting a *class* so numerous as to make it impracticable to bring them all before the court'.[10] When the new Rule 23 of the *Federal Rules of Civil Procedure* of 1938 extended class action to uniform legal and equitable relief and allowed damage actions, the Supreme Court decided definitely that

> there is scope within the framework of the Constitution for holding in appropriate cases that a judgment rendered in a class suit is res judicata as to members of the class who are not formal parties to the suit. (…) With a proper regard for divergent local institutions and interests, (…) this Court is justified in saying that there has been a failure of due process only in those cases where it cannot be said that the procedure adopted, fairly insures the protection of the interests of absent parties who are to be bound by it.[11]

The reform of 1966 established several criteria for certification such as the numerosity of the class (impracticability of joinder), the commonality of the questions of law and fact (predominance test), the typicality of claims and defences of the representative parties and the fairness and adequacy of representation. The reform facilitated 'civil rights litigation' and 'small claim class actions' for consumers and introduced an opting-out mechanism. The Supreme Court denied 'that the Due Process Clause of the Fourteenth Amendment requires that absent plaintiffs affirmatively "opt in" to the class, rather than be deemed members of the class if they do not

---

cases the decree shall be without prejudice to the rights and claims of all the absent parties.' For the role of Story (1836), see Yeazell (1987, pp. 218ff.).

[8] *Smith* v. *Swormstedt* 57 US 288 (1853): 'the decree binds all of them the same as if all were before the court.'

[9] See *American Steel & Wire Co.* v. *Wire Drawers & Die Makers' Unions* 90 F. 598, 608 (C.C.N.D. Ohio 1898). The term class was already used in *Willoughby* v. *Chicago Junction Railways & Union Stockyards Co.* 25 A. 277 (N.J. Ch. 1892) at 279: 'The practice has long been recognized of permitting suit to be brought by a few as the representatives of a numerous class, on behalf of themselves and all others of the *class*, when there is a common interest or a common right which the suit seeks to protect, and against a few as representing a numerous *class* subject to a common liability, which the suits seeks to enforce.'

[10] *Supreme Tribe of Ben-Hur* v. *Cauble*, 255 U.S. 356 (1921): 'Class suits have long been recognized in federal jurisprudence', at 336: '…being thus represented, we think it must necessarily follow that their rights were concluded by the original decree.'

[11] *Hansberry* v. *Lee,* 311 U.S. 32 (1940).

"opt out"'. The 'minimal procedural due process protection' would require 'best practicable notice', an opportunity to appear in person or by counsel, an opportunity to opt out, and adequate representation.[12] While special rules on the securities class actions were enacted in 1995, the Supreme Court opened the door to 'settlement only class actions' in mass torts cases.[13] The *Class Action Fairness Act* of 2003 and 2005 tried to strengthen the procedural guarantees (fairness hearing) and the control of judges over advocates.

The divergence of US-style class action from English representative action is first of all due to a practical success. Success could be measured in a statistics, but also in the political choices of other countries such as several Canadian Provinces (Quebec 1978, Ontario 1992, British Columbia 1995, Saskatchewan and Newfoundland 2001, Manitoba 2002, Alberta 2003), Israel (1988), Brazil (1990), Australia (South Australia 1987, Federal 1992, Victoria 1995).[14] Even the English trend to a more relaxed and flexible criterion of 'common ingredient' and to a new group litigation management have signed a re-convergence. Nevertheless the ongoing trans-atlantic debates on pros and contras of class action show that the common roots are not of a consistence that a worldwide consolidation of class procedures could become a short term policy goal.

2. THE EUROPEAN VARIATIONS OF THE CLASS ACTION THEME

The United States model of class action has grown in a specific system of justice with juries, big law firms, advocates that take a *quota litis*, judges that make judicial review and supreme courts that make their own procedural regulations and have a discretionary power in case selection. This system aims to perform a civil justice which includes more harsh forms of punitive damages and is embedded both in a common law culture and in a constitutional context of a market economy, not bound by specific social rights guarantees or welfare-state goals, and with a presidential democracy, not bound by specific political party guarantees or other group representation. The European legal cultures, on the other hand, have developed other alternative forms of collective protection for rights that strengthen the role

12 *Phillips Petroleum Co.*. v. *Shutts,* 472 U.S. 797 (1985).

13 *Amchem Prods., Inc.* v. *Windsor*, 521 U.S. 591, 619 et seq. (1997).

14 See Taruffo (2001). For the Chinese model of representative action see now Daffer (2006).

of public law and core institutions of the European social welfare state such as, for example, obligatory insurances.[15]

Alternatives can first of all be provided granting specific substantial rights by civil law or public law legislation. Mass claims can be managed through fiduciary cession to private agencies for '*incasso*' purposes. In order to avoid insolvency risks, they can also be transferred *ope legis* to public care bodies that realize social rights to services and resources to the claimants, or through specific public funds and foundations administering indemnities.

Public enforcement can be furthermore obtained by special, more or less independent authorities such as the 'state attorneys general' in US antitrust, the Office of Fair Trading in United Kingdom, the General para la defensa de los consumidores y usarios in Spain, the Bureau of Consumer Affairs and the State Financial Institutions Commission in Hungary etc. Such authorities for specific guarantee purposes can act as *parentes patriae*.

Private-public or 'social' forms of public interest litigation are finally the various experiences of 'organizational action' or '*Verbandsklage*', in Germany existing since 1898, in France since 1920 and even in Italy and other countries (incl. Czech Republic and Lithuania), embedded in a specific European history of corporativism. Such organisations, mostly corporate and often registered associations are acting in particular fields of individual and collective interests and can defend in their areas (only in the Netherlands even without material limits) their own procedural rights or the rights of their members through various forms of actions (injunctional and damages relief).

In this context have to be placed even the following European variations and surrogates or 'functional equivalents' of class action that have been developed over the last decades: 1) French *action en représentation conjointe* since 1992, 2) Portuguese *acção popular* since 1995, 3) Spanish *acción colectiva de grupo* since 2000, 4) English *group litigation,* with written rules since 2000, 5) Austrian-style *Sammelklage* since 2001, 6) Swedish *grupprättegång* since 2003, 7) Dutch *collectieve afwikkeling massaschade* since 2005; 8) German *Kapitalanleger-Musterverfahren* since 2005.

(1) The French 'action en représentation conjointe' (art. 422 Code de la Consommation) is a special action for licensed consumer protection organizations that need to be mandated by at least two consumers (not necessarily members), victims of the same practice, to represent

15 See Cafaggi and Micklitz (2007), Stuyck et. al. (2007), Michailidou (2007).

them before any civil or criminal court. The law allows no extension of the *res judicata* and prohibits any publicity through mass media.

(2) Art. 52.3 of the long constitution of Portugal adopted in 1976 provided a right to popular action that has been specified in 1982 and 1997 as follows:

> Everyone shall be granted the right of actio popularis, to include the right to apply for the appropriate compensation for an aggrieved party or parties, in such cases and under such terms as the law may determine, either personally or via associations that purport to defend the interests in question. The said right shall particularly be exercised in order to: a) Promote the prevention, cessation or judicial prosecution of offences against public health, consumer rights, the quality of life or the preservation of the environment and the cultural heritage; b) Safeguard the property of the state, the autonomous regions and local authorities.

Lei n. 83/1995 has precised that the popular action applies to all cases of civil and administrative justice. Actors do not need a personal interest, but represent the holders of rights or interests involved except those which exercise a 'direito de auto-exclusao' and therefore are not bound by the decree. They can be substituted by the Public Prosecutor in cases of withdrawal, settlement and damaging management.[16]

(3) The Spanish Constitution of 1978 provided that 'the public powers (poderes) shall guarantee the defence of the consumers and users, protecting their safety, health, and legitimate economic interests through effective procedures'.[17] The Spanish *Ley de Enjuiciamiento Civil* established that legally embodied consumer associations will be legitimated to stay in court in order to defend rights and interests of their members 'as well as the general interests of the consumers' (art. 15.1). In matters of group litigation for damages, if the members of the group can be identified easily, even unincorporated groups can be represented by a majority and all members can opt-in and become parties. Otherwise, the right to action is reserved to consumer associations. Once filed, the suit will be published in the media and for two months members can opt-in. In both cases, res judicata will be extended even to other consumers (art. 222.3).[18]

---

[16] See Chapter 16 and Teixeira De Sousa (2002), Lebre de Freitas (2003). An open question is whether the Court could decide on damages even 'ultra petita'.

[17] Art. 7.3 of the Ley Organica del Poder Judical of 1985 established that in order to defend collective 'derecheos e intereses legitimos', 'se reconocerà la legitimación de las corporaciones, asociaciones y grupos que resulten afectados o que esteem legalmente habilitados para su defensa y promoción.'

[18] Silguero (2003, pp. 337ff.)

(4) The English 'group litigation' or 'multi-party action' is based on a wide-ranging court power 'to provide for the case management of claims which give rise to common or related issues of fact or law' (Civil Procedure Rule 19.10). Group litigation differs from class action insofar as it produces binding decisions only for registered parties on the basis of an opting-in mechanism with a further option for parties to apply to the management court for the claim to be removed from the register. Furthermore, group litigation orders can give directives for test case procedure. Conditional fee agreements are allowed and legal aid funds can be used.[19]

(5) In Austria, the 'Sammelklage nach österreichischem Recht' (group action according to Austrian law) is a representative test action mechanism based on a joinder of causes of action (§ 227 Code of Civil Procedure) experienced since 2001. Specific corporate bodies under the control and with the funding of government, specially the Verein für Konsumenteninformation and the Federal Chamber of Labour, can aggregate several claims against one defendant.[20] Being a test case procedure similar to the Verbands-Musterklage created for injunctive relief, non-parties can benefit only indirectly and bear the risk of prescription.

(6) The Swedish Law on Group Proceedings of 2002 distinguishes three forms of group action: private, organisational and public. The second form refers to associations for consumer and worker protection, the third to authorities chosen by the government. Those members of the group which are named by the actor and declare in a time fixed by court to take part to the action are parties only in relation to the rules relating to their procedural rights, liable for the costs and bound by the decree. The court has to control settlements and fee agreements.[21]

(7) In the Netherlands, section 3:305a and 305b Dutch Civil Code, as modified in 1994, invests corporations, associations with full legal capacity and public bodies with the competence to bring a legal action for injunctive relief. Section 7:907–910 of the Dutch Code of Civil Procedure, as modified by the 'Law on the collective settlement of mass damage' in 2005, allows organizations representing victims of mass damages to negotiate a settlement and to ask the court to declare it binding on all victims. The judgment cannot be appealed,

19 Cfr. N. Andrews (2007), 291ff; R. Mulheron, (2004), 94ff.

20 Pirker-Hörmann and Kolba (2006), Stadler and Mom (2006, pp. 199ff.).

21 Cfr. Lindquist and Hammarskiöld (2007, pp. 98ff.), Lindblom (1997).

but during a given period of time, individual victims can opt out from the binding effect.

(8) The German 'Capital Markets Model Case Act' of 2005 provides for claims of damages due to false, misleading or omitted public capital markets information and claim to fulfilment of contract, which is based on an offer under the Securities Acquisition and Takeover Act, a test case decision of a Higher Regional Court if at least ten applications are made on an opting-in basis. Plaintiffs benefit only from sharing the costs of the model case ruling, being relieved of prepaying costs for the model case proceeding and gaining time from a speedy decision. The law will automatically be out of force on 1 November 2010 – unless the legislator decides to have it prolonged or even broadened to other mass civil case proceedings.

In conclusion, the diversity of legal cultures and the political debates in Europe show an increasing interest at the national level for new 'functional equivalents' to the American class action. Comparison is still ongoing, because the national experiences have still to be evaluated and it is difficult to find a common glossary. The main issues involved such as jurisdiction, court powers, corporative actors, foreign parties, notification, suitability requisites, individual issues, temporary relief, settlements, costs, timing still are a puzzle that a single consumer would be unable to make.

3. UNIFORM EUROPEAN RULES OR MULTIFORM NATIONAL EXPERIMENTS?

In the United States, class action rules are federal and state law, with notable diversity between states such as California and Virginia. Even in Europe 'classes' were perceived traditionally as parts of a society organized in a national state, but can be a concept also for understanding global markets and international communities. The first question, any assessment of the constitutional issues of class actions has to face, is thus what level of government has to make the choice of the rules.

Within Italian legal order, the central State has the exclusive competence to define 'jurisdiction and procedural laws' (art. 117 co. 2 let. l Const.). Within the Union and Community, *nulla quaestio* that 'community law, as it now stands, does not provide for a right to bring a class action before the

Community courts'.[22] A similar choice would need an amendment of the treaties and of the relevant statutes. On the other hand, the injunctions directive has established a common procedure to allow consumer bodies to stop unlawful practices that harm the collective interest of consumers anywhere in the EU and the Commission announced it will 'consider action on collective redress mechanisms for consumers both for infringements of consumer protection rules and for breaches of EU anti-trust rules in line with its 2005 Green Paper on private damages actions'.[23]

The competence in this sector has to be construed on the basis of Art. 153 EC-Treaty as amended in Amsterdam: 'In order to promote the interests of consumers and to ensure a high level of consumer protection, the Community shall contribute to protecting the health, safety and economic interests of consumers, as well as to promoting their right to information, education and to organise themselves in order to safeguard their interests'. The Community shall contribute to the attainment of these objectives through 'measures adopted pursuant to Article 95 in the context of the completion of the internal market' or 'measures which support, supplement and monitor the policy pursued by the Member States'. Group litigation could 'ensure a high level of consumer protection', but unlike the injunctional relief as provided under art. 3 law no. 281/1998, damages relief would protect first of all 'economical interest' and promote – at least – a better information for the safeguard of consumer interests.[24] In order to the principle of necessity under art. 3 B EC-Treaty, directive 98/27/EC has outlined two options of public or organisational collective action because 'the specific features of national legal systems must be taken into account to every extent possible by leaving Member States free to choose between different options having equivalent effect'. An additional burden of argumentation has now to be faced in order of the necessity today, ten years

[22] Tribunale di Primo Grado, Seconda Camera, decisione del 28. 11. 2005, *European Environmental Bureau (EEB) et al.* v. *Commission* T-236/04, T-241/04.

[23] EU Consumer Policy strategy 2007–2013. Empowering consumers, enhancing their welfare, effectively protecting them, SEC (2007) 321–323). See also Commission staff working paper – Annex to the Green Paper – Damages actions for breach of the EC antitrust rules {COM(2005) 672 final} (SEC/2005/1732): 'Option 25 : A cause of action for consumer associations. (…) It appears that there is scope to introduce additional means of collective consumer redress, such as a collective or representative action by consumer associations or other qualified entities. (…). A specific legal basis for actions to be brought by consumer associations or other qualified entities in the competition field would have the advantage of greater clarity, as well as possibly defining the relationship of such actions to other issues such as the standing of direct or indirect purchasers.'

[24] Cfr. Poncibò (2002).

later, of the imposition of a private enforcement with class action or group litigation scheme for damages actions. Neither the unspecified argument of a 'total underdevelopment'[25] nor the existing clashes between European and American Judges seem to be sufficiently substantiated arguments for such further harmonization. A new directive for a European wide consumer *class action* should furthermore respect the principle of subsidiarity if we consider art. 153 EC-Treaty as a source of a concurrent competence more than a provision that aims to save the exclusive competence under art 95 EC-Treaty for the special sector of consumer protection policies.[26] The first interpretation would imply the question whether 'the objectives of the proposed action cannot be sufficiently achieved by the Member States and can therefore, by reason of the scale or effects of the proposed action, be better achieved by the Community'. At this stage of the national experimentation of variations of class action, a negative prognosis could be hardly argued, except for those situations which would need a cross-border group action.[27] If the need for European uniform rules would rely on the 'cross-border implication' of a class action, the Community could adopt harmonizing measures 'eliminating obstacles to the good functioning of civil proceedings, if necessary by promoting the compatibility of the rules on civil procedure applicable in the Member States' under Art. 65 let. c EC-Treaty, using the procedure provided by Art. 67 EC-Treaty. That could be the way to build a uniform European class action, strictly limited to such cases that do invest the territory of more than one of the Member States of the Union and managed by the national judges.[28]

4. SOCIAL AND ECONOMIC FUNDAMENTAL RIGHTS AS JUSTIFICATIONS AND RESTRAINTS FOR CLASS ACTION

A transplant of the US-styled class in the European legal cultures action could raise questions of constitutional review regarding fundamental rights guarantees similar to those of the due process clause specified by the Supreme Court. European constitutional courts have sometimes faced

---

[25] See http://europa.eu.int/comm/competition/antitrust/others/private_enforcement/index_en.html#damages.

[26] Michailidou (2007, pp. 295ff.).

[27] Criticized Jaeger (2007, pp. 349ff.).

[28] A similar proposal has been made by Michailidou (2007, pp. 362ff.). A French-style civil procedure connected to a criminal action could fall under art. 31 EU-Treaty.

questions on collective actions through corporations and associations, but there are only a few decisions related more or less indirectly to class actions. It is worth to noting that these decisions have not embraced the classical justification of 'access to justice' and 'effectiveness of justice', but relied mostly on social and economical rights.[29]

The Austrian Constitutional Court has stated in 1994 that the preferential treatment given to the Austrian Sammelklage as a test case procedure does not violate the principle of equality. The institution was not created for the purpose of privileging the group of claimants represented by the acting association, but only in order to promote the general interest in the solution of the legal questions that have been raised.[30] One could argue that at least the interest in consumer protection itself could be a constitutionally qualified general interest, especially under constitutions with relevant social rights guarantees or with public policy clauses similar to art. 38 of the Nizza-Charter, that can justify a special preferential treatment for consumer class actions in judicial systems.

But class action rules can be not only a tool for access to social justice, they have also to respect the defendant's economical rights. The German *Bundesverfassungsgericht* suspended in 2003 the enforcement of a decision of the High Regional Court of Düsseldorf that authorized the notification, by way for international legal assistance, of a US class action for damages to the Bertelsmann AG (Napster case). Granting temporary relief to a constitutional complaint (*Verfassungsbeschwerde*) assisted by the constitutional law Professor Peter Lerche, the German Constitutional Court stated that the duty to respect foreign judgments is limited if the claim – at least in its amount – has evidently no substantial legitimacy: 'The German constitutional law could be infringed if procedures on state courts were obviously abused in a way to bring a market operator to heel through media pressure and the risk of a condemnation'.[31]

In 2007, an *obiter dictum* of the same court has explained that an abuse of law in case of judicial decrees incompatible with 'the irrevocable principles

---

[29] From the classical access to justice approach see the remarks on 'asymmetries and caseloads in the Welfare State' in E. Storskrupp / J. Ziller (2007), 188ff.

[30] Austrian Constitutional Court, decision of 15th December 1994, VfSlg 13.989 = Österreichische Juristenzeitung 1996, 474.

[31] BVerfG, 2 BvR 1198/03 of 25. 7. 2003 = BVerfGE 108, 238 ff. The case has been settled. Accademical critics from Stürner (2006, pp. 60ff.) and K. Hopt/R. Kulms/J. v. Hein, 'Rechtshilfe und Rechtsstaat. Die Zustellung einer US-amerikanischen class action in Deutschland', Tübingen 2006, see 7 *German Law Journal* No. 12 (1 December 2006). In 1994, after having granted temporary relief for an action for punitive damages, the final decision accepted notification: BVerfGE 91, 140ff.

of a liberal state governed by the rule of law' (*rechtsstaatlich*) could happen in cases of 'claims for damages for an amount that could compromise the economical existence of the defendant or of *collective actions* (*Sammelklagen*) with an unforeseeable number of actors and *petita* managed through a media campaign'.[32]

Finally, the most recent decision of the *Bundesverfassungsgericht* has furthermore explained that the institute of class action in itself is not questionable, even if one takes into account the pre-trial-discovery, that could be abused for improper investigation purposes, the lack of reimbursement of costs even in cases of completely pointless actions, the rules of joint and several liabilities etc.

> Even the decision of a law-making policy, decision that has to be generally respected from the German side, to allow class actions for mass torts whereby single class members have not to take an active role, does not infringe the irrevocable principles of a liberal state governed by the rule of law, as long as (solange) the class action procedure respects the unalienable rights of defence.

An abuse can be proved only on the basis of concrete facts, for example 'that the amount of the claim is evidently unreasonable, that the defendants evidently has nothing to do with the facts in question or that a pressure, even through media, is made in order to constrain the defendant to a settlement unreasonable in itself'.[33]

In this view, private enforcement has to respect not only 'unalienable' rights to defence, but also to avoid a sort of private abuse of the public power of the court in group litigation. Class action plaintiffs have the right to act in defence of their rights, but not the right to use an exceptional public proceeding for private power plays. They have a duty of fairness that could reflect a competition principle and a bona fide civilisation, but could be construed also as a principle of reasonableness and proportionality extended from public to private powers.

Significant is that the German Court faces the same risk of media pressure adopted by the French lawmakers of the *action en représentation conjointe.* The court seems to consider it unfair taking profit from the suspects and prejudices of the public, to 'pillory' the defendant instead of fighting with procedural arms in court. The public notice for the purposes of class certification itself will be not sufficient for a proof of abuse, but

---

32 BVerfG, 2 BvR 1133/04 of 24.1.2007, see Hein (2007, pp. 249ff.).

33 BVerfG 2. Senat 1. Kammer, BvR 2247/06, of 14.06.2007.

insofar as plaintiffs and advocates manage further publicity they make just a private use of information that should all be directed exclusively to the court.

From an economical point of view, the German jurisprudence has given to German defendants a symbolical barrier because they can use the ordinary and the constitutional complaint procedures in order to gain time and to accrue the risks of enforcements of decrees and settlements in class action litigation. There is another significant coincidence with the creation of a foundation for the forced labour victims under the Nazi-regime attacked by other complaints regarding the (perhaps arbitrary) exclusion of Italian military detainees ('Internati Militari Italiani') qualified (*ex post*) as prisoners of war.[34]

A similar concern, the necessity to bring mass litigation under a control and to protect even defendants' business interests has been articulated even in other countries. The Italian Constitutional Court faced in 1974 the question of constitutionality of a provision that reserved to the representative organs of trade unions at a local level the right to act against 'anti-trade union practices' (art. 28). The provision was considered not in violation of the right to act of the single workers because they could always defend their individual rights and a right of single workers to act would have generated a 'plethora of complaints' damaging the productivity and paralysing the management of business.[35]

5. THE IMPACT OF CLASS ACTIONS ON THE RIGHTS TO ACTION AND DEFENCE

European constitutional judges did never face directly the controversial issue of the opt-out mechanism. The 'Study on alternative means of consumer redress other than redress through ordinary judicial proceedings' did not analyse the question but stated: 'Indeed in Europe it is widely believed that the article 6 of the ECHR and the relevant constitutional principles guaranteeing access for each citizen to a judicial decision maker form an obstacle to the introduction of US type class actions based on an

---

[34] See BVerfG, 2 BvR 1379/01 of 28.6.2004 and BVerfG, 1 BvR 1804/03 of 7.12.2004, both based on an expertise of C. Tomuschat.

[35] Corte costituzionale, decision n. 54/1974. See V. Vigoriti, *Interessi collettivi e processo*, Milano 1979, 167ff.

opt-out system'.[36] At least from the point of view of the Italian constitution,[37] a more detailed analysis of the fundamental rights of process involved should distinguish the right to action (1.) from the right to defence (2.) (art. 24.1 Const.) and take into account even the additional guarantees (3.) such as legal aid (art. 24.3), the 'natural' judge pre-established by law (art. 25 Const.), equality and fair trial, as specified by the principles of 'dialectics' (contraddittorio) and 'reasonable length' (art. 111 Const.).

(1) The right to 'take judicial action in order to protect individual rights and legitimate interests' (art. 24 Const.) can be construed not only as a social right to have access to the public function of justice and the relevant services, but also as a subjective right of freedom. In the latter case it implies protection against prohibitions of judicial action and the imposition of duties to sue. A compulsory participation in plaintiff class actions or a rule that would exclude opting-out of class members from a party role would be unconstitutional. But even if class members are considered non-parties of the class action, the pending or concluded class action could imply for them a preclusion, i.e. prohibition for further action or 'relitigation' by virtue of the principles of 'litispendenza' and 'res judicata'.[38]

An effective freedom of *opting-in* could be respectful of the right to action of class members. An effective freedom of *opting-out* would leave the class member a choice whether to accept this prohibition or not, but the exercise of this freedom of choice would be restricted a) to a specific time period, b) to the court chosen by the plaintiff, c) to the legal burden of a valid declaration, d) to the factual burden of taking specific information and even legal counsel. On the other hand, the constitutional guarantee of the right to action doesn't cover either an immediate, or a perpetual relief.[39] If the right to act does not imply a freedom from burdens of declaration and counsel, the negative freedom from action could be restricted by similar burdens, if the burden itself is justified by a compelling public interest in economy

---

36 op. cit. p. 267.

37 A German scholar noted that class action can produce indirect and de facto unions with not freely chosen representatives. The freedom of association, indeed, has to be conceived even as a negative freedom from being associated by direct or indirect force of legislative acts. See R. Scholz (2003), 259ff.

38 *Dow Chem Co.* v. *Stephenson* 539 U.S. 111 (2003) left the question open whether the court's decision affirming adequacy of representation has to be considered binding for all class members, see Rubenstein (2007).

39 Corte costituzionale decision no. 251/2003: 'l'art. 24 Cost. non comporta necessariamente l'assoluta immediatezza dell'esperibilità del diritto di azione.'

and good timing of justice and proportional to the public benefits of the class action management. In light of foreign experiences, the discretionary power of the legislator could allow at least a temporary experimentation of similar procedures.

(2) The right to *defence* has been construed as a guarantee of the real opportunity to give voice to the proper reasons. That implies the right to be informed of all acts of a process, to become a plaintiff or defendant party in the process and to express through a lawyer and (in the Italian legal order) even personally own opinions on the facts and law that the judge has to take into account. This right is violated if the class action process is made without adequate information of the class members, if it is made *in absentiam* even when a class member would be able and willing to defend itself or when a party's comments on the facts and the law are not admitted to be heard.

The adequacy of information depends on whether a defendant can be identified or not. Only insofar as identification is impracticable, a notification to the unidentified through public proclamation (art. 150 Civil Procedure Code) could be justified as a reasonable compromise between the right to action and the right to defence.[40] Under the existing law public proclamation is allowed also for a great number of identified members, but all identified parties have to be listed in it.[41]

The class action can furthermore be a process *in absentiam* and even class members that do not opt out cannot defend themselves (if lawyers) or choose their own advocates in order to be heard individually. The opt-in system, on the other hand, can be organized in a way that class members become joint parties or remain 'represented' parties. In the latter case, the opting-in decision could be interpreted as a free will to not exercise the right to be heard if the class member is adequately informed and adequately represented by the leading plaintiff or defendant. The will would be free when the refusal of the opt-in leaves the non-participating class member free to act or defend itself in further proceedings, at least after the conclusion of the class action process.

An opting-out mechanism with a legal rule that presumes silence as acceptance of representation makes further burdens on the exercise of the right of defence. The choice to be not defended in the class action procedure and to make a defence through another separate

---

40 Corte costituzionale no. 151, 153/1980, 187/1987, 211/2001, 154/2006. See also Giussani (1996, pp. 392ff.).

41 Corte di cassazione 2005/121.

action, at least when the class action is concluded, would be limited to a specific time period through the legal burden of a valid declaration and through the factual burden of taking specific information and even legal counsel. Those burdens have to be again justified by a compelling public interest in economy and good timing of justice and widening access to it, being proportional to the public benefits of the class action management. The discretionary power of the legislator is thus not necessarily restricted to a choice of the opting-in model, but in the light of the principle of proportionality needs to search for balanced solutions that would be less restrictive of the procedural rights.

(3) Class actions have an impact even on other fundamental rights or principles of justice with constitutional guarantees in the Italian Constitution. Even the impact on these rights has to be included in balancing tests.

The right to legal aid means that 'the poor are entitled by law to proper means for action or defence in all courts' (art. 24.3. Const.). Insofar as class actions help the poor as a form of private assistance organized by the leading plaintiff or defendant, by virtue of a general principle of subsidiarity the legislator could be even allowed to exclude legal aid for separate action or defence of poor class members. On the other hand, if poor class members would like to be the leading plaintiffs or defendants, the legal aid has to be restricted just to the really poor members of the class and could not cover more expenses than those of a (fictive) individual suit.

The right to be not removed from a judge to another is not violated if connected cases of different judges (art. 40 c.p.c.) can be transferred to the judge that has been addressed first. Even a class action is inspired on the principle of 'simultaneus processus' as a further guarantee of the right to defence of the counterpart.

The right to be heard is guaranteed also by the principle that justice has to be administered through fair trial: 'Trials are based on equal confrontation of the parties before an independent and impartial judge. The law has to ensure a reasonable length of the proceedings'. (art. 111) These guarantees and the principle of equality could raise further questions on class action rules. First, equal confrontation on the parties means that the plaintiff and defendant should have equal procedural arms, equality which is difficult to reach under conditions of substantially asymmetric relations and access to media. Furthermore, the impartiality of a judge who has to control the 'adequacy of representation' of one party only could be questionable. On the other hand, class actions can help to guarantee the reasonable length of mass procedures, but then even a single class action process should take more time than an individual suit.

The foregoing considerations seem to be consistent with the American 'due process' clause if construed as an objective principle, as a 'functional' right or just as a duty of the judge. In the European context of more formalized constitutional and supranational 'rights to justice', a person could bind itself to not exercise the right to action and defence only insofar as the substantial rights can be an object of a negotiation and a settlement.[42]

We could also say that the European legislator has a specific duty to protect individuals from handing over the defence of fundamental rights, including the civil rights matters. That does not exclude that class actions play a role in the protection of all those interested in fundamental rights which have a merely economical interest. But class action should remain a subsidiary remedy for fundamental rights, especially if the protection of fundamental rights is a duty of administrations controlled by political representation and administrative justice. An open question is, whether this kind of protection could be more efficient than class action mechanisms with advocates controlled by judges.

6. THE IMPACT OF CLASS ACTIONS ON THE CONSTITUTIONAL CULTURE

The assessment of the constitutional impact of class actions imported to European countries has to take into consideration not only the prohibitions and needs of constitutional law, but also the effects such an institution could have on the constitutional culture. We have already seen that class actions applied to civil rights such as, for example, anti discrimination rights could even have effects on the architecture of constitutional justice. Test case procedures have been already experienced in the procedures of Verfassungsbeschwerde in Germany and mass procedures have been even realized for the amparo procedure in Spain. Even incidental mechanisms of constitutional review have to face the problem if a question that has been already raised allows other judges to suspend their processes without submitting the same question again to the constitutional court. Could class actions offer a procedure for challenging unconstitutional legislation or regulations in constitutional and or administrative courts?

42 See Schwab and Gottwald (1983, p. 40).

Another question to address is the impact class actions can have for the State, especially the rule of law and democracy and the more liberal or social and cultural concept of public sector action. For the first aspect, there can be no doubt that class actions increase the discretionary power of judges that should be subject to the law. From an Italian point of view, this might be a problematic issue, because a consistent part of the political class believes that judges usurped functions of political representation. Even the risk of increasing the corruption of judges should be taken into account. On the other hand, this fear is projected on criminal justice and strengthening judges' powers in civil justice might help to produce more distance from political parties, because classes can act without political parties. A demand for more civil justice could help to reduce the need for criminal justice. And the control over the adequacy of representatives in civil procedures could help even to empower the citizen to have a better understanding of the ways the powers of public prosecution can be exercised.

The Italian constitution designs a modern welfare state based on duties of solidarity (art. 2.2 Const.) and social rights, with the task 'to remove all economic and social obstacles that, by limiting the freedom and equality of citizens, prevent full individual development and the participation of all workers in the political, economic, and social organization of the country' (art. 3.2 Const.). In this regard, class actions could help to strengthen the sense for economic and social solidarity with the less protected classes, but also promote an increase of social conflicts. A class is not a 'social group expressing personality' (art. 2) and one might be sceptical that class actions have an 'added social value'.

Last but not least, further questions could arise from the Italian media culture. From a European point of view, a process has to be celebrated in court, not in the media. If the media will not respect secrets related to a class action proceeding, could they be threatened themselves?

7. POSTILLA 2007

The comparative analysis of the paper has to be enlarged to other EU-countries under reform, including Bulgaria (2006), Finland (2007),[43] Greece (2007), Italy (2007), Denmark (2008) and Poland (2009). Most European countries and citizens have nowadays specific remedies for collective redress. Excepting Belgium[44] and Romania, most bigger countries

---

[43] See Chapter 16.

[44] See a preliminary discussion in: Closset-Marchal, G, and B, Allemeersch (2008).

have developed more or less complex and differing national systems of collective redress, meanwhile only smaller states were less interested.[45]

The Italian Case is quite significant for the European trends because the legislation revised in 2009 goes beyond the traditional group action and tries to find a fair balance between the values protected by the constitutional guarantees of individual rights protection and the efficiency of a new procedure specially devoted to protection of small claims.[46]

A recent study of the European Parliaments points out that 'generally four types of instruments are used in the 16 Member States which apply collective redress schemes: group and representative actions, test case procedures and procedures for skimming off profits'.[47] The study holds that collective redress schemes provide added value and cost savings for consumers and businesses, but are 'not effective due to disparities and low participation rates, except for schemes running opt-out model'. As around 10 per cent of collective redress cases involve cross-border litigation, the need for further EU rules and harmonisation is perceived to be increasing.[48]

The European reluctance towards class actions in competition law and the preference for collective actions through associations in consumer protection are both criticised and under pressure. The ongoing European debate on collective 'redress' aims to compare and to combine more administrative with more civil justice based models, with more and more observers praising the virtues of informal ADR mechanisms. C. Hodges holds that the enrolment of consumer associations in enforcement mechanisms lacks of democratic accountability and has as an Achilles heel the '(un)availability of funding'.[49] On the one hand, the tension between legally imposed collectivisation through class action and the constitutional principles of liberal democracy has been perceived and criticised even for the US-model of class action.[50] On the other hand, a still open legal and

[45] For Ireland see the opinion of the Law Reform Commission 2003, http://www.lawreform.ie/archives/consultation-paper-on-multi-party-litigation.237.html. For Malta see the Draft Collective Proceedings Act https://opm.gov.mt/collective_proceedings.

[46] See R. Nahi (2010) and A. Pace (2011). For a German reform proposal with similar constitutional arguments see Lange (2011), 178.

[47] European Parliament (2011), 50.

[48] See 'Renforcer la cohérence de l'approche Européene en matière de recours collectif: Prochaines étapes, Note d'information de Mme Reding, M. Almunia et M. Dalli', 5 October 2010.

[49] Hodges (2008), 242.

[50] Redish (2009), 61. A. Lahav (2011), 993ff.

political question is whether a European funding for consumer protection associations at the European level could be a step forward.

REFERENCES

Andrews, N. (2007), *The Modern Civil Process*, Tübingen: Mohr.

Belli, C. (2007), *Le azioni collettive in Italia. Profili teorici ed aspetti pratici*, Milano: Giuffré.

Cafaggi, F. and H. Micklitz (2007), *Administrative and Judicial Collective Enforcement of Consumer Law in the US and the European Union*, available at http://cadmus.iue.it /dspace/bitstream/1814/6980/1/LAW-2007–22.pdf.

Cappelletti, M. and B. Garth (1983), 'The protection of diffuse, fragmented and collective interests in civil litigation', in W. Habscheid (ed), *Effektiver Rechtsschutz und verfassungsmässige Ordnung*, Bielefeld: Gieseking, pp.117–159.

Closset-Marchal, G., and B. Allemeersch (2008), *Vers une 'class action' en droit belge?* Brugge : Die Keure.

Daffer, T. (2006), 'Class Action Litigation As a Means of Enacting Social Change in China', *UMKC Law Review*, **75**, 227–43.

European Parliament Directorate General for Internal Policies, Policy Department A: Economic And Scientific Policy (2011), *Overview of existing collective redress schemes in EU Member States,* IP/A/IMCO/NT/2011–16 July 2011 PE464.433, http://www.europarl.europa.eu/document/activities/cont/201107/20110715ATT24242/20110715ATT24242EN.pdf

Giussani, A. (1996), *Studi sulle class actions*, Padova: Cedam.

Grossi, P. (1995), *L'ordine giuridico medievale*, Roma: Laterza.

Hein, J.V. (2007), 'BVerfG gestattet Zustellung einer US. amerikanische Klage auf Punitive Damages', *Recht der Internationalen Wirtschaft*, **53**(4), 249–55.

Hodges, Ch. (2008), *The Reform of Class Action and Representative Actions in European Legal Systems: New Framework for Collective Redress in Europe*, Oxford: Hart Publishing.

Jaeger, T. (2007), 'Gemeinschaftskompetenz "private enforcement"?', *Juristische Blätter*, **129** (6), 349–68.

Kaser, M. and J.K. Hackl (1996), *Das römische Zivilprozessrecht*, (2 ed.), München: CH Beck.

Lahav, A. (2011), 'Are class actions unconstitutional?' *Michigan Law Review* **109**, 993–1009.

Lange, S. (2011) *Das begrenzte Gruppenverfahren*, Tübingen: Mohr.

Lebre de Freitas, L. (2003), 'La acción popular en el derecho portugués', in: A. Gidi and E. Ferrer Mac-Gregor, *Procesos Colectivos*, Città del Mexico: Porrúa.

Lindblom, P.H. (1997), *Group Actions and the Role of the Courts: a European Perspective*, The Hague: Kluwer Law International.

Lindquist, Y. and P. Hammarskiöld (2007), 'Gruppenklagen in Schweden – erste Erfahrungen mit dem neuen Gesetz', *Recht und Versicherung*, **3**, 98–107.

Marcin, R. (1974), 'Searching for the Origin of the Class Action', *Catholic University Law Review* **23**, 515ff.

Michailidou, C. (2007), *Prozessuale Fragen des Kollektivrechtsschutzes im europäischen Justizraum*, Baden-Baden : Nomos.

Mulheron, R. (2004), *The Class Action in Common Law Systems: A Comparative Perspective*, Oxford: Hart.

Nashi, R. (2010), 'Italy's class action experiment', *Cornell International Law Journal* **43**, 147–173.

Pace, A. (2011), *Interrogativi sulla legittimità costituzionale della nuova 'class action'*, acailable at http://www.rivistaaic.it/articolorivista/interrogativi-sulla-legittimita-costituzionale-della-nuova-class-action

Pirker-Hörmann, B. and P. Kolba (2006), *Österreich: Von der Verbandsklage zur Sammelklage*, available at http://www.verbraucherrecht.at/development/typo/test/uploads/media/ Kolba_Pirker_Bamberg.pdf.

Poncibò, C. (2002), 'Le azioni di interesse collettivo per la tutela dei consumatori', *Rivista Critica del Diritto Privato*, **4**, 659–669, available at http://www.jus.unitn.it/cardozo/Review/ 2003/ponci.pdf.

Redish, M. (2009), *Wholesale justice: constitutional democracy and the problem of the class action lawsuit,* Stanford: Stanford Law Books.

Rubenstein, W. (2007), 'Finality in Class Action Litigation: Lessons from Habeas', *New York University Law Review*, **82**(3), 790–869.

Scholz, R. (2003), 'Individualer oder kollektiver Rechtsschutz?', *Zeitschrift für Gesetzgebung,* **18,** 248–263

Schwab, K.H. and P. Gottwald (1983), 'Verfassung und Zivilprozess', in W. Habscheid (ed), *Effektiver Rechtsschutz und verfassungsmässige Ordnung*, Bielefeld: Gieseking.

Silguero, J. (2003), 'Las acciones collectives de grupo en España', in A. Gidi and E. Ferrer Mac-Gregor, *Procesos Colectivos*, Mexico: Porrúa,

Stadler, A. and A. Mom (2006), 'Tu felix Austria? – Neue Entwicklungen im kollektiven Rechtsschutz im Zivilprozess in Österreich', *Recht der Internationalen Wirtschaft*, **5**(3), 199–205.

Storskrupp, E. and J. Ziller (2007), 'Access to Justice in European Comparative Law', in: F. Francioni (ed.), *Access to Justice as a Human Right*, Oxford : Oxford University Press, pp.177–203

Story, J. (1836), *Commentaries of Equity Jurisprudence*, Boston: Hilliard, Gray & Company.

Stürner, R. (2006), 'Die verweigerte Zustellungshilfe für US-Klagen oder der "Schuss übers Grab"' *Juristenzeitung*, **61**(2), 60–8.

Stuyck, J. et. al. (2007), *An Analysis and Evaluation of Alternative Means of Consumer Redress Other Than Redress Through Ordinary Judicial Proceedings*, The United States National Report, Leuven, available at http://ec.europa.eu/consumers/redress/reports_studies/ index_en.htm.

Taruffo, M. (2001), 'Some Remarks on Group Litigation in Comparative Perspective', *J. Duke. of Comp. & International Law*, **11**, 405–421.

Teixeira De Sousa, M. (2002), *Über die grenzüberschreitende Popularklage zum Schutz der Verbraucherinteressen*, in Festschrift R. Geimer, München: Beck, pp. 1317–1330.

Vigoriti, V. (1979), *Interessi collettivi e processo*.

Yeazell, S. (1987), *From medieval group litigation to the modern class action'*, New Haven: Yale University Press.

16. Introducing class actions in Finland: an example of law-making without economic analysis

Mikko Välimäki

1. INTRODUCTION

The Finnish Parliament accepted in February 2007 a new law on class actions (literally 'group actions'), which entered into force on 1 January, 2008.[1] The legislative process was particularly slow. Finland has been preparing a law on class actions since the early 1990s and this was – depending on the criteria of counting – the fourth try.

Some fifteen years ago the idea of class actions was something new in Europe. Time passes quickly, however, and the new Finnish law cannot be described as 'radical' by any meaning of the word. Many European countries, as described in other chapters in this volume, have changed their existing procedural codes and enacted new laws to make class action litigation possible.

The new Finnish class action law differs from the mainstream in fundamentally limiting its scope of application. Although the law is titled as being a general law on class actions, it only applies to consumer cases where the government-funded Consumer Ombudsman is acting as the lead counsel. This was not the case in the beginning. Years ago, the first law proposals had much broader scope of application but as the lobbying between potential defendants (the industry) and plaintiffs (consumer agencies etc.) became polarized, it became evident that there can be either a major compromise or no law at all. Indeed, the objectives and contents of the law proposals changed many times during the years

[1] Ryhmäkannelaki, 13.2.2007. The law is based on government's proposal nr. 154/2006.

This chapter analyses the Finnish law-making process from comparative and economic policy viewpoints. First, the chapter discusses how the Finnish legislative process ended up with a certain outcome. It is argued that neither well-founded economic nor empirical arguments had any relevant role. Instead, partisan claims on class action cases in the United States and their potential implications to companies were used as a strong argument to restrict the law's scope of application. The official preparatory documents did not present any study on experiences from the United States. There was non-partisan empirical evidence of the use of class actions only from Sweden.

Second, this chapter compares the claims presented in the Finnish law-making process to studies and legislative work made in other countries. Can one really claim, as was done during the legislative process in Finland, that other countries have made serious mistakes when they have not restricted the scope of application in class actions? Would a law on class actions also open doors to the misuse of the system through frivolous suits? Are class actions a totally foreign tool to continental European legal systems? The chapter concludes that these claims are mainly based on partisan opinions, not on well-founded studies. The examples of other Nordic countries show that there is nothing uncommon in implementing class actions in a Northern European legal system. Misuse of class actions is not likely to be due to, for example, fundamental differences in the substance of accident law and the rules regarding the indemnification of legal costs in litigation.

Third, this chapter argues that the main reason why the Finnish class action law 'failed' was the dynamics of the legislative process. The process may not aim to the best possible outcome for the society as a whole. In accordance with the theory of public choice, the result is often a compromise between conflicting interests. The idea of reaching a consensus in preparatory work before a law is submitted to the parliament means that if well-organized interest groups are able to form a strong opposition, the law may never enter the parliament no matter of the substantial arguments.[2] The result is that an unknown number of cases are not litigated at all in Finland because the scope of application of the law is restricted. Regulatory authorities have no resources to provide an extensive preventive threat as would a complementary private mechanism.

---

2 On the theory of public choice and interest groups see e.g. Mercuro and Medema (2006, pp. 191–5).

2. A HISTORY OF FINLAND'S CLASS ACTION LAW

2.1 Minimalist Approach

According to the first paragraph of the Finnish law on class actions, the law can be applied only in civil litigation in cases between *consumers and businesses*. In addition, the *Consumer Ombudsman* is the only party that can bring in and litigate cases on behalf of consumers.[3] The first paragraph then further clarifies that the law is not applicable in securities cases (stock owners are not consumers).[4] If a case is filed, the Consumer Ombudsman must inform all the individuals that can be considered to be in the relevant class. An individual must then submit a written acceptance to the Consumer Ombudsman that he wants to be a member in the suing class. This follows the so-called *opt-in* procedure.

In short, the Finnish law on class actions introduces at least three major limitations into its scope of application:

- The case must be between consumers and businesses; particularly securities cases are not allowed, however.
- The only party that can litigate on behalf of consumers is the Consumer Ombudsman.
- Consumers must submit written acceptances to the Consumer Ombudsman if they want to be members in the suing class (opt-in).

All these limitations support a *compensatory* rather than preventive objective. The limitations make sense if the law is to defend first and foremost the subjective interests of individuals. The limitations make the law an unsuitable tool for social engineering through private means. In other words, Finland still trusts on *regulation* rather than private enforcement. It is assumed that the Finnish state and its various governmental agencies keep on monitoring corporate behavior. Next, it is considered how and why did the Finnish legislative process end up with this outcome.

---

[3] In practice, the Ombudsman can delegate representation and according to the law even hire outside counsel as an advisor.

[4] It is unclear whether various kinds of modern investment instruments could be defined as securities based on the law's definition.

2.2 Early Law Proposals with Broader Approach Failed

Finland and Sweden were the first Nordic countries to start officially preparing class action legislation in the early 1990s.[5] The first Finnish preliminary investigation was published in 1992 concluding essentially that it was possible to introduce class actions in Finland following the United States model.[6] The Ministry of Justice set up a follow-up preparatory group, which published in 1995 a draft law proposal that argued for a new class action law with a broad scope of application.[7] The group consisted of a law professor, civil servants, members from the judiciary and the Consumer Ombudsman – but notably none from the industry and neither was any industry representative heard in the preparatory work. The group's proposal would have made it possible to initiate class action on any actionable claim under Finnish law. Anyone could have been the lead plaintiff with his chosen attorney. Class membership would have been based on the opt-out principle. Because of increasing critique from the industry representatives, the first draft never proceeded as a formal law proposal in the parliament. Instead, a new working group – now including industry representatives – published a new draft proposal in 1997 with some limitations in the scope of application.[8] Due to intense lobbying from the industry, the limited proposal did not proceed any further either.

Meanwhile Sweden adopted a law on class action that entered into force in 2003. Save for the opt-in principle, the Swedish law did not have any relevant restrictions in its scope of application. Norway and Denmark, which were not that active in the 1990s, followed quickly with their own law proposals based on the Swedish example.[9]

Finland continued the work as well. The Ministry of Justice set up the next governmental working group in 2004, which published its preliminary findings in 2005.[10] In addition to civil servants and members from the judiciary, two members came from the industry, two represented consumer protection interests, one environmental protection, one came from a labor

---

[5] One can say the initiative came from Sweden. See Section 4 below.

[6] Wihuri (1992).

[7] Anonymous (1995). Ehdotus ryhmäkannelaiksi. Työryhmän mietintö. Oikeusministeriön lainvalmisteluosaston julkaisu 1/1995. (In Finnish, 'Proposal for a law on class actions.')

[8] Anonymous, (1997). According to this proposal, private organizations such as workers unions could have not been claimants, class membership would have been based on opt-in principle, and it would have not been possible to sue for specified issues such as contract breach.

[9] See Section 4 below.

[10] Anonymous (2005).

union, and one was an attorney. Despite opposing comments by the industry representatives, the work finally resulted in a formal law proposal in the next year.[11] The 2005 working group did not take a certain position, for example, following the United States, Sweden, or other Nordic countries for that matter, but continued the work from where the previous groups in the 1990s had left it. Partly to mitigate industry worries, the group introduced possibilities to introduce an even further limited approach to class actions. From now on, it was a question about a minimalist class action law or no class actions at all.

2.3 The Art of Identifying Needs *a Priori*

The first main problem with the group's document was that it *did not empirically identify the needs for class actions in the first place*. The document did not present any data on the types of class actions in the United States or other countries, where the system had been in active use for decades. The only empirical data was from Sweden, where class actions had just been introduced. Necessarily, the data set was far from representative although one must admit it was indicative. During the first three years there had been only one case led by the Swedish Consumer Ombudsman among a total of six cases. None of them dealt with environmental issues.[12] For some unknown reasons, the group did not comment on that in any way or recognize a need to do a more comprehensive survey. Only consumer and environmental cases were discussed further as possible application areas.

The actual arguments used to limit the law's scope were rather formal and theoretical. Consumer protection was suggested to be the main application area because:[13]

- There are potentially an increasing number of consumer groups with similar small claims.
- A preventive function is important in the continuously evolving field of consumer protection.
- The scope of application in consumer protection law is clearly limited.
- There is Consumer Ombudsman, agencies, and voluntary dispute

---

[11] The follow-up draft law was Anonymous (2006a), which was then forwarded to the parliament with minor modifications as Government's law proposal 154/2006.

[12] The first Swedish cases include e.g. securities and civil rights. See Section 4 below.

[13] Anonymous, (2005, pp. 54–5).

resolution mechanisms, which means that litigation becomes actual only after other conflict resolution possibilities have failed.

The draft law proposal further motivated consumer protection with speculative statements describing the rise of 'global consumer society'. In addition, there was a reference to an earlier preparatory document from 1990s stating: 'from the case examples [discussed in the document] it is possible to conclude that class actions would be first and foremost actual in [selected consumer protection issues]'. The referred cases did not, however, represent any statistically meaningful set – the areas of law were selected first before the actual cases were searched for.[14] Environmental cases were also argued for although the motivations were briefer. Because the group had adopted a sector-focused approach to class actions, other areas of law did not receive any arguments for or against.[15]

Ministry of Justice received over 40 comments on the draft law.[16] The only parties that argued for no limits in the scope of application were three professors of procedural law and a consumer interest group. Professors referred to formal reasons and the examples of other Nordic countries. The consumer group agreed. Two labor unions also advocated extending the law's scope to employment cases.[17] Most of the commentators simply agreed with the chosen limitation on consumer cases, but were more cautious on environmental issues for both formal and substantial reasons. Industry representatives continued to be fundamentally against the idea of class actions in the first place. Based on the feedback the Ministry of Justice decided to drop environmental issues from the scope of application before the law was formally proposed in the parliament.[18] The law's scope of application did not change in the parliamentary process.

2.4 The Art of Identifying Economic Effects *a Priori*

Another major problem with the 2005 group's document was that it started with a statement that *they did not have at their disposal any economic*

---

[14] Anonymous, (2006a, p. 39), which referred to the law proposal from 1997. The selection of the cases in the 1997 proposal was 'exemplary' and it was specifically stated that 'no comprehensive study of case law has been done'. Anonymous (1997, p. 17).

[15] Interestingly, the 1992 investigation had some data from the United States (referred from Swedish studies) that indicated most of the class action cases there were about civil rights. See Wihuri (1992).

[16] Anonymous, (2006b).

[17] Anonymous, (2006b, p. 11).

[18] Government's proposal nr. 154/2006.

analysis of the effects of class actions.[19] This comment was perhaps more telling than any other. Namely, it did not restrict the group to document numerous claims about the negative economic effects of class actions in the United States. The only documented source on the effects of class action in the United States was an oral testimony and written brief from Nokia.[20] According to an article in a Finnish economic magazine:[21]

> The fight against class action legislation had its peak when Nokia director Rick Stimson gave his testimony to the working group in the Ministry of Justice. The American lawyer told how Finland should write its law. In the final minutes of his presentation he repeated six times that there are no reasons or needs to change the current practice… Stimson told to the working group several examples of the misuse of class actions in the United States. According to him, the ones benefiting from the system are attorneys, who share the millions of dollars in attorney fees. Claimants have received just little amounts of money or other benefits.

It is difficult to assess the overall impact of the Nokia brief to the outcome of the legislative process. The brief is, however, interesting reading since it collects almost all negative claims about class actions presented in the United States. According to the brief:[22]

> The United States Chamber of Commerce estimates that business in the US spend tens of millions of dollars each year defending against frivolous lawsuits and that the total cost of the US tort system (civil claims) to US businesses is more than $129 billion USD per year. While there has been no allocation of that to class action litigation, class action litigation is the most costly to defend and the most costly to settle, even when no product defect or injury has occurred or been proven.

In other words, the strategy was to blur any distinction between procedural law and substantial accident law as if a procedural class action instrument in Finland would also introduce American substantive law. Further, according to the Nokia brief, the argument that … :[23]

> … class action litigation is required to regulate business practices, presumes that a) there are current deficiencies in corporate behaviour that need to be regulated; b) alternative mechanisms to control behaviour do not function or exist; c) class

[19] Anonymous, (2005, p. xx).

[20] The document titled 'The US Class Action' is on file with the author. It is unpublished but public.

[21] Puustinen (2007).

[22] Document titled 'The US Class Action' is on file with the author. It is unpublished but public.

[23] Nokia's brief.

> actions are an effective deterrent; and 4) there is some cost benefit relationship between class action litigation and social benefit. Those four arguments do not survive close examination when applied to Finland or the European community.

The brief went on to argue that there was high ethics in the industry (low corruption rate), much regulation and government control already in place, and good access to justice for individuals because of the legal cost indemnification principle. Other industry groups followed up with vague references to 'legends' from the United States and argued that Finland would lose foreign investments if unlimited class actions were possible. In essence, the industry argumentation did not differ from the 1990s at all.

The Ministry of Justice answered in the draft law noting that the claims of negative economic effects are necessarily theoretic. There were no indications that the Swedish law on class actions would have had any effect on investments into Sweden. No new insurance products had been introduced on the market, nor had insurance premiums risen. They had no information that multinational Finnish companies would have avoided Swedish or even American markets just because of class actions. They also noted that there was no real possibility for frivolous suits because the only party having power to initiate a suit was the Consumer Ombudsman.[24] Although these arguments may sound like a general defense of class actions, they were modestly aimed at only defending the strictly limited draft proposal and make it possible to have at least some kind of law enacted.

As noted, the draft law received more than 40 comments. Maybe the most interesting one regarding economic effects was that of the Government's Institute for Economic Research.[25] Although short and informal, this was the only one from a research organization and the only one – save for some partisan industry comments – that focused on the economic effects. The Institute first noted correctly that *most of the claims for and against certain economic effects of class actions were based on theoretical conclusions or pure guessing*. Unfortunately, the comment itself also fell to the same speculation fallacy it first criticized. The comment did not provide any empirical or economic evidence, or even references, on class actions. It plainly went on to criticize the idea of legal entrepreneurship with the following statement:

---

[24] Anonymous, (2006b, pp. 74–8).

[25] Document titled 'Lausunto ryhmäkannetyöryhmän mietinnössä suoritetusta yritysvaikutusten arvioinnista' is on file with the author.

> If possible cases would be about compensating small claims, it is unclear what the benefits of class action would be. In this case the most important effect on companies would be the increase of law firm turnovers.

Further, the comment trashed specifically environmental class actions, just because ...:

> ... It is easy to think of cases, where well-resourced organizations (e.g. Greenpeace) could with weak grounds litigate against Finnish forest and energy companies. Suits would not necessary be accepted, but they would tie large companies to lengthy trials and could at the same time harm smaller subcontractors of these large companies.

The formal law proposal submitted to the parliament did not comment further on the Institute's claims although, as noted, environmental issues were left out of its scope.

> Perhaps the strongest argument against the idea of frivolous suits is the procedural rule that the losing party is subject to the legal costs of the winning party. For example if the Finnish Consumer Ombudsman loses a case where it has defended an individual consumer against a major industrial firm, it is not uncommon that a Finnish district court reimburses more than 100 000 euros of defendant's legal fees from the Ombudsman. Under these circumstances it is understandable that there will be no case unless the victory is almost sure.[26]

3. OTHER NORDIC COUNTRIES: ADOPTING THE AMERICAN MODEL WITH ADJUSTMENTS

Discussion on class actions in Nordic countries can be said to have started seriously when Swedish law professor Per Henrik Lindblom published a major book on the topic in 1989.[27] He carefully presented and rebutted numerous myths about class actions in the United States and finally concluded: 'No decisive barriers to a Swedish adoption appear to be at hand'.[28] The first policy meeting for all Nordic countries was arranged soon afterwards. According to the proceedings, 'There appeared to be

---

[26] Phone conversation with the Consumer Agency's lawyer Jari Suurla, 25 June, 2007. The Consumer Ombudsman has reserved only 20 000 euros for potential class actions in 2008. Thus, it is very likely there will be no class action cases in Finland in the near future.

[27] Per Lindblom (1989). The book has almost 800 pages.

[28] Ibid. p. 729 (English summary)

practically full agreement that the group action deserves special attention in the ongoing *de lege ferenda* discussion'.[29]

Sweden then went on to commission a working group to prepare an extensive three-volume legislative pre-investigation.[30] The working group was again led by professor Lindblom with members from the judiciary, government institutions, an attorney, a lawyer from a labor union, and even one from the industry who objected to particular issues such as the idea of private class actions and the opt-out principle.[31] This was just the beginning compared to the industry critique following the investigation's publication. The critique may have been even stronger than in Finland. Lindblom took the time to answer the industry claims and forcefully defended the proposal he had initiated. Lindblom's conclusion was that *the proposal had nothing to do with substantive law, which was the target of the critique.*[32] After all the dust had settled, the investigation led eventually into a formal law proposal in 2001 with little details such as the opt-out principle omitted.[33] The law was accepted and came into force in the beginning of 2003.[34]

Norway and Denmark followed the Swedish legislative work. Their proposals came after the Swedish law had already been accepted. At this stage, the industry critique did not stop the proposals from becoming law quickly. Both Norwegian and Danish national laws are entering into force 1 January, 2008.[35]

The content of these Nordic laws is rather identical and in many respects close to the American model. The scope of application is not limited to certain types of cases and standard rules on attorneys apply. The only major difference is that opt-in is mandatory in Sweden. In Norway and Denmark opt-in is the main principle as well, but opt-out can be applied

---

29 The meeting focused on the possibility of class actions in consumer protection issues. Per Lindblom (1990, p. 222) (English summary).

30 SOU 1994:151. Grupprättegång. Del A-C.

31 Ibid. Del B, pp. 685–9.

32 See on overview, see Lindblom (1996, pp. 85–107), which starts with the following statement: 'There is a strong, well-organized, well-funded and influential opposition to the proposal on class actions…' He identified the opposition to consist of a group of big companies ('storföretagsgruppen') who had further hired attorneys and a lobby organization to advance their cause.

33 According to Blom (2006, p. 96), the reason why the proposal was idle for so many years was not the critique but rather the administrative burden initiated by Sweden's EU membership.

34 Lag 2002:599 om grupprättegång.

35 Norwegian law: Lov 2005–06–17 nr 90: Lov om mekling og rettergang i sivile tvister (tvisteloven). Kapittel 35. Gruppesøksmål. Danish law: Lov nr. 181 af 28. februar 2007 om ændring af retsplejeloven og forskellige andre love (Gruppesøgsmål m.v.). Kapitel 23 a. Gruppesøgsmål.

when the individual claim is small enough and it is not likely that the claimants would bother to take the time to opt-in.

Table 16.1 A comparison of some key features of new class action laws in Finland, Sweden, Norway and Denmark (Finnish law is extremely restricted)

Country	Finland	Sweden	Norway	Denmark
In force	1.1.2008	1.1.2003	1.1.2008	1.1.2008
Scope	Consumer protection	Unlimited	Unlimited	Unlimited
Attorney	Consumer Ombudsman	No limits	No limits	
Opt-out	N/A	N/A	Small claims	Small claims

Sweden is the first Nordic country to have some data on class actions. There were a total of six class actions initiated during the first three years. Only one of them was led by the Consumer Ombudsman, others were private suits. As in the United States, case topics have varied from clear consumer protection issues to corporate governance and constitutional rights.[36] The low number and topical variety of cases speaks for the fact that *class actions complement the role of regulatory authorities.* In this sense, one could argue that class actions also minimize regulatory costs.

> One can find examples on the limits of government regulation also in its strong areas such as consumer protection. One recent example is a case when recording companies offered so called copy-protected CDs to consumers. Sony's particular copy protection system introduced a security vulnerability to the computers of thousands of consumers world-wide in 2005. Sony drew the CDs from the markets and settled a class action suit in the United States.[37] Meanwhile, hundreds of Finnish consumers protested openly against the problems of copy protections. After pressure from journalists, the Finnish Consumer Agency announced it would have a meeting with recording company representatives before it could make any statement of the case.[38] That statement never came.

[36] For statistics of different areas of class actions in the United States, see e.g. Deborah R. Hensler et al. (2000): *Class Action Dilemmas. Pursuing Public Goals for Private Gain,* RAND Institute for Civil Justice, especially section 3 and Willging and Lee (2007), with search term 'Class action litigation'.

[37] Information about the settlement can be found here: http://cp.sonybmg.com/xcp/

[38] Kuivalainen (2005).

Discussion on the principles of process law has differed somewhat from the United States. It is often argued that courts should decide individual lawsuits and not became arenas for social policy. Besides, lawmakers in the Nordic countries have traditionally had an active and strong role. On the other hand, there have been increasingly demands for direct democracy. Legislators and other government authorities have been criticized for being unable to react quickly enough to complex issues. It has been questioned where one needs third parties to enforce the rights of individuals that have been clearly defined in the parliamentary process. As one example, Finnish law professor Thomas Wilhelmsson has argued for class actions based on societal and economic reasons. He has presented that the functions of liability law should include regulatory, monitoring, service, and social security functions.[39] He argues that class actions can be used as a 'micropolitical instrument' in the Nordic market economies to further these 'modern' goals of liability law.[40]

4. CONCLUDING REMARKS: WHY DID THE FINNISH LEGISLATIVE PROCESS FAIL?

As this volume shows, it is evident that class actions are in Europe to stay. Their introduction, however, has not happened in a straightforward way. Many countries have adopted a very similar approach to the United States, but this has not been the case everywhere. The Finnish implementation is one example of a failed process.[41]

This chapter has presented that the main failures in the process were:

1. *Lack of empirical data of the various needs for class actions.* For some unknown reasons lawmakers focused only on consumer protection and environmental issues. They did not bother to survey empirical data from other countries but relied on theoretical speculations and submissions from selected interest groups. Comparative empirical data shows, however, that consumer protection and the environment are just two of the potential application areas for class actions. Issues such as constitutional rights could be considered fundamentally more important for the society as a whole. In the United States, these cases

---

[39] Wilhelmsson (2001, pp. 64–66).

[40] Ibid, pp. 176–7.

[41] As another similar example, Baumgartner (2007) criticizes how a class action law proposal in Switzerland was rejected with formal arguments without any empirical study on the various needs to have class actions.

account for about 15 per cent of all cases and even one of the first Swedish cases dealt with constitutional issues. To compare, no document in the Finnish legislative process mentioned the need to discuss constitutional rights or even any need to consult such interest groups.

2. *Lack of analysis of various economic effects of class actions.* True, it is difficult to estimate the economic effects of class actions but this should not be a reason to skip the issue. Perhaps the easiest way to start such analysis is to survey published empirical studies from other countries. Necessarily, one must collect this material from jurisdictions other than Sweden. Obviously the United States has been the leading 'test market' for *class* actions and there is an abundance of economic research material and empirical studies on the effects of class actions. Especially indicated in this regard is the final Finnish law proposal's *formal argument* of why American experiences were not surveyed in-depth: '... the process law in common law legal systems is not directly comparable to the process laws and other legislation regarding legal process in Finland ... likewise, substantial law is based on a different legal culture.' Also of note here is that Finnish lawmakers have traditionally been interested in other Nordic countries. In this case other Nordic countries took example from America. Indeed, the *economic problem* to which class actions have been tailored to give an answer is not totally different in Finland to the United States.

A critical commentator must now point out how little the Finnish process relied on substantive and verified arguments, especially when such arguments would have been available. Already the first government investigation from 1992 stated that empirical studies had proved most of the numerous claims against class actions as groundless.[42] For some reason, the preparation of the law continued years later as if that finding had never been published. In addition, the Ministry of Justice was able to construct good arguments to defend its draft law against industry claims in 2006. However, at that point their modest aim was to only defend a very limited approach to class actions.

A cynical commentator could now conclude that *the Finnish legislative process has fundamental flaws* if it cannot get clear issues right. As noted, in Finland laws are prepared in ministries where working groups discuss the political details before a formal law proposal is submitted to the parliament for review. The most important part of the process is the composition of the

---

42 Wihuri (1992, p. 13).

working group. In the case of class actions, industry representatives were able to maintain a polarized situation no matter of the merits of their arguments. The only way to reach 'a politically correct consensus' in this kind of situation was a substantially ill-founded compromise.

Interestingly, the result is *in accordance with the theory of public choice.* Industry representatives were able to influence the legislative process with effective coordination considerably more than groups with diverse interests, even though the latter groups may have had more to lose.[43] Some interests supporting class action were not heard in the process at all – it is, for example, difficult to name a certain group that would actively support constitutional rights in Finland. The state did not take the position of a referee but had its own interest to have at least some kind of law accepted and avoid among other things critique for the lack of authority.[44]

REFERENCES

Anonymous, (1995), *Ehdotus ryhmäkannelaiksi. Työryhmän mietintö*, Oikeusministeriön lainvalmisteluosaston julkaisu, **1**, Helsinki. (In Finnish, 'Proposal for a law on class actions.')

Anonymous, (1997), *Ryhmäkannelaki. Työryhmän 1996 mietintö*, Oikeusministeriön lainvalmisteluosaston julkaisu, **3**, Helsinki (In Finnish, 'Law on class action.')

Anonymous, (2005), *Selvitys ryhmäkanteesta*, Oikeusministeriön työryhmämietintö, **3**, Helsinki. (In Finnish, 'Investigation on class action.')

Anonymous, (2006a), *Ehdotus laiksi ryhmäkanteesta*, Oikeusministeriön työryhmämietintö, **4**, Helsinki (In Finnish, 'Proposal for a law on class actions.')

Anonymous, (2006b), *Ehdotus laiksi ryhmäkanteesta. Lausuntotiivistelmä*, Oikeusministeriön lausuntoja ja selvityksiä, **14**, Helsinki. (In Finnish, 'Proposal for a law on class action. Summary of responses.')

Baumgartner, S.P. (2007), 'Class actions and group litigation in Switzerland', *Northwestern Journal of International Law and Business*, **27**, 301–349.

Blom, M.O. (2006), 'Behovet av grupptalan – en argumentativ övning', *Tidskrift utgiven av Juridiska Föreningen i Finland*, **1–2**, 86–107.

Kuivalainen, J. (2005), 'Kuluttajavirasto vaikenee toistaiseksi kopiosuojauksista', *Digitoday*, November 11.

Lindblom, H. (1989), *Grupptalan. Det anglo-amerikanska class actioninstitutet ur svenskt perspektiv*, Stockholm: Nostedts.

[43] For example Olson (1971, pp. 141–3) why industry interests can be overrepresented in the legislative process: there are after all not that many politically active big companies (they have same opinions) and they have more resources compared to other interest groups.

[44] On public choice arguments for failure in legislative process see for example Mercuro and Medema (2006), pp. 186–95.

Lindblom, H. (ed.) (1990), *Grupptalan i konsumentmål*, NEK-rapport, 7, Nordisk Embetsmannkomité for konsumentspørsmål. Nordisk Ministerråd, Köpenhamn.

Lindblom, H. (1996), 'Grupptryck mot grupptalan', *Svensk Juristtidning*, **81**, 85–107.

Mercuro, N. and Steven G. Medema (2006), *Economics and the Law. From Posner to Post-Modernism and Beyond*, (2nd edn.), Princeton: Princeton University Press.

Olson, M. (1971), *The Logic of Collective Action*, Cambridge: Harvard University Press.

Puustinen, T. (2007), 'Ei sarvia eikä hampaita', *Talouselämä*, February 8.

Wihuri, A.J. (1992), *Ryhmäkanne. Perusselvitys käyttömahdollisuuksista Suomessa.* Oikeusministeriön lainvalmisteluosaston julkaisu, Helsinki. (In Finnish, 'Class action. Basic investigation on the usage possibilities in Finland')

Wilhelmsson, T. (2001), *Senmodern ansvarsrätt. Privaträtt som redskap för mikropolitik*, Helsingfors: Kauppakaari.

Willging, T.E. and E.G. Lee III (2007), *The Impact of the Class Action Fairness Act of 2005 on the Federal Courts, Third Interim Report to the Judicial, Conference Advisory Committee on Civil Rules*, Federal Judicial Center.

17. Class actions in Portugal

Mariana França Gouveia and Nuno Garoupa

In this chapter we discuss the introduction of class actions in Portugal. We start by looking at the current legal framework and making some important distinctions from the American version of class action. We then look at procedural rules concerning the adequacy of representation, notification of class members and calculation of damages. We further discuss some recent developments, including the introduction of consolidation in civil procedure. Some final remarks conclude the chapter.

1. INTRODUCTION

In Portugal, class actions exist in the current legal framework, but they are different from the American model to some extent, both in nature and in procedure. The legal framework for class actions (*acção popular*) is fundamentally established by Law 83/95, of August 31. Nevertheless, this law deals simultaneously with the right of the community to participate in the process of designing certain public policies (therefore establishing the procedural rules for such participation) and class actions per se.

The right to participation in designing public policies allows citizens to contribute to the decision process concerning certain matters of general interest such as zoning. In this chapter, we look exclusively at class actions as regulated by Law 83/95. Other relevant pieces of legislation are commented upon at the end of the chapter.

We should nevertheless emphasize that we define class actions in a very broad way, that is, an action interposed by a private party (natural or legal person) to determine rights and remedies where the private party is not the exclusive possessor of the right in question (in fact, the party might be only a partial possessor or might not be a possessor at all of that right).

In Portugal, the tradition of class action broadly defined is very old, going back to the Roman law. The Administrative Code of 1878 introduced for the first time the so-called supplementary class action (*acção popular supletiva*) allowing any citizen (member of the electorate) to interpose actions 'in name and in the interest of the district, city or parish' with the objective of demanding or recovering any misappropriated goods or rights.[1] This type of class action was to remain later in the following Administrative Codes (1886, 1896 and 1936). Another type of class action was the so-called corrective class action (*acção popular correctiva*) under French inspiration, directed to the impugnation of certain deliberations of local governments or to appeal certain decisions and electoral issues.[2]

Not surprisingly, class actions were contemplated by the democratic Constitution in 1976, under article 49 (currently 52, number 3) subject to the cases and under the terms foreseen in ordinary legislation. The constitutional formulation of class actions was extremely vague and only gained substance with the 1989 revision. According to Portuguese legal commentators, the 1989 constitutional reform approximated the concept of class action to the general Anglo-American notion.[3] The decisive step was taken some years later, in 1995, with the passing of the Law of Class Action (Law 83/95, of August 31).

2. GENERAL ASPECTS OF LAW 83/95

The Law of Class Action, now more than fifteen years old, establishes that any citizen and certain types of associations (those that are actively engaged in protecting the general interest in areas such as public health, environment, quality of life, consumers, cultural heritage or public domain) can interpose actions to defend rights and demand remedies whether or not they have a direct interest at stake.

The class actions can be purely compensatory in nature, for example, to demand the payment of damages in product liability cases. They can also be injunctions in order to prevent possible situations that might violate the rights in question, for example, to impede the entrance in the market of a potentially harmful product or to hold back the construction of a tunnel that might put future users in danger.

The scope of the possible affected interests encompassed by this legal framework is enormous and has been subject to discussion among legal commentators in Portugal. Usually we have three types of interests, where the rights in question are diffused, collective or possessed by a homogeneous well-defined set of individuals. In fact, two well-known and influential University of Coimbra constitutional law professors, Gomes Canotilho

---

1 de Freitas (2003, p. 17).
2 Martins (1999, p. 102).
3 Martins (1999, p. 103).

and Vital Moreira, have distinguished between individual interests and then public interests (those of the Government and other state agencies), diffuse interests (those that each citizen has as a reflection of the community membership), and collective interests (those of a certain category or group).[4]

Another author, Payam Martins, who has studied class actions in Portugal in detail, has argued that collective and diffuse interests have in common the indivisibility of the right and the individual interdependence. The substantive difference between these interests is in the nature of the relationship between the possessors. The holders of a diffuse right do not have any specific bond between themselves; they are drawn together by particular circumstances. The holders of a collective right belong to a well-specified group or category of people with a bond that is legally recognized or recognizable.

More recently, a University of Lisbon law professor, Miguel Teixeira de Sousa, has defended that the three types of interests are actually one. According to him, all are about diffuse rights, where these rights have two different dimensions, an individual dimension and a supra-individual dimension. Therefore collective and group (of homogeneous individuals) interests consubstantiate in fact diffuse rights.[5] The advantage of his reasoning is that it approximates the Portuguese way of looking at class actions to the American approach. However, it distances the Portuguese way from the more traditional Roman-Germanic model for which the super-individual attribute is much more relevant than any individual interest. Also, Teixeira de Sousa's rationale has obvious significant consequences for procedural rules in class action litigation.

3. PROCEDURE

3.1 Adequacy of Representation

The prerequisites for a class action in Portugal are therefore very mild. The option for such a model has been applauded by some commentators and the focus of severe criticism by others. Payam Martins makes the point that such a mild solution is a serious mistake because citizens cannot single handedly launch class actions for such widely diffused interests. Furthermore, there is no foreseen condition for representation, for example the

---

4 Canotilho and Moreira (2007, p. 698).

5 De Sousa (2003, p. 45).

North-American requirement of the adequacy of representation.[6] Miguel Teixeira de Sousa presents a different point of view by arguing that Portuguese law establishes two mechanisms that are enough to balance out any possible inconvenience caused by the adopted model.[7] First, the wide inquisitorial powers attributed to the judge and, second, the possibility for public prosecutors to take over the class action at some point. In fact, according to the Law of Class Action (article 16, number 3), within the scope of the powers exercised by the public prosecutors, they can decide to take over a class action if the plaintiff drops the lawsuit.

What is quite clear is that Portugal has not witnessed American-style class action litigation. Some of the few cases that have existed have been filed by citizens only very recently. Associations, in particular consumers' associations, have interposed the large majority of cases that have taken place. It might well be that the current rules do not promote adequate representation and that deters more class action litigation.

3.2 Notification

One other aspect that has deserved serious criticism is the procedural rule concerning notification of interested parties. According to the Law of Class Action (article 15, number 2) the notification is by poster (for geographically located interests) or in the press (for general interests) without any obligation of personal identification of the parties targeted by the announcement. The obvious problem is that neither a poster nor the press may be the best way to notify potentially interested parties when those interests might be diffused (specifically for well-defined homogeneous groups of individuals). Personal notifications are excluded by law when they make much more sense in group litigation.

The US model of personal notification when the members of the class can be pre-determined is not possible in Portugal. Another possible option could have been the Brazilian model by which there is no explicit rule of notification, although in that case public prosecutors have a more significant role.[8]

The Portuguese solution is, in some way, a sluggish solution. But, worse than sluggish, it is also a potentially dangerous solution. In fact, it has raised serious concerns with respect to its constitutionality. The notification rule does not guarantee effective knowledge by all potentially interested parties but presupposes it. Nobody can allege not to have had

---

6 Martins (1999, p. 112).
7 De Sousa (2003, p. 78).
8 See Gidi (2003, pp. 311–408).

knowledge of the interposed action that regulated his/her right or remedy. Portuguese law establishes that all interested parties are obliged by the final outcome of the lawsuit. This commitment is independent of the outcome of the litigation, being that favorable or unfavorable to non-intervening affected parties. There are only two minor exceptions, those described by article 19 of Law of Class Action, namely that the action is dismissed for lack of evidence or the outcome is justified on the basis of specific individual merits of the intervening plaintiffs.

A well-known law professor at the University of Lisbon, Lebre de Freitas, sees in these rules a clear contradiction with the constitutional right of access to justice. In cases where the outcome is unfavorable and the effective notification is not guaranteed, the missing potentially interested parties lose the right to use the courts to litigate their rights or demand proper remedies. His view is that only favorable outcomes should bind all parties.[9] The question has not been placed to the Portuguese Constitutional Court yet due to the very few cases so far.

3.3 Compensatory Damages

One other important aspect of class actions is the calculation of the compensatory damages. The Law of Class Action, in its article 22, states that compensation for the violation of rights not individually assigned is fixed at the overall level. It does not establish the exact criteria for this overall determination, but it has been deemed as necessary to find some criteria in order to limit judicial discretion. Thus, the compensation must be calculated as a function of the total damage generated, and not by looking at individual liability. The danger, however, given the difficulty of these calculations, is that the determination of such overall damage might introduce punitive damages which are not foreseen by Portuguese law, since they are criminal and not civil in nature.[10] Furthermore, the circumstance of individual compensation being capped by overall damages or apportioned according to some unspecified division rule might raise once again constitutionality questions as pointed out by Lebre de Freitas.[11]

3.4 Statutory Time Limits

A favorable outcome must be claimed within three years of adjudication; if not, the compensatory damages are paid to the Ministry of Justice. Not

---

9 De Freitas (2003, p. 21).
10 Martins (1999, pp. 119–120).
11 De Freitas (2003, p. 22).

surprisingly, this rule is criticized by some commentators including Payam Martins. He notices that it is conceivable in some circumstances that the potential claimants realize only later than this period that they were victims of a certain accident or injury. For example, the effects of contamination by certain products are only known many years later and, therefore, the injured party might not even know their condition within these statutory three years.[12]

This is an important point to distinguish between US and Portuguese class actions. The compensatory aspect of Portuguese class actions is diluted by the statutory limitation of three years. Precisely because they aim at overall damages and not individual losses, they should take into account the losses of the subset of individuals who take more than three years to claim the remedy. However, the statutory limitation reduces the likelihood of extremely large damages or punitive damages.[13]

3.5 Enforcing Judicial Decisions

Finally, a comment on the enforcement of judicial decisions: nothing in particular is foreseen in the Law of Class Action. Therefore, general rules of procedural law are applied. These norms do not seem, however, to be appropriate since they are tailored for individual actions. It would make more sense to rethink and specialize Portuguese procedural law for class actions.[14]

As we have seen, the Portuguese procedural rules in class actions have some problems. They are the balance found by the Portuguese legislator between the far-reaching US system (undesirable for the Portuguese legislator) and the weak European approach (for example, the Directive 98/27/CE excludes the interests of individuals that have been negatively affected by an illicit activity).

4. OTHER RELEVANT LEGISLATION

Although the Law of Class Action is the essential legislation that regulates class actions in Portugal, there are other relevant dispositions. First, the Law of Consumers' Protection, article 13; second, the Law of Contractual General Clauses, article 25 (promotes an anticipatory class action against the inclusion of forbidden clauses in contracts, *acção inibitória*); third, the

---

12 Martins (1999, p. 121).
13 De Sousa (2003, p. 117).
14 Martins (1999, p.121).

Law of Cultural Heritage Protection (article 9 attributes legitimacy to public prosecutors to litigate on the behalf of a class in this context). Clearly the second referred piece of legislation creates a substantive procedural rule for class action. Notice, however, that the rules developed by the legislator in this context seem to apply only to favorable outcomes (those where the judicial decision forbids the inclusion of certain clauses). The conclusion seems to be that unfavorable outcomes do not bind individual interests.[15]

5. CONSOLIDATION

Lately in Portugal there has been a new important legal development that, albeit not within the rules for class action, could make class actions more successful. This new development has been inspired by the US consolidation in civil procedure.[16] The Portuguese version of consolidation allows the temporary junction of different lawsuits that are on similar points of law or facts. It is different from the permanent junction of lawsuits (*apensação*) of Roman-German origin by which the lawsuits follow together until the end of the case. In the consolidation, once the points of law or facts have been established, the lawsuits follow their separate ways.

The consolidation is a procedural rule that applies to any act, individual or class. For example, in ten identical lawsuits relative to a standardized contract with an identical general contractual clause, the nullification of this clause is demanded. The judge can decide this question in a unique sentence; a definitive sentence for some cases (because no other questions were raised) and a partial sentence for other cases (because the lawsuits will follow in order for the judge to appreciate other matters). Another example, in eighteen actions interposed against the same defendant, a certain witness is the same. Instead of calling the same witness eighteen times, the court will be able to make it all at once, using the same hearing for all the lawsuits. The witnesses who are different, for example because they are indicated by different plaintiffs, will be heard by the court separately later. Yet another example, in several actions that have reference to the same accident involving several cars and vehicles, the evidence concerning the accident can be established together, allowing the appropriate damage to be calculated individually later on. A judge could decide to visit the place of the accident only once. The consolidation will be the easiest procedural way to justify only one visit to the place of the accident and produce evidence to multiple

15 De Freitas (2003, p. 24).

16 Gouveia (2006, p. 73).

lawsuits.[17] However, consolidation has also been criticized by some legal commentators for being a transplant completely misadjusted to Portuguese civil procedure.[18]

6. CONCLUSIONS

Class actions exist in Portuguese law. It is quite clear that they have different procedural rules than the American-style class actions. Some of these differences have been criticized by many commentators and might justify why so few class actions have actually been interposed. Nevertheless, we should not ignore that some of these differences have been explicitly endorsed by the Portuguese legislator to move away from the American model.

The effectiveness of class action litigation in Portugal is dubious to say the least. The small number of cases that have taken place does not allow a more comprehensive judgment. In fact, many of the questions raised by commentators have not even been addressed by the Portuguese Constitutional Court due to the fact that there have been very few cases so far.

A word of caution is necessary. We should not jump to the conclusion that just because we do not observe too many class actions, the legal framework and the procedural rules are improper. The reasons for the apparent lack of interest by the citizens for class actions in Portugal could lay elsewhere, namely the market for legal services (where contingent fees are still forbidden), the existing court congestion (that could deter individuals from filing lawsuits) or the allocation of legal costs to the loser.[19] Another important aspect is to recognize the lack of a litigation culture or mania in Portuguese society today for American standards (although litigation has expanded in the last thirty years which in part explains the current court congestion).

As the American and British experiences show, effective class action litigation presupposes some version of contingent fees in order to solve restrictions imposed by limited assets and to internalize substantial external effects (collective action problems to say the least). In Portugal, contingent fees are forbidden by the laws of the Law Society (*Ordem dos Advogados* Statute) and a possible reform of that rule is currently under debate.

---

[17] Ibid. p. 59.

[18] Lameiras (2007, p. 54).

[19] See on the impossibility of class actions without contingency fees and loser-pays legal costs rules, Rowe (2003, pp. 125–49).

REFERENCES

Canotilho, G. and V. Moreira (2007), *Constituição da República Anotada – Volume I* (4th edn), Coimbra: Coimbra Editora.

De Freitas, L. (2003), *A acção popular do direito português*, Coimbra: Sub Júdice number, **24**, 15–26.

De Sousa, M.T. (2003), *A Legitimidade Popular na Tutela dos Interesses Difusos*, Lisboa: Lex.

Gidi, A. (2003), 'Class actions in Brazil: A model for civil law countries', *American Journal of Comparative Law*, **51**(2), 311–408.

Gouveia, M.F. (2006), *Regime Processual Experimental Anotado*, Coimbra: Almedina.

Lameiras, L. (2007), *Comentário ao Regime Processual Experimental*, Coimbra: Almedina.

Martins, A.P. (1999), *Class Actions em Portugal,* Lisboa: Edições Cosmos.

Rowe, T.D. (2003), 'Shift happens: Pressure on foreign attorney-fee paradigms for class actions', *Duke Journal of Comparative and International Law*, **13**, 125–49.

18. The class action code: a model for civil law countries

Antonio Gidi

1. INTRODUCTION

This project's objective is to inspire the creation of the best possible code for class action suits, in light of the needs and peculiarities of civil law countries and international experience with class actions (or collective actions, as they are more appropriately called). The proposal offered below represents the author's choices among possible solutions to problems that arise in the judicial protection of group rights. Each possible solution has its own advantages, disadvantages, and opportunities for abuse.

Many rules herein recommended are repetitions, adaptations, or improvements of existing rules in other legal systems. Others are more innovative, and are the fruit of the author's vision of the class action process as a whole, influenced by comparative procedural law, both individual and collective, particularly derived from the law of Brazil, the United States, Canada, France, Italy, and Scandinavia.[1]

One of the project's contributions is to eliminate unjustified procedural differences in class actions. For example, such differences exist in Brazilian and American class actions as a result, merely, of chance and historical mistake. There is nothing that justifies why notice in American class actions for damages should be more rigorous than that in injunctive class actions, or why res judicata in Brazilian class actions should be a function of the type of claim involved. This is an opportunity to correct such distortions.

Some differences in class action proceedings, however, are legitimate in light of the peculiarities of various types of claim or fact pattern. For this reason, the proposal includes special Titles for the protection of 'transindividual rights' (indivisible rights belonging to the class as a whole) and for

---

[1] *See* Antonio Gidi, *Class Actions in Brazil. A Model for Civil Law Countries* 51 Am J. Comp. L. 311 (2003).

the protection of 'individual rights' (divisible rights belonging to individual members of the class). The amount of the claim and the type of controversy can also be legitimate basis for procedural differences in class actions. For example, mass toxic tort cases pose questions substantially different from questions resulting from single incident mass tort injuries such as a shipwreck. Civil rights and antitrust cases also present different issues that may require specific procedural approaches. These variations are beyond the scope of this project.

This project also does not address the more complex issues that have been troubling American class actions recently, such as mass toxic torts, future classes, multi-state claims, costs, and unethical behavior. Rather, the objective is more modest – to introduce a simple class action device for those civil law countries that do not have such a device, and to improve the systems that do. The project is not directed at a contemporary American audience, although Americans could find, in some provisions, inspiration for law reform in the United States as well.

In view of the multiplicity of legal systems and the diversity of legal vocabulary used in different civil law countries, the language used in drafting this Code is deliberately non-technical. The project also has an educational and informative purpose; its goal is to develop a self-explanatory system, avoiding the need for commentaries. It is anticipated that answers to questions that surface from application of this Code can be resolved in the use of the system itself.

TITLE I

General Provisions

Article 1. Applicability of class actions

1. A class action is suitable to protect transindividual rights and individual rights.

1.1 In particular, the class action may protect:

1.1.1 Transindividual rights – diffuse rights, of an indivisible nature, held collectively by a class of people linked among themselves or to the opposing party by legal or factual circumstances.

1.1.2 Individual rights – subjective rights belonging to each member of the class, and linked by legal or factual circumstances.

1.2 All types of suits capable of providing adequate and effective protection of the rights of the class and its members are permissible. In particular, the class claim may be a declaratory action, suit for damages, or for an injunction.

1.3 The class action is also suitable for protecting claims against a class of people, in accordance with the provisions of Title V.

Article 2. Standing to Bring a Class Action

2. Class actions may be concurrently brought by: (potential class representatives)

> **I** – the Office of the Attorney General;
> **II** – the Union, the States or Provinces, the Municipalities, or the Federal District;
> **III** – the entities and agencies of public administration;
> **IV** – non-profit associations legally constituted for at least two (2) years.

2.1 The class as a whole and its members are the party in the class proceeding, represented in court by the representative.

2.2 Whenever possible, the class will be represented in court by more than one representative, in order to promote an adequate representation of the rights of the class and of the class members. (See Articles 6, 9(IV), and 10.2.)

2.3 If the Office of the Attorney General does not file or intervene in the action, it shall nonetheless act as an overseer.

2.4 An entity or agency of public administration and the associations can only bring class actions related to their own institutional purpose (subject matter).

2.5 The judge shall dispense with the two-year prerequisite or the subject matter requirement or attribute class standing to class members, when there is no adequate representative interested in protecting the rights of the class in court. (See Articles 2(IV) and 2.4.)

2.6 The association represents the rights and interests of the class and of the class members, not of those of the members of the association.

2.7 The class counsel represents the rights and interests of the class and of the class members, not those of the representative that hired counsel.

Article 3. Prerequisites to a class action

3. An action shall only be conducted in class form if:

> **I** – there are common questions of fact or law, allowing for the uniform adjudication of the class claim;
> **II** – the representative and the class counsel can adequately represent the rights of the class and of the class members; (See Article 18(I))
> **III** – the class action is not a means manifestly inferior to other viable means for the protection of rights.

3.1 Upon evaluating the adequacy of the representative and the class counsel, the judge shall consider, among other factors:

3.1.1 their competency, honesty, capacity, reputation, and experience;

3.1.2 their past involvement in judicial and extra-judicial protection of class interests;

3.1.3 their conduct and participation in the class suit and in other previous lawsuits;

3.1.4 their financial capacity to maintain the class litigation; and

3.1.5 the duration of the establishment of the organization, and its level of representativeness of the class interests.

3.2 In case of groundless abandonment of the class suit or inadequate representation, the court shall give ample notice to the class, and another representative may continue the proceeding. (See Articles 5 and 6.) In the absence of an adequate representative interested in assuming the lead in the class action, the judge will dismiss the class action without prejudice.

3.3 When the group is too small, the members are easily identifiable, and the controversy can, in practice, continue in individual form, the court shall deny certification of the class action and permit the class members to intervene in the individual proceeding and litigate jointly.

TITLE II

Class Procedure

Article 4. Venue

4. In federal nations, class actions shall be brought:

I – in the forum where the injury occurred or would have occurred, for injuries of a local scale;
II – in the appropriate federal court in the Capital of the state, for injuries of statewide or region-wide scale;
III – in the appropriate federal court in the Federal District, for injuries of a national scale.

Article 5. Adequate notice

5. In the initial phase of the class action, the court shall provide, with the assistance of the parties, the best possible notice to the class and its members, in light of the circumstances of the specific case. (See Articles 3.2, 14.6, and 16.1.)

5.1 The notice should be economical, efficient, and broad, focused on informing the greatest possible number of potential representatives (see Article 2) and class members. The Office of the Attorney General, the Fund for Group Rights, the relevant entities and public agencies, the most representative national and regional associations, and a small sample of easily identifiable class members shall always be notified. (See Articles 5.10, 14.9, and 24.3.)

5.2 The court shall employ all available methods in order to provide adequate notice to the class. Such methods include announcements in the press, on the Internet, or other media compatible with the dimensions and type of the group.

5.3 The notice and the identification of the class members and relevant entities is the responsibility of both parties and the court, but in principle it will be borne by the representative. (See Article 5.12.) When identification or notice is difficult or costly for the representative and not for the party opposing the class, the court shall confer such duty on the party opposing the class, which may have the right of reimbursement for its expenses from the representative. (See Article 5.13.)

5.4 The notice shall be transmitted in simple, clear, and practical language in light of the circumstances, and shall include, among other information, the following:

5.4.1 the definition of the class;

5.4.2 the identification of the defendant;

5.4.3 the identification and the information for contacting the representative and the class counsel;

5.4.4 the description of the class controversy, with a summary of the facts alleged;

5.4.5 the class claim and the object of the proceeding;

5.4.6 the consequences of the class action for the class and its members;

5.4.7 the binding nature of the class judgment and the possibility of and period for the commencement of an individual suit, if the class member is interested in being excluded from the class (See Article 20.1);

5.4.8 a copy of the complaint, the response, and relevant documents, selected by the court with the assistance of the parties;

5.4.9 instructions on how to obtain more information about the class action;

5.4.10 any other information relevant to the specific case.

5.5 The notice shall be sent in the name of the court.

5.6 The notice shall be written in a neutral and impartial manner. The court may assign such duty to the class representative, under the scrutiny of the defendant and the control of the court.

5.7 The court shall reduce or eliminate the individual notification of a sample of class members if it is disproportionately costly or if the initiation of the class action has received adequate notoriety.

5.8 The class representative shall keep the class members continually informed of important aspects of the class action's development, or face disqualification for inadequate representation. If dissatisfied with the periodic notification provided by the representative, the court shall direct other notification of any procedural event.

5.9 The most significant potential class representatives, as identified by the court, shall receive, and those that so request may receive, notification of important acts realized in the process.

5.10 The court shall not provide notification if the class suit is manifestly without merit or unfounded.

5.11 In order to avoid prejudice to the defendant or in order to give the most complete information to the class, the court may postpone ample notification until convinced of the good faith of the class suit, initially limiting notice to the most significant potential representatives. (See Article 14.9.)

5.12 The court may order that the expenses, with ample notification and identification of class members, be fully or partially borne by the defendant, if there is a substantial likelihood that the class will eventually prevail on the merits. (See Article 5.13.)

5.13 If the party opposing the class sends correspondence to the class members, publishes newspapers or brochures, or maintains a site on the Internet, the court may order notice through that method, if there is a substantial likelihood that the class will eventually prevail on the merits, in order to adequately inform the class without substantially and unnecessarily increasing the expenses. (See Articles 5.3 and 5.12.)

5.14 The court may order the creation of an Internet site containing important information about the class proceeding and the facts that led to its commencement, with copies of the notice, complaint, answer, and principal statements, briefs, documents, and decisions. The site shall be updated frequently with the objective of informing class members about the case, and may contain important messages for the class and its members such as requests for information or evidence, and the announcements of an eventual settlement offer. The site's electronic address shall be made widely known. The court may order that a link to the referenced website be placed on the site of the class representative, class counsel, intervenor, and party opposing the class.

Article 6. Intervention (See Articles 2.2, 3.2, 10.2, 19, and 28.4)

6. Any potential representative (see Article 2) may intervene in the class proceedings at any time and at any jurisdictional level in order to demonstrate the inadequacy of the representative or to assist the representative in the protection of the class interests. (See Article 24.3.)

6.1 The potential representative may also intervene as assistant to the party opposing the class.

6.2 The class members may participate in the class suit as informants, providing new evidence, information, and arguments.

6.3 An intervenor shall be compensated for its expenses and attorney's fees in a measure proportional to its participation and contribution. (See Article 21.)

Article 7. The object of the class action suit

7. The object of the class action shall be as far-reaching as possible, including the entire controversy between the class and the opposing party, regardless of express request or claim by the representative, and including both transindividual claims, which belong to the class as a whole, and individual claims, which belong to the class members. (See Articles 9 (II), 10.3, and 16.)

Article 8. Tolling the Statute of Limitations

8. The commencement of a class action suit shall toll the statute of limitations period for individual and transindividual claims related to the class controversy.

8.1 The prescription period shall recommence to run upon notification to the class and its members of the final decision. (See Article 16.1.)

Article 9. Class certification

9. At the end of the pleading phase or at any early phase of the proceeding, after hearing the parties and intervenors, the court, in a reasoned and explained decision:

> **I** – shall decide if the action can continue as a class action;
> **II** – shall define the object of the class action in the broadest manner possible, regardless of request from the parties; (See Articles 7 and 16.)
> **III** – shall describe the class, with the precision necessary and possible;
> **IV** – shall select the most adequate representative to represent the class interests in court. (See Article 2.2.)

Article 10. Case management

10. While the court is neutral and impartial, it has the duty to protect the rights, interests, and substantive and procedural guarantees of the class and its members.

10.1 The court shall maintain direct control over the class proceeding and shall take appropriate measures for the speedy, just, and efficient progress of the class action suit.

10.2 The representatives and intervenors shall participate in the proceeding and present evidence, arguments, and motions jointly, to avoid repetitions and contradictions. The court shall only admit evidence, arguments, and motions separately produced if not repetitive. (See Articles 2.2 and 6.)

10.3 The court may sever the claims or the causes of action into separate class actions if such separation enhances procedural economy or facilitates the development of the class action suit. (See Article 7.)

10.4 The court may divide the class into subclasses with similar rights and interests for better decision-making and operation of the class action suit. If there are conflicts or substantial divergences of interests between class members, the judge may name a representative and an attorney for each subclass.

10.5 The court may limit the object of the class action to the part of the controversy that may be adjudicated collectively, leaving the issues that are not common to the class to be decided in individual actions or in a later phase of the same class action suit. In a reasoned and explained decision, the court shall indicate which issues will be part of the class action suit and which will be left out for individual actions or for a later phase of the class action suit.

10.6 The court decisions may be modified at any time during the proceeding, as long as doing so does not represent undue prejudice or surprise to the parties, and the right to be heard is preserved.

10.7 The court may increase time limits when there is a great number of representatives or intervenors, or when the questions of fact or of law are complex.

Article 11. Burden of proof

11. When the discovery of the truth of the facts depends on technical knowledge or on information that only one of the parties has or should have, the burden of proof falls on that party, if the allegations of the opposing party are credible.

Article 12. Cost of proof

12. When the production of proof is difficult or costly for one of the parties and not for the other, the court shall allocate its production to the opposing party, which has the right to be compensated for its expenses.

Article 13. Statistical proof

13. The use of statistical proof or proof by sampling is permitted as a complement to direct evidence, or when the production of direct evidence is costly, difficult, or impossible.

Article 14. Adequate settlement

14. The class representative may enter into a settlement agreement with the opposing party. If the terms of the agreement are adequate to protect the rights and interests of the class and its members, the court shall approve the settlement, and the agreement shall bind the class and its members. The decision must be accompanied by a reasoned explanation of its legal and factual basis. (See Articles 18 and 20.1.)

14.1 The settlement shall protect the interests of the class as a whole and may include aspects not related to the object of the proceeding. The settlement shall include a daily penalty which shall be assessed to the party that does not comply with its terms. (See Article 15.2.)

14.2 If the settlement is partial, the class action suit shall continue with regard to the rest of the controversy. (See Article 17.)

14.3 The Office of the Attorney General and the intervenors have the right to participate in all phases of the settlement negotiation.

14.4 In exceptional circumstances, the settlement may establish that the defendant will compensate the class members through discounts on future purchases of parts and products of the defendant's making. The discount coupons should be unconditional if possible. Limitations of any kind should be justified and can jeopardize the adequacy of the offer. Whenever possible, the option of receiving a discounted value in cash should be given to the class members. The benefit to the class, for purposes of the computation of attorney's fees, shall be calculated based on the settlement's cash value, not the face value of the coupons. (See Article 21.4.)

14.5 The parties shall present the proposed settlement agreement to the court. The motion for approval should describe the proposed settlement in a neutral and comprehensive manner, alerting the court to the strengths and weaknesses of the proposal, including potential prejudice to the class, and the reasons why the proposed settlement should be considered adequate despite any imperfections. The proposed settlement or the representative shall be considered inadequate if there are grave omissions in the motion for approval.

14.6 If the court considers the proposed settlement satisfactory, it shall provide ample notification to the class and its members about the agreement's terms. The court shall also set a public hearing date for comment on the adequacy of the proposed settlement. (See Article 5.)

14.7 The notice of the settlement offer shall include, among other information: (See Article 5.4)

14.7.1 a neutral and impartial description of the proposed settlement, with information about its favorable and unfavorable aspects;

14.7.2 the procedure and a reasonable time period for challenging the adequacy of the proposed settlement;

14.7.3 the date and place of the public hearing to evaluate the proposal;

14.7.4 the net value or advantage to be received by the class as a whole and by each member of the class;

14.7.5 instructions on how to obtain more information about the agreement and the class proceeding;

14.7.6 any other relevant information on the specific case.

14.8 Any interested person may present, with or without an attorney, the reasons against or in favor of the proposed settlement. The court may assign one of the interested persons or a reliable person the task of presenting a summary of all the arguments raised.

14.9 Before providing broad notice to the class, the court may provide limited notice to the most significant potential representatives (see Article 2) and to the intervenors that participated most actively in the class action suit, inviting them to comment on the settlement offer. (See Articles 5.1 and 5.11.)

14.10 The court shall carefully evaluate the proposed settlement, taking into consideration factors such as:

14.10.1 the arguments for and against the proposed settlement;

14.10.2 the issues of law and fact involved in the litigation;

14.10.3 the probability of success of the class claim;

14.10.4 the risks involved in the litigation;

14.10.5 the complexity, cost, and duration of the class action suit in the absence of a settlement;

14.10.6 the sufficiency of the available evidence and legal arguments on which the class claim is based at the time of reaching the settlement, and the possibility that other information or evidence may be discovered during the development of the suit; and

14.10.7 a comparison between an eventual favorable judgment on the merits and the terms of the proposed settlement.

Article 15. Injunction

15. In suits for the performance or non-performance of an obligation of an individual or transindividual character, the court shall order specific performance of the obligation or ensure a practical result that is equivalent to the performance.

15.1 The obligation shall only be converted into damages if the class agrees to it, or if specific performance or obtaining the corresponding practical result is impractical.

15.2 The court sua sponte may impose upon the defendant a daily fine that is sufficient and compatible with the obligation, fixing a reasonable time period for compliance. The court shall modify the amount of the fine or the frequency of its imposition, if it has become insufficient or excessive. The fine is independent from the damage award and from the penalty for noncompliance with the judicial order. (See Article 14.1).

15.3 The court may determine the necessary methods to achieve specific performance or the equivalent practical result.

Article 16. Class judgment

16. The class judgment shall decide the controversy in the broadest manner possible. The judgment shall address all individual and transindividual claims, including declaratory, injunctive, and damage claims on behalf of both the class and the class members, independently of express request by the representative, provided that it does not cause undue prejudice or surprise, and preserves the right to be heard. (See Articles 7 and 9(II).)

16.1 The class and its members shall be broadly and adequately notified of the class judgment, in accordance with the provisions of Article 5. (See Article 8.1.)

Article 17. Partial class judgment (See Article 14.2)

17. The court may decide part of the class claim, granting a partial judgment, when as to that part there is no need to produce proof or when the proof already available in the record is sufficient.

17.1 The partial judgment may be appealed and enforced in the same terms as the final judgment.

17.2 The class action shall continue with respect to the rest of the class controversy.

Article 18. Res judicata

18. Res judicata shall bind both the class and its members whether the judgment is favorable or not, unless the class action claim is deemed groundless due to:

> **I** – inadequate representation of the rights and interests of the class and of its members (See Article 3(II)); or
> **II** – the insufficiency of evidence.

18.1 If the class action is unsuccessful due to lack of evidence, any potential representative (see Article 2) may commence the same class action by making use of new evidence that could lead to a different outcome.

18.2 The challenges referred to in this Article may be decided either by the class action court or by the court where the individual action or class action is subsequently commenced.

18.3 In an individual action commenced by a class member bound by res judicata in the original class action, the court may only decide those issues of an individual nature and issues not covered under the class judgment. (See Article 20.1.)

Article 19. Lis pendens

19. The first class action suit shall prevail over other class actions related to the same class controversy. The subsequent class actions shall be dismissed, but their representatives may intervene in the first class action. (See Article 6.)

19.1 The defendant shall inform the court and the class representative about the initiation of another class action related to the same controversy.

Article 20. Class actions and corresponding individual suits

20. The class action does not prevail over corresponding individual actions related to the same class controversy. Individual actions shall not be dismissed.

20.1 The class member that brings an individual action to protect his or her individual rights before the date of the class judgment or before the approval of the proposed settlement shall be excluded from the class and shall not be bound by the class judgment. (See Article 18.3.)

20.2 The defendant shall inform the court presiding over the class action and the class representative of the existence of any individual actions relating to the same controversy, as they are commenced.

20.3 If a class member who is also the plaintiff in an individual action is notified of the existence of a corresponding class action, he or she may request a stay of his or her individual suit within a period of 60 days, if the class member wishes to be bound by the class action judgment.

20.4 If the class action is decided by a judgment on the merits, the member who requested the stay of his or her individual action shall be bound by the class judgment and, if it is the case, the individual action shall be dismissed. (See Article 18.3.)

20.5 If the class action is dismissed without a judgment on the merits, or if the class judgment otherwise has no res judicata effect (See Article 18.), the individual action shall continue.

20.6 In the absence of the notice referred to by Article 20.3, the class member who is the plaintiff in the individual action will be benefited but not prejudiced by the res judicata effect of the class judgment.

20.7 Before the class judgment is rendered or the proposed settlement is approved, the plaintiff in the individual action that had requested stay of his or her individual suit under the provisions of Article 20.3 may remove himself or herself from the class action and request continuance of the individual suit.

Article 21. Expenses and fees

21. In plaintiff class actions, plaintiffs shall not pay initial costs or any other expenses.

21.1 The judgment, regardless of request, shall order the losing party to pay to the winning party expenses and attorneys' fees.

21.2 In unsuccessful plaintiff class actions, the class representative and the intervenors shall not be liable for the winning party's attorneys' fees, costs, and expenses, unless the class action was initiated or maintained in bad faith, in which case the class representative, intervenors, and those directly involved shall be jointly ordered to pay attorneys' fees and up to ten times the costs and expenses, without prejudice to the responsibility for damages.

21.3 Payment of the class attorneys' fees may be conditional upon the result of the class action, but the attorney may not finance the litigation. (See Article 24.1.)

21.4 In the calculation of attorneys' fees, the court shall take into consideration, among other factors, the benefits obtained for the class, the quantity and quality of the work performed, and the risks and complexities of the case.

21.5 As an incentive for potential representatives (see Article 2) to bring class action suits and for representatives to take active control of the suit, the court may grant a form of financial gratification to the representative and to the intervenor whose performance was relevant in the protection of the rights, interests, and guarantees of the class and its members. This amount may be taken from the damage award, or may be paid by the defendant in addition to the damage award. In its evaluation, the court shall take into consideration the participation of the representative and the intervenor in the discovery of the harm and in the resolution of the conflict, among other factors that demonstrate the utility of their involvement and their exemplary conduct.

21.6 The court may retain part of the payment of the attorneys' fees or of the award of financial gratification of the representative until the defendant complies with the class judgment or settlement.

Article 22. Precedence of the class action suit

22. The court shall give priority to class action suits, when the public has an interest in the litigation, as evidenced by the scope and nature of the harm or by the significance of the legal claim to be protected.

Article 23. Motion for new proceeding

23. Class judgments on the merits with res judicata effect (see Article 18) may be rescinded through a proceeding initiated by one of the potential representatives (see Article 2) when:

> **I** – due to the scope, nature, or character of the offense or harm, an analysis of the adequacy or consequences of the settlement or decision was not possible at the time they were reached;
> **II** – due to the complexity of the issues, it was not possible to perform an adequate analysis of the evidence produced or of the legal arguments raised in the class suit;
> **III** – the decision or the settlement, after continuing relations, proves to be manifestly inadequate with the passage of time.
> **IV** – another event set out in the individual procedural law occurs.

TITLE III

Protection of Transindividual Rights

Article 24. Fund for group rights

24. In class actions for damages, a damages award for harm caused to the class as a whole shall be paid to the Fund for Group Rights. The Fund shall be managed by a commission formed by members of the Office of the Attorney General, judges, and members of the community. (See Article 27.)

24.1 The Fund's resources shall be employed in the restoration or reparation of the harms caused to the class. In case restoration or reparation is not possible, the Fund's resources shall be utilized in a discretionary, creative, and flexible manner in connection with the nature of the infraction or the harm caused, including use in financing and supervising other class actions, and for scientific, educational, informational, and research projects. (See Articles 5 and 21.3.)

24.2 The Commission administering the Fund for Group Rights shall be constituted within 90 days after this Code enters into effect. While the Commission is not duly constituted, the money eventually awarded to the Fund shall be deposited in a bank account with interest.

24.3 The Fund for Group Rights shall be notified about the commencement of any class action and about the most important decisions in such proceedings, and may intervene in any class suit at any time in order to demonstrate the inadequacy of the representative or to assist the representative in the protection of the class interests. (See Articles 5.1 and 6.)

TITLE IV

Protection of Individual Rights of Class Members

Article 25. Calculation of individual damages

25. Whenever possible, the class action court shall determine the amount of individual damages owed to each class member, and the enforcement of the class judgment shall be in the class form.

25.1 When the amount of the class members' individual damages is uniform, prevalently uniform, or may be reduced to a mathematic formula, the decision shall indicate the amount or the formula for calculating the individual damages.

25.2 A class member who considers his or her individual damage award, or the formula for calculating it, to be different from that contained in the class judgment may file an individual action for computation of his or her damages.

25.3 If the class action court cannot calculate the amount of the damages individually owed to the class members, the class judgment shall be general, setting forth the defendant's liability for the damages caused and the duty to pay damages, deferring the computation of the individual damages to individual proceedings brought by each member of the class. (See Article 26.) The class members shall have a period of two years, commencing from the date of the notice of the final decision, in which to file individual actions for computation of individual damages and enforcement against the defendant. (See Article 27.)

Article 26. Distribution of the money

26. When individual damages have been awarded, the money shall be distributed among the class members in a fast, economic, and effective manner.

26.1 Once the class judgment becomes final, the defendant shall voluntarily make payment to the class members, without the need for the filing of an action for the computation or enforcement of the individual damages, upon satisfactory evidence by class members that they qualify.

26.2 The class action court shall appoint one or more arbitration commissions to evaluate dubious cases. Appeals from arbitration decisions shall be directed to the class action court. The commissions shall be formed by one to three people, membership preference given to judges, attorneys, law students, or responsible citizens, recommended by the parties and appointed by the court. Individual suits may also be submitted to small claims courts or other appropriate tribunals.

26.3 The court shall determine the arbitrators' remuneration, which shall be borne by the defendant. The remuneration shall not be calculated in proportion to the amount given in the commission's decisions, but it shall be calculated as a function of the number and degree of complexity of the issues to be decided.

26.4 The arbitrators' decisions are not binding. Nevertheless, if the defendant refuses to voluntarily comply with individual claims that are clearly lawful, the court shall order the defendant to pay up to one hundred times the amount suggested by the commission, in addition to expenses and attorneys' fees. When deciding the amount of the fine, the judge shall take into consideration, among other factors:

26.4.1 the reasons for the non-compliance;

26.4.2 the degree of certainty of the class member's claim;

26.4.3 the number of times the defendant has repeated the conduct;

26.4.4 the necessity of restraining the defendant;

26.4.5 the good faith of the parties during the arbitration proceedings;

26.4.6 the defendant's financial condition.

Article 27. Aggregate individual compensation and the fund for group rights

27. If only a small proportion of class members has been compensated or has brought an action within the period prescribed in Article 25.3, the court shall calculate the aggregate value of the damages individually caused to members of the class, and the defendant shall pay that amount to the Fund for Group Rights. (See Article 24.)

27.1 The value of the overall harm caused to the class members may be calculated immediately, but the moneys may only be disbursed to the Fund after the period prescribed in Article 25.3.

27.2 The court may order the payment of part of the total award to the Fund before the period prescribed in Article 25.3, if the commencement of individual suits is realistically improbable due to, for example, the difficulty of proof, the reduced value of the individual claims, or the insolvency of the defendant.

TITLE V

Defendant Class Actions

Article 28. Defendant class actions

28. Class actions may be commenced against the members of a class represented by an association that constitutes them.

28.1 The association represents the class as a whole and the class members. All class members shall be bound by the class judgment whether favorable or not, even if the class member is not a member of the association that represented him or her in court. (See Articles 2.1, 2.6, and 18.)

28.2 If there is no such association, the defendant class action may be commenced against one or some of the class members, who shall function as representative(s) of the class. (See Article 2.2.)

28.3 The class members may form an association with the specific purpose of representing them in court in the defendant class action.

28.4 Class members may intervene in the defendant class action suit. (See Article 6.)

28.5 The representative shall have the right to be compensated by the class members, in proportion to the interest of each class member, for expenses related to the class proceeding.

Article 29. Plaintiff class action provisions as supplementary

29. The plaintiff class action provisions of this Code are applicable to defendant class actions, unless incompatible.

29.1 Whenever possible and necessary, the plaintiff class action provisions shall be interpreted with flexibility and adapted to the needs and peculiarities of defendant class actions.

TITLE VI

Principles of Interpretation

Article 30. Flexible interpretation

30. This Code shall be interpreted in a creative, open, and flexible way, avoiding extremely technical applications that are incompatible with the class protection of transindividual and individual rights.

30.1 The court shall adapt the procedural rules to the needs and peculiarities of the controversy and of the class, taking into consideration factors such as the amount and type of the claim.

Article 31. Class procedure as supplementary

31. The rules of this Code are applied to all class actions, unless incompatible with a specific kind of class action.

Article 32. Individual procedure as supplementary

32. The rules, principles, and guarantees of individual civil procedure (non-class action procedure) are to be applied supplementarily to class action proceedings, in a way that does not conflict with the spirit of class litigation.

32.1 Whenever possible and necessary, the rules, principles, and guarantees incompatible with the spirit of class actions should be adapted to the needs and peculiarities of class litigation.

TITLE VII

Final Provisions

Article 33. Effective Date

33. This Code shall come into effect on the date of its publication, being applied immediately to pending class action suits.

Index